INSIGHT GUIDES

ECUADOR
& Galápagos

Discovery
CHANNEL

APA PUBLICATIONS L
Part of the Langenscheidt Publishing Group

ABOUT THIS BOOK

INSIGHT GUIDE
ECUADOR

Editor
Rachel Lawrence
Editorial Director
Brian Bell

Distribution

United States
Langenscheidt Publishers, Inc.
36–36 33rd Street, 4th Floor
Long Island City, NY 11106
Fax: 1 (718) 784 0640

UK & Ireland
GeoCenter International Ltd
Meridian House, Churchill Way West
Basingstoke, Hampshire RG21 6YR
Fax: (44) 1256 817988

Australia
Universal Publishers
1 Waterloo Road
Macquarie Park, NSW 2113
Fax: (61) 2 9888 9074

New Zealand
Hema Maps New Zealand Ltd (HNZ)
Unit D, 24 Ra ORA Drive
East Tamaki, Auckland
Fax: (64) 9 273 6479

Worldwide
**Apa Publications GmbH & Co.
Verlag KG (Singapore branch)**
38 Joo Koon Road, Singapore 628990
Tel: (65) 6865 1600. Fax: (65) 6861 6438

Printing

Insight Print Services (Pte) Ltd
38 Joo Koon Road, Singapore 628990
Tel: (65) 6865 1600. Fax: (65) 6861 6438

©2007 Apa Publications GmbH & Co.
Verlag KG (Singapore branch)
All Rights Reserved
First Edition 1991
Third Edition 1998
Updated 2007

CONTACTING THE EDITORS
We would appreciate it if readers
would alert us to errors or out-
dated information by writing to:
**Insight Guides, P.O. Box 7910,
London SE1 1WE, England.
Fax: (44) 20 7403 0290.
insight@apaguide.co.uk**

www.insightguides.com
In North America:
www.insighttravelguides.com

The first Insight Guide pioneered the use of creative full-color photography in travel guides in 1970. Since then, we have expanded our range to cater for our readers' need not only for reliable information about their chosen destination but also for a real understanding of the culture and workings of that destination. Now, when the internet can supply inexhaustible (but not always reliable) facts, our books marry text and pictures to provide those much more elusive qualities: knowledge and discernment. To achieve this, they rely heavily on the authority of locally based writers and photographers.

How to use this book

The book is structured to convey an understanding of Ecuador and to guide readers through its sights and activities:

♦ The **Features** section describes Ecuador's history and culture in lively essays.

♦ The main **Places** section provides full details of all

crafts of Ecuador, and contributed to the Places section.

Sally Burch, one of the few full-time foreign correspondents in Quito, wrote about the Ecuadorian people; **Mary Dempsey** was your guide to Quito and Guayaquil; **Sean Doyle** contributed the chapters on history and the North Coast; **Rob Rachowiecki**, who is author of two other books on the country, has contributed chapters on the Oriente and the Western Lowlands; and **Betsy Wagenhauser**, former head of the South American Explorers, wrote about adventure travel. **Jane Letham** works for the South American Explorers in Quito, on which she wrote a short essay. **Mark Thurber**, a geologist and guide, contributed the chapter on Ecuador's economy and ecology.

The chief photographer for the book was **Eduardo Gil**, director of the prestigious Buenos Aires Cultural Center. Many of the portraits of indigenous life were taken by **Eric Lawrie** and **Stephen Trimball**. **André Bartschi** did much of the stunning wildlife photography for the Oriente chapters; and Galápagos resident **Tui de Roy** photographed some of the islands' extraordinary creatures.

This new and updated version was commissioned and edited by **Rachel Lawrence**. **Dominic Hamilton** updated the History section and **Nicholas Gill** updated the Features, Places, and Travel Tips sections. **Sylvia Suddes** helped with the text editing. **Neil Titman** and **Rachel Fox** proofread the book.

the areas worth seeing. The chief places of interest are coordinated by number with full-color maps.

◆ The **Travel Tips** listings section offers information on travel, hotels, shops, restaurants, and more.

The contributors

This edition, edited by **Pam Barrett** and **Christina Park**, builds on earlier versions edited by **Tony Perrottet** and updated by **Andrew Eames**. The chief contributor was US-born writer **Lynn Meisch**, who has lived for many years in the Andes. She wrote the essays on the customs, arts, and

Map Legend

—— ·· —	International Boundary
— —	Disputed Boundary
— — — —	Province/ State Boundary
⊖	Border Crossing
—·—·—	National Park/ Nature Reserve
— — — —	Ferry Route
✈	Airport
🚌	Bus Station
❶	Tourist Information
✉	Post Office
✝ ♂ ♀	Church/Ruins
∴	Archeological Site
∩	Cave
★	Place of Interest

The main places of interest in the Places section are coordinated by number with a full-color map (e.g. ❶) and a symbol at the top of every right-hand page tells you where to find the map.

INSIGHT GUIDE
ECUADOR

CONTENTS

Taking the
baby to
Pujilí
market

Insight on....

Information panels

Travel Tips

Places

THE BEST OF ECUADOR

From the Galápagos Islands to jungle lodges, and surfing to art galleries...
here, at a glance, are our recommendations, plus some tips
that even Ecuadorians won't always know

BEST WILDLIFE WATCHING

- **The Galápagos Islands** The most famous wildlife reserve in the world and the place where Charles Darwin formed his theory of evolution. *Pages 296–325*
- **Parque Nacional Machalilla** Most visitors come for the whale watching around Isla de la Plata, but you can also see iguanas, tortoises, and boobies. *Page 202*
- **Reserva de Producción Faunística Cuyabeno** Lagoons along the Río Cuyabeno attract fascinating wildlife species. *Page 224*
- **Parque Nacional Podocarpus** This isolated park near Vilcabamba sees few visitors and contains an area of remarkable biodiversity and several rare species, including the spectacled bear. *Page 120*
- **Parque Nacional Yasuní** Ecuador's largest nature reserve is home to the elusive jaguar and the vocal howler monkey. *Page 53*

ONLY IN ECUADOR

- **Devil's Nose Train** If you're brave, try riding on the roof of the train to the Devil's Nose near Riobamba like the locals do. *Page 237*
- **Cuy** On a spit or fried with potatoes, once you've tried guinea pig you'll never look back.
- **Surfing in the Galápagos Islands** Grab your board and head for one of the world's most unusual surf spots, but be prepared to share the waves with the resident sea lions.
- **Shaman Ceremony** If you're tired of western medicines, you could attempt a curing ceremony with a Tsáchila shaman. *Page 78*

BEST ART GALLERIES

● **Capilla del Hombre** Guayasamín's masterpiece in the Bellavista district of Quito is perhaps the most stunning example of Modernist Latin American art on the continent. *Page 162*

● **Museo de Arte Contemporario** Combined with the Museo de Antropológico on

Guayaquil's Malecón 2000, this modern museum has some of the best contemporary art in the country. *Page 282*

● **Museo Nacional del Banco Central** This Quito gallery showcases Ecuadorian art, from pre-Colombian artifacts to contemporary pieces. *Page 161*

BEST HOTELS

● **Kapawi Ecolodge** Deep in the Amazon on the border with Peru, a collection of thatched huts on stilts in a beautiful lagoon.

● **Hotel Plaza Grande** This restored colonial building looks directly over Plaza de la Independencia in the heart of Quito.

● **Luna Runtún** This luxury spa in Baños

is the place to get away from it all, with access to nature trails, horseback riding, and mountain biking.

● **Red Mangrove Adventure Inn** Conservation-focused hotel next to the Darwin Research Station in the Galápagos Islands. *See pages 335–340 for details of accommodations.*

ABOVE: *La Familia* (The Family) by one of Ecuador's most famous artists, Oswaldo Guayasamín.
ABOVE RIGHT: Eco-friendly paradise, the Kapawi Lodge.
RIGHT: A wall of ice on Volcán Cotopaxi.

BEST ADVENTURES

● **Hiking the Inca Trail to Ingapirca** This three-day trek is not nearly as crowded as its Peruvian cousin, but takes you to a magnificent Inca ruin just the same. *Page 117*

● **Climbing Cotopaxi** Over ice and snow, the 5–8 hour ascent takes you to the top of one of the world's highest active volcanoes. *Page 122*

● **Surfing in Montañita** Hang ten in this all encompassing surfing resort on the south coast. *Page 286*

● **White-water rafting in the Andes** Take a multiple-day rafting trip down the Class III and IV rapids at the eastern edge of the Andes mountains right into the heart of the Amazon jungle. *Page 122*

BEST HOT SPRINGS

- **Termas de Papallacta** Just 64 km (40 miles) east of Quito are the most developed thermal baths in the country. *Page 169*
- **Baños** The appropriately named town of Baños offers a range of options, from luxury resorts to secluded public parks. *Page 248*
- **Baños San Vicente** These thermal springs and mud baths on the Santa Elena peninsula are thought to have curative properties. *Page 286*

BEST RUINS

- **Ingapirca** Ecuador's most impressive Inca site was built by Huayna-Capac in the 15th century. The fine stonework on display includes storehouses, baths, a *tambo* (royal inn), and a sun temple. *Page 267*
- **Chirije** Located near Bahía de Caráquez on the Pacific coast, this little known archeological site dates back to the Bahía culture (500BC–500AD) for whom it was an important seaport. Ceramics, jewelry, and burial mounds have been found here. *Page 198*
- **La Tolita** These ancient burial mounds on the island of the same name are the archeological highlight of Ecuador's northern Pacific coast. *Page 189*

BEST FOR FAMILIES

- **Salinas** The most complete beach resort on South America's Pacific coast. *Page 287*
- **Oriente Lodges** Kids will love boat trips in the night to spot caimans or hiking through the jungle in search of jaguars during the day.
- **Telefériqo** Quito's cable car whisks you to the top of a hill, beside an active volcano, for awe-inspiring views of the city. *Page 150*
- **Museo Solar Inti Ñan** Located right on the equator, this small museum has interactive exhibits that will keep kids amused. *Page 167*

BEST MARKETS

- **Otavalo** The largest Saturday market in the Andes now runs almost everyday. This is the place to pick up handmade clothes and bags, pottery, and other crafts. *Page 175*
- **Riobamba** This is mainly a produce market where each Saturday local villagers trek down from the mountains to sell their goods. It's far less touristy than some of its better known competitors. *Page 252*
- **Saquisilí** Pens of llamas and sheep, produce, and various animal parts and products are spread out on plazas at what is generally considered to be Ecuador's most important indigenous market. *Page 245*

CLOCKWISE FROM FAR LEFT: natural relaxation at the Termas Papallacta; making friends with sea lions on the Galápagos Islands; colorful blankets in Otavalo market; the blue domes of Cuenca cathedral; the ruins at Ingapirca.

BEST CHURCHES

- **La Compañía** With gold-plated walls and ceilings, this cathedral in Quito is one of the most impressive churches in Latin America. *Page 153*
- **El Sagrario and Catedral de la Inmaculada Concepción** Cuenca's "old" and "new" cathedrals dominate the main plaza. The first dates back to the mid 16th century, while the second was built in the late 19th century and holds a famous crowned image of the Virgin. *Page 260*
- **Santo Domingo** Guayaquil's first church was built in 1548 in the Las Peñas district and is currently undergoing a major restoration. *Page 283*

TOP TIPS FOR TRAVELERS

Cheap eats The filling daily set lunch in many small, local restaurants is called the *menú* – the actual menu is called *la carta*. It is comprised of several courses, including a soup, main dish, and drink, and usually is just over a dollar.

Cheap to sleep Although they lack luxuries such as hot water or private bathrooms, many of Ecuador's cheaper hotels and hostels are clean, well-located, and can be had for between $5–10.

Traveling by bus Ecuador has an impressive bus network serving destinations all over the country. It is worth buying your ticket in advance around public holidays as buses can get very booked up. Always carry your passport with you as there are frequent police checks on roads leading in and out of main towns.

Spanish classes Ecuador is one of the best countries in South America in which to learn Spanish and there are dozens of schools in Quito and other popular tourist destinations. If you really want to immerse yourself in the language and culture, it is often possible to stay with an Ecuadorian family.

LATITUDE 0° 00'

Straddling the equator, Ecuador has become one of the
most popular holiday destinations in Latin America

The Republic of Ecuador took its name in the early 1800s from the equatorial line that runs through its heart. As far as the rest of the world was concerned, this geographical peculiarity would long remain Ecuador's major claim to fame. When outsiders did consider Ecuador, it was as a kind of giant natural laboratory. In 1736 Charles-Marie de la Condamine and Pierre Bouguer headed a pioneering expedition mounted by the French Academy of Science; almost 70 years later, the German explorer Alexander von Humboldt made discoveries here that were vital for the development of physical geography; and in 1835 Charles Darwin studied wildlife in the Galápagos Islands.

All these men, as well as the eminent English traveler Edward Whymper, who came here in 1879, published adventure-spiced volumes about their experiences, recounting a land of fantastic animals, ice-capped volcanoes, and impenetrable Amazonian jungles; but few of their compatriots followed in their footsteps. Had they done so, they would have found a harsh but beautiful country, in which the Catholic Church held considerable sway over people's lives, and where political assassination and periods of military rule were common.

Ecuador still does not come into the world's eye very often today – a fact that many Ecuadorians may feel thankful for, considering that it has been the chaos of war, revolution, and staggering debt that has made many of the country's neighbors internationally known. Since the latter part of the 20th century the Ecuadorians have lived in relative tranquility. The flamboyant nature of President Bucaram, the confusion surrounding his removal from office in 1997, and the removal of two subsequent presidents as a result of public demonstrations, including Lucio Gutiérrez in 2005, have made the West aware of the country's existence. But despite these upheavals, Ecuador is still one of the most politically stable countries in Latin America. It is also among the safest in which to travel, though pickpocketing and rare instances of armed robbery are on the increase in some tourist areas.

Ecuador is not, and has never been, a prosperous country, but it has largely avoided the most bitter extremes of poverty that afflict other Andean countries, such as Bolivia and Peru, and has been greatly helped by high prices for its oil exports. The Ecuadorians remain an approachable and easygoing people. They are a culturally diverse population, who include descendants of the Spanish *conquistadores* and of the original pre-Columbian inhabitants, many of whom still speak Quichua and maintain traditions from Inca times and earlier. Divided into 10 distinctly different communities, the original inhabitants prefer to be called *indígenas* (natives or indigenous people) rather than the Spanish *indio* (or "Indian" in English). Given the history of repression that has marked their country's evolution, they are remarkably open and friendly to foreigners.

Ecuador's cultural diversity is matched by its great geographical contrasts. Although only slightly larger than Colorado and somewhat larger than Britain, it contains the snow-capped Andes, a string of volcanoes, both extinct and active, the wide, largely deserted beaches of the Pacific Coast, and expanses of steamy Amazon jungle. Until recently Ecuador was almost entirely a rural country, but the past few decades have been marked by rapid urbanization, although about half of the population still lives in rural areas. Its two main cities – Quito, the capital, and Guayaquil, the industrial heart – are trying hard to cope with the problems that such expansion inevitably brings, and are all too obviously characterized by extremes of wealth and poverty. But they are vibrant, exciting places to explore, and visitors are generally welcomed.

Given all this, together with the relatively low cost of living, which makes traveling inexpensive, you can see why Ecuador has become one of the most popular destinations in South America. ❑

PRECEDING PAGES: clouds over the Western Cordillera; minding sheep in the windswept Sierra; patchwork fields in the Chimborazo province; cruising past Kicker Rock in the Galápagos Islands.
LEFT: young girl in typical Otavaleño dress.

COAST, SIERRA, AND JUNGLE

Sandy beaches, snowy volcanoes, Amazon rainforests, the Galápagos Islands...
Ecuador's vivid diversity is one of its greatest attractions

Straddled across the Andes on the most westerly point of South America, Ecuador is half the size of France (271,000 sq. km/103,000 sq. miles), making it the smallest of the Andean countries.

The Andean mountain chain divides the country into three distinct regions: the coastal plain known as the Costa, the Andean mountains, or Sierra, and the Amazon jungle, or Oriente. A fourth region, the Galápagos Islands, is a group of volcanic islands situated in the Pacific Ocean some 1,000 km (620 miles) due west of the mainland. The striking geographical and cultural contrasts between these regions in one small country are what make Ecuador such a fascinating place to visit.

Contrasting ecosystems

The gently rolling hills of the Costa lie between sea and mountains, varying in width from 20 to 180 km (12 to 112 miles). The low-lying areas and marshlands frequently become flooded, making access difficult in the rainy season. Much of this area was virgin coastal rainforest at the turn of the 20th century, but now it is devoted primarily to agriculture.

The shoreline offers long stretches of relatively unspoiled sandy beaches lined with coconut palms, and the sea is warm all year round. The river estuaries harbor mangrove swamps, important breeding grounds for land and marine wildlife, though many of these are being converted to expansive pools for commercial shrimp ranching. Further inland, particularly on the fertile lowlands irrigated by the Guayas and Daule rivers, there extend plantations of bananas, sugarcane, cacao, and rice. A low mountain range called the Mache-Chindul, near the coast, rises to a height of 800 meters (2,550 ft) and is one of the few spots that still supports virgin coastal rainforest and scattered indigenous communities, known as *chachis*.

VOLCANIC AVENUE

The term "Avenue of the Volcanoes" was coined by the German explorer Alexander von Humboldt in 1802.

The Andes consist of an eastern and western range, joined at intervals by transverse foothills. Nestling between the ranges are the valleys of the Sierra, with highly productive volcanic soils that have been populated and farmed for several thousand years. From the valley floors, a patchwork quilt of small fields extends far up the mountainsides, illustrating the intensive use that has been made of every available inch of land. The Quichua indigenous communities who own this land often hoe their own smallholdings by hand, producing a variety of crops such as potatoes, corn, beans, wheat, barley, and carrots.

The northern end of the Ecuadorian Andes is dominated by 10 glaciated volcanoes that tower to over 5,000 meters (16,000 ft). The Pan-American Highway follows the central valley, the Avenue of the Volcanoes, with excellent views over these snowy giants. Chimborazo, in the western chain, is the highest peak in Ecuador (6,310 meters/20,700 ft). A little further north, in the eastern range, is Cotopaxi, at 5,900 meters (19,350 ft) the highest active volcano in the world. The upper slopes of these peaks are covered by active glaciers that beckon mountaineers from all over the world.

Equally enchanting for trekkers are the surrounding sub-Alpine grasslands known locally as *páramo,* which host a diversity of wildlife, including the Andean condor, Andean fox, and spectacled bear, as well as hundreds of wildflowers. Lower down on the eastern Andean slope there is a dense cloudforest that remains largely unexplored because of cliffs, thick vegetation, and dismally heavy rains all year round.

The Amazon rainforest of the Oriente begins in the foothills of the eastern Andean slope. River systems flowing from this rainy wilderness become tributaries of the Amazon, the longest being the Río Napo (855km/530 miles). The banks of these wide and slow-moving rivers have traditionally been the location of settlements, and the river has been the principal

LEFT: the awesome Mount Chimborazo.

means of transport through a hilly and densely vegetated terrain. However, this lifestyle is rapidly being transformed by an expanding road network initiated by the oil industry in the early 1970s. Settlers, agricultural interests, and expanding indigenous communities are now converting once virgin rainforest into pastures and croplands. For the moment, much of the original forest survives and offers both magnificent scenery and ideal terrain for adventure.

The Galápagos Islands, home to the famous giant tortoises, blue-footed boobies, and marine iguanas, consist of 13 islands and 40 to 50 islets, some of which are no more than large rocks. The biggest island, Isabela, measures more than 4,000 sq. km (1,520 sq. miles).

The Galápagos are the product of a hot-spot volcanic center that actively erupts basalt lava on several of the islands. Since this archipelago never had direct connection to the mainland, the wildlife that exists here evolved in isolation, and many species are endemic. Because the area is biologically unique, all of the islands are protected within the Galápagos National Park and by the United Nations as a World Heritage Site, as well as by a Marine Reserve.

Land of sun and rain

Being right on the equator, Ecuador lacks the four seasons of the temperate zones. Every location in the country generally has a wet (winter) and dry (summer) season, but it is difficult to predict the weather on a day-to-day basis, especially during an El Niño year, when the whole country gets dumped on by heavy rains and the Sierra experiences a drought.

The rainy season for the Costa is between January and June. It rains most of the time in the Oriente, though December to February are usually drier. Both these regions are hot (above 25°C/80°F) all year round. The Galápagos Islands have a hot and arid climate.

Weather patterns in the Sierra are complex, and each region has its own microclimate. Generally, the central valleys are rainy between February and May, while the rest of the year is drier, with a short wet season in October and November. The climate overall is mild, and Quiteños brag about their perpetual spring, where gardens bloom all year round. The distinct ecological zones of this diverse country account for the

LEFT: sea lion on the Galápagos Islands.

broad variety of wildlife. For example, of the 2,600 species of birds existing in this part of the world, over 1,600 can be found in Ecuador.

A dynamic landscape

The forces of tectonic plates, volcanoes, and water have sculpted an exquisite array of landscapes, but have also caused devastating natural disasters throughout Ecuador's history. In 1996 an earthquake shook the province of Cotopaxi, causing 30 deaths and leaving thousands homeless. Another in 1987 destroyed parts of the Trans-Ecuadorian oil pipeline, the country's primary source of income, crippling the economy for six months. Thousands were drowned as floods of ice and mud were unleashed from glaciated peaks in the eastern Andean range.

In 1660, a century after the colonial city of Quito was founded, the nearby volcano of Guagua Pichincha erupted catastrophically, dumping several feet of ash onto the city. It began erupting again in 1999, causing the evacuation of villages near the crater. Geologists have indicated that Quito is safe from lava and pyroclastic flows: the crater opens to the west away from the city, and Rucu Pichincha blocks any potential flows. However, Quiteños will likely experience more eruptions over the next few years, and are learning to deal with the occasional ash fall as they would a snowy day.

Tungurahua started spitting out ash and incandescent rocks soon after Guagua and the town of Baños was evacuated from October to December 1999, and again in October 2005, in case of a major eruption. These eruptions are not related: volcanoes in between, like Cotopaxi and Quilotoa, are still sleeping.

Demographics

The population of Ecuador is around 13 million, about half of whom live in the cities. Population growth is around 2 percent annually. The country is divided into 22 provinces, many of them named after mountains (Chimborazo, Cotopaxi, Pichincha) or rivers (Guayas, Napo, Esmeraldas). The capital city, Quito, situated in the northern Sierra at an altitude of 2,800 meters (9,300 ft), has about 1.8 million inhabitants. Guayaquil is the largest city, with a population of over 2 million, and its seaport is the economic nerve-center of the country. ❏

LEFT: rainforest in the Amazon basin.

Decisive Dates

PRE-HISTORICAL 30,000–3000BC

Hunter-gatherer societies inhabit the Andes.
6000BC manioc is cultivated in the Amazon basin.

VALDIVIAN PERIOD 3500–500BC

The first evidence of permanent settlements and communities. Surviving pottery testifies to sophistication of the society.
3500BC earliest Valdivian site, called Loma Alta, is established.
1500BC ceremonial temples are built in Real Alto.

LA TOLITA PERIOD 500BC–AD500

A society of gold- and metal-workers.

MANTA PERIOD AD500–1500

Crafted objects of gold, silver, and pottery, plus cotton textiles.

SIERRA CULTURES 10TH–16TH CENTURY

10th century the Cara people, ruled by the Shyri, became established in the land of the Quitus. The Cañaris emerge as the most powerful and well-organized culture. The Puruhás are ruled by the Duchicela dynasty.
14th century Shyri and Duchicela familes intermarry, creating the greater kingdom of Quitu.

1460 Inca invasion. Tupac-Yupanqui subdues the Cañaris.
Late 15th–early 16th century the Incas consolidate their victories; the city of Tomebamba is built; the Inca Huanya-Capac builds Ingapirca (Inca Stone Wall); indigenous people are forcibly transferred from Ecuador to Peru and vice versa; the Imperial Highway is extended from Cuzco to Quito.
1492 the city of Quitu is taken by the Incas.
1527 Huascar, son of Huanya-Capac, ascends the Cuzco throne; war breaks out between him and his half-brother Atahualpa, heir to the Kingdom of Quito.
1532 war ends with Huascar's defeat.

SPANISH CONQUEST AND COLONIALISM

1526 first *conquistadores*, under Bartolomé Ruíz, land near Esmeraldas.
1530 Francisco Pizarro lands near Manabí.
1530–32 constant battles and massacres of indigenous people in the Spanish quest for gold.
1532 Atahualpa is captured and killed.
1534 Pedro de Alvarado lands in Manta.
1534 an army led by Simón de Benalcázar defeats the Incas when thousands of members of the Inca army stage a mutiny. Benalcázar founds the Villa de San Francisco de Quito on the ruins of the city the Incas have destroyed.
1535 the city of Guayaquil is founded.
1549 the Spanish conquest is completed but the *conquistadores* fight each other for gold until subdued by the Spanish crown in 1554.
1550s The land is divided up among the Spaniards and worked under a form of serfdom on huge estates. The Church becomes a major landowner. *Obrajes* (textiles workshops) using forced labor are established in Otavalo.
1563 Quito becomes the seat of a the *Real Audiencia* (colonial assembly).
17th century seminaries and universities are established in Quito and the city becomes an intellectual center.
1720 *encomiendas* are abolished, but *indígenas* become serfs on large *haciendas* under the *wasipungo*, or debt peonage, system.
1736 expedition by the French Academy of Sciences measures a degree of the meridian near the equator and determines the circumference of the earth; also conducts the first scientific exploration of the Amazon.
18th century Enlightenment ideals reach Ecuador. Eugenio Espejo (1747–95) campaigns against imperialism and dies in prison.
1802 Alexander von Humboldt arrives in Ecuador.

He is the first to identify altitude sickness.

1835 Charles Darwin spends five weeks on the Galápagos Islands where he makes many of the observations underpinning his theories of evolution.

1820 Guayaquil establishes a revolutionary junta.

1822 Battle of Pichincha: the forces of Antonio José de Sucre defeat the royalist army and liberate Quito.

1822 Simón de Bolívar arrives in Quito.

1823 Bolívar's ideal, Gran Colombia, incorporating Ecuador, Venezuela, and Colombia, is formed, but lasts only seven years.

1830 General Juan José Flores announces the creation of the Republic of Ecuador. Sucre is assassinated, and Bolívar later dies in exile.

1858–75 Gabriel García Moreno imposes a harsh dictatorship and is finally assassinated. The country's infrastructure is improved.

TOWARDS DEMOCRACY

1912 Eloy Alfraro, liberal president, is killed.

1922 crippling blight strikes the banana industry, in which Ecuador is the world's largest exporter.

1930s first oil explorations in the Oriente.

1934–61 José María Velasco Ibarra, a populist leader, enjoys five presidential terms.

1941 Peru annexes almost half of Ecuador's territory, taking much of El Oro, rich in gold and coffee.

1942 Rio de Janeiro Protocol ratifies the new borders. Ecuador will later renege on the deal.

1950s crisis in the *hacienda* system.

1964 Land Reform Act outlaws debt peonage system and gives *indígenas* title to their plots of land.

1972 oil becomes the major export.

1978 constitution grants the vote to 750,000 illiterate adults. The center-left government of Jaime Roldós increases wages and encourages unions.

1981 Roldós is killed in a plane cash. Osvaldo Hurtado takes over and continues reforms.

1982 devasting *El Niño* floods ruin crops and destroy roads and railways.

1987 earthquake sweeps away oil pipeline.

1988–92 Social Democrat Rodrigo Borja Cevallos heads a fair and progressive government.

1992–96 unpopular right-wing government under Sixto Durán Ballén.

1995 border dispute with Peru.

1996 Abdala Bucaram wins election but his popularity soon fades amid allegations of corruption.

PRECEDING PAGES: gold earrings and bracelets from the Carchi culture, 1400–500BC. **LEFT:** Francisco Pizarro, the Spanish conqueror who landed in 1530.
RIGHT: member of the palace guard.

1997–8 Bucaram is ousted. *El Niño* floods wreak havoc throughout the country.

1998 Jamil Mahuad Witt wins election. Peace Treaty between Ecuador and Peru is signed.

1999 economic crisis as inflation reaches 60 percent; bank accounts are frozen.

2000 Mahuad is forced to quit following attempted coup by military and indigenous groups. Vice President Gustavo Noboa becomes President. US dollar replaces sucre as the official currency.

2001 oil spill in the Galápagos but an ecological disaster is largely averted. The economy rebounds but chronic corruption continues.

2002 protests by indigenous peoples bring oil pro-

duction almost to a standstill. Lucio Gutiérrez, a leftist nationalist colonel and supporter of the indigenous movement is elected as President.

2003 Gutiérrez secures new IMF financing. Widespread unrest, primarily among the indigenous poor. Ex President Noboa is granted political asylum by the Dominican Republic.

2005 Congress votes to oust President Gutiérrez. He is succeeded by his Vice President, Alfredo Palacio.

2006 President Palacio declines to sign a Free Trade Agreement with the United States. Elections are held in October with a second round in December. Economist Rafael Correa emerges triumphant.

2007 Correa sets a radical agenda for reform, including a plan to replace Congress with a Constituent Assembly and rewrite the Constitution. ❑

LOST WORLDS

Ancient civilizations bequeathed a rich variety of cultural remains
which continue to intrigue both archeologists and visitors

The archeology of the Americas shines, in the public mind, with just a few specially bright stars: the Incas of Peru, the Aztecs of central Mexico, and the Maya of southern Mexico and Guatemala. The many pre-Columbian cultures beyond those centers are still relatively unknown, in spite of some astonishing recent discoveries.

Ecuador comprises one of those *tierras incognitas*, even though it has a fabulously rich archeological heritage. Because of the close proximity between coast, Sierra, and Amazonia, experts are able to study the movements that shaped civilization on the entire continent. It is becoming clear that many key developments defining pre-Columbian South America took place in Ecuador.

The oldest pottery in all of the Americas has been found here. Cultures have been discovered that worked in platinum, a metal unknown in Europe until the 1850s. Ancient trade links have been established between Ecuador, Mexico, and Amazonia. And it seems likely that pre-Columbian Ecuadorians sailed to and explored the Galápagos Islands.

The remote past

The first human beings who came to Ecuador were hunters and gatherers. The approximate period of their arrival is still debated among scholars, but it is certain that human beings have been in the Andes for 15,000 years, probably 30,000 years, and perhaps even for as long as 50,000 years. But the crucial question in Ecuador itself surrounds the gradual, all-important transformation from the hunting and gathering way of life to what archeologists call the "formative lifestyle."

While hunters and gatherers led a nomadic existence, formative cultures featured permanent settlements and communities. Most archeologists believe that this transformation in the Americas occurred over a 2,000- or 3,000-year

period, beginning around 3000BC in the most advanced areas. To the great surprise of many archeologists, the earliest pottery and other evidence of formative cultures in the whole of South America has been found on the coast of Ecuador, from a culture known as Valdivia.

The Valdivian culture stretched along the

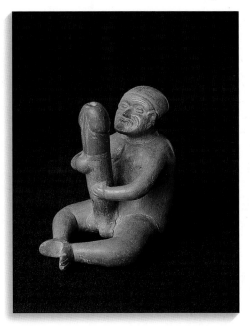

Ecuadorian coast of modern-day Manabi province, with its extensive, ecologically rich mangrove swamps, reaching inland to the drier hilly country. The earliest Valdivian site, dating back perhaps to 3500BC, is called Loma Alta. A range of extraordinary pottery has been found at this site, decorated with different carved motifs and a variety of colored clays. The Valdivian potters also formed multicolored female figurines that turn up in late strata in the archeological sites.

In Real Alto, a large Valdivian town continuously inhabited for over 2,000 years, archeologists have found the remains of over 100 household structures, each of which may have

---

LEFT: Jama Coaque figurine, 500BC.
RIGHT: priapic pottery from the Carchi culture.

housed 20 or more people. By 1500BC, the Real Alto people had built ceremonial temples on the tops of hills in the center of their town, where complex rituals obviously took place. A large number of female figurines have been found here, displaying sculpted hair and long, slender legs.

The problem for archeologists and historians was not that the earliest and most advanced formative culture was found in Ecuador, although that certainly surprised them. The real problem was that the Valdivian culture, with highly developed pottery, agricultural cultivation, and social organization firmly under its belt, could not have appeared out of nowhere. There must have been a long series of precursors, of trial-and-error development that led up to these cultural achievements.

The evidence to show that these developments occurred on the coast of Ecuador, ultimately giving birth to Valdivia, is not completely convincing. Investigations have uncovered earlier pottery on the coast, yet supporting data linking these oldest clay chips to Valdivia is lacking.

The daring and well-publicized voyages of Thor Heyerdahl encouraged such archeologists as Emilio Estrada (see panel below), even though Heyerdahl's rafts sailed from Peru to Polynesia, not from Japan to Ecuador. The acceptance of the Jomon–Valdivia connection was wholehearted in some quarters. Indeed, visitors to the Museum of the Banco Central, Quito's most important archeological museum, may still encounter this theory as an almost proven fact, presented as the most up-to-date hypothesis by many of the museum's guides.

THE JAPANESE IN ECUADOR?

The well-known Ecuadorian archeologist Emilio Estrada, at first working alone, and later with the collaboration of Smithsonian Institute archeologists Betty Meggers and Clifford Evans, postulated that Valdivia's origins were to be found on the Japanese island of Kyushu. The Jomon culture, which existed on Kyushu around 3000BC, produced pottery strikingly similar to that found at the Valdivian sites, with predominantly curved and zigzag lines and wedge shapes, and with combinations of ridges, lines, dots, and grooves. However, this theory never caught on and now it has been virtually abandoned.

But, in fact, the Jomon theory has been largely discarded. No single phase in the development of Valdivian pottery corresponds to a particular phase in the Jomon cultural development. In fact, the decorative motifs common to both Jomon and Valdivia are found all over the world, because the techniques that produced them are precisely those which potters choose almost automatically when they experiment with the results of applying a finger, a bone tool, a leaf, or a stone to the wet clay.

On a deeper level, the views of Estrada and his colleagues strike an important chord for all archeological studies in the Americas. There seems to be an irresistible tendency to assume that technological and artistic advances originated in the "discovery" of these lands by Asians or Europeans. The most vulgar expression of this tendency is to be found in the still popular theory of the writer Eric van Daniken, which connects advanced pre-Columbian civilizations with extra-terrestrials.

Origins in the Amazon

In the Oriente region of Ecuador, as elsewhere in Amazonia, the persistent presence of hunting and gathering peoples has led many observers to regard Amazonia as a historical backwater, incapable of supporting large populations and advanced civilizations.

The first hint that this could not be the case came from agricultural scientists investigating the domestication of manioc, which they concluded had taken place in the Amazon basin at least 8,000 years ago.

Archeologists believe that large cities of more than 10,000 people, supported by manioc cultivation, grew up on the Amazon's fertile floodplain as well as in the jungles on the eastern slope of the Ecuadorian and Peruvian Andes. These new historical concepts view modern tribes as being descended from the inhabitants of these undiscovered cities, the survivors of the plagues, wars, and forced dislocations caused by the Spanish Conquest.

The cultures of the Amazonian cities, which archeologists are now starting to find in Ecuador and Peru, gave pottery and manioc to South America. Manioc, along with corn (which came to Ecuador from Central America by way of trade), formed the agricultural foundation for a series of advanced coastal cultures, starting with Valdivia, according to current thinking. The

Andes, or Sierra, at first acted as a thoroughfare between the Amazon and the coast.

An important site near Cuenca, called Cerro Narrio, is situated at the crossroads of a natural, easy route, following the drainages of the Pastaza and Paute rivers. From around 2000BC, Cerro Narrio may have been a key trading center, where exchanges of technologies, products, and ideas from the coast, Amazonia, and the Sierra took place. Ceramics bearing unmistakably similar designs to those of coastal cultures have been found at Cerro Narrio, but archeologists are unable to determine whether these pots were imported from the coast or were

Amazonian societies were renowned for their ritual vessels, made for more than 3,000 years, and for their hallucinogenic potions.

Flowering of coastal activity

Following the establishment of formative cultures and of wide-ranging trade and exchange networks, stretching from Mexico to Peru and from the Amazon to the coast, archeologists describe a period of "regional development" (500BC–AD500) followed by a period of "integration" (AD500–1500). The final period culminated in the conquest of all of present-day Ecuador by the Inca Empire, which undertook

made at Cerro Narrio by potters who had come from the coast to live in the Sierra.

Archeologists now believe that a number of important items were traded between coast, Sierra, and jungle. Coastal societies collected spondylus shells, which were processed into beads in the Sierra and traded in Amazonia, where the shell design appears on much of the pottery that has been discovered. The Sierran societies cultivated the potato, which was used for trade, as well as coca – crucially important in rituals and ceremonies in the area. Meanwhile,

ABOVE: pre-Columbian copper pieces which have been found in the Sierra.

an extensive program of city-building and artistic creativity, before being itself destroyed by the Spaniards. A grand flowering of cultural activity preceded the Inca conquest of Ecuador, and the abundance of distinctive phases, especially on the coast, is overwhelming. The extraordinary achievement of these coastal cultures is embodied in the goldwork and sculpture of the La Tolita and Manta civilizations.

La Tolita civilization

The La Tolita culture reached its zenith around 300BC, and its star shone for perhaps 700 years on the coast of northern Ecuador and southwestern Colombia. The key site is a small, swampy lowland island in the mouth of the Santiago River in the coastal province of Esmeraldas. Now inhabited by Afro-Ecuadorian fisherfolk, La Tolita came to the attention of Westerners in the 1920s, when several European explorers announced the discovery of unprecedented numbers of finely crafted gold objects.

The merciless pillage of these priceless objects went on for years, and was even industrialized by prospectors, who mechanized the milling of thousands of tons of sand, from which gold artifacts were extracted and then melted down into ingots. Despite this, many gold objects are still found on La Tolita.

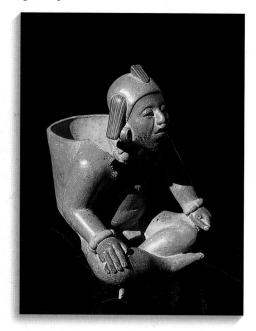

The magnificent mask of the Sun God, with its ornately detailed fan of sun rays, the symbol of Ecuador's Banco Central, was found on La Tolita. So much gold has been uncovered there that archeologists believe that the island was a sacred place, a pre-Columbian Mecca or Jerusalem, a city of goldsmiths, devoted to the production of holy images. It may have been the destination of pilgrims from the coast, the Sierra, and possibly Amazonia, who went there to obtain the sacred symbols of an ancient cult that influenced most of what is now Ecuador.

The quality and beauty of La Tolita goldwork is matched by the sculpture found on the island. The free-standing, detailed figures in active poses make La Tolita sculpture unique in pre-Columbian art. The sculptures depict both deities and mortals, the latter displaying deformities and diseases, or experiencing emotions of joy, sadness, or surprise.

La Tolita artisans also excelled in a form of metalcraft unknown in Europe until the 1850s. Metalsmiths on the island worked in platinum, creating intricate masks, pendants, pectorals, and nose-rings in a metal with a very high melting point.

Archeologists have puzzled over how La Tolita metalsmiths were able to do this, with only rudimentary tools and technology. One theory is that by combining pure platinum with bits of gold, which melts at a much lower temperature, the smiths created an alloy with which they could work.

The Manta culture

The Manta culture, in the modern province of Manabi, flowered during the period of integration, and also produced objects of outstanding beauty in gold, silver, cotton textiles, pottery, and stone. The great city of Manta housed more than 20,000 people, and by including the population of outlying villages, archeologists have arrived at very high numbers of people who lived during the Manta culture. This culture produced the greatest mariners of pre-Columbian Ecuador, and there is evidence that the Manta people settled extensive coastal areas, and traded with the coastal peoples of western Mexico and central Peru.

There is an intriguing theory held by some archeologists that Manteña mariners, along with pre-Columbian Peruvian sailors, discovered the Galápagos Islands. A quantity of ceramic shards, almost certainly of pre-Columbian vintage, have been uncovered on three of the islands; the presence of cotton plants, cultivated on the continent, also indicates some sort of contact between the islands and the mainland. Whether the contacts were only occasional, or perhaps accidental, as some believe, whether the islands were used as a seasonal fishing outpost, as Thor Heyerdahl and others favor, or whether they were settled by groups of Manteñas, as a few archeologists assert, has yet to be established.   ❑

LEFT: Jama Coaque drinking cup. RIGHT: figurine from the Bahía culture, 500BC–AD500.

ON THE SIDELINES OF HISTORY

Although never a major player on the world stage, Ecuador was
fought over and dominated by the Incas and the conquistadores

The forces of historical change have frequently been imposed on Ecuador from beyond its borders. Successive invaders – the Incas, the Spaniards, and, more recently, bellicose neighbors – have swept across the country in great waves of destruction, each seeking to remake it in their own image. Their success is reflected in the varied ethnicity of the Ecuadorian people – 40 percent indigenous, 40 percent *mestizos* (mixed European-indigenous blood), and the remainder an assortment of full-blooded or American-born Europeans *(criollos)* and the descendants of black Caribs and Africans *(morenos)*. Their legacy of brutal exploitation constitutes an ongoing struggle for modern Ecuadorians.

Sierra cultures

The land that is now Ecuador was first brought under one rule when the Incas of Peru invaded in the middle of the 15th century. By this time, the dazzling cultures of Manta and La Tolita on the Ecuadorian coast had flowered and faded, while an increasingly powerful series of agricultural societies had divided the region's highlands among them.

The greatest of these cultures was the Cañaris, who inhabited the present-day sites of Cuenca, Chordaleg, Gualaceo, and Cañar. Theirs was a rigidly hierarchical society. Only the Cañari elite were allowed to wear the fine, elaborate gold and silver produced by their metalsmiths. Among the Cañari artifacts, figures of jaguars, caymans, and other jungle animals predominate – showing their strong links with Amazonian groups.

Another advanced group were the Caras, forefathers of the modern Otavaleños. The Caras were under the rule of the Shyri dynasty. Arriving in Ecuador "by way of the sea," they ascended the Río Esmeraldas during the 10th century and established themselves in the land of the Quitus.

They worshiped the sun and believed the moon was inhabited by humans. They built an observatory to chart the solstices, and identified the equator as "the path of the sun." Their economy was based on spinning and weaving wool, and there was a traveling class of merchants who traded with tribes in the Oriente.

The Puruhás, ferocious warriors based around Ambato, were ruled by the Duchicela family, which intermarried with the Shyri in the 14th century and created the greater kingdom of Quitu. While little social or economic influence was exerted over the kingdom's lesser tribes, they nevertheless expanded the numbers of men who could be deployed in battle.

The Inca invasion

Onto this landscape of tribal identity marched the Incas – literally, "Children of the Sun" – who were to be the short-lived precursors of the Spaniards. Although established in the Peruvian Andes from the 11th century, it was not until

LEFT: Alexander von Humboldt and his fellow traveler, Aimé Bonpland. **RIGHT:** a fanciful European depiction of the Inca Atahualpa.

about 1460 that they attacked the Cañaris, with the ultimate objective of subjugating the kingdom of Quitu. Ecuador became brutally embroiled in imperial ambitions as armies dispatched from distant capitals turned the country into a battlefield.

The Cañaris fought valiantly against superior odds for several years before being subdued by the Inca Tupac-Yupanqui. His revenge severely depleted the indigenous male population: when the Spanish chronicler Cieza de León visited Cañari territory in 1547, he found 15 women to every

BATTLE DRUMS

The stomachs of enemies were turned into drums to be beaten at the next battle.

the Incas built an imposing fortress that also served as temple, storehouse, and observatory.

Inca conquest along the spine of the Andes continued inexorably. Quitu, which had fallen by 1492, became a garrison town on the empire's northern frontier and, like Tomebamba, the focus of ostentatious construction. Battles continued to rage: for 17 years the Caras resisted the Inca onslaught before Huayna-Cápac, Tupac's son, captured the Caras' capital, Caranqui, and massacred thousands.

The Incas at war were a fearsome sight.

man. Inca occupation was focused on the construction of a major city called Tomebamba on the site of present-day Cuenca. It was intended to rival the Inca capital of Cuzco, from where stonemasons were summoned to build a massive temple of the sun and splendid palaces with walls of sculpted gold.

But by the time Cieza de León arrived, Tomebamba was already a ghost town. He found enormous warehouses stocked with grain, barracks for the imperial troops, and houses formerly occupied by "more than two hundred virgins, who were very beautiful, dedicated to the service of the sun." At nearby Ingapirca, the best-preserved pre-Hispanic site in Ecuador,

Dressed in quilted armor and cane or woolen helmets, and armed with spears, *champis* (head-splitters), slingshots, and shields, they attacked with blood-curdling cries. Prisoners taken in battle were led to a sun temple and slaughtered. The heads of enemy chieftains became ceremonial drinking cups, and their bodies were stuffed and paraded through the streets.

Imposing the new order

Inca colonization brought large numbers of loyal Quechua subjects from southern Peru to Ecuador, and many Cañaris and Caras were in turn shipped to Peru. The Incas introduced their impressive irrigation methods and some new crops – sweet potatoes, coca, and peanuts – as well as the llama, a sturdy beast of burden and an excellent source of wool. The chewing of coca, previously unknown in highland Ecuador, soon became a popular habit. The Imperial Highway was extended to Quito, which – although 1,980 km (1,230 miles) from Cuzco – could be reached by a team of relay runners in eight days. Loyalty to the Inca, with his mandate from the sun, was exacted through the system of *mita* – imperial work or service – rather than taxation. As large areas came under centralized control for the first time, a nascent sense of unity stirred; but it was an alien and oppres-

cial part in the collapse of the empire, for Huayna-Cápac, seeking to unite his domain through marriage, achieved just the opposite.

Huanya-Cápac had been born and raised in Tomebamba; his favorite son, Atahualpa, was the offspring of the Duchicela marriage and heir to the kingdom of Quito. Atahualpa's half-brother, Huascar, was descended from Inca lineage on both sides, and thus the legitimate heir. In 1527, Huascar ascended the Cuzco throne, dividing the empire for the first time. Civil war soon broke out, and continued for five years before Atahualpa defeated and imprisoned Huascar after a major battle near Ambato.

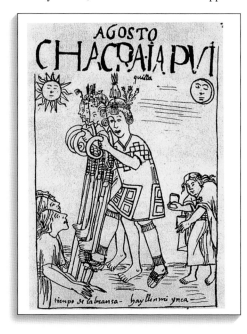

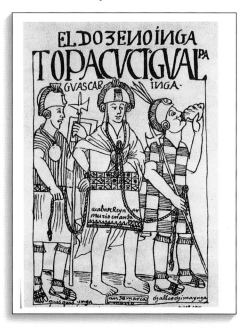

sive regime, attracting little genuine loyalty.

The Ecuadorian Amerindians who suffered Inca domination were proud, handsome peoples. Cieza de León spoke of the Cañaris as "good-looking and well grown," and the native Quiteños as "more gentle and better disposed, and with fewer vices than all Indians of Peru." Tupac-Yupanqui married a Cañari princess, and Huayna-Cápac, in turn, the daughter of the Duchicela king of Quito. This was to play a cru-

Atahualpa, an able and intelligent leader, established the new capital of Cajamarca in northern Peru. But the war had severely weakened both the infrastructure and the will of the Incas, and by a remarkable historical coincidence, it was only a matter of months before their death-knell sounded.

The bearded white strangers

Rarely have the pages of history been stalked by such a greedy, treacherous, bloodthirsty band of villains as the Spanish *conquistadores*. With their homeland ravaged by 700 years of war with the Moors, the Spanish believed they had paid a heavy price for saving Christian Europe

---

LEFT: famous Inca masonry at Ingapirca ruins.
ABOVE: Inca society had a well-ordered system of public works. **RIGHT:** the capture of Huascar during the Incas' bitter civil war.

Into the Amazon

O nce Quito had been settled, the *conquistadores* began to seek new lands and new adventures. Tales of El Dorado and Canelos (a Land of Cinnamon, supposedly to the east), filled the air. Francisco Pizarro appointed his brother, Gonzalo – "the best-beloved of any man in Peru" – to lead an expedition to find these magical destinations. On Christmas Day, 1539, Gonzalo left Quito with 340 soldiers, 4,000 Amerindians, 150 horses, a flock of llamas, 4,000 swine, 900 dogs, and plentiful supplies of food and water.

Surviving an earthquake and an attack by hostile natives, the expedition descended the Cordillera. At Sumaco on the Río Coca they were joined by Francisco de Orellana, who had been called from his governorship of Guayaquil to be Gonzalo's lieutenant.

Hacking their way through dense, swampy undergrowth, and hampered by incessant heavy rain, they were reduced to eating roots, berries, herbs, frogs, and snakes. The first group of natives they met denied all knowledge of El Dorado, so Gonzalo had them burned alive and torn to pieces by dogs. They met another group who spoke of an inhabited city, supposedly rich in provisions and gold, just 10 days' march away at the junction of the Coca and Napo rivers.

A large raft was constructed, and 50 soldiers under Orellana's command were dispatched to find the city and return with food: already 2,000 natives and scores of Spaniards had starved to death. Hearing nothing of the advance party after two months, Gonzalo trekked to the junction, but there was no city. The pragmatic natives had very sensibly lied to save their skins. In early June, 1542, the 80 surviving Spaniards from Pizarro's group staggered into Quito, "naked and barefooted." By then, Francisco de Orellana was far away. The brigantine's provisions were exhausted by the time the party reached the river junction: sailing back upstream against the current was impossible, and the difficulties of blazing a jungle trail would have killed the weary men. Hearing the call of destiny and whispers of El Dorado across the wilderness, Orellana sailed on.

For nine months the expedition drifted on the current, never knowing what lay round the next bend. Crude wooden crosses were erected as they progressed, purporting to claim the lands in the name of the Spanish king. They encountered many indigenous tribes: some gave them food – turkeys, turtles, parrots, and fruits – and ornaments of gold and silver; others attacked them with spears and poisoned arrows, claiming many Spanish lives.

On one occasion 10,000 natives are said to have attacked them from the river banks and from canoes, but the Spaniards' arquebuses soon repelled them. They heard frequent reports of a tribe of fearsome women known as "Amazons," who lived in gold-plated houses. Near Obidos, the "Amazons" attacked. These fearsome women were "very tall, robust, fair, with long hair twisted over their heads, skins round their loins, and bows and arrows in their hands." From this report, the great South American river and jungle area took its name.

Finally, in a lowland area with many inhabited islands, Orellana noticed signs of the ebb of the tide and, in August 1541, sailed into the open sea. For the first time, Europeans had traversed South America. Today, if you want to emulate this experience in style and comfort, you can take a four- or five-night cruise aboard the *Manatee Amazon Explorer*, a comfortable riverboat which began operating in 2002 on the Río Napo from the town of Francisco de Orellana, otherwise known as Coca. ❑

LEFT: *conquistadores* abuse one of their press-ganged porters.

from Muslim domination. When news reached Spain of the glittering Aztec treasury, snatched by Cortés in 1521, it fired the imaginations of desperate owners of ruined lands – and the Church – and spawned dreams of other such empires in the New World.

The first *conquistadores* to set foot on Ecuadorian soil landed near Esmeraldas in September 1526. They had been dispatched from Colombia by Francisco Pizarro to explore lands to the south. The party, led by Bartolomé Ruíz, discovered several villages of friendly natives wearing splendid objects of gold and silver, news of which prompted Pizarro himself, with

and jungles, and frozen, cloud-buffeted mountain passes. Arriving exhausted in Cajamarca in November 1532, they formulated a plan to trap the Inca Atahualpa. At a pre-arranged meeting, the Inca and several thousand followers – many of them unarmed – entered the great square of Cajamarca. A Spanish priest outlined the tenets of Christianity to Atahualpa, calling upon him to embrace the faith and accept the sovereignty of the Spanish king, Charles I. Predictably, Atahualpa refused, flinging the priest's Bible to the ground; Pizarro and his men rushed out from the surrounding buildings and set upon the astonished Incas. Of the Spaniards, only Pizarro

just 13 men, to follow a year or so later. Near Tumbes, he found an Amerindian settlement whose inhabitants were similarly adorned, and so planned a full-scale invasion. Late in 1530, having traveled to Spain to secure the patronage of King Carlos I and the title of governor and captain-general of Peru, Pizarro – this time with 180 men and 27 horses – landed in the Bay of San Mateo near Manabí.

For two years the *conquistadores* battled against the native peoples and against the treacherous terrain of mosquito-infested swamps

himself was wounded when he seized Atahualpa, while the Incas were cut down in their hundreds.

Atahualpa was imprisoned and a ransom demanded: a roomful of gold and silver weighing 24 tons was amassed, but the Inca was not freed. He was held for nine months, during which time he learned Spanish and mastered the arts of writing, chess, and cards. His authority was never questioned: female attendants dressed him in robes of vampire-bat fur, fed him, and ceremoniously burned everything he used. The Spaniards melted down the finely wrought treasures, and accused Atahualpa of treason. Curiously, Pizarro baptized him "Fransisco," and then garroted him with an iron collar.

ABOVE: 16th-century depiction of the Spanish advance during the Conquest.

Two worlds collide

To the Incas, the Spanish conquest was an apocalyptic reversal of the natural order. In the eyes of a 16th-century native chronicler, Waman Puma, these strangers were "all enshrouded from head to foot, with their faces completely covered in wool… men who never sleep."

The Incas had no monetary system and no concept of private wealth: they believed the only possible explanation for the Spaniards' craving for gold was that they either ate precious metals, or suffered from a disease that could be cured only by gold. Their horses were "beasts who wear sandals of silver."

LAMENT FOR ATAHUALPA

An elegiac lament was composed by the Incas upon Atahualpa's death: "Hail is falling/Lightning strikes/The sun is sinking/It has become forever night." Atahualpa is still considered by many people to have been the first great Ecuadorian. Curiously, Pizarro baptized him with his own Christian name, Francisco, before garoting him with an iron collar.

There are indigenous people today, in the Saraguro region, who are said to wear their habitual somber black and indigo ponchos and dresses because they are still in mourning for the death of Atahualpa, nearly 500 years ago.

Conversely, the Spaniards perceived the natives as semi-naked barbarians who worshiped false gods, and were good for nothing; Cieza de León's positive remarks *(see page 35)* only illustrate his unusual fair-mindedness.

While Pizarro continued southwards toward Cuzco, his lieutenant, Sebastián de Benalcázar, was dispatched to Piura to ship the Inca booty to Panama. But rumors of these treasures had traveled north, and Pedro de Alvarado, another Spaniard in search of riches, set out from Guatemala to conquer Quito. With 500 men and 120 horses, he landed at Manta in early 1534, and during an epic trek slaughtered all the coastal natives who crossed his path.

Hearing of this, Benalcázar quickly mounted his own expedition to capture Quito. Approaching Riobamba in May, he encountered a massive Quiteño army under the Inca general Quisquis. Fifty thousand natives, the largest Inca force ever assembled, were deployed, hopelessly outnumbering the Spaniards. But the natives, owing no loyalty to the Incas, mutinied and dispersed, and the best opportunity to defeat the Spanish was lost. Alvarado was paid a handsome sum by Pizarro to abandon his Ecuadorian excursion and return quietly to Guatemala.

Benalcázar marched northward with thousands of Cañaris and Puruhás in his ranks, for both tribes sought revenge on the brutal Incas. Arriving in Quito in December, 1534, he found the city in ruins; Rumiñahui, the Inca general, had destroyed and evacuated it rather than lose it intact. Atop Cara and Inca rubble, with a mere 206 inhabitants, the Villa de San Francisco de Quito was founded on December 6, and Guayaquil the following year. Rumiñahui launched a counter-attack a month later, but was captured, tortured, and executed.

By 1549, the conquest was complete: a mere 2,000 Spaniards had subjugated an estimated 500,000 natives. The number of casualties is impossible to ascertain, but tens of thousands died in this 15-year period, through starvation, disease and suicide, as well as in battle.

The Spanish yoke

With the restless natives quietened, the *conquistadores* fought each other for the prizes: not until 1554 did the Spanish Crown finally subdue them. In 1539, Pizarro appointed his brother Gonzalo governor of Quito, but when the first viceroy to Peru passed through shortly thereafter, he found the colonists in revolt. Gonzalo fought off the viceroy's forces in 1546, only to be deposed and executed by another official army two years later. During Gonzalo's governorship, an expedition was mounted to explore the lands east of Quito. The undertaking was a disaster *(see Into the Amazon, page 36)* but under the renegade leadership of Francisco de Orellana, the first transcontinental journey by Europeans was made in 1541.

When Cortés cried, "I don't want land – give me gold!" he spoke for all *conquistadores*. But the immediately available treasures were soon exhausted. The land and its inhabitants were

and slaves were brought from Africa to man the coastal cacao plantations. Ecuador escaped the grim excesses of mining that befell Peru and Bolivia, as the Spanish, to their disappointment, found few precious metals here.

As well as horses, pigs and cattle were introduced, and Ecuador nurtured the first crops of bananas and wheat in South America. The Spaniards also imported diseases such as smallpox, influenza, measles, and cholera. But with much of the highlands and all of the Oriente so inaccessible, Spanish settlement was relatively light, so geography saved the natives from extermination, if not from subjugation.

divided among the *conquistadores*, and the first settlers soon followed. Of the Quito region, in contrast to the damp, ghostly barrenness of Lima, Cieza de León wrote: "The country is very pleasant, and particularly resembles Spain in its pastures and climate."

The Avenue of the Volcanoes, the strip of land 40 to 60 km (25 to 40 miles) wide running the length of Ecuador between two towering rows of volcanoes, was ideal farmland. In addition, workshops were established to produce textiles,

LEFT: Francisco Pizarro, the conqueror.
ABOVE LEFT: colonial depiction of weaving.
ABOVE RIGHT: a *criollo* noble.

Colonial administration was based on the twin pillars of the *encomienda* system and the Church. The former effected the transition from conquest to occupation. The *encomenderos*, or landowners, were given tracts of land and the right to unpaid native labor, and in return were responsible for the religious conversion of their laborers. The natives were obliged to bring tribute, in the form of animals, vegetables, and blankets, to their new masters, as they had to the Incas. It was a brutally efficient form of feudalism whereby the Spanish Crown not only pacified the *conquistadores* with a life of luxury, but also gained an empire at no risk or expense. For centuries, the main landowner was the Church, as dying *encomenderos* donated their estates, in the hope of gaining salvation. Pragmatically, *indígenas* accepted the new faith, embellishing it with their own beliefs and rituals. Days after Benalcázar founded Quito, the cornerstone of the first major place of Christian worship, the church of San Francisco, was laid. Franciscans were followed by Jesuits and Dominicans, each group of missionaries enriching themselves at the natives' expense while claiming a monopoly on salvation.

Methods of conversion could be brutal: children were separated from their families to receive the catechism; lapsing converts were

protesting against increased taxes on food and fabrics. The authorities put an end to the agitation by executing 24 conspirators and displaying their heads in iron cages.

During the 18th century, the ideas of the European Enlightenment crept slowly toward Quito University. The works of Voltaire, Leibnitz, Descartes, and Rousseau, and the revolutions in the United States and France gave intellectual succor to colonial libertarians. The physician-journalist Eugenio Espejo, born in 1747 of an indigenous father and a mulatto (Afro-Hispanic) mother, emerged as the anti-imperialists' leader.

imprisoned, flogged, and their heads were shaved. Some priests took native women as mistresses, and their children contributed to the number of *mestizos*, people of mixed Spanish-native blood. Quito – seat of a Viceregal Court or *Audiencia* from 1563 – grew into a religious and intellectual center during the 17th century as seminaries and universities were established.

Push for independence

In reaction to the Spaniards' oppressive socio-economic actions there sprouted violent popular uprisings and nascent cries of "Liberty!" As early as 1592, the lower clergy supported merchants and workers in the Alcabalas Revolution,

Espejo was a fearless humanist. He published satirical, bitterly combative books on Spanish colonialism; and as founding editor of the liberal newspaper *Primicias de la Cultura de Quito*, was probably the first American journalist. He was repeatedly jailed, exiled to Bogotá for four years, and finally died, aged 48, in a Quito dungeon. From his cell, he wrote to the President of the *Audiencia*: "I have produced writings for the happiness of the country, as yet a barbarian one." His name now graces the National Library and countless streets in Ecuador. ❏

ABOVE: a contemporary depiction of the quay at Guayaquil.

Von Humboldt: the First Travel Writer

Simón Bolívar described Humboldt as "the true discoverer of America, because his work has produced more benefit to our people than all the *conquistadores*." Praise indeed from the liberator of the Americas. But how did this wealthy Prussian mineralogist come to play such a vital role in the history of the continent?

Alexander von Humboldt was born in Berlin in 1769. As a young man he studied botany, chemistry, astronomy, and mineralogy, and traveled with Georg Forster, who had accompanied Captain James Cook on his second world voyage. At the age of 27 he received a legacy large enough to finance a scientific expedition, and made such an impression on Carlos IV of Spain that he received permission to travel to South America – the first time a non-Spanish scientist had been granted this privilege since Charles-Marie de la Condamine in 1735.

With his companion Aimé Bonpland, Humboldt set off for Caracas in November 1799. During their five-year expedition the two men covered some 9,600 km (6,000 miles) on foot, horseback, and by canoe. They suffered from malaria, and were reduced to a diet of ground cacao beans and river water when damp and insects destroyed their supplies. Following the course of the Orinoco and Casiquiare rivers, they established that the Casiquiare channel linked the Orinoco and the Amazon. In 1802 they reached Quito, where Humboldt climbed Chimborazo, failing to attain the summit but setting a world record (unbroken for 30 years) by reaching almost 6,000 meters (19,500 ft). He coined the name "Avenue of the Volcanoes" and, after suffering from altitude sickness, was the first to connect it with a lack of oxygen. Between ascents he did a vast amount of work on the role of eruptive forces in the development of the earth's crust, establishing that Latin America was not, as had been believed, a geologically young country.

It was while in Ecuador that Humboldt began assembing notes for his *Essays on the Geography of Plants*, pioneering investigations into the relationship between a region's geography and its flora and fauna. He claimed another first by listing many of the indigenous, pre-conquest species: vanilla and

---

RIGHT: the young Humboldt, who received a legacy at the age of 27, enabling him to finance his research.

avocado, yucca, maize, and manioc, among others; and he was responsible for the birth of the guano industry, after he sent samples of the substance back to Europe for analysis.

Humboldt's contributions seem endless: off the west coast he studied the oceanic current, which was named after him; his work on isotherms and isobars laid the foundation for the science of climatology; he invented the term "magnetic storms," and as a result of his interest the Royal Society in London promoted the establishment of observatories, which led to the correlation of such storms with sun-spot activity.

Humboldt viewed the natural world through the

eyes of a 19th-century Romantic. He was also deeply interested in social and economic issues. Despite good relations with the Spanish Crown, he called himself "a Republican at heart"and was adamantly opposed to slavery, which he considered "the greatest evil that afflicts human nature." Goethe, a close friend, found him "exceedingly interesting and stimulating," a man who "overwhelms one with intellectual treasure;" while Charles Darwin had been inspired by the Prussian scientist's earlier journey to Tenerife, in the Canary Islands, and his description of the volcanic Pico de Teide and the dragon tree. Darwin knew whole passages of Humboldt's *Relation Historique* off by heart, and described him as "the parent of a grand progeny of scientific travellers." ❑

INDEPENDENCE AND AFTER

From the battle for independence to recent oil exploitation
in the Amazon, the history of modern Ecuador has been turbulent

As the Crown's grip on its colonies began to loosen, the ghost of the *conquistadores* stirred from its slumber. From the beginning of the Spanish era, money and muscle had meant power; laws, constitutions, and governments were subject to the greed of reckless individuals. Cortéz and Orellana disobeyed orders and attained greatness, and Pizarro answered to no one.

The ethos they bequeathed to those who came after them was devoid of ideas and morality. Through the age of caudillos in the 19th century, and of military dictators in the 20th, Ecuador was viewed as a treasure, like Inca gold, conveniently there for the taking.

The road to freedom

Ecuador's first step toward independence was also its first coup. In response to the fall of Spain to Napoleon in 1808, a new wave of repressive measures was enforced in the colonies, prompting members of the criollo oligarchy to seize power in Quito in August, 1809, and imprison the president of the *Audiencia*. Within a month, loyalist troops from Bogotá and Lima had displaced the usurpers, but the subsequent reprisals were so harsh that they prompted a second rebellion two years later. This time, a constitution for an independent state was formulated, but the uprising remained confined to Quito, and so was easily suppressed.

But the whole continent was moving inexorably toward liberation. With English support, Simón Bolívar – *El Libertador* – had taken on the Spanish loyalists in his native Venezuela, where he became dictator, and then in Colombia. In October, 1820, Guayaquil ousted the local authorities and established a revolutionary junta; and following the Battle of Pichincha in May, 1822, when forces led by Antonio José de Sucre resoundingly defeated the royalist army, Quito was liberated.

PRECEDING PAGES: political mural in Latacunga.
LEFT: a worker overlooking the Quito of the 1890s.
RIGHT: Simón Bolívar, *El Libertador*.

A few weeks later, Bolívar arrived in Quito. He was the archetypal criollo – ambitious, paternalistic, impatient, never doubting his methods or goals. His brilliance sprang from the singular intensity of his vision, which brought liberation to a continent, but he failed to appreciate the dynamics of the new nations. His

Argentine counterpart, José de San Martín, was stoic, taciturn, and self-effacing – Bolívar's ideal complement. But at their only meeting, in Guayaquil in July, 1822, to plot the future of a proposed Gran Colombia – they had a fundamental disagreement: Bolívar wanted a republic, while San Martín envisaged a monarchy. What happened at that meeting is not known, but Bolívar triumphed, and San Martín went into self-imposed exile in Europe.

Gran Colombia was formed in 1823, incorporating Ecuador, Colombia, and Venezuela. But the new, united nation lasted just seven years: in September, 1830, the military commander of Quito, General Juan José Flores – a

Venezuelan who had married into the Quiteño aristocracy – announced the creation of the Republic of Ecuador. The new republic's population now stood at approximately 700,000 and its ill-defined borders were based on those of the colonial *Audiencia*.

That same year, Marshal Sucre – Bolívar's chosen successor – was assassinated en route from Bogotá to his home in Quito, prompting Bolívar to grieve "They have slain Abel." On the northern shores of the continent that he had transformed, *El Libertador* died a broken man: overcome with frustration, he said of his life's work, "Those who serve the revolution plough the sea."

before being toppled by the Liberals.

In the subsequent period of chronic political disorder, the next 15 years saw 11 governments and three constitutions come and go, while the economy stagnated. Border disputes sprang up with both Peru and Colombia, with the mayor of Guayaquil actually ceding his city and southern Ecuador to Peru.

This morass was tidied up by one of the strong men of Ecuadorian history, Gabriel García Moreno, who had risen from humble origins to the rectorship of the University of Quito. During his decade in power, the nation became a theocracy where only practicing Catholics could vote.

False freedom

The inequalities of the colonial social structure were preserved with ruthless duplicity by the new Ecuadorian élite. While cries of "Fatherland" and "Freedom" echoed across the country, the poor remained enslaved in workshops, on haciendas and plantations. National power was up for grabs, and the struggle between the Conservatives of Quito and the Liberals of Guayaquil began immediately. Flores made a deal with the opposition Liberal leader, Vicente Rocafuerte, to alternate the presidency, with Flores retaining military control, but in 1843 he refused to step down from his second term and was bribed into exile. Flores held power for two more years

He renamed the best regiments "Guardians of the Virgin" and "Soldiers of the Infant Jesus" and frequently indulged in acts of self-humiliation: photographs capture him carrying a heavy wooden cross through the streets, followed by his cabinet.

Freedom of speech and the press were nonexistent, and political opponents were imprisoned or exiled. But while the country's mind was being repressed, its body matured: hospitals, roads, and railways were constructed; schools were opened to natives and women; Guayaquil's port facilities were improved; and new crops enhanced agricultural productivity. From this era there emerged a spirit of national identity.

García Moreno's critics were many, but they

trod a dangerous path, all too aware of the fate that awaited enemies of the regime. Quiteño journalist and leading intellectual Juan Montalvo railed against the president's tyrannical clericalism. From his enforced exile in Colombia, he rejoiced on hearing of the president's assassination in 1875, declaring: "My pen has killed him."

As the century turned, the Liberal President Eloy Alfaro managed to improve the natives' lot, modernize the legal code, and separate Church and state before an incensed pro-clerical mob tore him to pieces.

Political assassination has not been a feature of more recent years, but nepotism and mind-

each taken generously from its portion of Amazonia. In 1941, Peru snatched almost half of Ecuador's territory in an invasion that was largely uncontested, as President Arroyo, fearing a coup, kept most of his troops in Quito. Much of El Oro, a region rich in gold, oil, and coffee, was lost, though Ecuador subsequently reneged on the Rio de Janeiro Protocol of 1942, which ratified the new boundary. Several skirmishes broke out over the following years. One conflict in 1995 lasted three months, cost both sides several hundreds of casualties and had a damaging effect on the economy. A ceasefire finally took place, with Ecuador reluctantly accepting the Rio Protocol.

less populism have characterized the political landscape. José María Velasco Ibarra, who enjoyed five presidential terms between 1934 and 1961, was known as "The National Personification" for his ability to transcend regional barriers, and on one occasion cried, "Give me a balcony and I will be president again!"

War in the Amazon

Ecuador was originally more than double its present size, but Brazil, Colombia, and Peru have

LEFT : the victorious Marshal Sucre signing the Act of Independence in 1822. RIGHT: workers on a banana plantation in the 1880s.

In 1998 the leaders of Ecuador and Peru, both anxious for a real solution, agreed to submit the unresolved issues to arbitration by the guarantor countries of Brazil, Argentina, and Chile. In October, the historic Acta de Brasília Peace Treaty was signed, the conflict zone demilitarized and bi-national development plans put into place. Since then relations have improved dramatically between the two countries.

The economy has expanded from its original bases of cacao and textiles to include coffee, Panama hats, shrimp farming, fresh flowers, tourism, and, particularly, bananas. Under the iron fist of the Boston-based United Fruit Company, Ecuador became, and remains, the world's leading exporter of bananas. The accompanying ethos of rampant capitalism produced a crisis in the archaic hacienda system in the 1950s as, for the first time, money spread beyond the few hundred dominant criollo families. The long-overdue land reforms of 1964 further eroded traditional socio-economic ties, and the discovery of massive oil deposits in the Oriente has permanently shifted Ecuador's economic base away from agriculture. Oil is now the major industry, controlled by state-run Petroecuador and several multinationals. A controversial second oil pipeline, costing $1.5 billion, was completed in 2003, despite opposition from indigenous and environmental groups.

Democratic leaders

Ecuador was the first Latin American country to attain democracy. In 1978, the army drew up a constitution which extended the vote to the country's 750,000 illiterate adults. The center-left government of Jaime Roldós, elected the following year, launched massive literacy and housing programs. Emphasizing issues instead of personalities, the government increased workers' wages and encouraged the emergence of a politically articulate middle class, and of mass-based organizations such as peasant co-operatives and labor unions. But an economic crisis eventually loomed as oil prices dropped and payments on foreign debt fell due, and for a

while rumors of a military coup were rife.

In 1981, Roldós died in a plane crash. Vice-President Osvaldo Hurtado fulfilled his pledges to serve his full term, to continue Roldós' reforms, and to maintain civil liberties – despite the added difficulty of the great *El Niño* floods of late 1982, which ruined banana and rice crops and destroyed roads and railways. León Febres Cordero, a Conservative, won the 1984 elections. Febres oversaw sustained economic growth, but was brought down over charges of misuse of public funds, which he allegedly paid to an Israeli counter-insurgency adviser to help to dismantle a guerrilla movement.

Elections in 1988 brought to power President Rodrigo Borja Cevallos, a Social Democrat from Quito. He set an honest, competent political course: civil disturbances such as transport workers' strikes and student riots over price rises were handled leniently. Inflation fell, foreign debt was serviced regularly, and foreign investors continued to be attracted, both under Borja and under his successor, Sixto Durán Ballén of the Christian Social Party, who was elected in 1992. Sixto was not a popular president, although the border dispute with Peru did produce a temporary surge in support. One of his more unpopular policies was the introduction of a privatization program for telecommunictions, electricity, and parts of Petro-ecuador, but Congress stalled the program. Jaime Nebot, a right-wing Christian Socialist, looked set to lead Ecuador through the late 1990s, until Abdala Bucaram led the Ecuadorian Roldosista Party (PRE) in a surprise victory and formed a coalition government in 1996. Bucaram, a former mayor of Guayaquil nicknamed "El Loco" (the madman, a name he coined himself), gained support from the country's poor and disenfranchised.

After singing and dancing his way into office, newly elected President Bucaram continued his extravagance by recording a CD which many government employees were "encouraged" to buy. But the country soon became tired of the show. Bucaram introduced rigorous economic measures that caused steep price increases and those already living in poverty – the people he had promised to help – found themselves worse off. Most serious though was his blatant corruption in administering state funds.

In February 1997 a two-day general strike in protest against Bucaram brought the country to a standstill. The military maintained order but, exercising considerable restraint, refused to take sides.

By the end of the second day, Congress conveniently found a clause in the constitution that enabled them, by majority vote, to oust Bucaram on the grounds of mental incapacity. Confusion followed as both Vice President Rosalia Areteaga and Fabián Alarcón, President of Congress, claimed the presidency. Finally Congress officially voted in Alarcón as interim president pending democratic elections in August 1998.

Mismanagement and corruption continued and reform was delayed until the new President, Jamil Mahuad, a Harvard-educated centrist, took office in August 1998. His daunting task of reversing the economic slide was exacerbated by *El Niño* floods on the coast that had affected production of key agricultural exports.

Mahuad's success in bringing about peace with Peru was overshadowed by his unpopular introduction of austere economic reforms to secure IMF loans. The value of the sucre fell sharply as a result and, in an attempt to halt speculation, Mahuad ordered banks to freeze all existing accounts for at least a year. At the end of 1999, Mahuad announced his plan to replace the sucre with the dollar. The aim was to curb the 60 percent inflation rate, bring down interest rates, and spur investment. Many sectors accepted the measure but it incensed indigenous groups who rallied together and marched to Quito in protest. On January 21 2000, Mahuad was forced to flee as thousands of indigenous protesters stormed the Congress Building with the help of junior military officers. US warnings of isolating Ecuador internationally and withdrawing financial aid pressured the military chief in command of the new junta to back down in a matter of hours.

Power was ceded to the Vice President, Gustavo Noboa, who faced the challenge of a radicalized indigenous movement amid a general distrust of politicians and the country's worst economic crisis in 70 years. In less than two years there had been a transformation of Ecuador's economy, helped by low inflation since dollarization and millions of dollars of foreign investment in oil exploration and production.

In late 2002, Leftist and former coup leader Lucio Guitérrez won the presidential election, and soon secured IMF financing; by mid-2003 Noboa had fled to the Dominican Republic amid allegations of financial mismanagement.

In 2005 Guitérrez became the third president in eight years to be toppled and was replaced by Alfredo Palacio, his Vice President. Palacio steered a steady course, avoiding confrontation in view of his lack of legitimacy. In the election of late 2006, the banana millionaire Alvaro Noboa went through to the run-off with the former Finance Minister, Rafael Correa. Correa won by an easy margin, running on a platform of radical political reform and economic equality.

A former economics lecturer with a left-leaning agenda, he plans to replace the Congress with a Constituent Assembly which will draw up a new constitution. This model apes that of Hugo Chávez

of Venezuela, with whom Correa shares many ideological ties. He has vowed not to sign a free trade agreement with the United States and has said he won't renew the lease on the United States' military base in Manta in 2009. Correa has caused confrontation early in his administration, and will no doubt continue to do so for the coming years.

Despite the political turmoil of recent years, Ecuador's economy has not performed too badly, growing by 3.6 percent in 2006, mainly due to high oil prices and the stability brought by dollarization. It remains to be seen if Correa can steer a course between a more equitable sharing of Ecuador's resources (41 percent of the population still live in poverty) and more upheaval. ❑

LEFT: political graffiti in Otavalo. **RIGHT:** Rafael Correa, elected President in 2006.

ECONOMY AND ENVIRONMENT

*Ecuador has a difficult balancing act to perform if it is to
conserve the environment while boosting the economy*

The most significant event for the economy and ecology of the Oriente was the discovery by Texaco in 1968 of large petroleum reserves in pristine Amazon rainforest. The development of these oilfields spurred an economic boom in the 1970s but also resulted in profound damage to the rivers, rainforest, and the indigenous way of life. Today oil accounts for 56 percent of Ecuador's exports, and it will remain an important source of foreign income in the coming years.

The government of the day negotiated a profitable deal with the petroleum companies in 1972 when oil first started flowing through the Trans-Ecuadorian pipeline. At the same time, world oil prices rose dramatically. The government quadrupled its budget in three years, and public spending on social services was proportionally higher than in any other country in Latin America. Investments were made in education, health, and infrastructure that improved the lives of most Ecuadorians.

The history of the Oriente took a different course, however. Settlers, large corporations, and indigenous peoples competed for land and resources. Little thought was given to the potential impact on the environment, as drilling wastes and oil spills flowed directly into rivers and lakes. The native contingent had no concept of ownership and allowed oil companies to build roads and drill in exchange for gifts.

Settlers were awarded plots of land if they were willing to "improve" it, which meant clearing most of the native vegetation for agriculture or pasture. As their land was usurped by settlers, the indigenous peoples in the Lago Agrio area were forced to enter the new Ecuadorian society, often at the bottom social rung as laborers, domestic workers, and prostitutes. Or they fled deeper into the rainforest, coming into conflict with other tribes.

With the support of the environmental lobby in the 1980s, however, tribes such as the Quichua, Siona-Secoya, Cofan, Achuar, Shuar, and Huaorani began to raise awareness in Ecuador and abroad through protests, putting pressure on the government to recognize their land rights and for the oil companies to clean up their act. In the early 1990s a division within the Ministry of Energy and Mines was created to regulate the oil industry: today environmental-impact studies are required before each phase within an oil concession, although members of the local and international community would argue that these have little meaning. For example, in January 2000, the Ecuadorian government declared a huge area of Amazonian jungle (in the Yasuni and Cuyabeno-Imuya national parks) off-limits for mining, logging, and colonization in perpetuity. However, in the same month, the government gave permission to the City Investing oil company to begin seismic prospecting into the Cuyabeno Reserve.

Attempts at protection

One of the most controversial areas of oil production is in the petroleum concession of Block 16, part of which lies within the Yasuni National Park. The park was severely reduced in size after the Conoco oil company revealed plans to construct a pipeline. Intense pressure to abandon the project was exerted by indigenous Huaorani and international environmental organizations such as the Rainforest Action Network.

The block was sold to Maxus, which is a less visible Texas-based company and so less vulnerable to press criticism. Some efforts were made to minimize impact by using the latest technologies such as drilling 10 wells from a single platform, similar to offshore drilling methods; some of the water extracted from the wells was re-injected, avoiding the practice of polluting the rivers with high levels of toxic heavy metals and hydrocarbons. However, YPF, an Argentine company, purchased Maxus in 1996, and expenditures for environmental studies have been drastically reduced.

In October 2003, after 10 years of legal battles in US courts, attorneys representing 30,000 rainforest people of Ecuador charged Chevron Texaco with destroying their homeland by

LEFT: oilman on a dusty road through the Oriente.

dumping toxic wastewater and crude oil from 1971 to 1992. Pressure groups such as Oilwatch and Amazon Watch supported *indígenas* in their demonstrations against the OCP pipeline, which was completed in 2003, and carries crude oil from the Amazon to the Pacific, jeopardizing fragile ecosystems and local communities.

Economists initially estimated that the country would receive up to $3 billion of foreign investment upon completion of the pipeline, which could nudge the country out of its current economic crisis. While a period of high oil prices between 2003 and 2005 generated greater investment, it seems, however, that it is the IMF which

will most benefit from the new pipeline whilst Ecuadorians will become poorer and more debt-ridden than before. In 2006, President Palacio and Finance Minister Rafael Correa passed legislation diverting more funds to social programs and less to repaying the country's foreign debt. This displeased many lending institutions, including the IMF, but arguably set Correa on his course to become president in the elections of late 2006. In the meantime, much of the country's pristine rainforest and indigenous territories have already been irreversibly destroyed.

Another controversial project has been the construction of a 120-km (75-mile) long all-weather access road. Guard stations have kept settlers

from the Sierra out, but Quichua and Huaorani now use the road as the primary means of reaching the Napo River and are beginning to clear areas for agriculture. In addition, heavy rains in this hilly terrain have resulted in large and frequent landslides, which have silted up many small streams and threaten to break the pipeline.

Agriculture

The strong link between the need for economic development and environmental protection in Ecuador was made clear during the summer of 1997, when poor *campesinos* (peasants) burned forests and fields in the "greenbelt" that surrounds Quito to clear areas for grass to graze their livestock. Burning is common throughout the country and has been partially responsible for one of the highest rates of deforestation in Latin America (estimated at 300,000 hectares/750,000 acres per year). But it is hard to blame the *campesinos,* since their average wage is about $6 a day, and creating more pasture land with fire is purely an act of survival.

The agricultural industry, accounting for 40 percent of foreign earnings, is just behind petroleum in importance. Pesticides are used extensively to maximize production. Officially, the laws regulating pesticide use and residues on vegetables are strict, but they are rarely enforced. Most farmers have no training on what to use, nor use protective equipment.

Climate change

The rainfall record since the beginning of the 19th century shows a pronounced decrease. Glaciers along the Avenue of the Volcanoes have retreated on average 300 meters (950ft). The trend is most pronounced in the south. In 1995–6 Ecuador rationed electricity, because the Paute hydroelectric plant that provides 65 percent of the country's electricity was dry due to lack of rain as well as deforestation, which causes soil to absorb water less efficiently. Almost $4 billion in production was lost.

To save Paute from silting up completely, a new dam called Masar is being built upstream which will also provide vital electricity for the national grid. When rationing means you can't even turn on your lights, the vital connection between conservation of scarce resources and the health of the economy really hits home. ❑

LEFT: knocking a highway through the jungle.

National Parks

In an attempt to protect Ecuador's extraordinary variety of largely intact ecosystems, the agency INEFAN was created in 1992. It has since been incorporated into the Ministry of the Environment, which now manages and protects 22 national parks and protected areas that cover 17 percent of the total area of the country.

The entrance fees to the most popular national parks (Galápagos, Cotopaxi, and Cotocachi-Cayapas), help subsidize some of the less visited and more threatened reserves. For instance, many coastal mangrove swamps, which are vital breeding grounds for marine fish species, have been destroyed in the past 20 years by the construction of expansive pools for "shrimp ranching." The Cayapas-Mataje and the Manglares-Churute reserves were created to protect a small portion of these rapidly disappearing mangroves, but many locals are unaware that these reserves exist. There is a great need for community education on sustainable use of fish resources within these reserves.

Cloud forests were being cleared from the Andean central valley long before the Spanish conquered Ecuador in the first half of the 16th century, but the Andean eastern slope has never been cut because it is so wet, rugged, and inaccessible. However, as more roads are punched into the Oriente and colonists begin to fell the old-growth mahoganies and alders, protected areas such as Cayambe-Coca Ecological Reserve, Llanganates and Sangay national parks become important refuges for rare species such as the Andean spectacled bear, woolly mountain tapir, and Andean condor. The latest addition to the park system is the bi-national Parque Nacional Cordillera del Cóndor, which escaped deforestation and development because it was located along the disputed border with Peru. Although it is still mined and not yet set up for tourism, scientists are beginning to catalog its biological diversity.

Yasuni National Park in the Oriente is considered the most biologically diverse place in the world, where over 900 different species of trees have been identified in a single 2-hectare (5-acre) plot. Even with UNESCO Biosphere Reserve status, however, the howler monkeys and jaguars of Yasuni still have to share their habitat with oil companies and aggressively colonizing indigenous groups. Con-

servationists are extremely wary of this experiment, since the nearby Cuyabeno Reserve had its western half lopped off and the area is now filled with colonists and oil wells.

Mediating land-use conflicts perhaps presents the greatest challenge to the Ministry. Multiple and often environmentally damaging activities such as homesteading, timber harvest, grazing, water projects, mining, and oil production are permitted by other federal agencies in protected areas. The Ministry has benefited from financial assistance from several international aid agencies. Perhaps the most significant help came in 1995 in the form of a five-year "debt for nature" grant of $9 million from

the Global Environment Fund – which is a branch of the now "greening" World Bank. This grant supports high-tech research projects, such as a satellite image study to map out potential new parks in Ecuador's southern provinces, as well as providing funding for basic management in the field.

Cynics often refer to Ecuadorian protected areas as "paper parks" since essential environmental policing is still lacking, but it is remarkable that a country with limited resources has had the foresight to sketch out the natural areas that are worth saving in the future. If you are interested in the Ministry's work, its offices are at Amazonas and Eloy Alfaro, 8th Floor, Quito, tel: (02) 256 3429, or visit the Ministry of the Environment's excellent website: www.ambiente.gov.ec. ❏

RIGHT: a jaguar – one of the creatures in need of protection.

THE ECUADORIANS

The people of Ecuador inhabit a relatively small land, but they are as diverse and colorful as the landscape

Like other Andean countries, Ecuadorian society reflects divisions that can be traced back to the Spanish Conquest of the early 16th century. But the people have been shaped as much by Ecuador's wild geography as its history: the racial make-up, temperament, and outlook of Ecuadorians is radically different on the coast, in the Sierra, and in the jungle.

Until the discovery of oil in the early 1970s prompted an urban explosion, Ecuador was an almost completely rural society. To a large extent it still is, although roughly half the population live in towns or cities: how they behave and think is closely linked to their relationship with the land, and modern urban life conserves elements of traditional rural customs. To understand the differences between Ecuador's three regions, one should first look to village life.

Images from the countryside

The typical *campesino* (peasant) of the Sierra works hard to obtain a meager living from rocky, volcanic soil. Andean families live in a harsh environment, where bare mountains descend into shelving ravines and gentle valleys. The land is rarely flat, except on the valley bottom, which generally belongs to the rich landowners. The *campesino* must use ingenuity to terrace and cultivate the steep mountain sides on slopes with up to 60-degree angles, where the topsoil is easily washed away by rain.

In harmony with this environment, the typical *serrano* (mountain-dweller) tends to be tough, patient, frugal, and resigned to the difficulties of life. Yet *serranos* can be vivacious when their imaginations are fired. Andean music, with its plaintive tones, melodic pipes, and sorrowful lyrics, expresses the *serrano* temperament.

The peasants of the Costa live in contact with the abundant nature of the green lowlands,

PRECEDING PAGES: Otavaleñas selling handicrafts in Old Quito; light refreshment at Quito bullfight; steaming afternoon on the Amazon frontier.
LEFT: marcher in the Mamá Negra parade, Latacunga.
RIGHT: laundry in the Napo River.

where the warm climate and fertile soil make daily living easier. But life is also more uncertain because of the dangers of disease, floods, and other hazards. Like their environment, the *costeños* (coast-dwellers) tend to be easygoing and exuberant, but also quick-tempered, and unconcerned about what tomorrow may bring.

The Oriente is a case apart; it represents scarcely 4 percent of the population. Indigenous peoples have lived there for centuries in relative isolation, and their way of being is very different from that of the people of the Sierra who have suffered long years of discrimination. Light-hearted and self-confident, they are accustomed to a generous natural environment and a free lifestyle. This situation has begun to change with the presence of timber and oil companies that are endangering their environment, as well as encroaching colonization, which has brought about an accelerated process of assimilation.

Natural differences between the regions have been accentuated by slow, hazardous transport and difficult communications. But within each region, society is characterized by diverse racial and ethnic groups.

Traditional Andean society

The rigid social order that reigned in the Sierra from colonial times until the land reform of 1964 is the basis on which modern society was built. Cut off by the difficult mountain passes and under the strong influence of the Catholic Church, Andean society engendered a world of traditional values centered around the family.

The nucleus of rural life was the *hacienda*, or estate. These large properties were the main pole

population growth and increasing unrest among the peasants, who were pressing for more land, the authorities passed legislation to break up the larger estates and *haciendas* and hand over uncultivated land to the peasants.

Frontier settlements

While the Sierra has mainly produced food for local consumption, the Costa, with the advantage of its navigable rivers, seaports, and extensive fertile plains, has been developed over the past 100 years for export crops. Cocoa, bananas and, more recently, cultivated shrimps have each had their boom period.

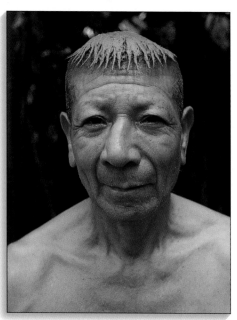

of production. Their owners were descendants of the Spanish *conquistadores* who controlled the country's economy and politics. They allowed indigenous families a small plot of land for their own subsistence in exchange for labor. This form of dependence still exists in a few areas, though it was officially abolished in 1971.

Mestizos (of indigenous and Hispanic origin) were employed on *haciendas* as managers, stewards, or clerks. The power they wielded over those under their authority fueled racial animosity between natives and *mestizos*.

The traditional social order of the Sierra began to disintegrate in the 1960s with the introduction of agrarian reform. In the face of rapid

CONFLICTING VALUES

The typical Spanish settler in the Sierra considered the act of work to be degrading, whereas the indigenous population valued it and disapproved of laziness. This was a further element that exacerbated racial tension, since the Spaniard expected the native to work for him, but then despised him for doing so.

These perceptions – Spanish intolerance and native incomprehension – still survive in diluted forms today, particularly within the realm of public service. It is this lack of mutual understanding that is largely to blame for the fundamental disunity which is so characteristic of Ecuadorian society.

Landless peasants from the Sierra traveled to the coast in search of work on the plantations or a piece of undeveloped land to till. Thus, in the space of a century, the inhabitants of the Costa changed from being a small fraction to slightly more than half of the total population.

The owners of the *haciendas* on the Costa tended to be more business-minded and enterprising than their *serrano* counterparts, and generally did not mind dirtying their hands alongside their wage-earning farmhands. This helped to create a more liberal and egalitarian society, which was accelerated by greater contact with the outside world via the seaports.

of 1964 had to leave the *haciendas,* and many of them sought work in the towns.

In just two decades, a quarter of Ecuador's population uprooted from a lifetime of rural living to the noise and pace of towns and cities, causing an urban explosion which the country was unable to support. Housing, and water and electricity supplies, could not possibly keep up with the huge increase in demand.

Today, Ecuador is short of an estimated 1 million homes; half of the existing houses lack running water and sewage facilities, and a third have no electricity supply.

With the foreign debt crisis of the 1980s,

Today the Ecuadorian Costa has a Caribbean flavor, which has led to Guayaquil being called "the last port of the Caribbean."

The urban explosion

In the 1970s, following the discovery of petroleum deposits in the Oriente, Ecuador began to export oil, which meant more jobs and the promise of new opportunities in the cities. At the same time, those peasants who had been unable to obtain land under the agrarian reform

LEFT: a Sierra *indígena* from Cañar; healer from Santo Domingo de los Colorados.
ABOVE: schoolgirls from Quito.

unemployment increased dramatically. The new urban population had nowhere to turn, except to the streets to scrape together a living by their wits. Vendors of trinkets, clothes, or electrical goods of doubtful origin throng the city centers, competing for the attention of passers-by. And on street corners, five-year-olds sell newspapers, shine shoes, or urge you to buy chewing gum in the hope of earning their daily meal.

Today, less than half the workforce has a steady full-time job; 38 percent are in the informal sector of street vendors and self-employed craftsmen, and 10 percent are unemployed. Unofficial sources put these figures even higher.

Meanwhile, the well-to-do find all the comforts of modern life in apartment blocks protected by armed guards. Shopping precincts display a broad variety of goods, and chauffeur-driven limos wait at the doors of luxury restaurants.

These contrasts are an expression of the erratic modernization of Ecuador, which has radically changed living and working conditions in scarcely two decades, without being able to answer the basic needs of its population. The most flagrant social contradictions are to be found in Guayaquil, center of the nation's wealth, which is surrounded by vast slum areas, the scene of abject poverty and rampant delinquency.

Chronic poverty

It is ironic that in Ecuador, a country rich in natural resources with its fertile valleys, abundant marine life, extensive forests, and reserves of oil and gold, most people face a daily struggle to scrape together the bare necessities. UNICEF estimates that about two-thirds of Ecuadorian families live below the critical poverty line, though until the recent economic crisis, Ecuador was not as badly off as Peru and Bolivia. The cost of living is relatively low, and as Ecuador produces most of its own food, few families are unable to get a square meal each day, and most do have a roof of some kind over their heads.

Hardship is not reserved to the towns. In rural areas, life is increasingly difficult for the peasants. Those who became small landowners cannot keep up with production costs, which rise faster than the price they receive for their crops, and they can rarely get cheap credit or adequate technical help. And once the paternalistic relations of the *hacienda* disappeared, the lack of social services became acute.

Successive governments have implemented social welfare programs in health care, aid to small farmers, food distribution, cheap housing, child care, employment, and other needs, but there are never enough resources.

All the same, in spite of hardship, the Ecuadorian people are on the whole patient, peaceable, and honest. The violence that has become typical in Colombia and Peru is less common here, and though the crisis has brought about a rise in delinquency and crime, the level of violent crime (with the possible exception of Guayaquil) is lower than in many of the industrialized world's big cities.

Indigenous groups

The visitor to Ecuador is readily seduced by the colorful costumes and skillful handicraft of the indigenous population: the women's embroidered blouses, the ponchos, the woven belts. But these are just the outward embodiment of a whole culture, an identity and a long history of resistance to assimilation by colonial society.

There are 10 different indigenous groups in Ecuador, each of which considers itself a distinct nationality, with its own language and culture. Together, they make up between a quarter and a third of the population. The most numerous are the Quichua, who live mainly in the Sierra and are related to the Quechuas of Peru and Bolivia.

In Ecuador, the terms *indígena* and *blanco* (indigenous person and white) are social and cultural rather than racial definitions. The term *mestizo* (mixed-blood) is not used frequently, although it is probably the most accurate description of the genetic heritage of most Ecuadorians. About half the population are self-identified as indigenous: people are considered *indígenas* if they live in an indigenous community, speak Quichua (or another indigenous language) and dress in a particular way.

Ethnicity in Ecuador is, to some degree, fluid. To some extent, over a generation or two, people can change their ethnic identity. An indigenous family can move to Quito, send their children to school dressed in Western-style clothes, and the children will generally be considered white. But these same children can return to their parents' community, and identify themselves as *indígenas* should they so choose.

Some Ecuadorian indigenous groups have been residents of the land for centuries, while others are descendants of people (called *mitmakuna*) who were moved around the Andes by the Incas: loyal Inca Quichua-speakers who were sent to recently conquered areas to serve as a teaching and garrison population, and people who were moved far from their home-

tacit resistance to the ill-treatment and discrimination practiced against them. The survival of indigenous culture and identity despite the odds is witness to their endurance.

The Quichuas and the native Amazonians in the Oriente have retained their own identities more than most. They lived for centuries in almost complete isolation from the rest of the world, apart from a few missions that were established there. But when oil companies began to dig pipelines and build roads into the region, settlers soon followed, and the natives with whom they came into contact were rapidly assimilated into modern society.

lands as a punishment for resistance to Inca rule.

Racism is deeply engrained in Ecuadorian society. Native people who become "white" by leaving aside their traditional dress, language, and identity are often those who show the most virulently racist attitudes. "Stupid Indian" or "dirty Indian" are typical epithets used about people who for years were excluded from public education, while their cultural heritage and language were treated with disdain.

Many *indígenas* have defied attempts to integrate them into *mestizo* society, manifesting a

LEFT: children have to earn a living.
ABOVE: woman selling roots for tea-making.

Recently, with international campaigning for protection of the Amazonian forest, indigenous groups who are still seeking to preserve their environment and lifestyle have found a worldwide audience for their claims, which gives them greater leverage on governments. In the late 1990s CONAIE (the Confederation of Indian Nations of Ecuador) gathered steam in its fight for economic reform and has become the most cohesive and influential indigenous organization in South America. The storming of the Congressional Building by thousands of indigenous protestors in January 2000 and the subsequent overthrow of President Jamil Mahuad demonstrated the growing influence that these groups are finally having on national politics. For more details, contact Survival International in London; tel: +44 (0)20 7687 8700; website: www.survival-international.org.

Afro-Ecuadorians

Many coastal people have curly hair and darkish skin, revealing their descent from African slaves. But in two areas, the warm Chota Valley in the mountainous province of Imbabura, and the northwestern province of Esmeraldas, there is a predominantly black population. In both areas there is a strong African cultural heritage, which has mixed with indigenous culture. The people of the Chota Valley, for example, play the plaintive native music of the Sierra on African-type instruments, while the native Awa from north of Esmeraldas have adopted the marimba, which is of West African origin.

Immigrant groups

There has been little immigration to Ecuador, apart from an influx of Colombians in the north, and a substantial number of Chinese who settled in Guayaquil. The only other sizeable foreign ethnic group is the Lebanese, popularly known as "Turks," who came to Ecuador at the beginning of the 20th century and have accumulated considerable economic and political power.

LEGACY OF SLAVERY

The origin of Ecuadorian blacks goes back to the slave trade. Historians believe that a Spanish frigate loaded with slaves was shipwrecked off the northern coast of Ecuador around the middle of the 17th century, and that the Africans who survived the wreck spread gradually across the province of Esmeraldas, living practically in isolation there for many years.

The black population of the Chota Valley, on the other hand, are the descendants of people who were brought to Ecuador to work on the sugar-cane plantations at the height of the slave trade, and who were given their freedom when slavery was finally abolished in the region.

Religious fervor

Since the arrival of the early missionaries, Ecuador has been under the strong influence of the Catholic Church. The word of the local priest or bishop still holds great weight, especially in the rural Sierra. However, since the end of the 19th century, when the anti-clerical liberal movement of the Costa took power, state and Church have been separated. In state schools, the curriculum does not include religion.

In recent years, the Catholic Church in Latin America has reaffirmed its intention to work on behalf of the poor. Some Catholic groups have taken this attitude further and are promoting political organization among the rural and urban slum populations as a means of seeking solutions to their grave problems.

Meanwhile, Protestant groups are engaged in active evangelization, particularly among the native population. Their success is due partly to the funding they provide for development projects and infrastructure, but also to the Protestant work ethic, which has been favorably received in many communities, as it has much in common with the indigenous belief in the dignity of labor. For several Protestant sects, however, the priority is to counteract the work of progressive sectors of the Catholic Church.

countries, such as wanting to live alone, is considered a strange and antisocial aberration.

But this sense of community operates only within the immediate group of family and acquaintances. Outside, in the cement jungle of the cities, the rule is everyone for himself.

The family unit

Middle-class families in Ecuador are typical of Latin countries: they value strong family ties and the close supervision of womenfolk, while men tend to take their sexual freedom for granted, priding themselves on their gallantry and their *machismo*. Among the poorer urban

Community life

Native culture greatly values the community. For example, indigenous peoples advocate communal ownership of land – a concept that often comes into conflict with Ecuadorian tenancy laws. Another facet of the community spirit is the *minga* – a collective work effort inherited from Inca times via the hacienda system *(see page 76)*.

Ecuadorians are generally glad to share whatever they have with family and friends, whether there is abundance or scarcity. The kind of individualism typical in northern

classes, especially those in the Costa, family relations are often far more informal, and it is not unusual for a man to have several families with different women, with whom he lives in turn, rarely contributing much to their upkeep. Young indigenous couples often have a "trial marriage" before formalising their relationship with wedding vows.

The status of women

Although Ecuador was the first country in South America to grant women the right to vote, it has been one of the slowest to embrace the principle of equality of the sexes in the workplace and at home. However, attitudes are beginning to

LEFT: an *indígena* couple admire an amusement park in Riobamba. **ABOVE:** Holy Week Passion Play, Otavalo.

shift. In 1989 a law prohibiting all forms of discrimination against women was introduced, and in 1995 an inter-American law against violence to women was written, signaling increased recognition of women's rights.

Another legal breakthrough has been free legal assistance to women when proceeding with charges of violence against them. However, domestic violence continues to occur at an alarming rate, with 80 percent of women in relationships having suffered some form of violence. In Quito and Guayaquil an average of 70 domestic abuse cases are reported daily.

The number of women's organizations work-

ing toward making the laws effective in practice is increasing. CEPAM (Center for the Promotion and Action of Ecuadorian Women) is one of the largest. Notably, there has been active participation of indigenous women in promoting such issues in the Sierra. The migration of more men than women from the Sierra to urban areas has led to indigenous women taking on new responsibilities in their communities. Organizations are focusing on providing education and health care for women.

Approximately 40 percent of women are now economically active. Many started work due to financial pressure, but as family size has decreased to an average of two or three children in urban areas, women are freer to pursue careers. They have entered most fields, although you will not see a female bus driver or welder. In 1990 women made up 5 percent of the police force. At high school, many girls take a premilitary training course, but very few pursue it as a career. The number of women and men studying at university level is more or less equal.

Despite engrained attitudes about traditional gender roles in Ecuadorian society, women are making inroads into national politics. The first female vice president of Ecuador, Rosalia Arteaga, was elected in 1996. There were two women ministers during Jamil Mahuad's presidency in 1999. In a decisively pro-woman stance, President Correa named seven women to his first 17-strong cabinet, although, tragically, the new Minister of Defence, Guadalupe Larriva, died in a helicopter crash soon after taking office. Indigenous women are also gaining a political voice. Over the past few years Nina Pacari became one of the most prominent indigenous female leaders, and in early 2003 she was elected as the Minister of Foreign Affairs of Ecuador.

Urban youth

Lifestyles in urban Ecuador are rapidly modernizing and changing the face of Ecuadorian culture. A middle-class teenager from Quito or Guayaquil probably identifies more with peers from the United States or Europe than with those in an isolated mountain village. These young people have access to cable TV, videos, internet, and MP3s. Western rock and pop are often more popular than traditional Latin music.

Shopping malls have become popular seeing places for teenagers before a night out at one of the modern multi-screen cinemas or meeting friends at a Burger King or Pizza Hut. On weekends *discotecas* playing salsa and rock music are bursting at the seams until 3 or 4am.

The best jobs for young professionals are often with foreign companies. As a result, night schools are as full as the *discotecas*, with students studying English and computer programing. As Ecuadorian yuppies enjoy their symbols of success – cellphones, credit cards, espresso coffees, and copies of *Newsweek* – they are worlds away from the rural *campesino* who still earns about $5 a week. ❏

LEFT: growing up in the city.
RIGHT: a stallholder at the Otavalo market.

THE BRIGHT COLORS OF EVERYDAY WEAR

The distinctive clothes of Ecuador's indigenous peoples are not just worn on high days and holidays, but can be seen in any market or village street

The diversity of Amerindian dress in Ecuador is witness to the strong sense of identity which the various groups have retained throughout the centuries. Some of the clothes that the *indígenas* wear so proudly today are in fact adaptations of the 16th-century Spanish-style costumes which were once a kind of uniform, indicating which *hacienda* they belonged to.

INCA INSPIRATION

Some items go back much further: it is said that the indigo and black clothing of the Saraguro people is worn as a sign of perpetual mourning for the Inca Atahualpa, killed in 1533 at the beginning of the Spanish conquest. Hats, too, date back to before the colonial period. Even the Panama is an adaptation of the headgear worn by the Manabí people at the time of the conquest. Fragments of *ikat* tie-dyed textiles from the pre-Hispanic period have also been found.

Traveling around the many markets in Ecuador, you are bound to notice the wide variety of colors and styles of shawls, ponchos, and *macanas*, the ubiquitous carrying cloths which are used to carry various items from kindling to babies.

▷ **WOMEN OF THE CLOTH**
Carrying traditional cloth, these Otavaleñas are dressed in their habitual finery: intricately embroidered cotton blouses, hand-spun skirts, and shoulder wraps. Their luxuriant black hair is bound with brightly coloured ribbons called *cintas*. Teeth are often capped with gold.

△**MEN'S BRAIDED HAIR**
The men of Cañar, Otavalo and Saraguro province wear their hair in a thick braid, bound with cloth.

▷ **SILVER TRINKETS**
Large, intricate silver filigree earrings and stunning indigo-colored ponchos are worn by the women of Pujilí in Cotopaxi province.

◁ **CHAPS WITH CHAPS**
Shepherds of Cañar province, north of Cuenca, wear sheepskin chaps, along with deep red ponchos. Broad brimmed white felt hats are worn by all Canãri men.

COLORS TO DYE FOR

ECUADOR

The rich colors of the ponchos, shawls, and scarves are the most striking thing about the dress of Ecuadorian Amerindians.

Many of the shades come from natural dyes: the deep indigo blue worn by the Saraguro Amerindians comes from the Indigofera, a tropical bean-producing plant; and the rich red of the scarves and wraps worn by *indígenas* of Salasaca is produced from cochineal, which is extracted from the crushed bodies of female insects *(Dactylopius coccus)* which live on the Opuntia cactus. *Ikat* textiles – ponchos, shawls, and belts – are also richly colored. They are made by a process of tying and dyeing *(see far left picture)* before the garment is woven.

The indigo-dyed cotton shawls called *paños*, which are made around Gualaceo, are the best-known of the *ikat* products. These shawls have macramé fringes which are an art form in themselves, as they can take many months to make.

△ **SEED-BEAD STATUS**
The color and number of rows of the Saraguro seed-bead necklaces indicate the community to which a woman belongs.

▷ **SHIGRAS**
Shigras are brightly colored bags made of agave fiber, which are hand-made in the central Sierra and found nowhere else in the Andes.

LIFE AND LORE IN THE SIERRA

Ancient values, traditional healers, and Christian festivals
are all part of life in the Sierra

Every valley of the Ecuadorian highlands is populated by distinct indigenous groups, some descendants of original Ecuadorian tribes, others descendants of the Incas or of people imported by the Incas from other areas of the country. Any guidebook that assures you "the people lead lives unchanged since Inca times" should be tossed right out of the window, because indigenous Ecuadorians don't live in a static universe any more than others do.

Europeans and Ecuadorian *indígenas* have been in contact for nearly 500 years, and Europeans have influenced the lives of *indígenas* in profound ways. Language, clothing, food, housing, and religion all have a European imprint. The influence has also worked the other way round: for example, more than half the food crops consumed in the world today were domesticated in the Americas before the arrival of Europeans. Most significant are corn (maize) and potatoes, which were the economic foundation of the Inca Empire.

Distinctive subcultures

Indigenous people still retain a number of customs of pre-Hispanic origin. Although the various groups have distinctive subcultures, they share a number of traits. Some might argue that a poor, evangelical Protestant family in Chimborazo that ekes out a living on half an acre of bad land has nothing in common with a wealthy, Catholic weaving family in Otavalo that has just finished the construction of a four-story apartment building in town. Yet both families consider themselves *indígenas*, both wear a distinctive dress that identifies them as members of a particular ethnic group, and both families speak Quichua inside their homes.

To paraphrase Sir Winston Churchill, the *indígenas* of Ecuador are separated by the barrier of a common language: Quichua or Runa Shimi (The People's Tongue). Quichua is part of the Quechua language family. There are five

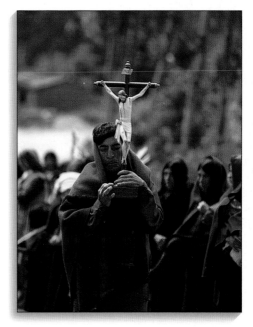

Quechua languages spoken today in Peru, and two or three different Quichua languages spoken in Ecuador. This means that *indígenas* from different regions of Ecuador do not necessarily understand each other. The origins of Quechua are unknown, but we do know that it was spoken around the time of Christ by the Chinchay, a trading group on the coast of Peru. The Incas adopted Quechua from the Chinchay and spread it throughout the Andes as they expanded their empire in the 14th and 15th centuries. Then the Spanish employed Quichua as a lingua franca to help them Christianize the *indígenas*.

The Quechua language family is growing; more people speak it now than in Inca times, including several million people in Ecuador. Today most *indígenas* are bilingual in Quichua and Spanish, but some older people, especially in remote communities, speak Quichua only.

Quechua and Quichua were not written languages when the Spanish arrived. Various alphabets have been devised over the centuries,

---

PRECEDING PAGES: market day, Saquisilí.
LEFT: market stalls. **RIGHT:** Easter procession in Cacha.

and this accounts for inconsistencies in spelling. The Quichua word for baby, for example, can be spelled *wawa*, *guagua*, or *huahua*.

Co-operative values

If there is a core value in indigenous society it is reciprocity, and naturally there are Quichua words that express this. One such word is *minga*, a collective work effort, which operates in various ways. In community *minga* the leaders organize an effort to repair the roads, or clean the irrigation channels, and every family must furnish several workers. If they fail to show up, some communities levy a fine.

Then there is a private *minga*. If a family needs to roof a house, for example, they invite the neighbors to a roofing *minga,* supplying copious quantities of food and *chicha* (a local beer made from *yuca*) for the workers, and people come because they know they'll need help themselves one day.

In the same way, *compadres* (two couples who are ritual kin because they are godparents to one another's children) also know they can call upon each other for help – anything from a loan of money to working in the kitchen at a fiesta.

Before the Spanish Conquest, money did not exist in indigenous societies. Items were bartered or labor was traded. Under the Incas, people paid their taxes in the form of labor *(mita)* or goods, and in return were taken care of with food from central storehouses in times of famine. In many places, reciprocity still means the exchange of goods or services rather than money. It is useful, as a tourist, to bear this in mind: for example, if you have a Polaroid camera, giving people photographs is much better than paying them to let you take their picture. However, this is not always applicable in public places such as markets, where you're likely to draw a huge crowd. Sharing food or gifts of food is culturally appropriate in most situations.

Sacred mountains

Indígenas throughout the Andes have worshiped mountains for millennia. In Ecuador, mountains are seen as male or female individuals, inhabited by powerful spirits. Mountains are also believed to control the rain and therefore the fertility and well-being of the entire region. The highest peak in any area was considered to be a *waka (huaca)* or sacred spot by the Incas. The Spanish constructed Catholic shrines over Inca sacred places, which is why you will see so many isolated chapels on hilltops.

Chimborazo, in the western *cordillera* of central Ecuador, is the highest mountain in the country, an enormous snowcap that looms over the province like a giant ice cream. It is known as Taita (Father) Chimborazo, while slightly to the north and in the eastern *cordillera* is Mama Tungurahua. Lesser peaks in the region are also seen as male and female pairs. Offerings such as guinea pigs, *trago* (a fierce sugar-cane liquor), or plants are sometimes made to the mountains to propitiate them.

In Imbabura province, Mama Cotacachi reigns to the west of Otavalo while Taita Imbabura dominates the east. When Cotacachi's peak is snowcapped the *indígenas* say it is because Taita Imbabura visited her during the night. Needless to say, this encounter resulted in a baby, Urcu (Mountain) Mojanda, which lies just to the south of Otavalo. The connection of mountains with fertility is obvious here, and many *indígenas* carry it even further. When, for example, people who live on the flanks of Imbabura plant crops they first ask Taita Imbabura to give them an abundant harvest. And when it rains in the region people say that Taita Imbabura is peeing on the valley below. If the mountains send the rain, Mother Earth (Allpa Mama or Pacha Mama) feeds the people by producing crops. It is customary to throw the last few drops of an alcoholic drink on the ground as an offering to her.

It was not uncommon for the Incas to sacrifice humans on the mountain tops, most often teenage girls who were told from a young age they were the chosen ones. The ritual was considered a great honor.

Shamanism and healing

Virtually every Ecuadorian community has a man or woman who knows the healing proper-

intestinal parasites, or because they believe an envious neighbor has cast a spell on them *(envidia),* or because they are looking for success in love or business. In addition, many people in the highlands have combined the Quichua belief in an inner and outer body, which must be kept in balance, with the medieval European belief in humoral medicine. This ancient tradition held that the body was composed of four humors: yellow bile, black bile, phlegm, and blood, whose relationships determined a person's disposition and health.

ties of various plants, or who can diagnose and cure by correcting spiritual imbalances or undoing spells. Healers are known by various Spanish names: *curanderos* (curers), *brujos* (witches), or *hechiceros* (sorcerers, witches). In Quichua, traditional healers are called *yachaj mamas* or *yachaj taitas* (knowledgable mothers or fathers). There are also midwives, who are known as *parteras*. The details of healing vary among the different ethnic groups, but in the Sierra people might go to a local healer for a number of reasons: it might be because they have

LEFT: a smile in the Sierra.
ABOVE: family sifting grain in Guamote.

Today people believe that such illnesses as infant diarrhea occur because the baby has had a fright, which caused the inner and outer bodies to become unbalanced. If the inner body actually flees, then death can result, so the healer performs a ceremony known as "calling the soul" to bring back the baby's inner body. Bodies can also become diseased because of bad air (*wayrashka* in Quichua), known as *mal aire* in Spanish. *Mal aire* gave us our word malaria, because people initially believed that the disease came from swamp vapors rather than from the bites of mosquitoes that lived in the swamps.

Calling the soul involves a cleansing, in which the patient's body is rubbed with a raw egg. The egg is shaken, and the sounds it makes indicate that the bad air is being absorbed. After the cleansing a child is sent to hide the eggs in the fields near by. Calling the soul also includes prayers in Quichua to God the Father, Son, and Holy Spirit, the Virgin Mary and the saints. The healer tells the patient's heart to rise up (that is, to come back), passes alcohol to all present, and smokes cigarettes, blowing the smoke on the patient. Tobacco has long been used by indigenous Americans in healing. There are many early Spanish accounts of its use among the Maya, and it is still used in healing and religious rituals throughout the Americas.

While most communities have their own healers, several areas are famous for their *curanderos*. People in the Sierra believe that the Shuar people have special healing powers, as do the Taschila *indígenas* of Santo Domingo de los Colorados on the western slopes of the Andes. The healers of Iluman, outside Otavalo, are also famous, and people come from all over the highlands to be treated by them.

These healers rely on centuries of knowledge passed down from their ancestors. In *ayahuasca* rituals, a psychotropic plant is given to the patient allowing the shaman to enter the sick person's body, find the illness, and cure it. These

NATURAL REMEDIES

How effective are these spiritual healers? It depends entirely on your belief system and on what kind of results you expect.

A positive attitude is tremendously important in healing of any kind. Western doctors say that 80 percent of all illnesses are self-healing – it's the other 20 percent that need medical intervention. If local healers have an 80 percent success rate, that looks pretty impressive. We should also bear in mind that many Western drugs, such as cocaine, curare, and quinine, come from plants that local healers know well and have used in their remedies for centuries.

medicine men are well-respected members of their communities and are given credit for saving many tribes from death. The practice is making a comeback as Ecuadorians and international tourists frustrated with modern medicines look for alternative methods of treating disease and mental anguish.

A calendar full of fiestas

Latin America's reputation for partying and festivities has a long history. In pre-Hispanic times community fiestas were organized around the agricultural and solar cycle. After the Spanish Conquest, the Church cleverly turned many traditional indigenous religious celebrations into Catholic feast days on the grounds that people were going to celebrate anyway, so they might as well observe a Christian occasion. Heavy drinking of *chicha* (local beer) is associated with nearly all Andean festivals, despite the Catholic Church's efforts to phase it out.

While a number of civic festivals are observed throughout the year in Ecuador, the most interesting fiestas by far are the traditional celebrations in the country. These mainly occur in the spring and summer, especially after the harvest and during the dry season. Every community has its own ritual calendar, so you might at any time of the year wander into a town in the

lage. Ambato, however, has outlawed water-throwing and has a fiesta of fruit and flowers that includes street dances and folkloric events. Hotels fill up early, but Ambato is only an hour from Quito by bus, so it's well worth a day trip.

Holy Week (Semana Santa, the week before Easter) begins with Palm Sunday (Domingo de Ramos). Throughout Ecuador people buy palm fronds in the market, weave them into different shapes and take them to church. Four days later, on Maundy Thursday, families visit the cemetery and bring food and drink for the dead in an observance similar to that of the Day of the Dead *(see page 82).*

middle of a fiesta in honor of its patron saint. However, here are a few of the major Sierra fiestas that are well worth catching:

Carnival (February or March) is held during the week before Lent begins on Ash Wednesday. *Carnaval* is a transplant from Europe, and represents a last fling before the austerity of Lent. Carnival in Ecuador is not like the one in Rio. In the Sierra the main activity is throwing water, and it is definitely not fun to be hit in the back with a water balloon or to have a bucket of water dumped on your head in a chilly mountain vil-

In Quito on Good Friday there is an enormous, spectacular procession through the streets of the city, complete with flagellants, men dragging huge wooden crosses, and penitents dressed in what look rather like purple Ku Klux Klan outfits. There are also impressive Good Friday processions, with costumed penitents in such Chimborazo towns as Yaruquies, Tixán, Chambo, and Chunchi.

Corpus Christi, in honor of the Eucharist, is a moveable feast, held on the Thursday after Trinity Sunday, usually in the first half of June. It is a major fiesta in the central Sierra, especially in Cotopaxi and Tungurahua provinces, but it is celebrated in many places, including

LEFT: Semana Santa procession, Quito.
ABOVE: Corpus Christi dancers.

some communities in Chimborazo province and in Saraguro, Loja province. Dancers with ornate headdresses and spectacularly embroidered costumes are now found only in such communities as Pujili, Cotopaxi, and San Antonio de Pillaro, Tungurahua. In Salasaca, the *indígenas* wear plaster masks, bright ribbons and feathers on their hats, and dance from Salasaca to the nearby town of Pelileo.

The winter solstice, Inti Raymi, celebrated on June 21, was once a major event in the Inca festival calendar. In the Cuzco area, south of the equator, the winter solstice is the shortest day and longest night of the year. Closer to the equa-tor, the differences in the length of the day and night are less dramatic, but astute indigenous astronomers still recognized them.

Today, **Saint John the Baptist** (San Juan Bautista, June 24) is the major fiesta in the Otavalo Valley and probably replaced an ancient, pre-Inca solstice festival.

Among the Otavaleños, San Juan is a male fiesta lasting the better part of a week. On the night of the 23rd, the male vespers *(la víspera)* dress up in costumes. The dancing begins after dark both in Otavalo and in the outlying towns.

The variety and ingenuity of the costumes is a sight to see – Batman, Káliman, North Ameri-

RITUAL BATTLES

Also connected with the festival of San Juan is a ritual battle with rock-throwing, which takes place at the chapel of San Juan, located on the west side of the Pan-American Highway from the town proper. Until the 1960s people were sometimes killed during these fights, and there are still some nasty injuries sustained. The point of spilling blood seems to be a payment or sacrifice to Mother Earth (Pacha Mama), in gratitude for the corn harvest.

Similar ritual battles (called *tinku*), fought with rocks and fists, still occur in the highlands of Peru and Bolivia, with corresponding casualties.

can Plains Indians with feathered headdresses, Mexicans with giant sombreros, women, soldiers. Some *indígenas* even parody gringos by wearing blond wigs, down jackets, jeans and running shoes, and carrying backpacks. The dancing goes on each night for a week, with groups of musicians and dancers moving from house to house and dancing (actually stomping) in a circle, with sudden reversals of direction which may represent the movement of the sun.

Saints Peter and Paul (San Pedro y San Pablo, June 29) is a major fiesta which takes place in Imbabura province, and in many towns and villages the San Juan and San Pedro y Pablo festivities run together.

On the night of June 28 bonfires are lit in the streets throughout the province. This seems to be a combination of indigenous and Spanish customs. Young women who want to have a child are supposed to leap over the fires. San Pedro is especially important in Cotacachi, where there are also ritual fights, and in Cayambe. While San Juan is important to the Otavaleños, San Pedro is the big event for the other main ethnic group in Imbabura, the people who live on the east side of the mountain in Zuleta, Rinconada, La Esperanza, and Angochagua.

Because San Pedro is the patron saint of the canton of Cayambe, hundreds of *indígenas*

is most often performed for the indigenous sponsor (called the *prioste*) of local fiestas.

The feast of the **Virgin of Carmen** (La Virgen del Carmen, July 16) is a notably larger celebration in the southern provinces than in the north. There is a fair *(feria)* in front of the church of that name in downtown Cuenca. In Chimborazo this fiesta is celebrated in Pumallacta and in Chambo.

Chambo, located just outside Riobamba, is the site of a miraculous shrine and fountain, one of those instances where a Catholic church was built on a mountain over what was undoubtedly a pre-Conquest holy site. The shrine is dedicated to the Virgen de la Fuente del Carmelo de

come into town and parade under the banners of their communities. The groups dance down the streets, around the main plaza, and past a reviewing stand, where local officials award prizes to the best groups. Among the dancers are men and women carrying roosters in wooden cages or tied to poles for a ceremony called the *entrega de gallos* (delivery of roosters). In the days of *wasipungo* (serfdom) the indigenous people on the haciendas had to show their loyalty to the landowner by making a ceremonial gift of roosters at this time. Today the ceremony

---

LEFT: fiesta of San Pedro celebrated in Cayambe.
ABOVE: All Saints' Day at a graveyard near Zumbahua.

Catequilla. *Indígenas* from throughout Chimborazo, in their finest traditional dress, visit the shrine and chapel on July 16. There is also a small fair at the base of the springs where food, drink, candles, and holy items are sold.

Saint James (Santiago, July 25) is the patron saint of Spain, and his image (on horseback with a raised sword, killing Moors) was carried into battle by the Spanish during their conquest of the Americas. The Spanish had firearms, which were unknown to *indígenas*, who associated Santiago with their powerful god of thunder and lightning (called Illapa by the Incas). Today Santiago is the patron of many communities, and there are many fiestas in his honor.

The feast of the **Virgin of Mercy** (La Virgen de la Merced, September 24) is a major two-day fiesta in Latacunga (Cotopaxi province), where a local dark-skinned statue of the Virgin is known as La Mamá Negra, the black mother. La Merced is also celebrated in Columbe (Chimborazo province).

All Saints' Day and the Day of the Dead (Todos Santos and Día de Difuntos, November 1 and 2). These two Catholic feast days are another example of the blending of Andean and European traditions. In pre-Conquest burials, food and drink were placed in graves to feed the dead in the next life. Some people believe that the spirits of the dead return to earth for 24 hours and will be unhappy if they aren't remembered.

If you are in Quito in early December you'll get swept along in the fesitivities that celebrate **The Founding of Quito** (December 6). There are parades, bullfights, dancing in the street, and general merriment.

Finally, there are many beautiful **Christmas** (**Navidad**, December 25) pageants and celebrations throughout Ecuador; it's a wonderful time of year to be traveling there. Christmas is a religious holiday, not a commercial one, and for the most part such European and North American

SPIRITUAL FOOD

All over Ecuador, little human and animal figures are baked from bread dough and taken to the cemeteries on November 2, where they are placed on graves along with paper wreaths and other offerings of food and drink. It sounds as if it would be a very sad occasion, but in fact it is often quite cheerful and festive.

In a nice local variation on the theme of "waste not, want not," poor people often come to the cemeteries and offer prayers at each grave site in return for some of the food. It's a sensible idea, as they need the food more than the departed – and, of course, a few extra prayers never go amiss.

customs as decorating Christmas trees and the exchange of gifts are virtually unknown. Among the local Christmas customs is the Pase del Niño (Presentation of the Christ Child). Families who own statues of the baby Jesus carry them in a street procession to the church, accompanied by musicians and by children dressed as Mary, Joseph, and other Nativity figures. The baby Jesus statues are blessed during a special Mass and then taken back to the household cribs.

The most famous Pase del Niño occurs in Cuenca, on the morning of December 24. It begins at the churches of San Sebastián and Corazón de Jesús and converges on the cathedral on the Plaza de Armas. Families from around the region bring their children, some dressed as *indígenas* and mounted on horseback, their horses decked with gifts of food, liquor, sweets, and fruits. Other children are on foot, dressed as Nativity figures or as gypsies, gauchos, or Moors, each group carrying its own statue of Jesus. Inside the cathedral the children are given *chicha* and bread, then the participants wind their way through the streets to celebrate Christmas at home.

In Saraguro, Loja province, each indigenous community owns a statue of the Christ child which is carried in a procession on Christmas Day from the main church to the home of the

Fiesta etiquette

There are appropriate and inappropriate ways to behave at fiestas, and everyone will have a better time if you know how to act. If you want to take photographs, for example, you will be less conspicuous and find it much easier at the larger and more public events. If you are the only outsider at a small village event, then circumspection is the word. Put your camera away, watch the festivities, talk to people, and then ask if you can photograph them. *Indígenas* have been pushed around by people for nearly 500 years, and they're pushing back. They resent the arrogance of some outsiders who assume they

Christ child's "godparents," the *marcan taita* and *marcan mama*. The procession is led by violinists and drummers and accompanied by costumed dancers. At the *marcan taita*'s house the statue is placed on a decorated altar, and the entire community assembles for a huge meal and an afternoon of music and dancing.

Other Christmas observances include the fiesta of the Holy Innocents (Santos Inocentes) on December 28 (in Quito), and the feast of Epiphany or Three Kings (Tres Reyes or Reyes Magos), on January 6.

LEFT: dancing partners at a highland fiesta.
ABOVE: a festival to inaugurate a new mayor, Salasaca.

can photograph anything, anywhere without asking permission. Remember, you're a guest here, not Sebastián de Benalcázar.

Ritual drinking is customary at all fiestas, and by late in the day many participants are hopelessly looped. It is insulting if you refuse to drink when the *trago* bottle is passed around, so join the revellers in a drink or two and throw the dregs on the ground as an offering to Pacha Mama. One of the best ways to enjoy a fiesta without causing or taking offense is to arrive fairly early in the morning and leave by about 2pm, before things get seriously out of hand and before you've shared so many drinks that you can't find your way back to the bus stop.   ❏

SOUNDS OF THE ANDES

Andean pipes happily coexist with brass bands and salsa clubs.
And then there are the weekend marimba parties...

What's a party without music? Making a joyous noise seems to be a universal human activity, and the Ecuadorians are no exception. At fiestas in Ecuador, two kinds of music are usually played: traditional, pre-Conquest indigenous music and Spanish (or more generally European) music. Naturally, after almost 500 years there has been a considerable blending of the two.

You can hear traditional music groups (*grupos* or *conjuntos*) at many indigenous fiestas and in folk-music clubs (*peñas*). There are also local and national traditional music competitions, which are usually free to the public, with an amazing variety of talent (or lack thereof).

Ancient instruments

Pre-Hispanic vocal and instrumental music was based on a pentatonic (five-note) scale, which gives Andean music its distinctive haunting, melancholic sound. Pre-Hispanic instruments were of three basic varieties: wind (flutes, pan pipes, conch shells), percussion (drums), and rattles and bells.

Flute-like instruments used today include the *quena*, a notched bamboo with six finger holes and a thumb hole, and a smaller flute (*pingullu*), which has three or four holes. When condors were more plentiful in the Andes, *quenas* were sometimes made from their leg bones. The pre-Hispanic flutes were always held vertically; flutes (*flautas*) which are held horizontally are modeled on the European instrument.

The pan pipe (*rondador*) goes back at least 2,000 years. Its modern Spanish name comes from that of the nightwatchman in colonial Ecuador who played the instrument on his rounds. A typical *rondador* is made of varying lengths and widths of cane or bamboo tied together in one long row; the different lengths and diameters producing distinct tones. Many Ecuadorian musicians now use *zampoñas*, the

pan pipes typical of Peru and Bolivia. The *zampoña* is tuned differently from the *rondador* and usually has two rows of pipes lashed together, which musicians say makes it easier to play. The large *zampoñas* have a deep, breathy sound that has been likened to a gentle wind off Chimborazo. There are many kinds and sizes of *zam-*

poñas with different names in Quichua and Aymara, but *zampoña* seems to be the generic name given to southern Andean pan pipes.

The frequent use of Peruvian and Bolivian instruments by Ecuadorian musicians is indicative of the cross-fertilization that occurs as Ecuadorians travel in Peru and Bolivia, and southern Andean musicians (or their tape cassettes) come north. The musicians teach one another songs and trade instruments. One of Bolivia's premier folk-music groups, Los Kjarkas, toured Ecuador some years ago, and their music has been emulated ever since. If you go to Ecuadorian *peñas* you are likely to hear some of their songs.

PRECEDING PAGES: *indígena* dance performed for tourists. **LEFT:** musicians at a fiesta near Otavalo. **RIGHT:** school of music in Riobamba.

Percussion instruments include drums (*bombos*) and gourd rattles (*maracas*). Bells (*campanas*) are still used, especially by dancers. In Imbabura province, for example, 10 or 12 cowbells are attached to a piece of cowhide and are worn over the shoulder by dancers at the fiestas of San Juan and San Pedro (June 24 and June 29).

Spanish influences

Stringed instruments were introduced by the Spanish and were soon incorporated into the traditional repertoire. These instruments include the guitar (*guitarra*), violin (*violín*), mandolin (*bandolín*), *charango* and Andean

monica (*rondín*) were introduced in the 19th century. The most recent addition is the portable Yamaha organ. Today, a mix of instruments is used to play both old and new music.

Brass instruments are another European introduction. Trumpets, trombones, clarinets, cymbals, French horns, and tubas, many battered beyond repair or the possibility of producing a harmonious note, are hauled out for occasional use. It is traditional for brass bands to play at small-town fiestas and civic events, during which musicians pass round a bottle and are soon beyond repair themselves. Volume and enthusiasm often surpass musicianship.

harp (*arpa criolla*). The *charango* originated in Bolivia and looks like a ukulele, but has five pairs of strings and eight frets. The body is sometimes made of wood, but more often from an armadillo shell. The Andean harp is a homemade version of the European harp, beautiful to listen to but difficult to make and transport, which is why few musicians use them.

After the Spanish introduced cattle into Ecuador, the indigenous peoples made a unique instrument from cow horns, called a *coroneta* or *bocina*. Between 16 and 20 horns are joined and then the joints are bound. The tone of the *coroneta* depends on the number of horns used. The accordion (*acordeón*) and har-

Another venerable musical tradition is the weekend concert in the park. Many towns have municipal bands which assemble on Sunday mornings and rouse the populace from their Saturday-night torpor. It's not exactly indigenous music: you are quite likely to get a rendition of the theme tune from the latest hit television series. In traditional music groups, men usually play musical instruments and sing, while women are only vocalists. Some types of music, including the *wayñu* (or *wayno*) and the *yaraví*, were probably introduced by the Incas and are almost always sung in Quichua. But the most common is

ABOVE: impromptu sidewalk concert.

the *sanjuanito*, which qualifies as Ecuador's national dance music. *Sanjuanitos* can be both instrumental and vocal and are played by folk-music groups and modern bands at most fiestas.

At a *peña* a typical group will be composed of young men playing the guitar, mandolin, *charango*, violin, drum, *quena, pingullo, zampoña,* and *rondador,* or a combination of these instruments, and they will alternate purely instrumental music with songs with musical accompaniment. Many of the songs will be in Quichua. Some you will hear all over the country, others are specific to certain provinces.

Festival music

To foreign ears much traditional fiesta music sounds like an obsession with one theme. The same refrain is repeated over and over, endlessly hypnotic and great to dance to. During San Juan, the musical groups literally dance all night (to *sanjuanitos* naturally), moving from house to house throughout the village.

Increasingly, traditional musical groups are being replaced by ones which use amplified instruments, especially for such occasions as weddings and other large parties. Into the house come the musicians in traditional dress, but instead of guitars and *quenas* they carry an electric sound system including microphones, amplifiers, speakers, maracas, and a Yamaha organ, which will prevent any sleep in the *barrio* for days. The musicians will tune up and launch into "La Rasca Bonita," a *sanjuanito* with a catchy tune and upbeat tempo that qualifies as the national party melody. The band alternates *sanjuanitos* with *cúmbias*, music of Afro-Caribbean origin from the coasts of Colombia and Ecuador. Everyone from grandparents to toddlers dances at these parties.

A dance which is done less and less at parties and now seems to be performed mainly at folk-music events is the *cueca*. It's a Spanish dance derived from the *jota* and is performed by any number of couples holding handkerchiefs.

Marimba and salsa

In the Esmeraldas region marimba is still very much alive. The Afro-Ecuadorians who settled freely in the area retained many of their customs, including their dance and music. The marimba instrument itself, the *chonta*, is similar to a xylophone, and was adapted from the African marimba using local hardwood. It is accompa-

nied by *bombos* (drums), *cununeros* (small tamborines), and *guasos* – bamboo stalks filled with seeds. In the villages near Borbon, north of Esmeraldas, every single house has its own marimba. At weekends and important holidays people head out to marimba parties. The local firewater *(aguardiente)* is often thrown on the instrument itself, to signify the beginning of the marimba. Each song tells a story, moralizing, instructing, illustrating daily life, or recognizing death. The haunting, passionate music goes on until dawn and sometimes for several days.

Salsa, merengue, and cúmbia, essentially dance music from Caribbean countries, is particularly big on the coast. Among the most popular artists from Ecuador are Los Duques, Medardo y sus Players, Los Chigualleros, and Los Embajadores.

In the modern shopping malls it is easy to find good recordings of salsa on CD. Music stores have rows of salsa compilations.

Rap, reggae, and Andean chill

In larger cities popular Latin music is more likely to be played. Reggaeton is big in Ecuador, as it is in many Latin American countries. Along with a mix of 1980s pop music, a blend of rap and Latin pop music is what you are most likely to hear in a *discoteca*, much of it originating in Puerto Rico and Panama. The lyrics are often ridiculous, but if you are in the mood to dance, nothing will get the disco moving faster. Andean chill is one of the more respected genres that have emerged in the Andes in recent years, albeit on a minor scale. The genre fuses traditional native songs, tunes, and instruments, with electronic music. Miki González is one of the premier artists of the genre. ❑

TAKING PART

Segundo Quintero and Carmen González are two of the better-known marimba artists, but recordings of marimba are hard to find. The Centro Cultural Afro-Ecuatoriano, Tamayo 985 and Lizardo García, Quito, tel: 02-252 2318, has videos of some of these frantic dances and information about the bigger festivals.

If you have time, there are plenty of schools in Quito where you can learn to dance to the tropical rhythms of salsa and merengue, in individual or group lessons. Once you've learnt the basics, head to Seseribo in Quito (Veintimilla and 12 de Octubre) on Thursday or Friday nights and join in.

PEOPLES OF THE AMAZON

The Amazonian people preserve many of the old ways,
but are learning how to live with contemporary changes, both good and ill

When Westerners think of indigenous Amazonian peoples, they conjure up strings of age-old stereotypes. The popular image is of naked men and women slipping through the jungle with Stone Age tools, isolated until recently from history and the outside world. According to this school of thought, they have always hunted for their food rather than grown it, and often engaged in brutal wars, shrinking their enemies' heads and occasionally eating their flesh. Conversely, they are held to be ecological saints, protecting their delicate environment at all costs.

Not surprisingly, the image has little to do with reality – as anthropologists in the Ecuadorian Oriente are rapidly finding out.

Coping with change

Far from being unchanging, undeveloping societies – and therefore "idyllic" – all Amazonian peoples have their own histories, and very dynamic histories at that.

Because Amazonians did not possess writing systems and, even more importantly, because their rainforest home is particularly unconducive to preserving the remains of past civilizations, there is little data with which to reconstruct Amazonian history. However, archeologists can now show that human beings have lived in the Amazon since at least 10,000BC, and that major technological breakthroughs occurred in the Amazon basin.

Amazonians domesticated manioc around 8000BC, and probably invented clay pottery around 4000BC, before any other indigenous cultures in South America. Migrations, new languages, and vast cultural and religious transformations characterize the history of the Amazon basin. Archeologists believe that cultural advances moved out of Amazonia into the Andes, not the reverse.

After the arrival of the Portuguese and Spanish *conquistadores*, Amazonian societies

changed tremendously, whether they had direct contact with the invaders or not. Plagues of diseases to which indigenous peoples had no resistance moved in waves from the coast, over the Andes, into the rainforest, drastically reducing the population. Migrations of peoples away from regions conquered and colonized by the

Spanish and Portuguese provoked chain reactions of indigenous peoples being forced off their original lands into unfamiliar territories.

New technologies reached the Amazon as well, again brought by intermediaries, so that no direct contact occurred with Europeans. Steel tools and new foods (especially the banana, plantain, and papaya, which originated in Southeast Asia) were traded from one people to the next throughout the jungle, transforming the ways of life throughout the Amazon. In this way, the pressures created by the Spanish Conquest of Ecuador and Peru transformed Amazonia, and the pre-Conquest jungle lifestyle will for ever remain a mystery to modern man.

LEFT: Shuar woman in traditional dress.
RIGHT: at work in the Oriente.

A range of jungle groups

The Ecuadorian Amazon is small compared with the vast jungles of Brazil, but it is nevertheless an important, even crucial, part of the region. It is inhabited by six major ethnic groups (the term "tribe," with its primitive implications, has been discarded). The largest grouping is the Quichua people (60,000), followed by the Shuar (40,000), Achuar (5,000), Huaorani (3,000), Siona-Secoya (650), and the Cofan (600).

The Huaorani people remain the most nomadic of Ecuador's indigenous Amazonians, and the least interested in cultivation, but during the 20th century they too partially adopted horticulture. Because they customarily went about naked, and relied so much on hunting and gathering wild foods, the Huaorani were originally called "Aucas," which means savages in the Quichua language. The Huaorani have rejected this name, which they, quite understandably, consider highly derogatory.

It appears almost certain that the Huaorani, who are composed of a number of discrete groups (Guequetairi, Pijemoiri, Baihuairi, Huepeiri, etc) are an amalgamation of survivors from many different groups diminished by disease, war, and migrations. For this reason, anthropologists view the sparse material culture

of the Huaorani, not as evidence of "backwardness," but as the basic survival mechanisms of those forest cultures that endured the most intensive stresses.

The Amazonian Quichuas are closely related to the people of the same name who dominate the Andean highlands of Ecuador. Anthropologists surmise that Quichua-speakers migrated down into the rainforests after the Spanish conquered the highlands in the early 1500s. The most numerous of the indigenous Amazonians, the Quichuas are composed of two distinct ethnic groups, the Canelos and the Quijos. These peoples brought the knowledge of well-developed agricultural systems from the Andes to the jun-

MYTH AND REALITY

Although the popular Western image persists of Amazonians surviving by hunting wild game and gathering fruits and nuts, the truth is that most indigenous peoples are no longer true hunter-gatherers. In the 21st century they obtain nearly all their foodstuffs from cultivation.

They are either horticulturists, which means that they establish moderate-sized, temporary gardens; or agriculturalists, planting crops on a permanent basis and usually on a much larger scale. The only partial exception to this is the Huaorani group, the most nomadic of the Ecuadorian Amazonian peoples.

gle, although they had to learn how to grow very different crops in their new territory. Living in dispersed, permanent settlements on individually owned plots of land, the Quichua men clear land and plant crops, while the women maintain, weed, and harvest them. They use a rotation system, resting the plot for three years after approximately five years of cultivation.

In the northern Oriente

The small ethnic groups that live in the northern region of the Ecuadorian Amazon are the Cofan (who call themselves the A'I) and the Siona-Secoya, a combination of two once sepa-

allow it to rot and mulch the exposed earth.

These peoples are semi-nomadic, which is to say that they move about within defined territories, abandoning old plots for new ones located in richer hunting grounds. They most frequently locate their gardens close to their houses, but sometimes plant smaller, less complex gardens at some distance from home. Siona-Secoya and Cofan farmers are women, and the profundity of their knowledge about soils and maintaining their fertility, about weather patterns, plant behavior and diseases, and crop combinations (beans and corn, or corn and manioc, for example) is truly astounding.

rate groups with very similar customs that unified when their numbers dwindled drastically in the 20th century. These peoples practice what anthropologists call "slash and burn," a technique of creating small clearings in the forest which produces food for two or three consecutive years and then must be abandoned to replenish their fertility. The Siona-Secoya usually leave big trees standing, especially those that produce fruits, and they do not always burn off the vegetation they have cut, but sometimes

LEFT: missionaries at work in the early 1900s.
ABOVE: a Huaorani spokesman accepts land title agreement in 1990.

The Shuar people of the southern region of Ecuadorian Amazonia, and their closely related cousins the Achuar, practice a horticultural system heavily dependent upon one crop plant – sweet manioc. Women harvest the tuber 12 months or more after planting it, and they simultaneously re-sow small tuber cuttings as they harvest. When manioc is mature, it can be left in the ground to continue growing without any risk of spoilage, which has obvious advantages in tropical Amazonia. The Shuar and Achuar may perhaps be described as semi-settled, rather than semi-nomadic. In recent years, Shuar and Achuar men have started raising cattle in increasing numbers, converting jungle to pasture. This income-earning strategy is probably not sustainable considering the fragile soil and subsoil ecology of the jungle, yet the Shuar and Achuar are finding increasingly sophisticated methods of planning their survival in the rainforest.

Movements through the forest

It is still true that hunting, gathering, and fishing determine the movements and rhythms of life for indigenous peoples. Anthropologists once assumed that hunting was the most important of these activities, but the gathering of wild fruits, honey, nuts, roots, grubs, and insects – a task

the planet's ecology, coupled with a romanticization of Amazonian life. In fact, it is fairly obvious that the indigenous people of the Oriente kill animals for food until those animals become scarce. Then they move on.

Yet the nomadic and semi-nomadic lifestyles of most indigenous Amazonians have prevented and continue to prevent the extermination of game animals upon which indigenous peoples depend. The horticultural groups have always placed an overwhelming social emphasis upon having small families with no more than two children. Population stability unlocks the door to ecological stability. Amazonian belief-

performed exclusively by indigenous women – actually provides the largest part of the diet. The origin of the "hunting" myth was probably due to the fact that the mostly male Western anthropologists talked almost exclusively to indigenous men, who would have discussed their own activities, and not those of their womenfolk.

Another, more recent, myth held about indigenous Amazonians is that they never kill more than they need in the rainforest, that they revere the jungle's animals, and are attuned to the natural balances of their environment. There is some validity to this view, but much of it stems from the industrialized nations' recent awareness of how they themselves have abused

BENEFICIAL TABOOS

The Shuar and Achuar people believe that deer, owls, and rabbits are the temporarily visible embodiments of the "true soul" of dead human beings, and therefore they do not hunt these animals.

The Siona-Secoya will never eat deer for similar reasons, and they prohibit the hunting of tree-sloths, black monkeys, opossums, and weasels. They also revere and fear the pink river dolphins, and never harm them.

The Quichua honor the jungle puma, a very rare feline, and would never shoot one. It is thanks to these beliefs that many of these creatures still flourish in Ecuador's jungles.

systems also encompass a number of iron-clad taboos against hunting and killing certain animals *(see panel opposite)*.

Crafts of the Oriente

For all groups except the Huaorani (who wore nothing, even though men would use string to tie their penises up by the foreskin), a major craft used to be clothes-making. Shuar men and Achuar women spun homegrown cotton, wove it into cloth and dyed it with vegetable-based colorings. The men wore wrap-around kilts, tied in place by bark string, and the women fastened their dresses over their right shoulders,

of natural materials in the tropics because they are much heavier, induce food to rot, and are not nearly so versatile. The normal carrying basket of the Amazon is a plaited, openwork cylinder, no more than a meter high, tightly woven and very sturdy. The finest baskets are woven by the Shuar, for holding personal ornaments and other finery; they are lined with smooth banana leaves, and have an attached cover.

The tourist market has almost completely transformed another craft, pottery, which has always been the domain of women. Quichua women make clay vessels for household use, as well as sacred vessels with ritual character.

using a belt around their waists. The Siona-Secoya and Cofan men wove ultra-lightweight knee-length cotton smocks, called *cushmas*, which they dyed blue or red. The Quichuas adapted the forms of clothing their highland cousins wore. All of these peoples now usually wear trousers, shirts, and blouses, dresses, skirts, and shorts that are indistinguishable from those of other Ecuadorians.

Basket-weaving, a male craft, has survived a lot better than the production of clothes. Plastics simply do not perform as well as baskets made

---

These vessels are meticulously executed, elaborate, and eggshell-thin, with geometric and zoomorphic shapes and motifs. Shuar women lavish intricate geometrical adornments on the jars used to boil and serve the hallucinogenic beverage, *ayahuasca (see page 97)*. Tourist demand for Amazonian pottery has transformed its production into something resembling an assembly line, where duplicates are produced with patterns that have no significance. The income derived from the sale of ceramics is, relative to the overall monetary income of indigenous Amazonians, quite considerable, and has given women a degree of power over their lives in the midst of ongoing cultural transition.

Most fantastic of all Amazonian arts are the feather and beadwork crowns, necklaces, earrings, and other ornaments, which rely upon the plumage of toucans, parrots, macaws, hummingbirds, and other magnificent birds. These stunningly beautiful works of art have always possessed enormous ritual and spiritual significance for Amazonian peoples, directly linked to their use in the *ayahuasca* ceremony *(see page 97)*. Today, tourist demand for such ornaments, to take home as souvenirs, is encouraging indigenous Amazonians to kill the most colorful, and usually the most endangered, birds at an accelerated rate.

Amazonian shamans

It was in the realm of spiritual and mythical creativity that indigenous Amazonians made their greatest strides and their most momentous discoveries. Because the Amazonian storehouse of knowledge and wisdom has always been transmitted orally, a great deal of the complexity has been lost. Indigenous spirituality has been mercilessly attacked by missionaries ever since the Spanish Conquest. In recent years Protestant groups, such as the Summer Institute of Linguistics, have worked to blot out the legacy of thousands of years, preventing the transmission of traditions from the old to the young. Never-

DON'T EVEN THINK ABOUT IT

Don't buy anything made from the plumage of Amazonian birds.

Because the importation of products which cause the death of any endangered species is prohibited by the United States, Australia, and all of Western Europe, tourists who are irresponsible enough to attempt to take their "trinkets" home will inevitably have to surrender them at the customs office. This makes the death of these magnificent birds, and the devaluation of the traditions of Amazonian peoples, a tragic exercise in futility. The lower the demand for such souvenirs, the fewer birds will be killed.

theless, the enduring center of that legacy, shamanism, survives among the six principal peoples, albeit by ever more slender threads.

Shamans are the individuals who preserve the oral histories, myths, legends, and other belief systems of their peoples. Among the Siona-Secoya, Quichua, and Cofan groups shamans are usually men, but female shamans are not unknown in the Shuar and Achuar cultures. Many shamans devote their time to curing diseases through elaborate rituals. There are shamans who bewitch others, causing disease and misfortune to their enemies, or to the enemies of those who pay them to do so. Shamans enact the ceremonies of initiation, the rites of passage of young men and women into adult-hood; and they train others to take on the role, passing on the knowledge and the rituals.

The tools they use vary. Quichua shamans own magical stones, which act as their famil-iars. The Shuar and Achuar shamans utilize magical darts called *tsentsak*, to bring about both healing and harm. But the most important tools they all employ are hallucinogenic sub-stances extracted from jungle plants. The vine known as *ayahuasca*, Quichua for "vine of the soul," is the hallucinogen par excellence.

Using drum rhythms and other musical pat-terns, vocal incantations, the light of fires, and

The power of the family unit

In indigenous Amazonian society the most important organizational unit is the extended family. The rules of kinship define the individ-uals' rights of inheritance, whom they should marry, and where they should live.

The Huaorani, with their very loosely defined kinship rules that do not even insist on the authority of older people over younger, can be seen, again, as a society pared down to essen-tials in its struggle to survive. Cofan and Siona-Secoya men may only marry women allowed to them by a patrilineal system: couples live with the family of the man's father, or in a house built

the colors provided by feather ornaments and body paint, the shamans guide those who have drunk potions derived from *ayahuasca* to see visions based on the symbolism and mythology of their cultures. The jaguar, anaconda, and harpy eagle recur over and over again in such visions. This communion with their ancestral past and the supernatural is a continuous source of social and cultural cohesion for indigenous Amazonians, and has nothing in common with the often self-destructive use of drugs encoun-tered in Western cultures.

LEFT: Cofan family in traditional dress.
ABOVE: young Cofan *indígenas*.

close to the father's home, and they inherit prop-erty and privileges from the man's father.

Shuar men initially live close to their wives' families, before moving to their own houses, but inherit through their fathers' line. Achuar men permanently reside near their wives' families, inherit through their mothers' lines, and marry women according to matrilineal relationships. The Quichua people possess a patrilineal sys-tem, but one which is broader and more com-plex, defining a kinship group called the *ayllu*, several of which compose a community.

Amazonian cultures have no single leader or chief. Instead, leadership has always been pro-vided in crises by shamans and military men.

While Quichua farmers did not wage wars or carry out raids as much as they suffered from them, the lives of all the other groups were defined by feuds, raids, and war. The Siona-Secoya, Cofan, and Huaorani raided to capture women and to avenge raids against them, but never for territory. For the Shuar and Achuar, warfare symbolized the spiritual quest for power: by killing a designated enemy a man could gain the visionary magical soul called *arutam*, and possess the power to lead others.

The practice of severing an enemy's head, removing the skull, and shrinking the skin is a source of great notoriety for the Shuar and

Achuar. As gruesome as this practice may seem and as perverse as it became in the early 1900s due to Westerners' fascination with it, the rituals associated with shrinking heads were an integral part of the shaman-leader complex that defined war and peace among these peoples. Today, far from shrinking heads, the Shuar and the Achuar have organized the most successful ethnic federation in the Amazon basin, a model for groups in Ecuador and other nations.

Twenty-first century politics

Oil development over the past forty years has forever changed the rainforest environment. The indigenous Amazonians have no choice but to adapt and develop stagies in order to survive.

In the Federation of Shuar Centers, shamans no longer use their powers for vengeful purposes, but are organized around health and community issues. In addition to fighting for Shuar and Achuar land rights, the federation is involved in the protection of the environment in the southern region. The Shuar Federation has also published scores of books about the Shuar and Achuar oral traditions, which will make them far more accessible to future generations.

For the Quichuas, organizational models are available from their highland cousins, who have become intensely political. The Quichua regional federations have helped to link indigenous Amazonians and the peoples of the highlands; as a result, an Amazonian and highlander confederation, CONAIE, has been formed at national level.

For the smaller groups, the specter of demographic disappearance is real and terrifying. The Siona-Secoya community on the edge of the Cuyabeno Fauna Reserve has resisted oil development in its territory and worked with the Ministry of Environment in putting together a sustainable development plan for the reserve and buffer zones. This tribe is committed to maintaining its close relationship with and dependence on the rainforest.

Faced with the multinational oil companies and the subsequent influx of outsiders, a small number of the Cofan people, the tiniest of the groups, are developing their own survival mechanisms in the village of Zabalo (*see The Gringo Chief, facing page*).

Meanwhile, working through CONAIE, the Huaorani have struggled with the Ecuadorian government to gain title to at least part of their former lands. In the territory they have regained, about 600,000 hectares (1½ million acres), they theoretically have enough land to create a way of life that retains some elements of hunting and gathering. Although the Ecuadorian government maintains the right to exploit deposits of oil under some of these lands, much of the area near the Peruvian border was declared "untouchable" by an act of congress in 1999.

In early 2007, President Palacio signed a decree to formerly create the 809,000-hectare (two million-acre) zone to the south of Yasuní National Park which goes someway to making up for the lack of protection from oil exploration. ❑

LEFT: making a canoe in the Oriente.

The Gringo Chief

Randy Borman looks like many other guides catering to the boom in Amazon tourism as he leads groups of Westerners down the Aguarico River to visit a small Amerindian village, Zabalo, home to a splinter group of indigenous Cofan who have moved downriver, by motorized dugout canoe, from their main community of Dureno.

But Borman is different: brought up among the Cofan people by his missionary parents, he found it difficult to settle in the United States, and returned to the Amazon where he developed his own tourism business. Now he is the elected president of Zabalo, a village he founded and whose economy is based entirely on the North American tour groups he brings to observe the traditional hunting and fishing lifestyle. The village sits on a small island separated from the shore by a narrow channel where stingrays live. During flood season, the huts are up to their stilts in water. Five of the huts are inhabited by the Cofan, two by visiting tour groups. Downstream from the central clearing are five more Cofan huts and a schoolhouse.

The Cofan and their neighbors, the Siona-Secoya, are the two peoples indigenous to the Aguarico who are facing cultural extinction. Their combined populations number just over 1,000, but in the years since 1972, when Texaco's first well in the region began pumping oil, some 30,000 *mestizo* colonists have settled in the Lago Agrio area alone. A mere hour's bus ride from Dureno, Lago Agrio has mushroomed into a rough-and-tumble regional center linking the Amazonian Oriente district to the world. Unfortunately for the Cofan, their hunting land on the Lago side of the Aguarico River was cut to ribbons by a 504-km (315-mile) oil pipeline.

Borman organized local efforts for the Cofan to win legal title to their land. Pressured by a coalition that included missionaries and US academic leaders, the government finally recognized 8,000 hectares (20,000 acres) on the Dureno side of the river as a Cofan *comuna*. While *comuna* status offers only tenuous protection, the victory did give the Cofan the confidence to fight for their rights.

Even if no more roads are built or wells dug, Borman believes the damage has been done. While the Aguarico's oil-eating bacteria have been able to handle the dumping and the spills, there is no such handy solution to the problem of the colonists, who

RIGHT: Randy Borman guides a group through an Amazon tributary.

have used the oil company roads to gain access to the jungle, transforming it into a patchwork of small coffee farms.

"So many of the bases of culture in Dureno have been knocked away," Borman says. "The Cofan now support themselves by growing coffee for export, just like the colonists. The majority of kids there feel kind of directionless.They tend the coffee plants, play volleyball, and get drunk." He regards Zabalo as a way of giving the Cofan control over the pace of change, enabling them to retain their language and their sense of themselves as a people.

"The tourism business is a wonderful way of robbing the rich and giving to the poor," says Borman.

Semioticians would have a ball with Zabalo, a traditional Cofan village that supports itself by looking like a traditional Cofan village. Borman is ready to answer the unspoken charge that he is selling culture, not preserving it. "A traveler will gain a deeper appreciation of the jungle, but also of the people. The Cofan are not selling themselves, they are enhancing their integrity."

Some might see a contradiction in the fact that Zabalo's tourist economy is dependent on the motorboat, and thus on oil. "I call it realism," says Borman. "Trying to keep the Indians in a pristine showcase denies them their dignity." Of course, Zabalo is a showcase of a kind, but at least it's one co-produced by the Cofan people themselves. For more information, look at www.cofan.org ❏

ARTESANÍAS

*The ancient arts and crafts of the indigenous peoples of Ecuador
have become much sought after by Western visitors*

There are no words in the indigenous languages of Ecuador for art, nor is there a distinction between fine arts and crafts. Seduced by their beauty, Westerners have included many traditional Ecuadorian *artesanías* in our own category of fine art, particularly textiles, ceramics, and jewelry. If you have the time, there's something particularly satisfying about buying things from the artisans themselves or shopping in the market, but products from throughout the country make their way into Quito and to the famous market in Otavalo.

Woven textiles

Four or five thousand years ago, some genius in the northern Andes invented the stick loom, which is still in use and generally called the backstrap loom (local names include *awana, macana,* and *telar*). This loom, sophisticated in concept and simple in form, is made of sticks and poles, with one end fastened to a stationary object and the other to the weaver's back.

When the Incas made a census of their empire they counted humans first, cameloids (llamas and alpacas) second, and textiles third, before precious metals, gemstones, ceramics, or food. The pre-Hispanic Andeans were textile-obsessed, and the Spanish were amazed by the superb hand-woven cloth made of cotton, and from the wool of the cameloid that they found in Inca storehouses.

Ecuador's damper climate has not been as conducive as Peru's to the preservation of organic materials, but the few pre-Hispanic textile fragments that exist suggest a tradition as venerable and as exquisite as that of Peru. The Spanish introduced the treadle loom, spinning wheel, handcarders, wool, and silk; much later came electric looms and synthetic fibers. But an amazing number of weavers still use the stick loom. Even in Otavalo, where most weaving is

done on the treadle loom, some ponchos and virtually all belts are made on the backstrap loom. In Saraguro, blankets *(cobijas)*, grain sacks *(costales)*, and most items of traditional dress are hand-spun on simple spindles of the kind you see throughout the Sierra, and hand-woven on the stick loom. These pieces are difficult to come by, but some are sold in Quito stores. In Ecuador, the majority of weavers are men, although many women also weave.

The Cuenca region is famous for its *ikat* textiles. *Ikat* (*amarrado* or *watado*) is a dyeing rather than weaving technique, where the warp threads are tied and dyed *before* the piece is woven. Pre-Hispanic *ikat* fragments have been found in Ecuador, so we know the method is an ancient one.

The best-known *ikat* textiles are *paños*, indigo-dyed cotton shawls with elaborate macramé fringes, made in and around Gualaceo. A newer style is black and red with a macraméd, embroidered fringe. It takes only

---

PRECEDING PAGES: weavings made by Salasaca *indígenas;* handmade belts in Otavalo; weavers in Chimborazo province. **LEFT:** local ornaments. **RIGHT:** weavers learn their skills as children.

hours to wrap the design, dye and weave the shawl, but up to three months to knot the fringe. *Paños* were traditionally worn by Amerindian women, but young women no longer wear them, so fine ones are becoming rare. If you want to see the older women in their finery, proud as queens, visit the Gualaceo Sunday market.

The skilled dyers and weavers have switched to making *ikat* woolen belts, scarves, and shawls without fringes, usually dyed black or brown over red, blue, green or purple. Some of these shawls are made into high-fashion clothing, available in Quito.

Ikat carrying-cloths called *macanas* are made

around Salcedo and in Chimborazo province. The Salcedo *macanas* are of deep indigo like the Cuenca *paños*, but the designs are coarser and they have a short fringe. *Macanas* are used throughout the Sierra as carrying-cloths, to haul everything from a baby to a load of firewood.

Ikat ponchos are made and worn in the Sierra from Cañar to Natabuela, north of Otavalo. The poncho is a post-Conquest garment, an adaptation of the Inca tunic. Various kinds of plain ponchos are woven for daily wear, while the *ikat* ones are reserved for weddings and fiestas. Especially beautiful *ikat* ponchos are made in Cañar, Chordeleg, Cacha Obraje (outside Riobamba), and Paniquindra (near Otavalo).

Like ponchos, *ikat* blankets are made in every highland province, but these are for daily (or nightly) use. A good one of hand-spun wool, woven in two sections and sewn together weighs 4.5kg (10 lb) and will keep you warm in a tent on top of Chimborazo.

Belts *(chumbis)* are woven on the backstrap loom throughout the Sierra. Double-faced belts with motifs ranging from Inca pots to farm animals are woven from hand-spun wool or commercial cotton thread in Cañar. These are among the finest belts made in Ecuador, rivaled only by those of Salasaca.

Salasaca belts are still made of hand-spun wool, and many are dyed with cochineal, a natural dye made from crushed female insects which live on the Opuntia cactus. Running a close race are a number of double- and single-faced belts with woven motifs made in Chimborazo and Bolívar provinces, followed by belts made in Otavalo and Paniquindra in Imbabura province.

Tapestries

In the late 1950s the Andean Mission embarked on one of those craft projects that usually die a slow death. But this one was a resounding success. Weavers from Salasaca and Otavalo were taught how to make tapestries *(tapices)* on the treadle loom. This technique, in which the weft threads interlock, gives tapestries a painterly quality. Today the stores around the main plaza in Salasaca and half the Otavalo market are filled with tapestries, including wall hangings, handbags *(bolsas)*, and pillowcases *(cojines)*.

Hand-knit clothing

While Ecuadorian women have been knitting since the colonial era, a Peace Corps project in the 1960s got the modern industry off the ground. Today sweaters *(chompas)*, vests *(chalecos)*, and hats *(gorros)* of hand-spun wool are made in Cuenca and in the northern towns of Ibarra, Mira, San Gabriel, San Isidro, and Atuntaqui. Exporters and Quito craft-store owners work with the knitters on the production of exclusive designs, some of which are knitted in cotton. The highest-quality ones are usually sold in Quito or abroad, although some fine ones do show up in the Otavalo market. Wherever you buy a sweater, try it on. The knitter's idea of size may not necessarily be the same as yours.

Embroidery

If you look carefully in the Otavalo market you will see women from an ethnic group other than the Otavaleños, wearing pleated skirts and blouses with extremely fine, intricate embroidery on the bodice and sleeves. The women come from communities on the south and eastern sides of Imbabura Mountain, such as Gonzáles Suárez, Zuleta, La Esperanza, San Isidro de Cajas, and Rinconada. You can buy these blouses in the Otavalo and Ibarra markets. In addition, the women embroider a range

> **PRECIOUS TEXTILES**
>
> When the Incas conducted a census they rated textiles more highly than precious metals, gemstones, ceramics, or food.

introduced other items such as Nativity sets and Christmas tree ornaments to help tide the *paja* weavers over hard times in the hat industry.

Shigra means sack in Quichua. *Shigras* are made of *cabuya* (agave) fiber in the central Sierra provinces of Cotopaxi, Tungurahua, and Chimborazo. These bags, made by hand with a buttonhole stitch, are found nowhere else in the Andes. Tied over the shoulders, they serve as a carry-all for *indígena* men and women. While originally meant for local use, *shigras* found ready accep-

of more commercial items, such as dresses, napkins, towels, and tablecloths.

Hats, baskets, and bags

Contrary to popular belief, Panama hats aren't made in Panama; they're made in southern Ecuador, where they're called *sombreros de paja toquilla* after the palm fiber from which they are woven. They have been made here for more than a century, with the industry going through cycles of boom and bust *(see Panama Hats feature, page 204).* In the 1960s the Peace Corps

tance in the tourist and ethnic arts markets and the best of them are true collectors' items. Baskets *(canastas)* made from various plants including cane and *totora* reeds are made throughout Ecuador and found in every market. Giant ones with lids come from Cuenca, smaller ones from around Latacunga, and fine two-color baskets from the Oriente.

Leatherwork

Cotacachi is the main center for wallets, purses, knapsacks, and clothes made from leather *(cuero).* The main street of the town is lined with shops. Leather items can also be found in the Otavalo market and in many Quito shops.

LEFT: making *shigras* (woven bags).
ABOVE: bread figures for sale.

The leatherwork is usually good, but be sure to check the quality of zippers and clasps before you make a purchase.

Jewelry

One look at the pre-Hispanic gold, silver, and platinum objects in the Museo del Banco Central in Quito and you know the ancient Ecuadorians were master metalworkers. In indigenous communities jewelers make silver, nickel, and brass shawl pins *(tupus)*, with the finest coming from Saraguro. Contemporary gold and silver filigree jewelry is a specialty of Chordaleg, where jewelry stores *(joyerías)* line the road into

town and the main plaza. The workmanship is excellent and the prices are reasonable. In pre-Hispanic times the Ecuadorian coastline was the source of the prized, coral-colored spondylus shell, traded throughout the Andes. Beads are still an essential part of women's traditional dress. The preference for red or coral-colored beads goes back to the days when spondylus was queen.

Ceramics

The most beautiful ceramics in Ecuador – perhaps in the entire upper Amazon – are made by the Canelos Quichua *indígenas*, or Sacha Runa (jungle people), who occupy the territory between the Napo and Pastaza rivers in the Oriente. Women make the bowls and pots for household and ceremonial use, by hand-coiling. The finest pieces are eggshell-thin, with painted designs representing various aspects of their life and mythology. Some beautiful ceramics are now also made for the ethnic arts market.

There are several ceramic factories with showrooms in Cuenca, turning out handmade dinner sets and tiles. The Cuenca *barrio* of Corazón de Jesús, and the towns of San Miguel and Chordeleg, are also traditional producers of pottery, which is sold at the Cuenca market. These potters use the imported wheel, and in San Miguel and Chordeleg you can see their wares drying in the shade outside their houses. The Sierra around Latacunga and Saquisilí is another pottery center, where enormous Inca-style amphoras *(tinajas* or *ollas)* for making *chicha* are produced in the town of Tejar. Pujilí, noted for its Corpus Christi celebration, also has potters who make figurines of birds, animals, and fiesta scenes.

Woodcarving

There are two main centers of woodcarving: the Canelos Quichua region and San Antonio de Ibarra north of Otavalo. The Canelos Quichua woodcarvings of tropical birds and animals are designed expressly for the ethnic arts market, and were not made until 1975. Most of the carvings are made from balsawood, painted and lacquered. Some are works of art evincing an intimate knowledge of jungle fauna.

Woodcarvings in San Antonio de Ibarra run the gamut from elaborate furniture to Nativity sets, boxes, wall plaques, and statues of the Virgin, saints, and beggars. Some are kitsch, but there are some treasures, and you can watch the carvers at work in the rear of their shops, which line the main plaza in San Antonio.

Bread figures

Producing brightly dyed dough figures of humans and animals for sale and export is a main industry in Calderón at the southern edge of Quito. They are placed on graves as offerings to the dead on the feasts of All Saints (Todos Santos) and the Day of the Dead (Dia de Difuntos) on November 1 and 2 respectively. ❏

LEFT: a typical figure-carving of an old man.
RIGHT: tapestries hanging in Otavalo market.

A NATION OF PAINTERS

Quito has a thriving artistic scene which may yet rival the
accomplishments of its 16th-century precursor

Until early in the 20th century, art in Ecuador was mainly associated with the colonial School of Quito *(see page 165)*, but the first three decades of the 1900s saw the rise of a school called *indígenismo* (indigenism).

Because Ecuadorian artists have not been isolated from currents in the international art world and many of them have studied or traveled in Europe and North America, the unifying factor of the indigenist school has not been the style of painting, which ranges from realist to impressionist, cubist, and surrealist, but the subject matter – Ecuador's exploited indigenous population.

Inspired by a Sierra life

Eduardo Kingman is perhaps the prototypical indigenist. From the 1930s until his death in 1998, he painted murals and canvases, and illustrated books exploring social themes and the use of color. *Juguetería* (Toy Store), an oil painted in 1985, shows the back of a barefoot *indígena* girl peering into the window of a brightly lit toy shop. The toys are rendered in cheerful primary colors, while the girl outside in the shadows, the picture of longing, is painted in somber burgundy, black, and blue.

Such paintings as *Mujeres con Santo* (Women with Saint), *El Maizal* (The Maize-Grower) and *La Sed* (Thirst) are characteristic of Kingman's work: the indigenist subject matter and highly stylized, semi-abstract human figures with heavy facial features and huge, distorted hands. These paintings convey powerful images of oppression, sorrow, and suffering.

Camilo Egas, who died in 1961, lived in France for long periods of time and moved through a range of styles. *Desolación* (Desolation), painted in 1949, is extremely Dalíesque, with a walking eyeball and distorted women supine on a brown, barren landscape.

LEFT: Oswaldo Guayasamín, Ecuador's most famous painter, in his studio.

Then, in a surprising switch, Egas produced the most beautiful of all the indigenist works with a series of realist paintings in the 1950s. In *Indios* (Indians), three long-haired men lean diagonally into the picture, using ropes to haul an unseen burden. The painting is executed in a few bright, clear colors: blue sky, black hair, brown skin, red, white, and yellow clothing. Neither the bodies nor the features of the men are abstract or distorted, and the impression conveyed is one of dignity and strength rather than misery. He also produced *El Indio Mariano*, a beautiful profile portrait in the same idiom.

Finally, in another stylistic switch during the last years of his life, Egas painted a series of abstract expressionist oils in various tones of blue and gray.

Manuel Rendón was a prolific painter who produced a remarkably diverse body of work. Artistic talent evidently ran in his family, for the paintings of his paternal grandmother, Delfina Pérez, were included in the 1900 Paris Exposition. Rendón spent his youth in Paris, where his father was the Ecuadorian ambassador, and he was greatly influenced by the modern art movement in France. Rendón is considered an indigenist artist, but he is equally well known for his cubist-style paintings of men and women in the 1920s and for a series on the *Sagrada Familia* (Holy Family) in the 1940s. He also painted pointillistic figurative and abstract works, and did many sketches in pencil and pen and ink. No matter what the medium, he has shown a continuing fascination with line.

Ecuadorian maestro

Oswaldo Guayasamín, who died in 1999, is the best-known of the generation of artists who came of age in the 1930s and 1940s. His father was an *indígena*, and Guayasamín consistently and proudly emphasized his indigenous heritage. Few people are neutral about Guayasamín's work, with its message of social protest. His admirers see him as a gifted artistic visionary and social critic, while his detractors see him as a third-rate Picasso imitator whose innumerable paintings of *indígenas* with coarse features and gnarled hands have become parodies of the genre. Make up your own mind by visiting the Museo Guayasamín in Quito (*for address see panel opposite*).

Anyone familiar with the graphic paintings and statues of Christ, agonized and bleeding, in Spanish colonial churches can trace this theme of suffering in Guayasamín's work, although his figures are secular rather than religious.

One of his early works, the 1942 painting *Los Trabajadores* (The Workers) is realistic in a

Nineteen of the panels are in color, four are in black and white. The latter depict the first Ecuadorian president to enslave the *indígenas*, Ecuador's civilian and military dictators, and a skeletal face wearing a Nazi helmet emblazoned with the letters "CIA."

While Ecuadorians took the mural in their stride, the United States was outraged. The US ambassador called for the letters to be painted out and various US congressmen discussed cutting off economic aid to Ecuador. Guayasamín regarded this as exactly the kind of bullying that he was protesting against, and the panel has remained unchanged.

manner similar to that of the Mexican muralist José Clemente Orozco. The similarity is more than coincidental, as Guayasamín worked with Orozco in Mexico. Guayasamín went on to develop a style influenced by cubism, with its chopped up and oddly reassembled images, notably in his series of monumental paintings *La Edad de la Ira* (The Age of Anger), *Los Torturados* (The Tortured), and *Cabezas* (Heads).

In 1988 Guayasamín continued to make visual political statements with his enormous mural in the meeting hall of the Ecuadorian Congress in Quito, in which 23 panels convey episodes from Ecuador's history; Guayasamín produced anything but a romanticized picture.

Perhaps what will become his most famous work was only finished after his death at the insistence of his family. *La Capilla del Hombre*, in the Bellavista neighborhood of Quito, is rapidly becoming known as his masterpiece. The stone temple resembles an ancient pre-Columbian one on the outside, but the inside it is very modern, with fine woodwork and architectural design. A mural depicts the Latin American man from pre-Columbian times to the present. An eternal flame marks the altar on the lower level, which burns for peace and human rights. The minimalist chapel shows the dreams, fears, anguish, inspirations, and love of this great artist.

An artistic immigrant

Olga Fisch arrived in the country more than half a century ago as a refugee fleeing from Hitler, bringing with her a background in the visual arts. Fisch was among the first to recognize the value of Ecuadorian *artesanías* as art, and the design potential of traditional motifs. A talented painter, Fisch is best-known for her work in textile design, especially rugs and tapestries, based on her interpretations of pottery, embroidery and weaving motifs. She also designed clothing and jewelry, available at her two stores in Quito (*see Travel Tips page 347 for details*).

abstract people are delineated by swift, black brushstrokes. They lean against storefronts in what looks like a seedy downtown neighborhood and the use of yellows and reds contributes to a carnival-like atmosphere. Jácome's 1990 oil *A la Cola* (To the End of the Line) depicts a slashing rainstorm in which three bright-yellow taxis outlined in black divide the canvas diagonally. They are balanced by a mass of frantic people in the upper left, rendered in swirling lines of black and white. The painting effectively conveys the feeling of desperation familiar to anyone who has ever tried to catch a taxi in Quito in the rain. ❑

Modern-day artists

The younger generation of painters has moved away from *indigenismo* to more personal, idiosyncratic themes and subject matter. In the 1970s Ramiro Jácome was part of the neo-figurative movement, a return to works with recognizable figures. In the early 1980s he changed his style, painting a series of abstract oils, characterized by deep, rich colors. Later in the 1980s he returned to figurative works. In *Barrio* (Neighborhood), painted in 1989, three semi-

LEFT: an example of the indigenist painting style, by Eduardo Kingman. **ABOVE:** recent canvases by Jaime Romero *(left)* and Washington Iza *(right)*.

OUTDOOR ADVENTURES

Climbing, trekking, rafting, or biking – the astonishing variety of terrain is a big attraction for many sports enthusiasts

Outdoor enthusiasts of all types have discovered that the diverse topography of Ecuador provides an ideal environment for "adventure travel." The small size of the country makes getting around a logistical dream: nothing is too far away from anything else, and there are roads to almost everywhere.

Yet, for so small a country, Ecuador has an amazing assortment of terrain, while the climate is favorable for almost year-round excursions. Except for February and March, when it seems to be raining everywhere, good weather conditions can be found in one region or another throughout the year.

Trekking in the Sierra

Trekking is one of the most popular adventure activities, and there is a surfeit of places in the Andes to explore. A number of national parks offer uninhabited areas for days of wandering, while the populated highlands of the Sierra are dotted with small villages whose inhabitants usually offer a welcome to backpacking gringos.

One of the most popular treks in Ecuador is the easy three-day hike to the ruins of Ingapirca, the finest example of Inca stonework in the country. The hike begins in the charming village of Achupallus, north of Cuenca, 15 km (9 miles) off the Pan-American Highway. A dirt track eventually gives way to a cobbled footpath leading to a pass. You have to squeeze through a small cave to get to the other side. After a brief descent, the trail starts to climb again and traverses a mountain slope above the green valley of the Cadrul River. An excellent site for the first night's camp is beside the sparkling waters of the high mountain lake, Laguna Las Tres Cruces (Lake of the Three Crosses).

After about a half-day walk on the second day – crossing rocky ridges and skirting boggy valleys – the trail drops below the peak of Quil-loloma. The remains of the old Inca road appear in the valley below. There is an excellent place to camp near Laguna Culebrillas and some minor Inca ruins, aptly named Paredones ("ruined walls") because of the surviving crude stonework. A final three- to four-hour hike on the third day follows the grassy Inca road to the ruins of Ingapirca (*see pages 267–8*).

BE PREPARED

Buy topographical maps at the Military Geographical Institute (IGM) before setting out from Quito to go trekking.

National parks

Several national parks within the highland region of Ecuador are especially popular with trekkers because of the ease of accessibility, established trail systems, and marvelous scenery. In most cases, day hikes supplant longer treks for those who prefer to see the sights with a lighter load. Facilities within the parks are at a minimum, if they exist at all, but that's part of traveling in a developing country. A small park entrance fee is usually charged, and in some cases, permission from the local ex-INEFAN office must be obtained in advance (*see page 53*).

Cotopaxi National Park not only attracts climbers who come to scale the Cotopaxi volcano, but also its wide open *páramo,* which is ideal for cross-country treks. The lower slopes (called the Arenal – a word that comes from the Spanish *arena* meaning sand) are an interesting landscape of volcanic sand and boulders from an eruption and associated mud flows in the late 19th century. The Trek of the Condor is a three- to four-day hike from the village of Papallacta to the base of Cotopaxi. It passes several mountain lakes harboring Andean teal, Andean lapwing, *caricari,* and wild horses. The glaciers off Antisana loom over the *páramo,* and condors can sometimes be seen soaring around Sincholagua.

Parque Nacional El Cajas lies about 32 km (20 miles) west of Cuenca. Within its 30,000 hectares (74,000 acres) there is a huge variety of landscapes, ranging from granite rock outcrops to barely penetrable cloud forests, where mountain toucans and tropical woodpeckers make their home. With the exception of day-hike trails

---

PRECEDING PAGES: scaling Mount Cotopaxi.
LEFT: a climber at the summit of Mount Chimborazo.

around the ranger station, most of the area is totally without marked trails, yet a cross-country trek of several days is quite feasible. The region is dotted with some 250 lakes of various sizes and colors, and fishing for trout is encouraged.

Podocarpus National Park, south of Loja, is very popular with hikers. The area is largely cloud forest and is home to the reticent spectacled bear, the flamboyant Andean cock-of-the-rock, and the mountain tanager. A trail system includes several day hikes from the park headquarters, and there are various options for overnight camping. Contact the conservation groups Arcoiris, tel: 07-257 7499; www.arcoiris.

bag), a communal kitchen with gas stove, and the services of a hut guardian who knows the present conditions and route descriptions. Bringing your own stove during peak climbing periods is a good idea, as the huts can get crowded and the communal kitchen overused. Water is available at the *refugios*, but must be treated with purification tablets or boiled before drinking.

Good climbing weather is possible almost year-round, but normally the best months are June through September and during a short dry spell in December and January. Being a tropical mountain range at the equator, the Ecuadorean Andes generate unusual weather conditions.

org.ec; and the Fundación Ecológica Podocarpus, Olmedo and Juan José Peña, Loja, tel: 07-258 5924 for more information.

Mountaineering

The Andean mountain range in Ecuador comprises one of the largest concentrations of volcanoes in the world. It is possible to gain valuable high-altitude experience on moderate routes that do not require technical ice-climbing skill. With proper acclimatization, most peaks can be conquered over a weekend. Huts, or *refugios*, have been constructed on many of the higher and more popular climbs. Some of the huts are equipped with bunks (bring a sleeping

One part of the *cordillera*, or range, may be inundated with rain, while the next section will have clear skies and perfect conditions. This, at least, makes for plenty of options.

Proper equipment is essential for safe climbing, regardless of how straightforward most routes may appear. Any climbs which involve ice or glacier travel are considered to be technical and require special equipment and knowledge of its use. Crampons, an ice axe, and rope are necessary, along with the warm clothing demanded by high-altitude mountain conditions.

A rucksack with plenty of water, food, and extra-warm clothing is essential for a summit attempt. Flag markers, or wands, are used during the ascent for route-finding, as cloudy conditions will often obscure the descent. In addition, a good headlamp with spare batteries is essential, since all climbing begins in the early hours of the morning. All mountaineering gear can be hired in Quito, but, as with the trekking equipment, quality can vary.

Many climbs are so short that the need for proper acclimatization is often underestimated, but with major peaks above 5,700 meters (18,000 ft), it should not be overlooked. The best way to accustom your system to altitude is to stay in a relatively high city or town, and take a few day hikes to higher elevations. Quito is a

where climbers go to get acclimatized. Iliniza Norte is a rocky 5,126-meter (6,800-ft) peak about 55 km (34 miles) southwest of Quito, offering splendid views of the complicated and challenging glaciers of its sister Iliniza Sur. Iliniza Norte can be scaled in two days, and the climb is straightforward when the going is dry. If there is ice or snow, crampons and an ice axe are necessary.

A truck can be hired in Machachi or El Chaupi to get up to the parking area called La Virgen, named after a blue statue of the Virgin Mary. There is a three- to four-hour hike to the refuge. Climbers first follow a rutted road onto an

good choice, and there are several strenuous hikes that can help the climber get in shape. Pasachoa makes an ideal warm-up hike as far as the rock face at 4,100 meters (13,400 ft), and on a clear day gives you fabulous views over the Valley of the Volcanoes.

Easier climbs

Climbers recently arrived have several options for warm-up peaks. The most popular was Tungurahua until it erupted in 1999. Now Iliniza Norte, Corazón, Atacazo, and Imbabura are

---

LEFT: a trekker on the Inca Trail.
ABOVE: steaming crater of Guagua Pichincha.

YOU GET WHAT YOU PAY FOR

Mountain guides are available for inexperienced climbers, but caution in selecting the proper guide is strongly recommended. There are people who claim to be guides when they do not have the appropriate experience, and the result is potentially dangerous. A decent guide charges a decent price, and it is not something that you should economize on.

It is best to go with an adventure outfitter or agency which specializes in mountain excursions, or you could hire a guide recommended by one of the climbing shops or the South American Explorers Club in Quito *(see page 125 for more details).*

exposed ridge, then up a sandy slope to the saddle where the refuge sits between the two Iliniza peaks. The refuge is basic, but has a stove and bunks, and usually a good mix of international climbers preparing for Cotopaxi.

The next morning, around sunrise, climbers head up the rocky ridge to a cliff. There is a traverse named Paso de la Muerte (Death Pass), which is as difficult as it sounds, and a final scramble on loose rock to the summit.

Mountain highs

For climbers with greater technical experience, the volcanoes of Cayambe, at 5,790 meters

(almost 19,000 ft), Cotopaxi (5,900 meters/ 19,340 ft), and Chimborazo (6,310 meters/ 20,700 ft), are the main attractions. At weekends during the peak season, the *refugios* are packed with climbers preparing for the rigors of the climb ahead.

Start the climb at around midnight for a round trip of about 10 hours. Often large numbers of climbers set out at the same time, and the flickering light from their headlamps is all that is visible as they ascend through the darkness.

Cayambe is the most difficult of the three peaks, but also perhaps the most beautiful, with its rugged glacial terrain and views of the Oriente rainforest.

Cotopaxi has gentle, curving snow slopes and the massive rock wall of Yanasacha just below the summit. It's a pleasurable ascent as the dawn rays of the sun set the whole glacier sparkling. The summit crater seems perfectly formed against the deep blue Andean sky.

Chimborazo holds the attraction of being Ecuador's highest peak. After several hours of negotiating one steep slope after another, the process becomes something of a slog, and one begins to wonder if the summit will ever appear. In the end, the persistent achieve their goal, and the final summit views are well worth the effort.

White-water rafting

The attraction of running untamed rivers draws world-class rafters and kayakers to Ecuador. Those with little or no experience can also safely enjoy the thrill of white water with the growing number of travel adventure companies operating out of Quito, Tena, and Baños.

Many of Ecuador's rivers can be run year-round, while some of the more technically difficult ones are possible only during certain seasons. The most accessible and commonly run ones are the Río Toachi and the Río Blanco, both two to three hours from Quito. These rivers traverse the Western Cordillera of the Andes, passing through forested canyons interspersed with small farming villages. The best time to go is from February to May.

A popular Class III rafting trip, suitable for both beginners and experienced rafters, is along the upper Río Napo. It starts near Tena and is a fun trip through tropical rainforest descending the upper slopes of the Amazon basin and passing several indigenous Quichua communities. The trip is possible all year round, but the best months to do it are between March and October.

For the experienced rafter and kayaker Ecuador has many challenging Class IV and V rivers. One of the most exciting is the Río Misahuallí, but beware of the Casanova Falls. The river can be run safely only from October to March in the low-water season when, after a set of Class IV rapids, rafters must be able to stop themselves before the falls.

It is a beautiful trip through virgin rainforest – parrots, oropendulas, and other tropical birds abound. The combination of spectacular natural scenery and a strong feeling of isolation makes the adventure all the more exciting. Trips down the Río Misahuallí are organized out of Tena.

Horseback riding

Horseback riding across the lush valleys and hills of the Sierra has become a popular leisure activity throughout Ecuador. Several agencies offer organized trips out of Otavalo, Baños, and Cuenca *(see Travel Tips page 349)*. Ride Andes offers a wide range of trips, including one-day rides around Quito as well as *hacienda* tours, cattle round-ups, and volcano treks. Longer trips can be arranged into the Podocarpus Reserve in the very south of Ecuador from the village of Vilcabamba. Make

THE MISAHUALLÍ

The time to attempt the exciting Misahuallí river trip is in the low water season, between October and March.

If you stay off the main paved roads such as the Pan-American Highway – the Ecuadorians are known for their unsafe driving – the unpaved routes selected from a good topographical map will usually offer solitude and pleasant surprises.

A good place to get acclimatized to the elevation is the market town of Otavalo. Using this as a base for exploration, day trips can be made to the surrounding small villages known for their *artesanías*. Several outfitters in town will rent you bikes for the day and give advice about

sure the agency knows what your experience is, particularly if you are a beginner.

Mountain biking

The best way to get off the beaten track is on a mountain bike exploring the extensive dirt and cobbled roads that pass through villages rarely visited by tourists. The high elevation, hilly terrain, and poor road conditions are challenging, but the views and the colorful local communities make cycling well worth the effort.

LEFT: rafters tackling the white water on one of Ecuador's mountain rivers.
ABOVE: taking a break in the *páramo*.

some good routes to follow. A more ambitious ride takes you 600 meters (2,000 ft) up a paved road to the Laguna de Cuicocha, a spectacular collapsed volcanic caldera now filled with water. A labyrinth of unpaved roads leads back to Otavalo.

A popular day trip is a mostly downhill ride from Baños, where bikes of dubious quality can be rented, to the jungle town of Puyo. You follow the cliff-hugging road along the gorge of the Pastaza River, passing several inspiring waterfalls. In the town of Río Verde bikes may be left with a local shopkeeper while you visit the falls. Buses pass at half-hourly intervals, and you can heave your bike on top of the bus and avoid the long, punishing climb back to Baños.

A popular three- to five-day ride takes you past the volcanic crater lake of Laguna de Quilotoa. A long climb from the Pan-American Highway to the indigenous village of Zumbagua (this can be avoided by taking a bus) is rewarded by views of a volcanic landscape decorated by wheat fields at different stages of growth, from deep greens and golden yellows to the dark-brown earth ready for planting. A dirt track leads to the lake. The next day, after a cold night on the crater rim, you wind along the edge

of a deeply eroded pumice plain to the town of Siglos, where a bus can be taken back to Quito.

Paragliding

The topography of Ecuador is well suited for paragliding. One popular launch site is at the refuge (4,200 meters/13,800 ft) on Mount Cotopaxi, where you can ride thermals to the top of the highest volcano in the world. The best time of year to fly is December. Equally exciting is a flight from La Crucita on the coast, catching winds off the ocean, and following a ridgeline nearly 10 km (6 miles) long, staying airborne for three to five hours. Some enthusiasts take off from the slopes of Mount Pichincha and soar over the

---

EXTREME ECUADOR

Baños is the place to go for extreme sports. Try rafting, canyoning, or even *puenting* – bungee-jumping from bridges.

---

city of Quito. The best times to fly are during August and September. There is a paragliding school with an excellent safety record *(see Travel Tips, page 349).*

Surfing

Ecuador has much to offer as a surfing destination thanks to the Pacific storms which send waves directly towards its coast. In 2004, the country hosted the World Surfing Championships, in which more than 27 countries participated.

Montañita, in Guayas province, is Ecuador's surfing mecca and a popular backpacker hangout, with dozens of bars, hotels, jewelry stands, seafood shacks, and tour outfitters. In the north, Mompiche (Esmeraldas province) is renowned for its north break and 300-meter (985-ft) ride. South breaks can be caught from June to October, while the north-facing breaks are better from December to April.

The Galápagos Islands are another well-known surf spot. On San Cristóbal the waves are best from November to March, while Santa Cruz is best between April and August.

Scuba diving

With a spectacular diversity of sea life, Ecuador is home to some of the world's best diving sites. In the Machalilla National Park, humpback whales can be seen around the Isla de la Plata from June to September when they come to mate and give birth to their calves. The coral is in good condition here and attracts porcupinefish, parrotfish, and broomtail groupers, as well as eels, rays, starfish, sea cucumbers, and green turtles. The waters of the park are best explored from June to September, as the drop in water temperature allows for greater visibility.

Diving in the Galápagos Islands is an unforgettable experience. The reefs around Wolf and Darwin islands are home to dolphins, eels, marine turtles, hammerhead and whale sharks, and moray eels, while schools of tropical fish can be seen at the Devil's Crown on Isla Floreana. At Estrada Point in Academy Bay, on Isla Santa Cruz, it is possible to see marine iguanas, sea lions, white-fin reef sharks, and at the nearby Caamaño islet pods of friendly sea lions eager to play will sometimes approach divers. ❑

LEFT: surfers on the beach at Montañita.

South American Explorers

The Quito Clubhouse of the South American Explorers (SAE) is a valuable information center for travelers, outdoor enthusiasts, and members of scientific expeditions. If your ambition is to climb Cotopaxi, look at orchids, find a reliable boat to the Galápagos Islands, go white-water rafting, or simply to meet up with compatible hiking companions, then this is the place to come.

The club was founded by Don Montague and Linda Rojas in Lima, Peru, in 1977. Following its huge success, the Quito club was opened in 1989. New clubhouses were built in Cuzco, Peru, in 1999 and Buenos Aires, Argentina, in 2006. Montague still runs the US headquarters in Ithaca, New York, and edits a 64-page quarterly journal, *The South American Explorer*, an informative and topical magazine. Articles range from archeology, anthropology, and geology to mountaineering, indigenous peoples, and languages.

The non-profit club is funded by membership dues. A well-invested $50 a year (or $80 for a couple) allows you use of all its facilities in the clubhouses in Peru, Ecuador, and Argentina. You have access to an extensive library, equipment storage, book exchange, email, postal mail, phone message services, and bulletin boards. There are also first-hand trip reports written by members, which provide personal accounts of hotels, transport, guides, and agencies, plus advice and directions for a proposed trip, trek, climb, or any other activity; and there are plenty of useful books and maps for sale.

Besides the general services it offers to its members, the club's mission is to support scientific field exploration and research in the social and natural sciences. Its aim is to awaken greater interest in and appreciation for wilderness conservation and wildlife protection. The Quito club also holds bimonthly pub quizzes, yoga classes, and organizes visits to area prisons.

With this aim in mind it invites guest speakers to give presentations on their specialist subjects and encourages follow-up activities. Talks cover a wide spectrum, from the intellectual property rights in relation to medicinal plants, to climbing the active volcanoes of South America, or giving detailed information about wildlife in the Galápagos.

RIGHT: scaling the snowy heights.

Over the years the club and its members have built up close ties with orphanages, environmental organizations, and community aid projects. If you are interested in volunteering for one of these projects during your stay, check out the club's Volunteers Resources Desk. You'll find a mine of information on the types of opportunities available, how to get in touch, and a realistic idea of what the projects involve.

If you join the SAE before you head to Ecuador you will have the advantage of being able to ask for specialist advice on planning your trip. For a small fee to cover the cost of photocopies and postage, the staff at the Ithaca headquarters will recommend,

select, and mail trip reports to members. The club also has its own catalog, offering books, maps, CDs, language tapes, and handicrafts, with discounts for members.

The SAE headquarters in the United States can be contacted at 126 Indian Creek Road, Ithaca, NY 14850, tel: 607-277-0488, fax: 607-277-6122. The email address is: explorer@saexplorers.org; or visit www.saexplorers.org.

The Quito Clubhouse, which is open Mon–Fri 9am–5pm, Thur 9.30am–8pm, and Sat 9.30am–1pm, is located at Jorge Washington 311 and Leonidas Plaza (near the US Embassy) in Quito New Town. The mailing address is Apartado 17-21-431, Eloy Alfaro, Quito; or email quitoclub@saexplorers.org. ❑

FOOD

There's no escaping bananas. But Ecuador's topography has led to the development of some very distinctive dishes in different regions

There is no single Ecuadorian cuisine, but several different ones corresponding to the geographical regions of the country: Costa, Sierra, and Oriente. And what you'll find in good restaurants is quite different from what most people eat in rural areas and what you will find in market booths and small cafés throughout the country.

Bananas, however, are ubiquitous. Several varieties are grown on the coast and in the Oriente, from tiny finger bananas *(oritas)* to large, green cooking plantains *(plátanos* or *verdes).* The yellow bananas of the kind Westerners are accustomed to are called *guineos* in Ecuador. Short, fat red bananas called *maqueños* are also good to eat raw. Bananas and plantains are trucked up to every highland town and market, so you'll have no trouble finding them.

Staple foods

Rice *(arroz)* is not an indigenous food, but it is also ubiquitous, although potatoes *(papas)* will often substitute for it in the highlands. You can count on one or the other to come with every meal. And sometimes, for a complete carbohydrate overload, noodles *(fideos),* potatoes, rice, *yuca* (a white starchy tuber), and *plátanos* will be served, and that's the meal. This is poor people's food, and a partial explanation of why many Ecuadorians are short in stature: besides a genetic component, they don't consume much protein.

Ecuador is overflowing with fruit of all kinds, from enormous papayas to more exotic treats like passion fruit *(ayatacso, maracuyá,* and *granadilla* are just a few varieties to try). Then there are sweet custard apples *(chirimoyas)* and tart tamarinds *(tamarindos),* melons *(melones)* of all kinds, mangoes, pineapples *(piñas),* oranges *(naranjas),* tangerines *(manderinas),* avocados *(paltas),* and lots more. The *naranjilla,* a tiny fruit that looks like a fuzzy, orangey-greenish crab apple, makes a tasty drink that is

often served instead of orange juice. Don't be put off by the strange color – the juice is absolutely delicious. Lemons are called *limas* and limes are called *limones.* If you're uncertain about how to eat a fruit, try it as a juice *(jugo).* You can ask for juice without water *(sin agua)* and without sugar *(sin azúcar).*

Visit a market as soon as possible after your arrival in Ecuador. Don't be intimidated by the strange-looking array. Instead, buy every fruit you've never seen before, then go back to your hotel or *hostal* and ask the owner to share them with you and tell you the names of the different varieties. You'll discover some delicious fruits, which you can then enjoy for the rest of your trip.

LAND OF BANANAS

Ecuador was the original banana republic. For many years bananas were its principal export, and the country is still among the world's largest exporters.

Pacific flavors

Many of the coastal dishes are typical of the entire Pacific Coast from Chile to Mexico. They include *ceviche,* which is fish *(pescados)* or seafood *(mariscos)* marinated in lemon or lime juice, onions, and chili peppers. *Ceviche* can be made with shrimp *(camarones* or *langostinos),* lobster *(langosta),* sea bass *(corvina),* crab *(cangrejos* or *jaibas),* oysters *(ostiones),* or mixed seafood *(mixto).* The dish has been around since Inca times, when they marinated raw fish in *chicha.* The Ecuadorian version is often soupier than the Peruvian one, and uses oil and tomatoes and is served with popcorn on the side.

Ecuador's superb sea bass is served a number of ways, including fried *(frito),* breaded and fried *(apanada),* and filleted and grilled *(a la plancha).* Try any seafood cooked in *agua de coco* (coconut milk). Besides the varieties already mentioned there are clams *(almejas* or *conchas),* grouper *(cherna),* mackerel *(sierra),* marlin *(picudo),* snapper *(pargo),* tuna *(atún),* and squid *(calamares).* The *dorado,* or dolphinfish, which is not a mammal like the true dolphin, is also a popular dish and not to be missed.

A thoughtful Ecuadorian custom for regulating the spiciness of food is to serve hot sauce

LEFT: *ceviche* can be made from a variety of seafood.

(*salsa picante*) made from chili peppers *(ají)* in a little side dish so that you can add as much or as little as you like.

Tastes of the Oriente

Coastal and Oriente foods are similar because of the two regions' low elevation and tropical climate, although there is more game hunting in the jungle (everything from monkeys to tapir and *paca*, a large rodent) and freshwater fish instead of seafood. In both places you'll find lots of *plátanos* (plantains), *yuca*, rice, and fried fish. There are several dishes served exclusively in the Oriente, however. One is piranha, although it sur-prises many visitors that the notorious carnivorous fish is itself good for eating. The Oriente rivers also have lots of catfish (*challua* or *bagre*), which people make into a stew with plantains, chili peppers, and *cilantro* (leaf coriander).

For a jungle salad, try *palmitos* (palm hearts) or chonta palm fruits (*frutas de chonta*), both considered delicacies. *Chucula* is a tasty drink made with boiled and mashed plantains, which resembles a banana milkshake.

Serrano cuisine

As we climb to the highlands, a word about the tuber, that traditional mainstay of indigenous

ANDEAN FESTIVAL DISHES

Andean festivals are a great place to try local foods. *Fanesca* is an incredibly rich soup served only during Holy Week (the week before Easter). You name it and *fanesca* has it: fish, eggs *(huevos)*, cheese *(queso)*, corn, and every imaginable grain and vegetable, but no meat. *Cuy*, or guinea pig, is often eaten on special occasions, and you can almost always find it in some form during Andean festivals. Whether it's fried, roasted with potatoes, or in a spicy sauce, *cuy* is a delicacy. *Yahuarlocro* is a hearty potato soup made with sheep's innards seasoned with oregano and peanuts and served with avocado, chopped red onion, and tomato.

life in the Andes. There are a lot of tubers in the Andes, beginning with dozens of varieties of potatoes. The potato was cultivated around Lake Titicaca, the region that still has the most varieties – some of which are so specialized they grow only at altitudes above 2,400 meters (8,000 ft). Potatoes are served with almost every meal in the highlands, usually boiled, but sometimes cut up and added to thick soups. If you don't like potatoes you're in for trouble in Ecuador. They are the food of the common people, and, as in Inca times, everyone plants and eats them. The great Inca terraces, however, used to be reserved for another crop – corn, which was usually made into *chicha*.

Besides regular white potatoes in many sizes and varieties, you will come across the sweet potato *(camote)* as well as the *oca*, which looks like a long, skinny, lumpy potato. One Ecuadorian potato specialty is *llapingachos*, potato pancakes made with potatoes, cheese, and onions. A better lunch cannot be had.

Soups are the essence of meals in the Sierra. Before the Spanish Conquest *indígenas* did not have ovens for baking, which meant that most food was boiled, a custom that survives today. Soup is called *caldo, sopa, chupe,* or *locra.* Generally, a *sopa* or a *caldo* is a thin soup with potatoes and various unidentified floating

Mazamorra is a thick soup made with a ground corn base and cabbage, potatoes, onions, and spices. *Sancocho* is a stew made with *plátanos* and corn. Most soups and stews are liberally seasoned with *cilantro* and many are given a yellow or orange color by the addition of *achiote* seeds.

Corn *(maíz* or *sara)* is another staple, especially in the Sierra. Unlike in Mexico and Central America, corn in the Andes is not ground and made into tortillas. In northern Ecuador corn is most commonly served on the cob *(choclo)*. Ecuadorian corn has enormous, sweet kernels arranged irregularly, and it's the best corn-on-the-

objects of the faunal variety. A *locro* or *chupe* is a thick, creamy soup. *Sopa seca* or just plain *seco* (which means dry) is more of a stew than a soup, with meat and vegetables added according to the budget and whim of the cook. One of the most common *locros* is *yaguar locro* (blood soup), containing the heart, liver, and other internal organs (which is to say tripe, or *mondongo*) of a cow *(vaca* or *res)*, pig *(chancho)*, or sheep *(borrego)*; the soup is sprinkled with blood sausage or the animal's dried blood.

cob imaginable. In the north, corn is also eaten as parched kernels *(kamcha)* or as popcorn *(cangil)*. In southern Ecuador it is commonly served as boiled kernels *(muti* or *mote)*. *Humitas* are corn *tamales*: cornmeal seasoned and steamed in the leaf. Don't eat the leaf – unwrap it and eat what's inside. *Tostadas de maíz* are corn pancakes that make a good breakfast or snack.

Miracle grain

Other grains grown locally include *quinua*, wheat *(trigo)*, and barley *(cebada)*. *Quinua* is native to the Andes. This tiny, round grain is an amazingly nutritious food, consisting of 15 percent complete protein, 55 percent carbohydrate,

LEFT: *anticuchos*, a type of kebab, ready for the grill.
ABOVE: Quito has an increasingly diverse selection of restaurants to choose from.

and only 4 percent fat. The Incas regarded *quinua* as sacred, and it was their second-most important food crop. *Quinua* is usually served in soup, but it can also be eaten as a side dish, in the same way as rice. The grain has become a staple in Novo Andina, New Andean food which blends traditional Andean recipes with contemporary cooking methods. *Quinua* is often served as a risotto or used to encrust a fish or meat.

Most barley is ground up and used in soup, but wheat flour is used to make a variety of good breads and rolls (*pan* and *panecitos*) and *empanadas*, which are baked pastries filled with cheese or meat. Around Latacunga you'll hear

and *churrasco* or *lomo montado* is meat (usually beef) topped with fried eggs. You can also order veal *(ternera)*, lamb *(cordero),* or pork (*puerco* or *chanco; kuchi* in Quichua). *Lechón* is suckling pig. *Salchicha* means sausage, while *chorizo* refers to pork sausage. Bacon is called *tocino*, ham is *jamón*.

Asado, which means roasted, always refers to whole roasted pig in Ecuador, unless otherwise modified. *Fritada* (fried pork) is cooked in large copper and brass *pailas* (wok-like pans), visible in the markets or in the doorways of small restaurants throughout the country. *Chicharrón* is fried pork skin, crispy and delicious.

women at street stalls calling *allullas*, *allullas* (pronounced azhúzhas). These are home-made rolls, good when hot and fresh, but hard when they get cold.

Broad beans are called *habas*. These beans, which are much larger than you may have seen at home, are boiled and served hot, dipped in salty *campo* cheese, or cold in a salad dressed with butter and lemon juice.

In search of meat dishes

You should ask for *lomo* or *bifstec*, or *chuleta* if you want a chop. *Parrilladas* are steakhouses or grills, where the meat is sometimes charcoal-grilled at your table. *A la parrilla* means grilled,

FROM PET TO POT

If you'll settle for something smaller than a sirloin, try guinea pig *(cuy)*. Until the arrival of the Europeans, *cuy* was the main source of meat in the Andes. Every family had guinea pigs running around the kitchen, and some still do.

Cuy is eaten only on special occasions, when one is scooped up, killed, gutted, cleaned, rubbed with lard and spices, put on a spit, and roasted in the fire or baked in the oven. If you can bring yourself to try *cuy*, you'll find that there's not much meat, but what there is is delicious, and, as the Ecuadorians put it, what else are guinea pigs good for?

Other sources of dietary protein include chicken *(pollo)* or hen *(gallina),* and eggs served in the usual ways, as well as pasteurized cow's milk *(leche),* which is sold in unwieldy liter-sized plastic bags, and excellent cheese *(queso),* the quality of which has soared in recent years with the arrival of Swiss and Italian immigrants who have introduced European varieties. As for fish, in the Sierra many streams and lakes have been stocked with tasty, if rather bony, trout *(trucha).*

QUICHUA CONTRIBUTION

The Quichua language has contributed one word to English: "jerky," derived from *charqui,* meaning dried meat.

Slaking your thirst

Bebidas is the term for beverages in general, alcoholic or otherwise. Ecuadorian wine *(vino)* is unlikely to win any international awards, although occasionally bottles can be quite good. Argentinian and Chilean wines are often excellent, but expensive. You're better off sticking to soft drinks *(gaseosas),* mineral water *(agua mineral)* – among which Güitig (pronounced wee-tig) is the most common brand, or beer *(cerveza).* There are a number of locally brewed beers, the best and most popular of which is Pilsener.

There is also tea *(té),* herb tea *(agua aromática),* hot chocolate *(chocolate caliente),* and coffee *(café).* This last is usually boiled until it becomes a sludge, then set on the table in a small carafe. Known as *esencia* (essence), it looks just like soy sauce and causes some interesting culinary confusion in Chinese restaurants *(chifas).* The *esencia* is poured in your cup and hot water or milk is added. Sometimes instant coffee substitutes for *esencia* but the taste, unfortunately, is the same. Black coffee is *tinto,* coffee with milk is *café con leche,* and coffee with hot water and milk is *pintado* (which literally means "painted"). *Api* is a hot drink made from ground corn, and sometimes so thick it might be considered a soup. *Chicha morada* is a sweet, non-alcoholic drink made from purple corn.

When it comes to liquor, what you get is the most potent intoxicant with the highest imaginable octane rating: a distilled sugar-cane liquor known as *trago,* which burns with a clear blue flame. Local brands include Cristal and Sinchi Shungu ("strong heart"); there are several nameless varieties that are produced illegally in the countryside. Tequila is another highly intoxicating drink which is cheap and popular.

Hervidas are hot drinks served at every fiesta, consisting of *trago* mixed with honey and *naranjilla* or blackberry juice; *guayusa* is *trago* mixed with sugar and hot *guayusa* tea, while *canelazo* is *trago* spiced with cinnamon, sugar, and lime. As they say in Ecuador: *¡Buen provecho!* ❑

A VERY SPECIAL SPECIALTY

One jungle specialty is *chicha* (or *aswa*), a fermented beer made from yucca, which is also known as manioc *(mucuna).* In order to make the *chicha* ferment, women chew the manioc, spit it into a large jar and add water – the enzymes in the saliva cause the fermentation. In the highlands, however, *chicha* is not made by mastication; instead yeast and sugar are added to make it ferment.

Generally, the drink will only be offered to you in people's homes, so if you find the thought of it unpalatable you needn't worry about encountering *chicha* in the course of ordinary travel.

LEFT: whole suckling pig, called simply *asado*, is sold in many markets. **RIGHT:** mountains of fresh vegetables in the domestic market at Otavalo.

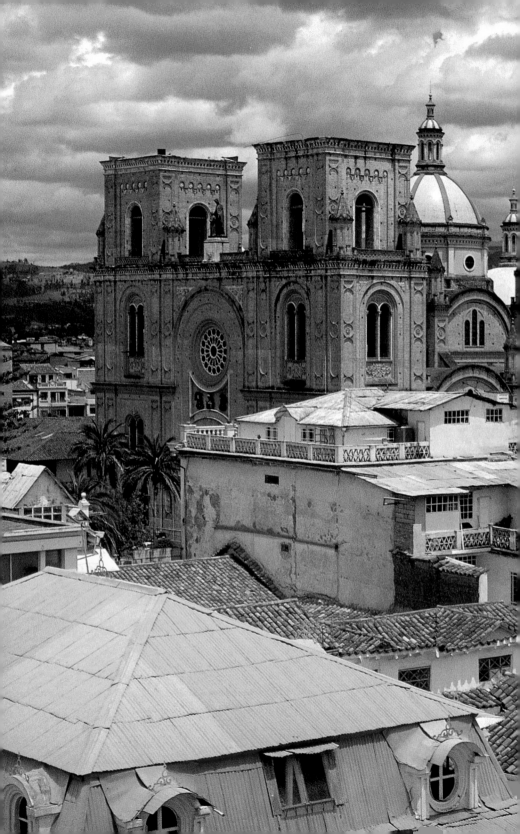

PLACES

A detailed guide to the entire country, with principal sites cross-referenced by number to the maps

Ecuador is the smallest of South America's Andean republics and without doubt the easiest to explore. The capital city, Quito, is the perfect base for travelers – and, for most, their point of arrival. Located only 24km (15 miles) south of the equator, Quito's Andean setting ensures that it has a pleasant, spring-like climate all year round. Unlike other Latin American capitals, Quito has not been totally swamped by a population explosion: its elegant colonial heart is preserved in the 18th century, while the modern "new town" offers every comfort of the 21st.

The Andean highlands remain Ecuador's heartland. The classic excursion from Quito, and one of the country's most famous attractions, is a short hop north for the Saturday handicraft market in Otavalo. Then, stretching south of Quito, is the lush mountain valley that the German scientist Alexander von Humboldt dubbed "the Avenue of the Volcanoes." The city of Cuenca, considered Ecuador's most beautiful colonial relic, marks the beginning of the Southern Sierra – a remote and strongly traditional region that has some of Ecuador's most distinctive *indígena* communities and the country's only Inca ruins.

But Ecuador offers much more than *serrano* cultures and the spectacle of ice on the equator. Just 20 minutes west of Quito by air is the Pacific coast. Moving to a more languid rhythm of life than the highlands, the Costa is washed by warm sea currents from the northern Pacific making the coastline lusher and swimming more pleasant than in the icy waters of Peru and Chile. Comfortable resorts are dotted along Ecuador's north and south coasts, which travelers often reach directly rather than passing through the tropical city of Guayaquil, Ecuador's chaotic and rarely attractive commercial heart.

Twenty minutes by air east of Quito is the Oriente region, one of the most accessible sections of the Amazon basin in South America. Jungle lodges, boats, and canoe trips explore the farthest reaches of this endangered region which, paradoxically, is fast becoming one of the continent's greatest travel attractions.

Finally, the Galápagos archipelago is in a class of its own. Easily reached on tours or independently by three-hour flights from Quito, this naturalists' paradise alone can justify the journey to Ecuador. Several days' cruising – either in a luxury liner or small chartered boat – is an expensive treat, but remains one of the world's great travel experiences. ❑

PRECEDING PAGES: view from the summit of Mount Cotopaxi; old-style locomotion across the tropical lowlands; a Quito mural; the colonial splendor of Cuenca.
LEFT: Mount Sangay erupting.

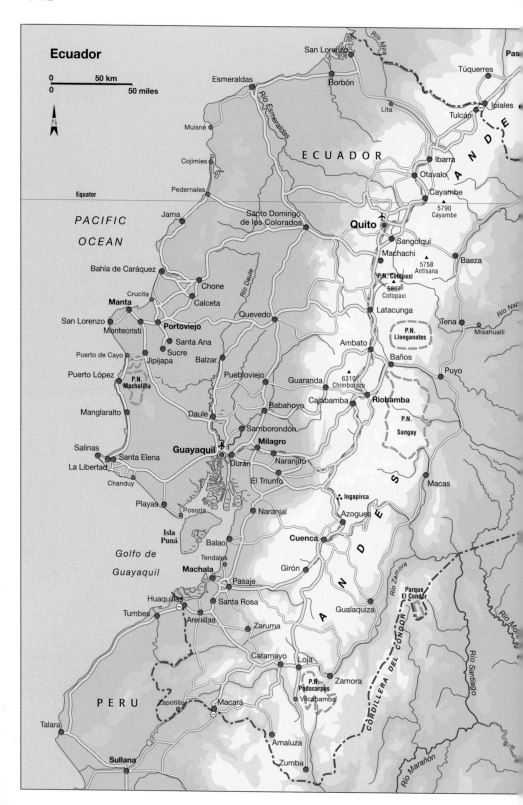

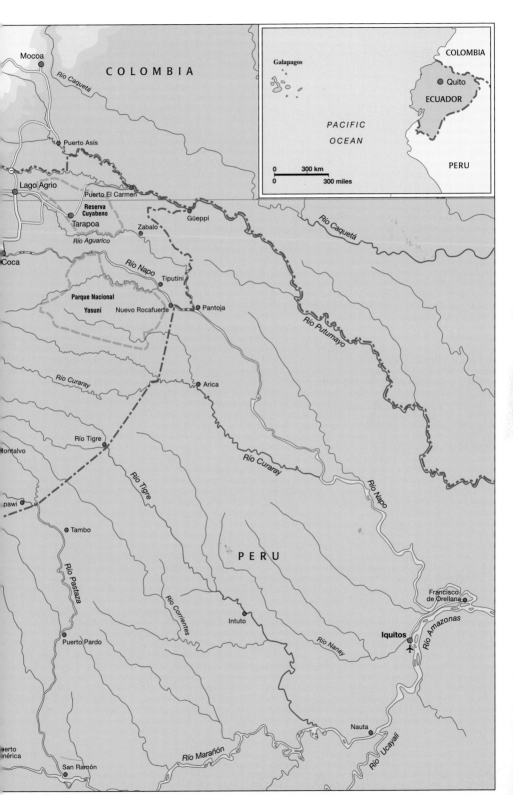

QUITO

Latin America's most beautiful church is here, along with splendid colonial buildings and some bargain shopping. A grid system makes it easy to find your way around

Surrounded by snowcapped volcanoes but only 24km (15 miles) from the equator, Quito is a strange and beautiful city with a spring-like climate all year round. Although an important city in Inca and pre-Inca times, its original buildings have been erased and today it is divided between the colonial architecture and sculpture of its Spanish conquest days and the clean lines of its modern section. This combination of superb well-preserved colonial churches and convents and shining glass and sleek contemporary architecture makes Quito one of the most beautiful cities in the whole of Latin America.

Nestled at the foot of 4,790-meter (15,710-ft) high Rucu Pichincha, Ecuador's capital owes its name to the Quitua Amerindians. When the Inca Empire spread as far as Ecuador under the leadership of Huayna-Capac, the Amerindians living in what is now Quito put up impressive resistance to the invaders from Cuzco (in modern-day Peru). But, in the end, Huayna-Capac not only added the area to the empire but he married a beautiful princess from the conquered tribe and set up the Incas' northern capital in Quito. A road was built to link Cuzco with Quito, from which Huayna-Capac preferred to rule.

His decision to divide the Inca kingdom into northern and southern regions – and his fathering of sons in both – were key factors in the downfall of the empire. When Huayna-Capac died, his legitimate heir in Cuzco, Huascar, claimed the throne at the same time as the leader's illegitimate (but some say favorite) son, Atahualpa, declared himself Inca in Quito. The rights to the throne were clouded, too, by the Inca line of succession – which was not based solely on birth order. In many instances, the first son of an Inca was passed over for younger siblings who showed greater leadership skills, wisdom, and courage. And, in the case of Huascar and Atahualpa, their subjects at each end of the kingdom supported the local son.

PRECEDING PAGES: Quito and Cotopaxi seen from Pichincha. LEFT: statue of the Virgin of Quito. BELOW: art for sale in El Ejido park.

A razed city

A year after Francisco Pizarro had Atahualpa executed in the main plaza of Cajamarca, now in northern Peru, Sebastián de Benalcázar, accompanied by *conquistador* Diego de Almagro, arrived to claim Quito for the Spanish crown. They skirmished with Atahualpa's general, Rumiñahui (Face of Stone), and when it became clear he would be overcome, he angrily set the Inca palace on fire. The flames spread and the city the Spanish finally claimed was razed. (Rumiñahui, meanwhile, was captured and executed.) For that reason Quito has no Inca structures; all that remained of those magnificent buildings perched on the city's beautiful high plain were massive rock foundations. On those bases, the Spanish conquerors built churches, convents, and palaces in the exuberant style of the Latin American baroque.

By the end of the 16th century, the new colonial city's population reache‹ 1,500 and it was declared the seat of the royal *Audiencia*, a legal subdivision o‹ the New World colony. The proliferation of churches, convents, and monaster ies won Quito the nickname "The Cloister of America" and, in 1978, the sam‹ colonial buildings prompted the United Nations to declare the city a Worl‹ Cultural Heritage Site.

In early colonial Quito, changes came slowly but steadily as wheat farmin‹ was introduced, the indigenous population was converted to Christianity, an‹ colonial rule and laws replaced the native culture. In the centuries that followe‹ Quito became a center for art and sculpture in the New World, with the Schoo of Quito *(see page 165)* producing an art form characterized by violent Christ ian themes, such as saints drawing their last breath in horrifying and blood scenes of martyrdom, painted in rich dark colors and gold brushwork, similiar t‹ the work of the School of Cuzco, Peru.

The growth and development of Quito was not problem-free. There was bloody rebellion against a royal sales tax in 1592 and another in 1765, when

Urban transport.

Quito Old Tow‹

0   200 m
0   200 yds

rumor spread that government-dispensed rum had been poisoned to eliminate the poorer classes. But things remained relatively peaceful until full-scale insurrection occurred when the winds of independence spreading across the continent reached this city. In August of 1809 the first sparks of revolution ignited in Quito and, on May 24, 1822, the city fell into the hands of the independence troops, led by Marshal Sucre, after a bloody battle in the foothills of Pichincha shadowing the city. May 24 is now a national holiday. For eight years Ecuador was part of La Gran Colombia – modern-day Colombia, Venezuela, and Ecuador united under a single government – but, in 1830, separated itself to become independent under the presidency of Juan Flores.

Map
on page
148

Colonial buildings, modern problems

Although Quito's old town, the *casco colonial*, with its churches, convents, and whitewashed houses with red-tile roofs, has not changed much physically since colonial times, social upheavals have been frequent, and it is experiencing many of the problems common to urban areas worldwide in the early years of the 21st century. In its narrow cobbled streets, traffic pollution is thick during the day. And behind the doors of the great mansions that once housed the city's richest residents in the oldest part of Quito are now the divided-up homes of the poor.

Quito flies the flag.

Quito today extends far beyond the old town's borders, even spreading up the slopes of Pichincha on the west side. The city has grown to a length of 35 km (22 miles), with a width of just 3–5 km (2–3 miles). On the eastern side of the city is the **Los Chillos** valley, which has experienced considerable urban development in recent years due to a new highway connecting it with the city. In northern Quito, huge business centers have sprung up complete with banks, shopping arcades, embassies, and government buildings. This part of Quito is also where upper-class residential areas are concentrated. The homes of the poor are largely on the city's south side, together with the factories and heavy industry that stretch along the Pan-American Highway, known locally as the Pana.

BELOW: posing for the camera in the old town.

The city's rapid growth has brought serious problems, including street crime, marginal housing, pollution, and a lack of basic services, such as water and electricity. The population has swelled to more than 1.5 million, though the squatter villages common in many other large cities on the continent are almost non-existent. However, Quito is still one of the few Latin American capitals where living conditions, as well as being extremely good for the wealthy, are sustainable, if nothing more, for working-class people. Although there has been a disturbing increase in the number of beggars in the plazas in the past few years, many tourists prefer to make the modern town their base.

Quito from above

In order to get an idea of the city's layout before you start exploring, it's a good idea to go to a spot that offers a fine panoramic view of Quito and the surrounding volcanoes. **Cerro Panecillo**, a hill dominating the old city and topped by a statue of the Virgin of the Americas with an observation deck, lures those who want to survey the basin in which Quito sits. A series of steps

and paths from García Moreno and Ambato enables you to walk up the hill but assaults are frequent and visitors are strongly advised to ascend El Panecillo only by taxi. The hill is where an Inca site for sun worship was once located. An even more splendid view is available from the **Cima de la Libertad**. Founded on the site of the 1822 Battle of Pichincha, this spot has a **museum** dedicated to the independence era in Quito. The museum exhibits flags, weapons, a model of this pivotal battle, and a sarcophagus containing the remains of its heroes. Dramatically, their tomb is guarded by an eternally burning flame.

Quito's newest attraction, the **Telefériqo** (www.teleferiqo.com; admission charge), starts at the base of Volcán Pichincha and transports visitors by cable cars 4,270 meters (14,000 ft) to the top of Cruz Loma. The views over Quito and of the surrounding mountains are stunning. From there, you can hike to the summit of Rucu Pichincha and back in 5–6 hours. It can get quite cold and the altitude can leave you breathless so be prepared; there is an oxygen bar though. At the base, Volcano Park has a number of restaurants, a disco, gift shops, and a small amusement park. The line to get on the cable cars tends to grow as the day goes on, so try and get there early. Free buses carry tourists to and from the site, although a taxi ride there is quite reasonable.

Strolling through the past

The center of Old Quito was made a UNESCO World Heritage Site in 1978 and, thanks to a large-scale restoration project, it is now one of the most attractive colonial centers in Latin America. Much of the area's former grandeur has been restored, and boutique hotels, restaurants, and galleries continue to appear. Walking around the hilly, narrow streets is the best way to see old Quito, the heart of

In 1534 the layout of the city was designed with 48 blocks, and divided by streets 10 meters (33ft) wide. The checkerboard outline was not completely regular due to slopes and ravines.

LEFT: the Telefériqo cable car.
RIGHT: view over Quito.

which is the **Plaza de la Independencia** , which has recently had a facelift on all sides. The ECH (Empresa Centro Historico) conducts walking tours through the historical center that leave from the tourist stand in the plaza (Tues–Sun 10am, 11am, and 2pm), accompanied by a bilingual member of the Tourist Police. Also known locally as the Plaza Grande, this palm-shaded square is dominated by **La Catedral Metropolitana** (Metropolitan Cathedral; open daily, except during Mass; free). The other sides of the plaza are flanked by the Palacio de Gobierno, the Archbishop's Palace, and the City Administration Building, which was erected in 1978 to replace a colonial structure that was beyond rescue. At the center of the plaza is a bronze and marble monument to liberty. Since 1998 there has been a new street-numbering system based on N *(norte)*, S *(sud)*, E *(este),* and O *(oeste)* followed by a street and building number, but many businesses still use their old address.

The cathedral is believed to have existed first as a wood and adobe structure before the official church was built on the site in 1565. Earthquake damage has forced restoration on three occasions, including after the 1987 tremors that damaged many of the city's colonial buildings. The cathedral is filled with paintings by some of Ecuador's finest early artists from what became known as the School of Quito *(see page 165)*. Outstanding among these is the *Descent from the Cross* by indigenous artist Caspicara. Like many churches built in Quito (and Cuenca) during the 16th and 17th centuries, the cathedral shows Moorish influences. One of the side altars contains the remains of Venezuelan-born Marshal Antonio José de Sucre, leader of the liberation army. Left of the main altar is a statue of Ecuador's first president, Juan José Flores, and behind the altar is a plaque showing where President Gabriel García Moreno died on

Map on page 148

BELOW: the Plaza de la Independencia.

August 6, 1875, from gunshot wounds he received while returning to the Presidential Palace after Mass. He was carried back across the street to the church but attempts to save his life were futile. This was not the only murder committed within the sanctuary of the cathedral. In 1877 a bishop of Quito died during Mass when he drank poisoned altar wine.

Detail from a Kingman painting.

The **Administration Building** is worth visiting to see the huge brightly colored *naïf* murals of Quito life, but you'll have to get past the plethora of children seeking to shine your shoes in order to do so. Around the corner from the cathedral on Calle García Moreno is **El Sagrario** **C**, built between 1657 and 1706 as the cathedral's main chapel but now used as a separate church, and with recently restored frescoes painted by Francisco de Alban in the cupola.

Roller-coaster politics

On the northwest side of the plaza is the **Palacio de Gobierno** **D** (Government Palace), also known as the **Palacio Presidencial** (Presidential Palace; access only to entrance area), with Ecuador's flag atop it and the entrance flanked by guards in red, blue, and gold 19th-century-style uniforms, which seem somewhat anachronistic in contrast with the automatic rifles they carry, and which they used during a 1976 coup attempt. This building has seen a great deal of activity, especially in the early days of the republic. From 1901 to 1948 alone, Ecuador had 39 governments and four constitutions, and at one point there were four presidents in a span of 26 days.

BELOW: entertaining the crowds in Plaza San Francisco.

Sightseeing is usually limited to the courtyard with its fountain and columns (the iron balconies were a gift from the French Government) and Oswaldo Guayasamín's famous mosaic mural depicting explorer Francisco de Orellana's

jungle voyage to the Amazon. It was Orellana's journey, which began in Ecuador and culminated in his naming of the Amazon River near what is now Iquitos, Peru, that led Ecuador to declare itself "The Amazon Nation." The palace, nearly 400 years old, is an unusual mix of formal and informal and must be one of the world's few presidential offices where the street-level floor has been converted into small shops that sell souvenirs.

Half a block from the plaza, at Eugenio Espejo 1147, is the **Antiguo Cuartel de la Real Audiencia** Ⓔ (Old Headquarters of the Royal Audiencia – now part of the Centro Cultural Metropolitano and commonly known as the Museo de Arte e Historia Alberto Mena Caamaño; Tues–Sun 9am–4.30pm), in an early Jesuit house that later served as barracks for the royal Spanish troops in Quito. The stone column in the patio was the pillory. Underneath it is the dungeon where 36 revolutionaries of the 1890 uprising were imprisoned for 9 months before being executed. Wax figures in the museum graphically illustrate their deaths. The museum contains ecclesiastical art from the 16th and 17th centuries, as well as a handful of works from the 1900s.

Latin America's most beautiful church

Almost next door to the museum is the impressive 16th-century church of **La Compañía de Jesus** Ⓕ (Mon–Fri 10am–5pm, Sat 10am–4pm, Sun noon–4pm; admission charge). This Jesuit church took 163 years to finish and is the most ornate in the country. It was severely damaged by fire, but FONSAL, the Cultural Heritage Protection Fund, finished extensive restoration in 2002. Richly intricate both inside and out, it is a masterpiece of baroque and Quiteño colonial art. Its altars are covered in gold leaf and the fine paintings on its vaulted ceiling have

Map on page 148

BELOW: guarding the Palacio Presidencial.

earned it the nickname "Quito's Sistine Chapel." The walls are covered with School of Quito murals. The designs on the columns inside the church clearly show a Moorish influence and the columns themselves are said to be copies of those by Bernini in the Vatican; they are reproduced in the main altar. However, the church's most precious treasures, including an emerald- and gold-laden painting of the *Virgen Dolorosa* (Our Lady of Sorrow), are kept in the country's Central Bank vaults and taken out only for special religious festivals. And the church's original holdings were far, far richer than what exist now. In 1767, when a decree banned the Jesuits from Spanish domains, the treasures in La Compañía were put into 36 boxes and shipped to Spain to pay war debts. What remained – mostly silver – was put up for sale but the devout Quiteños refused to buy it, saying that the items in question belonged to God.

At the foot of the altar in La Compañía are the remains of Quito's saint, Mariana de Jesús. In 1645, a combination of measles and diphtheria epidemics and an earthquake killed 14,000 people in Quito, prompting a frantic attempt to break the city's streak of bad luck. It was then that 26-year-old Mariana de Jesús stepped in. The orphaned daughter of an aristocratic family, she had already given all her wealth to the poor and was said to have miraculously healed the sick. Now she made a bargain with God, offering him her own life if the rest of the city's population could be saved. As the story goes, she fell ill immediately and, with her death, the plagues on the city ended. Just before she died, doctors bled her – as was the custom – and threw the blood into the garden of her home. It was said that a lily grew where the blood touched the earth and, for that reason, when the Pope canonized Mariana, he called her the "Lily of Quito."

Quito was severely damaged by an earthquake in 1987. FONSAL, the Cultural Heritage Protection Fund, has since carried out over 400 restoration projects in the colonial quarter.

LEFT: Olga Fisch, businesswoman and artist, in her home.
RIGHT: lavish gold interior, La Compañía church.

When you come out of La Compañía, go left down Avenida de Mariscal Sucre and between the streets of García Moreno and Venezuela you will find the **Museo Histórico Casa de Sucre** Ⓖ (Tues–Thur 9am–4pm, Fri–Sat 9am–1pm, tel: 295 2860; admission charge), with its collection of weapons, clothing, furniture, and documents from the independence era. This was once the home of Marshal Antonio José de Sucre. A statue of Sucre, pointing in the direction of Pichincha where he led independence troops to victory in 1822, is two blocks away at Bolívar and Guayaquil on the busy little Plaza Santo Domingo. Also in this square is the **Iglesia de Santo Domingo** Ⓗ (open daily; free), a church that is especially attractive in the evening when its domes are illuminated against the sky. FONSAL has completed the restoration of the church, including the beautiful wooden *Mudéjar* coffered ceiling. Santo Domingo has fine religious sculptures, especially those of the Virgen del Rosario, donated by Spanish King Charles I.

The Dominican **Museo Fray Pedro Bedón** (Mon–Sat 8.30am–5pm, Sun 9am–4pm, tel: 228 0518; admission charge), attached to the church, also has an impressive collection of art (the friar himself was a painter). The museum is home to the astonishing silver throne used to carry the Virgen del Rosario during religious processions.

Roaming La Ronda

From Plaza Santo Domingo, turn down Guayaquil to Calle Juan de Dios Morales. This is **La Ronda**, the neighborhood offering the most romantic slice of colonial Quito, with its bright white buildings trimmed with blue window frames and doors and brightened with pots of red geraniums. Narrow streets of polished cobble stones are bordered on both sides by beautiful old houses with

Map on page 148

BELOW: the house of Marshal Sucre, now a museum.

balconies. This graceful maze of passages and stairways runs from Carrera Venezuela to Calle Maldonado under two bridges. Its name comes from the guitar serenades – or *rondas* – that drew crowds here during colonial days. At intervals along the way are tiled portraits of famous Ecuadorian musicians and composers. However, this area is not as safe as it once was. Due to poverty, theft has become something of a problem, particularly at night, when a saunter down these streets is a near guarantee of robbery or assault.

From here it is only three blocks to the Plaza San Francisco, but en route you will pass Calle García Moreno. The **Museo de la Ciudad** (Tues–Sun 9.30am–5.30pm, tel: 228 3882; admission charge) opened in 1995 at Rocafuerte 572 and García Moreno. The building, with two large courtyards, functioned as the San Juan de Dios Hospital from 1565 until 1973 and has since been beautifully restored. Exhibits show the stages of Quito's development and daily life from the pre-Hispanic era to the present day.

Riding the bus to school.

Grand tribute to a patron saint

The expansive **Plaza San Francisco ❶** is named for its monastery church, **El Monasterio de San Francisco ❿** (Mon–Fri 8am–noon and 3–6pm, Sat & Sun 9am–noon; admission charge), honoring Quito's patron saint. The Flemish missionary, Fray Jodocko Ricke, directed construction of the church and monastery on the site of the Inca palace only 50 days after the city's 1534 founding – making this the American continent's oldest church. Fray Ricke, who was also responsible for introducing wheat to Ecuador by planting the first seeds in this plaza, is honored by a statue, which is situated in front of the church.

BELOW: faded grandeur in Old Quito.

The San Francisco religious complex with its 104 Doric columns is the largest structure in colonial Quito, with a sumptuous Spanish baroque interior. But the indigenous heritage of Quito is represented in this Christian enclave; the church ceiling is decorated with images of the sun – the Inca divinity. Its main altar is spectacularly carved and the side aisles are banked with paintings by School of Quito masters, including the *Virgen Inmaculada de Quito* by Bernardo de Legarda. This is reportedly the only winged image of the Virgin Mary to be found in either Europe or the Americas.

The complex's finest artwork, including paintings, sculptures, and furniture from the 16th and 17th centuries, is found in the **Museo Franciscano** to the right of the main entrance to the church, in a building that was originally established by Fray Ricke as a school of art and religious instruction for indigenous children. Note the details of the intricately wrought furniture: some pieces have thousands of mother-of-pearl mosaics in their construction. To one side of the San Francisco atrium is the **Cantuña Chapel**, which is believed to have been built by the indigenous Cantuña, a Christian convert, and financed by treasures from the Inca Empire. Cantuña's remains lie in the church. The chapel has a magnificent carved altar – the work of Bernardo de Legarda – and its walls display finely carved wood.

Not far away is another of Quito's churches – there are more than eighty in all. This one is **La Merced ⓚ**, located at the corner of calles Cuenca and Chile. Its monastery contains the city's oldest clock, built in 1817.

Other non-religious features of this complex include the statue of Neptune, which sits on the fountain in the cloister's main patio. Visits to the cloister must be arranged in advance with a representative at the monastery. The castle-like La Merced – constructed from 1700 to 1734 – was one of the last churches built during Quito's colonial period, and it has the old city's tallest tower (47 meters/154 ft) and its largest bell. The walls are decorated with pink and white reliefs displaying more than three dozen gilt-framed School of Quito paintings, among them several with unusual scenes of erupting volcanoes and an ash-covered city. Bernardo de Legarda carved the main altarpiece in this serenely beautiful church.

From here, the recently restored **Museo de Arte Colonial** ● (Museum of Colonial Art; tel: 228 2297; Tues–Fri 10am–6pm, Sat 10am–2pm; admission charge) is just a block away at calles Cuenca and Mejia. Located in a beautiful 17th-century colonial house, the museum provides a splendid and appropriate setting for the works on display. The former home of the Marquis of Vallacis now exhibits selected artwork from the School of Quito. Among its paintings, sculptures, and crafts are works by Samaniego, Caspicara, and de Legarda.

Quito's gold convent

If you are in the mood for more history and architecture, turn down Calle Mejía when you leave the museum, and at the corner of Mejia and Flores streets you will find the **Monasterio de San Agustín** ⓜ (Mon–Sat 7am–noon and 1–6pm; admission charge), where Ecuador's first (short-lived) Act of Independence was signed in August 1809. Inside its flower-filled patio, robed monks pray against a backdrop of oil paintings by Miguel de Santiago, who spent most of his life

LEFT: street in La Ronda.
RIGHT: enjoying the sunshine in the Plaza de la Independencia.

in the monastery illustrating the life of St Augustine. The third floor of one wing of the cloister, which is open to the public, houses restoration workshops of the Cultural Heritage Institute. The interior of the church is an intriguing mixture of Gothic and arabesque styles. The room where the independence document was signed is called the Sala Capitular and contains a portable altar in 18th-century baroque style attributed to the indigenous artist Pampite. In San Agustín's catacombs are the remains of the independence leaders killed by the Spanish loyalists a year after they joined the revolution.

Northeast along Calle Flores (toward the New Town) is the **Teatro Nacional Sucre** (tel: 228 0982), the city's most beautiful theater, where concerts and plays are staged. This is the home of the National Symphony Orchestra; extensive renovations were finally completed in 2003.

Quito's modern trolley system is 11km (6 miles) long with 40 stops, and carries 14,000 passengers an hour.

Where old meets new

From here, Calle Guayaquil, with its 19th-century buildings, leads toward the area where the past is left behind. The **Monasterio de San Blas** is one of the last colonial complexes before you come to modern Quito lying ahead at the point where old meets new. The landmark is the long, triangular **Parque La Alameda**, with an impressive monument of the liberation leader Simón Bolí-var. The park contains a number of other busts and statues in honor of famous Latin Americans. Among them is Manuelita Saenz – the Quito-born woman who was Bolívar's companion throughout the revolution. There are also monuments here commemorating the French mission that traveled to Ecuador in 1736 to measure the arc of the equatorial line in order to work out the circumference of the earth. Charles-Marie de la Condamine, the expedition's leader, and Pedro

BELOW: watching the world go by in colonial Quito.

Maldonaldo, an Ecuadorian, are the best-known members of the team.

It was in 1598 that Spanish officials in Quito obtained permission to build the Alameda, an area for recreation, brightened by well-tended gardens, flowers, and shade trees. The consensus was to place this park at the junction of a natural lagoon – nowadays used by canoeists. At the center of the park is South America's oldest observatory, the **Observatorio Astronómico ⊙** (Mon–Fri 9am–noon, 2.30–5.30pm; tel: 257 0765; admission charge), begun in 1864 and completed 23 years later. It is used by meteorologists and astronomers, but can also be visited by members of the public.

The small church of **El Belén ⊕** (open daily; free) on the park's north side is a favorite subject of Quito's artists. It marks the site where the first Mass in Quito was said after the city was taken over by the Spanish. Simple and graceful, this church's lone nave contains a magnificent Christ believed to be the work of indigenous artist Caspicara. Two blocks up Avenida 6 de Diciembre and right on Calle Montalvo is the **Palacio Legislativo ⊙**, a new government building with the history of Ecuador immortalized in carved stone along its north side. If you take Avenida Gran Colombia from here to Avenida Paz and Calle Miño, you can see the hill-top home of the **Instituto Geográfico Militar** (Geographical Military Institute; Tues–Fri 8am– 4pm; tel: 250 2091; admission charge). There is a museum, and the planetarium (Mon–Fri 9–3pm, Sat 9–11am) – distinguishable by its white dome – has shows lasting for about half an hour that take place several times a day. If you turn right, however, from the Palacio Legislativo, and continue up Calle 6 de Diciembre, you will come to the **Parque El Ejido** (Communal Park). This park, the largest in central Quito, is a favorite spot – especially at weekends – for Otavalo *indígenas*, picnickers, soccer players, couples out for a stroll, energetic

Maps,
pages
148 & 160

BELOW: the Casa de la Cultura Ecuatoriana.

Modern reflections.

children, and street vendors seeking the park's shady trees as respite from the warm sun. Here women carry huge trays of food balanced on their heads, offering for sale *fritada, papas, y mote* – grilled meat, potatoes, and corn. At the weekend there is a large art market, popular with tourists staying at the nearby Hilton Colón.

Banks, boutiques, and bargains

At the north end of El Ejido, from Avenida Patria to Colón, lies Quito's modern tourist and business area with hotels, offices, banks, and restaurants. **Avenida Amazonas** is home to travel agencies, art galleries, money exchangers, outdoor cafes, and the double-decker airport buses. This is the best spot for strolling and shopping, with stops for cool drinks or snacks at the many restaurants and pastry shops along the route. Shopping bargains range from well-made handicrafts to clothing in boutiques carrying the latest fashions. In the **Hilton Colón**, at the south end of the street, is a shopping gallery with a branch of Libri Mundi, the city's top book store carrying English-language titles and maps. You should also follow the parallel street, Juan León Mera, another good place for cafes and shopping, to the book store's main branch, and the popular Art Forum Café. Most of the shops in Quito close on Saturday afternoons.

Officially a part of Mariscal Sucre, the area north of Veintimilla and south of Luís Cordero is nicknamed "Gringolandia" because of the number of backpacker hostels and tour operators there. Many of the city's most lively discos are found here, filled with a mix of locals and tourists almost every night of the week. On the eastern edge, Plaza de Quinde has recently undergone a major renovation and is now home to the city's trendiest cafes, restaurants, and bars.

Head eastward from the park, along Avenida Patria, to the **Casa de la Cul-**

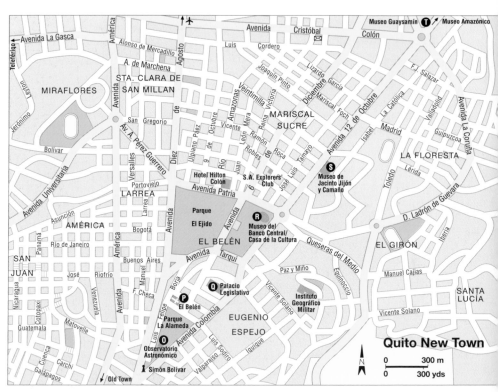

Quito New Town

Map on page 160

tura Ecuatoriana, a large circular glass building that houses the **Museo del Banco Central** ❼ (Tues–Fri 9am–5pm, weekends 10am–4pm; tel: 222 3259; admission charge), which was inaugurated in June, 1995. This stylish presentation of Ecuadorian history, demonstrated through its artworks, should not be missed. The spacious museum includes five connected salons, devoted respectively to archeology, gold, colonial art, republican art, and modern art.

As you walk through the collections in chronological order you will gain a sense of Ecuador's proud history as seen through the eyes of its artists. Each of the pre-Columbian cultures is represented by artifacts – including pottery, tools, and jewelry – and well-constructed dioramas. The highlight of the gold room is a ceremonial mask fashioned from gold and silver. The transition to the colonial collection is marked by a gold sun – the god of the Incas, and a silver cross inlaid with precious stones – an early piece fashioned by the conquering Spanish. The museum also contains pieces from the Quito School, including one of only two known sculptures of the pregnant Virgin Mary.

The republican art collection has wonderful paintings of mountain and jungle landscapes, as well as themes exploring national identity and social change. The indigenous peoples' struggle for freedom is forcefully presented in the paintings of Eduardo Kingman in the modern collection. The museum also displays many works by Camilo Egas, one of Ecuador's best-known contemporary artists, who died in 1961 at the age of 73 *(see A Nation of Painters, page 113)*. Another salon is reserved for presentations of works that are rotated every month – it's certainly worth checking what is on while you are in the city. Written explanations throughout the museum are in Spanish and English and guided tours are available in Spanish, English, German, and French.

Most tourists gravitate toward Amazonas.

BELOW: cafe culture in Plaza del Quinde.

The **Museo de la Casa de la Cultura Ecuatoriana** (opening hours as for the Museo del Banco Central, above) is housed in the same building, and contains a less comprehensive collection of art from the colonial period to modern times. A separate room of the museum displays musical instruments, many of them several centuries old, gathered from all over the world. There is also a display of traditional dress from various indigenous cultures. A movie theater and concert hall are also housed in the Casa de la Cultura.

Just two blocks away, another fine museum with archeological artifacts is run by the Universidad Católica on Avenida 12 de Octubre. The **Museo de Jacinto Jijón y Caamaño** ❾ (Mon–Fri 8am–6pm; tel: 256 5627; admission charge) contains the private collection donated by the family of the aristocratic archeologist after his death. It was the work of Jijón y Caamaño that provided the basis for the modern-day theories on how pre-Hispanic peoples lived in Ecuador; his books on the subject are valuable rarities.

The museum's collection includes *aribalos*, the graceful fluted-mouthed jars with pointed bottoms that are synonymous with pre-Inca cultures throughout the Andes, as well as a wide assortment of religious idols, masks, weapons, and shell and bone works. The museum also houses a small collection of School of Quito colonial art.

Art and artifacts

Continue for a few minutes along pleasant, tree-lined Avenida 12 de Octubre to the **Museo Amazónico** (12 de Octubre 1430 and Wilson; Mon–Fri 8.30am–12.30pm and 2–5pm; tel: 256 6327; admission charge). This interesting little museum is run by the Salesian Mission, and has a collection of artifacts from native Amazonian tribes and a number of cultural publications.

The **Museo Guayasamín** ⓣ (Mon–Fri 10am–5pm; tel: 244 6455; admission charge), at Calle Bosmediano 543 in one of the city's most beautiful modern houses, is perched on a hill side overlooking Quito, in the Bellavista district. The museum is quite a trek uphill and it might be better to take a taxi – most drivers know where to find the museum – or catch a Bellavista bus. The museum houses perhaps the most intriguing colonial art collection in the city. Set up by artist Oswaldo Guayasamín, the complex is divided into three: a colonial art gallery (housing Guayasamín's own collection), the artist's gallery, where he displayed and sold his artworks, and a studio used by himself and his students. Provocative and political, Guayasamín's art made him perhaps the country's best-known artist and the gallery of his works should not be missed. Born of an indigenous father and mestizo mother, his work delves heavily into themes connected with his mixed heritage and this museum complex represents 30 years of planning (*see A Nation of Painters, page 114*). A fine collection of sculpture is displayed on the flower-splashed tile roof.

The artist began what would later be considered his masterpiece in 1995 and it was finished after his death in 1999 at the insistence of his heirs. The **Capilla del Hombre** (Pasaje Lorenzo Chávez and Mariano Calvache; tel: 244 8492; Tues–Sun 10am–5pm; admission charge) is located a few blocks away and is

BELOW:
Guayasamín's
sculptures at the
Museo Guayasamín.

one of the most exciting contributions to Latin American art in recent years. There is a large collection of the artist's work including paintings, sculptures, and an eternal flame set in the center in defense of peace and human rights. The museum, modeled on an Inca temple, is dedicated to the values of the pre-Columbian man and his struggle against colonization. Set in picturesque gardens, the chapel overlooks the city. There's a small cafe and gift shop where you can buy prints of Guayasamín's work. If you plan to visit the Museo Guayasamín as well, it's best to take a taxi here first and then walk the five blocks to the museum.

After your visit to the museum, take a stroll through the fragrant eucalyptus forests in the **Parque Metropolitano**, which has splendid views of Quito city and the nearby volcanic peaks of Cotopaxi and Cayambe, before going back into town. If you would like to see what Quiteños do in their spare time, you could wander back down Bosmediano to the large **Parque Carolina**, located just off Avenida Eloy Alfaro. The playing fields on weekends are crowded with soccer and volleyball players and runners, and there are usually noisy groups of people picnicking. During August, Sunday outdoor concerts are given by the Banda Sinfónica.

The **Museo de Ciencias Naturales** (Natural History Museum; Mon–Fri 8.30am–4.30pm, Sat 10am–2pm; tel: 244 9824; admission charge) is on the south side of the park, at the corner of Rumipamba and Los Shyris. It has a good collection of endemic fauna and is worth a visit before you go to see the flora and fauna in the wild, as it will help you to identify some of the species you may find. Nearby a game of giant outdoor chess can be enjoyed at the Café Ajedrez (Chess Cafe). ❏

BELOW: the Banco de Azuay in Quito's New Town.

Map on page 160

COLONIAL ARCHITECTURE

Catholic concepts, indigenous motifs, and inspiration blend together with Arabic influences to create the Colonial style that has been carefully preserved in Quito and Cuenca

When the Spanish conquered Ecuador they brought with them priests from different monastic orders: Franciscans, Augustinians, and Dominicans, and later the Jesuits. Within 50 days of the foundation of Quito in 1534 the Franciscan monks had begun constructing their own church. This was the first classic example of Colonial architecture.

Each religious order was assigned land by the Spanish Crown and each competed against the other in the construction of churches, convents, and plazas. Brother Jodocko Ricke, a Flemish Franciscan, set up an informal school for indigenous children to teach them religion and art. It was the first school of fine arts in South America.

The Franciscans discovered the creative skills of the indigenous people and also brought over talented converted Muslims. Sun motifs (the Sun being the principal Inca god) are commonly found alongside Madonna and child representations, and ceilings often show *Mudéjar* influence. This blend of European and indigenous ideas created the Quiteño school of art and architecture.

The Jesuits strengthened the arts movement when they arrived in 1586. In the following 250 years ornate churches with richly adorned sacristies, carved choirs, and fine paintings flourished. Workshops and guilds were established and by the middle of the 18th century 30 guilds in Quito controlled all artistic production.

ALTAR ▷
As the influence of baroque art became more prevalent the altar pieces grew more and more elaborate. Some were overpowering three-dimensional structures, decorated in gold leaf with rich paintings and statues.

△ **STAINED GLASS**
This stained-glass window depicting Moses, which brightens Cuenca cathedral, is a fine example of the florid Colonial style.

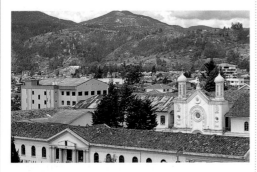

△ **CUENCA: A COLONIAL INHERITANCE**
The center of Cuenca, founded on the site of the Inca city of Tomebamba, has numerous 16th- and 17th-century churches which demonstrate the apogee of Colonial architecture.

THE SCHOOL OF QUITO

The niches of early Colonial altarpieces were first decorated with paintings, but polychrome statues became dominant later additions. When the first Colonial buildings were constructed, statues were shipped over to Ecuador from Andalucia in Spain. However, by the 18th century a distinct style of Quiteño art had emerged.

Baroque, rococo, and neo-classical styles from Europe reached Quito and were interpreted in a new way. Artists used different mediums: stone, ivory, tagua, clay, porcelain, and metal, but polychrome statues made from wood were the most popular. Pictured above is a typical 17th-century figure from the church of San Francisco.

Native cedar wood and sometimes alder from the hills surrounding Quito were used. Smaller figurines were usually made from balsa wood. Trees were cut only at the full moon so that the sap would have risen to the highest level possible, making the wood stronger for carving. First the artists primed the statues and then painted directly on them with bright primary colors. They developed attention to detail and realism, reddening the cheeks, using false eyelashes and nails, and glass eyes. The figures were sometimes dressed from head to toe in sumptuous fabrics with floral designs.

◁ **DOMES AND BELL TOWERS**
The domes and bell towers of the 17th-century building boom dominate the whitewashed buildings of Quito in Renaissance and baroque styles with many later neo-classical additions.

△ **PILLARED PORTAL**
This doorway in Cuenca's old cathedral illustrates another intrinsic facet of Colonial architecture: the great variety of columns, spiral, smooth, and striated, which were used in portals, facades, altars, and towers. The building was begun in 1557, the year the city was founded.

△ **FLOURISHING FIGURES**
By the 18th century, as artistic individuality flourished, secular figures, including nudes, were incorporated with religious themes.

DAY TRIPS FROM QUITO

Mountains, forests, thermal springs, and wildlife sanctuaries are all within easy reach of the capital – and the Virgin of El Quinche is renowned for her miracles

Map on page 168

ECUADOR
Quito

Q uito makes a good starting point for many day-long excursions into the lush surrounding Andean Sierra. By hiring a car, taking a tour, or using public transport or taxis, there are several popular trips into a region crowded with mountain views, waterfalls, thermal baths, and peaceful villages.

Buses to the Equatorial Line Monument, **La Mitad del Mundo ❶**, run every half hour on Avenida America in the New Town. It's about a half-hour trip (22 km/14 miles) to the north of Quito, located on latitude 0°, and provides an irresistible opportunity to straddle both hemispheres. The monument is a rather clumsy-looking thing, topped by a huge brass globe, but it's a very popular spot, particularly at the equinoxes (March 21 and September 21) when the sun is directly overhead and neither monument nor visitors cast a shadow. The monument forms the focal point of a park and leisure area with gift shops and restaurants (including the Equinoccio, which distributes certificates recording your visit), and there is a good museum inside (Mon–Thur 9am–6pm, Fri–Sun 9am–7pm; tel: 239 4806; admission charge). An elevator leads to the top for fine views. Just next door is the **Museo Solar Inti Ñan** (9.30am–5.30pm; tel: 239 5122; admission charge), which marks the true spot of the equator as measured by GPS. Interactive exhibits demonstrate how water drains in different directions on either side of the equator. This small museum is less touristy than the Mitad del Mundo, but far more informative.

About 4 km (2 miles) beyond the monument, toward the village of Calacalí, at Km 4 to the right, is the **Reserva Geobotánica Pululahua ❷**, centered on the biggest volcanic crater in South America. A paved road leads to the rim of the volcano. A rough path leads down from the rim, and the interior of the crater has its own microclimate, with rich vegetation and diverse bird life. Nearby is the excellent El Crater restaurant and art gallery, with fantastic views. Also to the north of Quito is the **Reserva Maquipucuna ❸** (contact the Quito office at Baquerizo 238 and Tamayo, tel: 250 7200, www.maqui.org). To get there, take the coast road through Calacalí to Nanegalito (61 km/35 miles), then take a right turn in the village. It is 19 km (12 miles) from Nanegalito, signposted along the way. The reserve consists of steeply sloped cloudforest, with a great diversity of fauna and flora. The **Reserva Bellavista** is on the road to Mindo at Km 68, also located in lush forest, with great views over the valley. The **Bosque Mindo-Nambillo**, near Mindo, is a protected reserve that is home to a range of birds, orchids, and bromeliads. The 20,000-hectare (49,420-acre) forest covers land of varying altitudes which makes for a very diverse ecosystem. Some 325 species of bird have been recorded here including cock-of-the-rocks, toucan-barbets, and several species of quetzals.

LEFT: Cotopaxi, seen from Quito.
BELOW: the equatorial line monument, La Mitad del Mundo.

Just below the Hotel Quito lies the tiny village of **Guápulo** with its four-hundred-year-old church containing works by some of the country's best-known 17th-century artists, for this was the founding spot of the School of Quito *(see page 165).* This church and former convent has a pulpit carved by indigenous sculptor Juan Menacho that is unquestionably the loveliest in Quito. Carry on down the mountain, crossing the Machángara River, and onto the Nuevo Oriental bypass. Going right will take you to Cumbayá, a modern suburb of Quito. Just after Cumbayá you can take the road branching right to Guangopolo and into the valley of Los Chillos, through unpopulated country along the winding San Pedro River. Otherwise, continue on to the town of **Tumbaco** ❹ with its many weekend houses. The bungee jump off the bridge here is claimed to be the longest in the world.

For horseback riding enthusiasts, trips can be arranged from the Reserva Geobotánica Pululahua.

Miracles and hot springs

The road through the Tumbaco valley passes through the sanctuary of **El Quinche** ❺, a point of attraction for pilgrims from the northern Sierra. The Virgin of El Quinche is renowned for her miracles, and is a favorite among drivers and transport workers. Devout Catholics come to ask the Virgin's blessing whenever they undertake a new venture. Many also make the yearly pilgrimage to Oyacachi where the Virgin Mary statue originated. This small isolated community has some hot springs set in a lush valley at 3,200 meters (3,500 yards) in the Cayambe Coca Reserve, just beneath the *páramo.* It is connected to Cayambe and Quito via Cangahua.

Descend the main road from El Quinche to the south (unpaved but well-maintained). The view is wonderful, and snow and subtropical forests lie close together. At Km 59, the small **Lago Papallacta** ❻ is renowned for trout fishing.

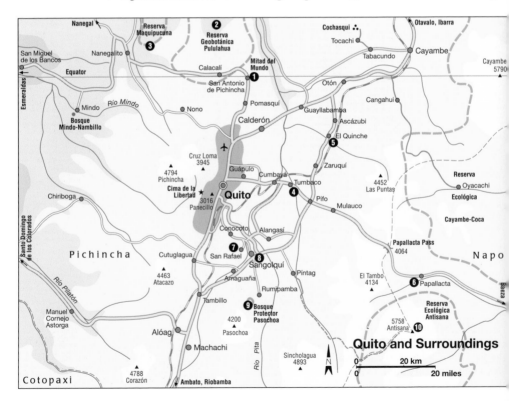

Quito and Surroundings

(The village of Papallacta is better known for the oil pipline that emerges here.) At Km 60, a road branches off to the springs of Huanonumpa, commonly known as the thermal springs of Papallacta. Recently renovated and expanded, these are the most attractively developed hot springs in Ecuador. Stay overnight in the comfortable Termas de Papallacta hotel *(see Travel Tips pages 335–340)* and go for a dip in one of its private pools. The public pools by the restaurant are crowded at weekends.

The **Valle de los Chillos**, an area of thermal springs, lies east of Quito. There is a fine descent into the valley on the Via Oriental and the Autopista de Los Chillos. The highway crosses the valley's main road in **San Rafael** ❼ (12 km/8 miles). Stop here to visit **La Casa de Kingman Museo** (Thur–Fri 10am–4pm, Sat & Sun 10am–5pm; tel: 286 1065; admission charge), the former home of the artist Eduardo Kingman. It is now open to the public and displays his works alongside other notable colonial and modern art. Ahead lies the village of **Sangolqui** ❽, known for its Sunday market. Nearby, at La Merced and El Tingo, are thermal springs (turn left at San Rafael). To get there from Quito takes only 30–40 minutes.

To the south of Sangolqui is the village of **Amaguaña**, which can be reached by bus from Quito (about an hour's drive). A few kilometers from Amaguaña, set around an extinct volcano, is the **Bosque Protector Pasochoa** ❾. This small protected area has Andean vegetation and is a sanctuary for birds and native plants (orchids bloom from February to May). For excursions, contact Fundación Natura, *(see Travel Tips page 350 for details)*. The road to **Volcán Antisana** ❿ goes through Pintag. The volcano has four snowy and glaciered peaks, which are very difficult to climb. To use the road you must get the permission of the Fundación Antisana, tel: 243 086. In the surrounding ecological reserve condors, rainbow ducks, and other birds can be seen. ❑

LEFT: the church at Guápulo.
RIGHT: miracles recorded at El Quinche.

GOING NORTH

From Otavalo, Ecuador's greatest market,
to the surrounding lakes and artisans' villages
and up to the Colombian border

Maps
on pages
174 & 178

The province of **Imbabura**, just a short step north of Quito, is one of Ecuador's most popular destinations. Its numerous Andean volcanoes, lakes, and valleys combine to make a landscape of extraordinary beauty, while the variety of local indigenous groups means that the northern Sierra is one of the most culturally vibrant regions in the country. Even more beguiling for many travelers is that Imbabura province is a rich source of handicrafts: it is home to the woodcarvers of San Antonio, the leatherworkers of Cotacachi, and the weavers of Otavalo.

Beyond the capital

Leaving **Quito ❶** behind, most visitors take the shortest route to Imbabura, some 100 km (60 miles) along the paved Pan-American Highway passing straight through the barren landscape of northern Pichincha. But for those who have time to explore, there are a number of ways of reaching the province and several places worth visiting en route. There are buses from Quito to the towns numbered on the map on page 174. Getting to some of the villages takes a little more ingenuity if you don't have your own transport, but many are walkable from the nearest town, and round-trip taxi journeys are not expensive.

The main road passes through **Guayllabamba**. Surrounded by dry rocky hills, and sparsely covered with tufts of grass, the Guayllabamba valley is warm and fertile, famous for its orchards and local fruit, such as the *chirimoya* (custard apple) and the local variety of avocado, which is small, roundish, and black-skinned. Visitors are pressed to buy the produce, and local women compete by offering a *yapa* (one extra for the same price). A specialty is the tasty *locro de cueros* (potato soup with pork rind) with avocados on the side.

Two roads lead out of Guayllabamba toward Cayambe: the left-hand one, via **Tabacundo**, follows a deep ravine, with curious rock formations. After crossing the Río Guayllabamba it is possible to make a detour along the riverside down to the tranquil villages of **Puellaro** and **Perucho**, where oranges grow and little seems to have changed for decades.

Another option is a visit to the archeological site of **Cochasqui**, on the southern slopes of **Mount Mojanda**, a short distance from Tabacundo. Some 15 flat-topped pyramids and 30 mounds are believed to have been built by Caranqui Amerindians around the 13th century, although some date from AD900. Take a guided tour from the resident guardian, and learn about religious and funeral practices, living styles, and even the astronomical discoveries made in that era.

The small town of **Cayambe**, under the perpetual vigilance of the extinct volcano of the same name, is worth

PRECEDING PAGES:
Otavaleña displays rich tapestries.
LEFT: headgear of Otavalo women.
BELOW: Saturday market in Otavalo.

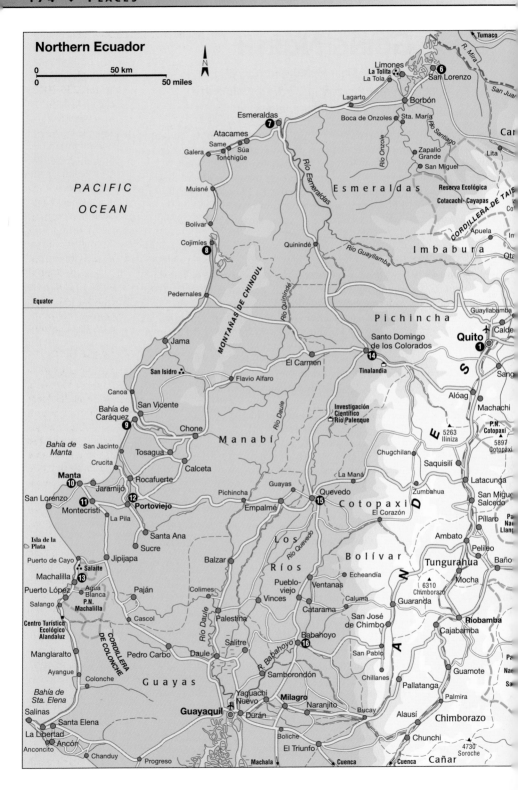

Northern Ecuador

0   50 km
0   50 miles

N

Tumaco
R. Mira
Limones
La Tolita
La Tola
6
San Lorenzo
San Juan
Lagarto
Borbón
Boca de Onzoles
Sta. María
Esmeraldas
7
Cañ
Atacames
Río Santiago
Same
Río Onzole
Galera
Súa
Zapallo
Lita
Tonchigüe
Grande
San Miguel

**PACIFIC
OCEAN**

Muisné
E s m e r a l d a s
Reserva Ecológica
Cotacachi- Cayapas
CORDILLERA DE TAIS
Co

Bolívar
Apuela
Im
Cojimíes
8
Quinindé
Río Guayllamba
I m b a b u r a
Ot

MONTAÑAS DE CHINDUL
Río Quinindé
Río Esmeraldas

Equator

Pedernales
Guayllabamba

P i c h i n c h a
Calde

Jama
Santo Domingo
de los Colorados
Quito **1**

El Carmen
14
Tinalandia
Sang
San Isidro
Flavio Alfaro

Canoa
Alóag
San Vicente
Río Daule
Machachi
Bahía de
Caráquez
9
Chone
Investigación
Científico
Río Palenque
P.N.
Cotopaxi
5263
Iliniza
5897
Cotopaxi
Bahía de
Manta
San Jacinto
M a n a b í
Chugchilan
Crucita
Tosagua
Calceta
La Maná
Saquisilí
Latacunga
Manta
10
Rocafuerte
Guayas
Quevedo
Zumbahua
San Miguel
Jaramijó
Pichincha
15
Salcedo
San Lorenzo
11
12
Portoviejo
Empalmé
C o t o p a x i
El Corazón
Pillaro
Pa
Montecristi
Nai
La Pila
Llang
Isla de la
Plata
Santa Ana
L o s
Ambato
Sucre
Río Quevedo
Peleleo
Puerto de Cayo
Jipijapa
Balzar
R í o s
B o l í v a r
Tungurahua
Baño
Machalilla
Echeandía
Mocha
Salaite
13
Puerto López
Agua
Blanca
Pajan
Colimes
Pueblo-
viejo
Ventanas
6310
Chimborazo
Salango
P.N.
Machalilla
Vinces
Caluma
Guaranda
Centro Turístico
Ecológico
Alandaluz
Cascol
Palestina
Catarama
San José
de Chimbo
Riobamba
CORDILLERA DE COLONCHE
Manglaralto
Pedro Carbo
Daule
Salitre
Babahoyo
16
San Pablo
Cajabamba
Pa
Ayangue
R. Babahoyo
Guamote
Na
Colonche
Samborondón
Chillanes
Pallatanga
Sa
Bahía de
Sta. Elena
G u a y a s
Palmira
Salinas
Yaguachi
Nuevo
Milagro
Chimborazo
Santa Elena
Guayaquil
Durán
Naranjito
Bucay
Alausí
La Libertad
Ancón
Boliche
Chunchi
Anconcito
Chanduy
El Triunfo
4730
Soroche
Progreso
Machala
Cuenca
Cuenca
Cañar

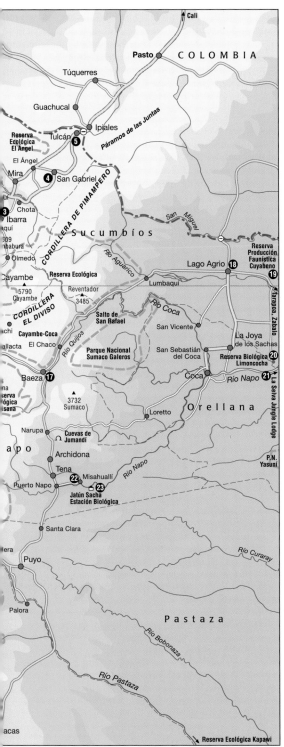

a stop-over to try its famous local cheese, especially *queso de hoja*, and the *biscochos*, a savory shortbread.

A few kilometers south of Cayambe is the **Hostería Guachala** (tel: 236 3042; www.guachala.com), a hacienda dating to 1580. It was renovated and converted into a hotel in 1993. Set in pleasant grounds with a swimming pool and opportunities nearby for horseback riding, it is an attractive place where it is easy to conjure up the rich history that its owner, Diego Boniface, is more than willing to reveal to you.

Going north from Cayambe, a turn in the main road unexpectedly brings into view Laguna San Pablo and, towering behind it, **Volcán Imbabura**, with its concave slopes covered in tiny fields. Opposite, though often enveloped in clouds, is its sister mountain, **Cotacachi**, and on the flat valley floor between the two, known as "the valley of the dawn," lies Otavalo.

Ecuador's greatest market

At dawn on Saturday mornings, the market square (called the Poncho Plaza) in **Otavalo** ❷ gets busy as the stallholders set up their displays. Handicraft workers from the outlying districts come to negotiate their wares with traders before the tourists arrive. By 9am the square is a feast of colors and textures: bolts of cloth, thick blankets, tapestry wall hangings, embroidered blouses and dresses, chunky hand-knitted sweaters, long patterned belts or *fajas,* such as the indigenous women wind round their waists, and *cintas*, tapes they use to bind their long hair. The square is a maze of stands and narrow alleys with just enough room to pass.

Tourists making day trips from Quito arrive by bus at around 10am, and the haggling begins. The *indígenas* are experienced in business, can size up their customer, and know just how far to lower their price. Several of them speak English.

Despite the crowds, the atmosphere is calm and relaxed – muffled, perhaps, by the walls of cloth. Most of the handicrafts are tailored to foreign tastes, although some of the designs are reworkings of traditional motifs. The style of clothing sold to the public is adjusted each year accord-

A young Otavaleña in typical distinctive dress.

BELOW: the colonial Hacienda Cusín near Otavalo, now a hotel.

ing to fashion and demand, and many high-quality handicrafts are sold in Quit(or abroad, and never appear at all at the Otavalo market. But there is plenty t(choose from: Otavaleño work is usually well made (though finishings are some times careless), and at prices that seem a dream to most foreigners.

Saturday is also market day for the local population. At the north end of Ponch(Plaza you'll find hot prepared food and a corner market for such animals as *cuye* (guinea pigs) and rabbits. The market plaza for the larger farm animals is at th western edge of town. Just follow the unmistakable evidence left by these ani mals along Calle Morales and across the Pan-American Highway.

In parts of Poncho Plaza and along Calle Jaramillo vendors sell every item o Otavaleño traditional dress, including the intricate hand embroidery of th(indigenous women's blouses, as well as fleece, yarn, loom parts, aniline dyes and carders. Vendors also sell clothing worn by other indigenous groups i Imbabura province and by mestizos and criollos. Although Saturday is the larges market day in Otavalo, its popularity has led to there being some sort of touris market every day of the week. Saturday has the widest selection of goods, bu prices tend to be a bit higher and the crowds can be overwhelming.

The incredible food market

Calle Jaramillo runs south into the permanent food market, which overflow on Saturdays with a mind-boggling array of vendors and food. You'll fin(every kind of fruit, vegetable, grain, and meat imaginable. Don't become s(engrossed in your shopping spree in Poncho Plaza that you miss the food mar ket because if weaving represents one means of subsistence, agriculture rep resents the other.

Outside the town

While day tours to Otavalo from Quito are popular, many independent travelers arrive on the Friday night before the market and stay for the weekend to explore the lush surrounding country. There are several unusual accommodations that make good bases for exploration. Just north of Otavalo, the elegantly restored **Hacienda Pinsaqui** provides all the modern comforts you could wish for. Also restored to its former splendor is the 17th-century **Hacienda Cusín** near Laguna San Pablo. The rooms are crowded with antique religious paintings, wooden armchairs, and candelabra, while outside are elegant gardens, with ponds and banks of glorious flowers. *(See Travel Tips, pages 335–340, for details.)* The crystal-clear **Laguna San Pablo**  is easily accessible from here. A favorite place for water sports, it has an annual swimming race across its width during September – though it takes courage to plunge into the lagoon's icy waters.

For fabulous views of the Otavalo area and Cotacachi and Imbabura volcanoes, head a few miles out of town to the ecologically oriented inn and farm, **Casa Mojanda**. Its friendly family atmosphere and excellent home cooking make it ideal for relaxing in a tranquil natural setting *(see Travel Tips, pages 335–340, for details)*. Further up are the beautiful **Lagunas de Mojanda** and the peak of **Fuya Fuya**, about 18 km (11 miles) south of Otavalo. A dirt road leads to the lakes, divided by hills inhabited by wild rabbits. Go in a group, as robberies have become a problem near the lake.

Artists at work

The villages close to Otavalo provide a chance to see another aspect of the handicraft trade: the craftsmen themselves at work. In nearby **Carabuela**, they

Map on page 178

BELOW: one of the Lagunas de Mojanda, near Tabacunda.

Handicrafts strictly for the tourist market.

make scarves, woolen gloves, ponchos, and belts, some still using the pre-Hispanic loom. Other craftsmen here specialize in making Andean harps. The village of **Peguche** ❸ too, has its weavers, and is well worth a stop. Peguche is about 3 km (2 miles) northeast of Otavalo, and is the home of several indigenous musical groups.

About 3 km (2 miles) east of Peguche, **Agato** ❹ is worth a visit if you are interested in textiles. The Tahuantinsuyo Workshop uses traditional looms and natural dyes and makes some lovely items, which are often for sale at the Hostería Cusín. You can reach Agato by bus or taxi from Otavalo.

Another nearby village of artisans is **Ilumán** ❺ (there are occasional trains and buses, or it's an easy walk from Otavalo). The inhabitants make double-sided ponchos, felt hats, and tapestries. But Ilumán is also famous for its traditional healers or *curanderos*, who use guinea pigs, candles, and ritual stones, as well as herbs and alcohol, to diagnose sicknesses and chase away evil spirits or negative energy.

The best-known shaman of the region is "Taita Marcos," who lives in **San Juan de la Calera** near Cotacachi. His house is worth a visit: he uses an altar built with thousands of bottles donated by grateful patients from all over the world, and adorned with pictures of saints.

West of Cotacachi lies **Laguna Cuicocha**, a distinctive, sparkling blue crater lake situated at the southern end of the Reserva Ecológica Cotacachi-Cayapas. A well-marked hiking trail circles the lake; it takes 4–5 hours to walk around the lake. Two small islands are plied by motorboats and there are a few small restaurants and shops at the visitor center (open Tues–Sat). Another option is to take a taxi here and walk the scenic route back to Otavalo

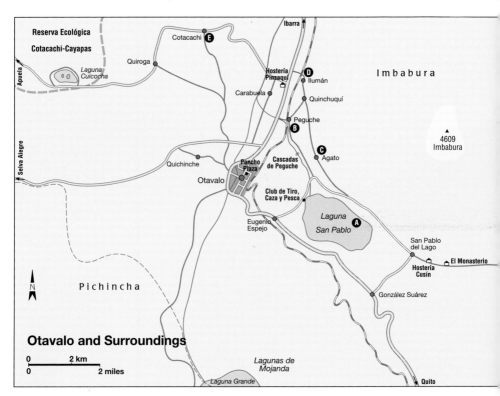

Otavalo and Surroundings

through unspoiled Andean villages and farmland. It is advisable to visit the lake in groups, however, as robberies have occurred in the area.

Master leatherworkers

About 15 km (10 miles) north of Otavalo is the village of **Cotacachi** Ⓔ, Ecuador's leatherwork center. Mostly made of tough cowhide, the goods have increased in quality recently, and there is an excellent choice of jackets, skirts, and boots, as well as briefcases, bags, riding equipment, and wallets.

It is worth tasting the typical dish of Cotacachi: *carne colorada*, made of sun-dried and fried pork or beef, colored with *achiote* (a red seed), and served with avocados, jacket potatoes, a cheese, onion, and egg sauce, and corn.

Further north

The highway northward from Otavalo curves around Volcán Imbabura and descends toward Ibarra, passing through **Atuntaqui**, which is said to serve the best *fritada* (deep-fried pork) in the region. Just before Ibarra, a right-hand turn leads into **San Antonio**, the home of expert woodcarvers. You can watch the craftsmen at work and buy the finished articles. Typical examples are the carved figures of people and animals, furniture, chess pieces, lamps, and mirror frames.

A shorter, much slower, but very attractive route to Ibarra is along the old Pan-American Highway from Cayambe, heading around the far side of Volcán Imbabura via the villages of **Olmedo** and **Zuleta**. This narrow cobbled road, full of potholes, winds through several of the region's oldest haciendas. Along the way, it presents an image of the traditional rural structure of Ecuador, mixed with modern farming techniques.

Maps on pages 174 & 178

BELOW: final touches to a carving at San Antonio.

The white city

The provincial town of **Ibarra** ❸, about 22 km (13 miles) north of Otavalo, is quite large, with a population of 100,000, and enjoys one of the best climates of the Sierra – neither too hot nor too cold – due to its moderate altitude of 2,225 meters (around 7,000 ft). Despite severe damage and destruction in at least two earthquakes, Ibarra has retained a colonial style. Its streets are cobbled, and the town's low red-roofed buildings all have white-painted walls, which has earned Ibarra the nickname of "the white city." The population is a cultural mix of *indígenas*, *morenos*, and mestizos. Typical foods made in the area include *arrope de mora* (blackberry syrup) and *nogadas* (a sweet made with walnuts). And the original *helados de paila* (water ices) can be found at the Rosalia Suárez ice-cream parlor. These ices are made by continuously beating fruit juice in a copper *paila* or round-bottomed pan, while it sits on a pile of ice.

Close to Ibarra is **Lago Yaguarcocha**. Its name means "blood lake" in Quichua, because in the 15th century the tough inhabitants of this region held out against the Inca invaders for some 16 years, until they were finally defeated and massacred on the shore. Today the lake is sometimes used for sailing, but is mainly known for the motor-racing track that surrounds it. Car races take place on this circuit during the September festival celebrations.

Sugar-cane valley

On the other side of the mountain lies the warm **Chota Valley**, the lowest point in the northern Sierra, where sugar cane, vines, and tropical fruits grow. There are several thermal springs in this valley, such as **Chachimbiro**, though the road to them is somewhat arduous.

You may hear Ibarra's nickname "the white city" translated into Spanish as La Ciudad Blanca.

LEFT: trinkets for sale at Otavalo market.
RIGHT: bargaining for a cow.

The Chota Valley is the only zone of the Sierra that has a predominantly black population. Today they are farmers, but the older inhabitants tell tales of their ancestors who fought against slavery on the plantations of Colombia. In the village of **Chota** (about an hour's drive from Ibarra) a concert hall regularly presents the *bomba negra* music of the local black population, which is a mixture of the music of the Sierra with African-style instruments and rhythms. One of the typical "instruments" is played by blowing tunes on a leaf held between the hands.

Map on pages 174–75

On the Colombian border

The highway north from the Chota Valley climbs steeply with twists and turns into the province of **Carchi**, over the high pass of **El Angel**, and down to the frontier town of Tulcán. This is rich agricultural country, which produces dozens of varieties of potatoes. It also has a thriving trade in contraband goods with Colombia. Carchi is the only province of the Sierra that has practically no indigenous population. The **Reserva Ecológica El Angel** preserves a large expanse of this region, where Andean condors can sometimes be seen.

From El Angel you can hike down toward the coast through the **Reserva Cerro Golondrinas** (www.fundaciongolondrinas.org). About 40 km (25 miles) south of Tulcán is Carchi's sanctuary, the **Grotto of La Paz**, near the village of **San Gabriel ❹**, where pilgrims visit the statue of the Virgin sheltered in a natural cave. There are two splendid waterfalls just outside the village. In **Tulcán ❺**, the border town, the main attraction is the topiary garden in the cemetery, where huge cypress hedges are clipped into the shapes of animals, houses, and geometric figures. It is a bizarre and impressive sight, and worth a visit if you are staying here or are on your way to Colombia. ❑

BELOW: topiary at the Tulcán cemetery.

THE WEAVERS OF OTAVALO

Ecuadorians have kept their traditional dress, but some can now afford more luxurious fabrics. The weaving families of Otavalo have transformed this demand into an impressive business

Typical Otavalo tapestry work.

BELOW: an Otavaleña takes her baby to market.

F or as far back as anyone knows, the people of the high, green Otavalo Valley have been spinners, weavers, and textile merchants. Because Ecuador lacks the mineral wealth of Peru and Bolivia, the Spanish were quick to exploit the country's human resources, and this included their textile skills. Under the *encomienda* system the colonizers were given the right to use forced indigenous labor in return for christening the workers, and by mid-1550s an *obraje* (textile workshop) using forced indigenous labor was established in Otavalo. While the Spanish were busily exploiting the native population, they also introduced the European technology that has formed the basis for the present prosperity: carders, spinning wheels, and treadle looms.

Between 1690 and 1720 the *encomiendas* were abolished by the Spanish Crown, but native land fell into white hands, and many *indígenas* entered into a system of debt peonage *(wasipungo)* whereby they were virtual serfs on large *haciendas*, many of which continued to operate weaving workshops.

The modern industry got its start in 1917 when *indígenas* on the Hacienda Cusín were encouraged to make imitations of imported British tweeds *(casimires)*. These proved successful in the national market, and *casimir* weaving spread to other families and villages in the Otavalo Valley. In 1964 the Agrarian Reform Law outlawed debt peonage and granted *wasipungeros* title to their plots of land, leaving *indígenas* free to weave at home or to hire out their labor. Many of the most prosperous contemporary weaving families are descendants of the *wasipungeros*.

The Agrarian Reform Law coincided with an increase in tourism to the region. In 1966 there was one crafts store in Otavalo; by 1990 there were about 80, most of them *indígena*-owned and operated. It's a mistake, however, to think that the textile industry is mainly dependent on tourism. It's a rare Ecuadorian who doesn't own something from Otavalo, and most textiles are sold to other South Americans. There is also a substantial export business to North America, Europe, and Japan, which brings several million dollars a year into the region.

About 85 percent of the estimated 45,000 Otavaleños in the valley are involved in the textile industry either full or part time as spinners, weavers, knitters, finishers wholesalers, or retailers, including store owners, market vendors, and traveling merchants. Almost all families have at least one spinning wheel or loom in the house. Involvement ranges from women who spin 2 kg (5 lb) of yarn a week, to families weaving a few ponchos a month on a backstrap loom, to the Tejidos Rumiñahui company in Otavalo, which produces up to 300 ponchos a day on electric looms.

Each weaving and merchant family seeks an economic niche to occupy, and the marketing acumen they evince

impressive. One family in Quinchuquí makes several hundred acrylic ponchos each month, which are exported to Venezuela; a family in Iluman produces
acrylic dresses and shawls which they market in Guayaquil; a family in Peguche
weaves woolen scarves, ponchos, and capes that are sold to a North American
exporter. Another family in Peguche makes high-quality *tapices* (tapestries),
which are sold to the major folk-art stores in Quito, to visitors to the family
home, and at a kiosk in the Otavalo market.

Increased prosperity has not meant the abandonment of traditional dress, but
the use of more luxurious fabrics. The women's skirt wraps *(anakus)* and shoulder wraps *(fachalinas)* were traditionally made of hand-spun wool or cotton;
today wealthy women wear velvet. The women's dress, incidentally, is one of the
closest in form to the costume of Inca women worn anywhere in the Andes
today. The men's dress is less conservative, being a mixture of colonial and
modern elements, although the custom of wearing long hair and the use of *alpar-
gatas* (espadrilles) are pre-Hispanic.

Although some older *indígenas* and residents of remote communities are
monolingual Quichua speakers, most *indígenas* are bilingual in Quichua and
Spanish and a few will surprise you by speaking fluent English, French, German,
or Portuguese.

The Saturday Otavalo market *(la feria)* is the high point of the week, not only
for the hundreds of travelers who come from around the world (including many
Colombians and people from other parts of Ecuador), but also for the thousands
of *indígenas* who come to buy, sell, and socialize. The market takes place in the
three main plazas and the surrounding streets. For more detailed information
on this colorful event, *see the Going North chapter, page 175.* ❑

Map
on page
178

BELOW: traditionally
dressed Otavaleñas
selling fine rugs.

THE PACIFIC COAST

Palm-fringed beaches are the lure. But there's much more to a coastal trip: marimba *rhythms, mangrove swamps, the bustling port of Manta, and an echo of Africa*

Map on pages 174–75

The north coast of Ecuador, extending as far south as Guayaquil, is one of the best places on the continent to take a break from the often demanding rigors of travel. Much of this varied coastline consists of largely empty, palm-fringed beaches, presenting the ideal opportunity to practice one of the foremost customs of ancient Ecuador: sun worship

This area bore the brunt of the devastating El Niño floods of 1982–83 and 1998–99, when roads, beaches, trees, crops, and a significant number of dwellings were washed away. Recovery has in many cases been slow, for in the tropical languor of a sweltering landscape, the tendency to consign things to *mañana* is pervasive. As a string of holiday resorts springs up along the coast, however, the last signs of destruction fade. This development testifies to Ecuador's growing stature as a tourist destination – due partly to its own charms, and partly to its neighbors' ill fortunes. A holiday in Colombia, with its cocaine-related civil disturbances, is not for the faint-hearted, while the Peruvian coastline is endlessly washed by the Humboldt Current, bringing damp, misty weather and ice-cold waters. Because of this, Ecuador has cornered the market in tropical beaches along South America's west coast.

PRECEDING PAGES: fishing boats on the tropical coast. **LEFT:** idyllic beach on Isla de la Plata. **BELOW:** enjoying a day by the Pacific.

Land of two seasons

The wet season on the Ecuadorian coast runs from December to June, the remainder of the year being dry – or perhaps not-so-wet. During the wet season, when flooding is commonplace and high levels of humidity make life uncomfortably sticky, the beaches – despite being below par – are well patronized. All things considered, August to October is the best time to visit this relaxed region.

The coastal topography consists of a thin lowland strip which turns from forbidding mangroves in the north to dry scrubland on the Santa Elena Peninsula, west of Guayaquil. A short distance inland runs a range of low, rounded, crystalline hills. The region is cut by numerous rivers meandering down from the Andes, which regularly flood the alluvial plain that lies to the east of the hills. Huge alluvial fans, often consisting of porous volcanic ash eroded from highland basins, spread out from the major river mouths, providing very fertile soil.

The province of Esmeraldas is one of dense, luxuriant rainforest characterized by two main botanical strata: a high canopy of towering evergreen broadleaf species sprinkled with palms; and at eye level, clusters of giant ferns, shrubs, and vines. Among these are spectacular smaller plants such as orchids and bromeliads which proliferate in the Amazonian forest.

South of Esmeraldas is a zone of deciduous scrub woodland that drops its leaves during the dry season. A

narrow strip of tropical, semi-deciduous forest lies just north of Manta; and from here down to Guayaquil, this mangrove forest is broken only by the infertile scrubland of Santa Elena. Among the commercially used plants of the coastal forests are the balsa tree, source of the world's lightest timber; the ivory-nut palm *(tagua)*, used to make buttons; and the *toquilla* reed, from which the renowned Panama hat is manufactured.

The coastal region, which contains almost half of Ecuador's 13 million people, is populated by a veritable melting pot of ethnic groups. Here, more than in the Sierra and the jungle, the trails of history incorporate all the colors of the rainbow. At the time of the Spaniards' arrival, the centers of coastal indigenous habitation were Esmeraldas, Manta, Huancavilca, and Puná; these peoples were either exterminated outright, or else they interbred to the point where their racial purity was completely extinguished.

A century or so later, the Spanish-Amerindian mixture (called mestizo) was infused with African blood as slaves were brought from West Africa, creating the mulatto (Afro-Hispanic mix) and *montuvio* (Amerindian-African mix) races. Indigenous Caribs were also shipped to Ecuador to work the plantations, adding a fourth element to this ethnic conglomeration. Mestizos comprise the majority of the coastal population, but the black influence is one of the region's most interesting features, pervading all aspects of life.

From the Colombian border

BELOW: tranquil waterways near San Lorenzo.

A journey that begins in **San Lorenzo ❻**, in Ecuador's northwestern corner, can only get drier. The sea is the town's raison d'être, and fresh, salty breezes fill the potholed streets. The land around San Lorenzo is mostly mangrove

swamp, navigated by motorized dugout canoes, while the town itself is frequently sodden with rainwater that has nowhere to run off. A road was recently constructed, linking San Lorenzo to Ibarra and Quito, and there is a bus service. However, many travelers who find themselves here may have come up the coast by boat. San Lorenzo used to mark one end of the spectacular, day-long train trip from Ibarra; unfortunately this line currently only runs from Ibarra to Primer Paso. It should be noted that San Lorenzo has no immigration office, nor any official currency exchange, so crossing the Colombian border to Tumaco is a somewhat risky proposition.

Despite its isolation, San Lorenzo can generate a certain amount of bustle. It possesses the best natural harbor on the Ecuadorian coast, and a hinterland still largely untouched due to its inaccessibility. The population has grown from 2,000 in 1960 – when, in the days prior to the discovery of oil in the Oriente, this was Ecuador's El Dorado, the alluring, untapped frontier – to 20,000 today. Timber traders have made profitable incursions into forests rich in mahogany, balsa, and rubber, creating industries and bringing itinerant laborers to this long-neglected outpost. However, illegal logging has put the forests under threat.

African legacy

Despite all this, San Lorenzo still has the feel of a town invented by Gabriel García Márquez. The descendants of people from distant continents have been washed up by history on this forbidding shore, and made the most of their displacement. African slaves transported in the 17th and 18th centuries were unloaded in Cartagena (Colombia) and marched southward to man the coffee, banana, and cacao plantations; less than half of this human cargo survived the privations of passage to reach their destinations.

Despite multifarious interbreeding, the legacy of Africa lives today in the form of ancestor worship and the voodoo rituals of *macumba*, whereby spirits are summoned to cure and curse. Beneath the Latinized veneer of regular Sunday Mass lies an ancient belief in macabre spirits or *visiones* such as *La Tunda*, who frightens bad children to death and then steals their bodies, or *El Rivel*, who feasts on corpses.

African rhythms anchor the up-tempo beat of *marimba* music, which can be heard in San Lorenzo. Esmeraldeña *marimba* retains purer links with its origins than does the Colombian style, which has borrowed heavily from the Caribbean jingles of *salsa* and often resembles Western pop music. Talented musicians and dancers of both *marimba* styles can be seen rehearsing on Wednesday nights, and when they hit the downtown bars, San Lorenzo starts jumping. Men are said to come of age when they begin to *andar y conocer* – literally, "to walk and to know," or "to travel and learn." In black idiom, this commonly used phrase means "to strut," and is heavily loaded with sexual innuendo.

To get to the coast road you have to go by boat from San Lorenzo to **La Tola**. Services are cheap and regular and take about 2½ hours. En route to La Tola lies the island of **La Tolita**, an important ceremonial center from 500 to 100BC. Tribal chiefs were buried here, their tombs filled with artifacts of gold, silver, platinum, and copper.

Map on pages 174–75

BELOW: blue and yellow macaw from the coastal rainforest.

In recognition of its historical significance, La Tolita has been declared an Archeological National Park and is undergoing extensive excavation. Like many such sites in South America, La Tolita has been savagely plundered by thieves, its treasures sold on the international black market. Fortunately, however, the government's attention was attracted in time to salvage a substantial portion of the relics, and another gap in the jigsaw puzzle of ancient Ecuador is slowly being filled. An archeological museum has been erected on the site, showcasing finds from the digs and recovered artifacts.

Frontier town

Opposite La Tolita at the mouth of the Río Santiago is **Limones** (which must also be reached by boat). It is a small town of some importance as the center of the local timber industry, but without a lot to offer tourists. Wood is floated downriver to the sawmill here, and processed for further distribution.

The mask of the sun god, found on La Tolita, is the symbol of the Banco Central.

The timber camps, isolated in the dense, upriver jungle, were quite notorious in their early days during the 1960s for a form of outpost exploitation worthy of the author Joseph Conrad. The mestizo owners forbade their workers – mostly *morenos* (a generic term for blacks) – to leave camp. Instead, prostitutes and alcohol were shipped in to the camps each pay day – a kind of slavery with overpriced and monopolistic fringe benefits.

This delta region is the home of the Cayapa or Chachi, who – along with the Colorado of Santo Domingo – were the only indigenous coastal tribe to evade extermination by the Spaniards. In both cases, survival was due to the inaccessibility of their homelands. Today, the Cayapa number approximately 4,000. They are sometimes seen selling their finely woven hammocks and

BELOW: bringing home the bamboo.

basketwork in the markets of Limones and La Tola – and occasionally Esmeraldas – but they prefer the privacy of Borbón and the inhospitable upper reaches
of the Río Cayapa. A turn-off on the La Tola-Esmeraldas road runs to **Borbón**,
but this country is decidedly off the beaten track, and travel can be numbingly
difficult, especially in the wet season.

A better option is to take a motorized dugout from El Bongo restaurant in
Limones upriver to Borbón. From here expeditions continue up to **Boca de
Onzoles**, at the confluence of the Cayapa and Onzoles rivers. In this far-flung
village, a Hungarian émigré called Stefan Tarjany runs a comfortable lodge –
Steve's Lodge, postal address: Casilla 187, Esmeraldas – and organizes trips to the
mission stations of **Santa María** and **Zapallo Grande**. He also arranges boat
trips to the **Reserva Ecológica Cotacachi-Cayapa**s, but the usual starting point
for this trip is **San Miguel**, the last settlement on the river. It is advisable to check
that these trips are still running before journeying to this remote location.

The reserve covers some 204,400 hectares (505,000 acres) and its habitat
varies from lowland tropical forest, in this region, to cloud forest, to windswept
plain, and accordingly has an enormous range of flora and fauna. It is also the
home of the Cayapa who continue to live in their traditional way, trying to avoid
the encroachment of Western values and influences. The reserve receives protection from the Ecuadorian Government and from international conservation
organizations. Guided tours in dugout canoes can be arranged with the park
rangers. There is excellent information to be found at www.ambiente.gov.ec.

Travel in other parts of Ecuador is rarely as adventurous as in these alluring
backwaters, which few visitors make the effort to explore. The Cayapa people's
counterparts in the Oriente – Stone Age tribes such as the Jivaro and the

Map on pages 174–75

LEFT: a quiet street in Puerto Lopez.
RIGHT: fish doesn't come any fresher than this.

Huaorani – have received far greater international exposure, which in turn has attracted more tourists. This exposure may, however, prove beneficial as the search for oil in the Amazon basin is a much greater threat to indigenous lifestyles than anything the Cayapa are up against.

Difficult highways

Esmeraldas took its name from the emeralds found in the river here.

The road from La Tola to **Esmeraldas** ❼ is rough and never ready: *rancheros*, which are open-sided trucks fitted with far too many wooden benches, take 5 hours to cover the 100 km (60 miles); regular buses do the journey in 3 hours. The northern half of this road may suffer severe flooding during the wet season, but otherwise it is a carefree, breezy ride past cattle farms and swamps teeming with bird life. A few small towns are strung out along the way, but offer little reason to pause.

It was near Esmeraldas that the *conquistador* Bartolomé Ruíz and company landed, the first Spaniards to set foot on Ecuadorian soil. Esmeraldas is named after the precious stone found in bountiful quantities in the like-named river, at whose mouth the city lies. The native Cara, who inhabited this area before migrating to the mountain basins around Otavalo during the 10th century, worshiped a huge emerald known as Umina. Today, the treasures are more industrial than geological: Esmeraldas is the major port of the north coast, whence timber, bananas, and cacao are shipped abroad. The 500-km (300-mile) trans-Andean oil pipeline ends here, and the construction of an oil refinery has brought new jobs and money to the city.

BELOW: a typical thatched beach hut.

The treatment of previously fatal tropical diseases has contributed significantly to the growth of Ecuadorian ports, notably Guayaquil, Manta, and Esmeraldas. The eradication of yellow fever from these towns early in the 20th century was the first step, followed by the discovery and availability of quinine as an antidote for malaria, which as recently as 1942 accounted for one quarter of all deaths in Ecuador. The treatment of tuberculosis, cause of almost one-fifth of deaths in Ecuador just a generation ago, completed the region's health improvements, providing the basis for the international maritime trade, although the area is one of the poorest in the country.

Black capital

Esmeraldas' population of nearly 120,000 consists of mostly mestizos and *morenos*, with a surprising minority of mountain *indígenas* looking forlorn and far from at home. Esmeraldas is the center of black culture in Ecuador. It is here that the visitor is most likely to encounter a full *marimba* band, complete with huge *conga* drums, led by the *bomero*, who plays a deep-pitched bass drum suspended from the ceiling. Esmeraldas is, like its music, a vibrant city that embodies the distinctive elements of coastal urban life. The people are gregarious and no-nonsense, playing with far greater enthusiasm than they work. Nothing is high-brow, all culture is popular, and most would rather watch the opposite sex sway by than observe a religious ritual. The energy level on the streets soars as the sun dips into the Pacific, and bars and restaurants – serving dishes of deli-

Map
on pages
174–75

cious *cocado*, fried fish in a spicy coconut sauce – fill to overflowing.

For the more cerebrally inclined, the **Museo Arqueológico** (Tues–Fri 8.30am–12.30pm and 2.30–5.30pm, Sat 10am–6pm) has exhibits on many of the region's pre-Inca cultures: Bahía, Valdivia, Chorrera, and Tuncahuan, as well as some small golden masks from La Tolita. There is also the **Casa de la Cultura Ecuatoriana** (Mon–Fri 8.30am–12.30pm and 2.30–5pm; tel: 06-272 7080) with a collection of colonial and contemporary art, but don't be surprised if you are the only visitor. Discotheques far outnumber museums in Esmeraldas, which is a fair reflection of the hedonistic spirit of the ancient peoples whose suggestive figures are on display here.

Golden sands and palm trees

To the immediate southwest of Esmeraldas begins a stretch of coastline containing the finest and most peaceful beaches in Ecuador. The beach suburb of **Las Palmas** is a more pleasant alternative to staying in the rather unattractive downtown area of Esmeraldas but the beach is polluted and reported to be a dangerous place for tourists and single women. The road to the other, less-visited beaches passes the Petro Ecuador oil refinery and a luxury hotel, the Hostal La Pradera (tel: 06-2712 2677; www.hostallapradera.com) – complete with swimming pool, tennis courts, and a statue of the Virgin of the Swan in a garden grotto – before reaching the coast.

The road from Esmeraldas is reasonable and there is a bus service down the coast to Muisné. The small, friendly resort town of **Atacames**, 30 km (18 miles) from Esmeraldas, is popular with Ecuadorian and foreign tourists alike. In recent years it has gained a reputation as a noisy party town, where the music blasts

BELOW: a kick-about on Atacames beach.

out 24 hours a day, particularly during the June–September high season. The town has blossomed into the largest resort on the north coast, with countless hotels, resorts, cabins, and lodges. Atacames has a cooperative of artisans, presided over by *El Tío Tigre* (Uncle Tiger), which manufactures and sells bracelets and necklaces of black coral, found just offshore to the south. Buying such artifacts cannot be encouraged, however, since in many areas the coral has been pillaged to the point of virtual extinction.

While the beach at Atacames looks harmless, there is a powerful undertow. There are no lifeguards, and the current sweeps some swimmers to their deaths every year. Sea snakes washed up on the beach pose another risk: they are venomous and should be avoided. A less avoidable problem is theft, which has been steadily increasing in Atacames in recent years. There have also been several reports of assault on the beach late at night, so solitary midnight strolls are not recommended. Despite these warnings, however, the probability of a visitor encountering any trouble remains slim. Some 6 km (3 miles) farther south lies **Súa**, a small, beautifully situated fishing village, somewhat more friendly than Atacames. The fishermen haul their catch right up on to the small beach, which immediately becomes an impromptu local market. The sky fills with sea birds such as frigates and pelicans, who do a fine job gobbling up fish heads and guts. While a stay in Atacames is chiefly a matter of relishing the elements, Súa offers glimpses of life in a small seaside town with its eye less on tourists than on the next catch.

Luxury and adventure

A further 8 km (5 miles) along the ocean road lies an unpaved side track to the beach of **Same** (pronounced Sa-may), perhaps the finest along this stretch.

TIP

The Hotel Súa has rooms with balconies and sea views. The restaurant is recommended both for fish and a wide variety of other meals.

BELOW: guest apartments at the Club Casablanca in Same.

There is little here other than a collection of mostly expensive and tasteful hotels. Same does have the air of a place on the verge of over-development, as it has become a resort for wealthy Quiteños who have erected an endless line of high-rise condos, but it remains the quintessential "away-from-it-all-in-comfort" destination.

The completely undeveloped villages of **Tonchigüe** and **Galera**, both with lovely beaches nearby, lie a short distance west of Same. At this point, the road leaves the coast and cuts southward through undulating banana plantations before re-emerging at the shoreline opposite the island of **Muisné**, 83 km (51 miles) from Esmeraldas. Motorized dugouts ply the short distance from the mainland to Muisné and, since few visitors bother to come this far from Esmeraldas for just another beach, Muisné exudes the alluring, timeless languor characteristic of any remote tropical island. The beaches here are enormous and empty; there is a handful of cheap, basic hotels and good seafood restaurants, and nothing more. The ghost of Robinson Crusoe may well haunt Muisné's beaches; if you see another set of footprints in the sand, it must be Friday. Inland from Muisné there is an isolated community of native Cayapa, some of whom may be seen around town at the Sunday market.

From Muisné to **Cojimíes** ❽, 50 km (31 miles) to the south, there is no road. One or two motorized dugouts make the 2-hour journey each day, some continuing as far as Manta; the boats hug the coastline all the way, making it a safe and picturesque trip. An adventurous alternative is to head off under your own steam: the town of **Bolívar**, from where boats depart for Cojimíes, is about 23 km (14 miles) from Muisné, making a feasible, if challenging, day's walk. There are several rivers to be forded en route, but locating a ferry is usually easy, and an early start should bring you to Bolívar, where there are no hotels, in time to catch a boat to Cojimíes before dark. The wildlife along this pristine, largely uninhabited coastline is unsurpassed on Ecuador's mainland shore: jellyfish and crabs proliferate, as does the full gamut of pelagic birds.

Cojimíes lies at the northern end of the road that follows the coast down to Manta. It is a quiet and welcoming town, the site of a pre-Columbian settlement that still awaits comprehensive excavation. Transport connections are delightfully whimsical: the unpaved road is impassable in the wet season, and the daily *rancheros* usually run along the beach in a race against the rising tide. Just south of Pedernales, the road crosses the equator – marked by a small monument – and then forks. The left-hand turn runs through more farms and plantations to **Santo Domingo de los Colorados**, while the coastal road continues on to the small market town of **Jama**. Another 50 km (31 miles) south lies **Canoa**, center of a fast-developing deep-sea fishing industry and with one of the widest beaches in the country.

Scenic roadway

The inland loop through Santo Domingo returns to the coast at Bahía de Caráquez, and is a refreshing change for anyone suffering from an overdose of empty, sun-drenched beaches. This route through the heartland of

Map on pages 174–75

BELOW: coconut milk makes a refreshing drink.

Freshly caught crabs in Bahía.

Manabí province is among the most scenic in the coastal region, and passes several interesting stop-offs. Past more banana plantations and cattle farms, the road runs to **El Carmen**, whereafter green hills rise from the plain. Much of Manabí, particularly the southern area, suffers a dearth of rainfall, due primarily to the lifeless winds of the Humboldt Current. Nevertheless, the province is the agricultural core of Ecuador, with coffee, cacao, rice, cotton, and tropical fruits cultivated widely. The Poza Honda Dam, built mostly with German finance, is fed by the Río Portoviejo and irrigates large areas of previously uncultivatable lowlands.

Chone (population 41,000) prospers on the strength of these industries, as well as the manufacture of leather saddles and a type of straw hat called a *mocora*. The banks of the Río Chone, twisting through the undulating **Bálsamo Hills**, sustain increasing numbers of shrimp farms, an indication of Ecuador's modern industrial diversification, although they have also led to the destruction of mangrove forests. The road climbs to a vantage point offering splendid views of Bahía de Caráquez and the mangrove islands dotting the bay, and then slides down to the coast.

The resort village of **San Vicente** stands at the mouth of the Río Chone, opposite Bahía de Caráquez. The recently constructed church of **Santa Rosa** has an ornate, eye-catching facade and mosaic and glasswork by the Ecuadorian artist Pelí, but otherwise there are few diversions except for the beach. About 70 km (43 miles) inland along a makeshift road is the important archeological site of **San Isidro**. The prehistoric inhabitants of San Isidro excelled in the art of ceramics, and imitations of their beautifully crafted figurines are today sold throughout Ecuador.

BELOW: idyllic coastal vista.

Banana centers

Bahía de Caráquez ❾ is named after the native Cara who, legend has it, came "by way of the sea" and settled in this bay. Formerly an important export center for bananas and cacao, Bahía entered semi-retirement when the focus of banana exporting – in which Ecuador continues to lead the world – shifted south to Guayaquil and Machala. The cacao industry, in turn, has been steadily declining since it was struck down by a crippling blight in 1922–23, at which time Ecuador was the world's foremost producer. In 1999 Bahía became an eco-city in recognition of its strong green movement and the efforts made by the local community to rebuild the city in an ecologically sound way after the disastrous El Niño floods and earthquakes of 1997–8. A stroll along the palm-fringed riverside Malecón *(jetty)*, past rows of stately old mansions, some of them in Victorian "gingerbread" style, reveals remnants of former prosperity. Nevertheless, Bahía's strategic river-mouth location ensures its continued existence as a minor port, and it remains the largest coastal town – with 20,000 inhabitants – between Esmeraldas and Manta.

Much of Bahía's energy today is devoted to tourism: unlike many of Ecuador's north-coast towns, it is easily accessible on good roads from Quito, and is one of the most popular resorts in the country. While there are few noteworthy sights in the town, it does offer some simple pleasures. An ascent of **La Cruz hill** is rewarded by sweeping views of the river and coastline, and a sojourn to a riverside café affords relief from the burning sun. There is also a collection of pre-Columbian Manabí pottery in the Casa de Cultura. Ferries across to San Vicente depart frequently, providing a means of transportation as well as a scenic way to cool off in the midday sun.

Map on pages 174–75

To learn more about eco-projects in and around Bahía de Caráquez, visit www.planet-drum.org

BELOW: a typical house, built on stilts.

From Bahía, tours can be arranged to the **Río Muchacho Organic Farm** *(see Travel Tips, pages 335–340 for details)*. While many farms in the area have destroyed the ecosystem and rendered the land desertlike, Río Muchacho is covered with vegetation. You can go horseback riding around the farm or try shrimp fishing. Multiple-day tours can include Spanish lessons and the opportunity to interact with the Montubios, the local indigenous people. Beach tours are also available on open-sided *chivas* buses, which tour the bay, stopping at a number of sites of interest.

Venturing slightly further afield, launches can be hired to visit **Isla de los Pájaros** and **Isla Corazón** in the bay. These two islands, as the former's name indicates, have raucous sea-bird colonies. A boardwalk has been constructed on Isla Corazón, which leads right over the mangroves. Some 20 km (13 miles) south of Bahía de Caráquez are the friendly, peaceful fishing villages of **San Clemente** and **San Jacinto**; driving along the beach at low tide may look tempting, but is inadvisable as many cars have died a watery death here. Instead, follow the Portoviejo road and turn off just before **Rocafuerte**; this route leads to San Jacinto, and on to San Clemente 5 km (3 miles) away to the north. Along this road, which is notable for the giant ceibo trees lining the way, lies **Crucita**, a beach resort and a perfect spot for paragliding. Shortly thereafter, and just 15 km (9 miles) east of Manta, is the fishing village of **Jaramijó**. This is the site of an extensive pre-Columbian settlement and where Eloy Alfaro, one of Ecuador's best-remembered presidents, lost an important naval battle against conservative forces in December 1884: the wreck of his ship, the *Alajuela*, can still be seen. Also near San Clemente, is the archeological site of Chirije, which dates back to the Bahía culture (500BC–AD500). A small museum on the site has finds from the ongoing excavations of the area and there are beach cabins nearby.

The ancient city of Manta had a population of 20,000 and traded with the coastal peoples of Mexico and Peru.

BELOW: the deep-blue Pacific.

Pre-Columbian hedonists

For 1,000 years prior to the arrival of the Spaniards, **Manta** ❿ was the center of one of Ecuador's pre-eminent indigenous cultures. It was known as Jocay – literally, "fish house" – by the local inhabitants, whose exquisite pottery was decorated with scenes of daily life. And what a life it was. The exuberant hedonism of contemporary coastal Ecuadorians can be traced back directly to the ancient Manteños with their pervasive fertility cult and enjoyment of coca. Their concept of physical beauty was expressed by the practice of strapping young children's heads to a board in order to increase the backward slope of their chins and foreheads. The desired effect – an exaggeration of the rounded, hooked nose – was quite Neanderthal.

The Manteños sacrificed their prisoners of war by ripping out their still-beating hearts. Their culture was part-settler, part-wanderer, as they cultivated fruit and vegetables while also trading with highland tribes – their source of precious metals – and navigated the ocean in rafts and dugouts as far as Panama and Peru, and possibly the Galápagos Islands. Their skill extended to the arts of stonemasonry, weaving, and metalwork – in short, a cultural sophistication of great breadth and depth. *(See the Lost Worlds chapter, page 27.)*

The Spaniard Francisco Pacheco founded the modern settlement of Manta just ten days before Portoviejo in

1535. Nine years earlier, however, Bartolomé Ruíz had encountered a balsa sailing raft with 20 Manteños aboard: 11 of them had leapt into the sea in terror, while the remaining nine served as translators before being set free. Perhaps this rare instance of Spanish tolerance has contributed to the unique character of modern Manta, for it is the most relaxed and habitable city of the entire coastal region.

In its previous incarnation as Jocay, the main thoroughfare of Manta was lined with statues of the chieftains and head priests of the "Manta Confederation." The Catholic Church ordered their place to be taken by inoffensive jacaranda and royal poinciana trees. Today, with a population of approximately 180,000, Manta is a major seaport, with coffee, bananas, cotton textiles, and fish comprising the bulk of the exports. For all this, the city feels much smaller than similarly sized Esmeraldas, the pace of life being much slower. Large numbers of Ecuadorian tourists vacation here.

Manta is divided by an inlet into a downtown and a resort district, the latter called Tarqui. Along the expansive **Tarqui beach**, local fishermen unload and clean their catch – tuna, shark, dorado, eel, and tortoise – whipping the attendant gulls and vultures into aerial frenzy. A towering statue of a Manabí fisherman overlooks the proceedings, noticing few material changes from earlier times.

The **Museo Banco Central** (Tues–Sat 10am–6pm) houses the finest collection of Manteño artifacts in Ecuador and is well worth a visit. Manta's outdoor theater is the venue for occasional performances, especially during the agriculture and tourism exposition held each October. **Playa Murciélago** is an unprotected surfing beach a few kilometers west of town, site of the comfortable Hotel Manta Imperial. In Tarqui, the Hotel Haddad Manabí, dating from 1931, offers central accommodations with a slight touch of faded grandeur.

Map on pages 174–75

BELOW: repairing Panamas is still a thriving trade.

Ecuador's "Panama" hat

Straddling the highway between Manta and Portoviejo is the deceptively non-descript town of **Montecristi** , for more than a century the home of the renowned Panama hat. Until recently the majority of Montecristi's 9,000-odd inhabitants were engaged in the weaving of these remarkable headpieces, made from the straw fronds of the *Carludovica palmata*s. Large numbers of them still are, but Montecristi has had to move with the times, and some have switched to making fine wickerwork furniture and decorations. It is the quintessential cottage industry – many houses contain a rudimentary factory and showroom. The lack of any signs of wealth in Montecristi is sad testimony to the inequitable distribution of the industry's hefty profits. Like Portoviejo, which we will come to next, Montecristi owes its existence to pillaging pirates: in 1628, a group of Manteños left the coast in search of an inland refuge following pirate raids. Their colonial-style houses, now in a state of chronic disrepair, line the quiet, dusty streets and, in combination with the non-mechanized weaving, this physical neglect creates the air of a town stuck in another time.

Montecristi's religious atmosphere is similarly dated: the beautiful church contains a famous statue of the Virgin to which several miracles were once attributed. And Montecristi's favorite son is now long dead: Eloy Alfaro, president of Ecuador at the turn of the 20th century and a committed liberal reformist, was born here. His statue overlooks the main plaza, and his house is now a mausoleum, with his library and many personal effects on display. Almost alone among towns in coastal Ecuador, Montecristi survives as a relic – an impression heightened by the sight of modern-day tourists and Panama hat dealers roaring into town in search of a bargain.

TIP

If you are into fruit salads and smoothies, try La Fruta Prohibida on Avenida Chile in Portoviejo.

BELOW: a fisherman mends his nets at Machalilla.

Portoviejo's memories

From Montecristi it is only 24 km (15 miles) to **Portoviejo** ⓬, a town with a long history. In coastal Ecuador, where the *conquistadores* began their epic trek to victory in the relocated Inca capital of Cajamarca, surprisingly little remains of the colonial past. The monuments, which are few and far between, are generally quite recent erections in honor of heroes of the Liberation or favorite republican presidents. It is as if a wilful forgetfulness has descended on the pre-republican centuries: those long years of disease and brutality bequeathed a legacy of military dictatorship and silence.

Descendants of the few hundred *criollo* (pure-bred European) families that have dominated political and economic life since the origins of the *Audiencia* still stalk the corridors of power. Since Ecuador returned to civilian government in 1978, however, historians have cast revealing eyes on the excesses of Spanish colonialism. The people whose transplanted lives are a direct product of that time have thus been able to understand the original forces that have shaped them, their community, and their country. Portoviejo was in fact one of the earliest Spanish settlements in Ecuador. It was founded on March 12, 1535, just three months after Benalcázar re-founded Quito atop abandoned Inca ruins. Guayaquil, founded in January 1535, was the first Spanish coastal community, but the local people, based on the nearby island of Puná, repeatedly launched marauding raids of such ferocity that alternative sites were sought.

The original settlement, founded by Francisco Pacheco on the orders of Francisco Pizarro and Diego de Almagro, was, as its name ("Old Port") suggests, located on the coast. The omens, however, were far from auspicious: in 1541, a fire destroyed the town, and 50 years later the local indigenous population staged a fearsome uprising. Finally, when English pirates ravaged the port in 1628, it was decided that a spot further inland would be out of harm's way. Since then, Portoviejo has existed in the shadow of Manta, though as capital of Manabí province it remains an important administrative and educational center. Its population has recently topped the 170,000 mark, most of which is engaged in commerce, industry, and the rich agricultural pickings of the hinterland. Portoviejo's bustling streets are prettily bordered with rows of flora, and a stroll through the **Parque Eloy Alfaro** is perhaps the most pleasing pastime. Opposite the park is one of Ecuador's starkest modern cathedrals. Could the Catholic Church have been short of cash for once? Beside it stands a statue of Pacheco, the city's founder.

There are two museums: the **Casa de la Cultura Ecuatoriana**, with a collection of traditional musical instruments; and the **Museo Arqueológico**, which is not as good as its counterpart in Manta. Portoviejo has a few old colonial buildings still standing, but otherwise little testimony to its long and tumultuous history.

Leaving Portoviejo, go back the way you came for 14 km (8 miles) then turn off the Guayaquil road to the village of **La Pila**, which is an interesting stop-off. In the wake of the discovery of exquisite pre-Columbian ceramics in the area, the resourceful inhabitants of La Pila began producing indistinguishable imitations to

Map on pages 174–75

BELOW: strolling along the Pacific Coast.

Map on pages 174–75

TIP

Puerto López is a popular place for whale-watching between June and September, when humpback whales visit the waters of the Machalilla National Park to mate and calve.

BELOW: lone fisherman casts his net.
RIGHT: statue of a fisherman in Manta.

cash in on their forebears' artistry. Nowadays they have embraced originality and appear to have inherited not only the enterprise but also the considerable artistic skill of their ancestors.

In contrast, **Jipijapa** – a town of 30,000 inhabitants situated another 40 km (25 miles) along the highway to Guayaquil – appears to have been swallowed up by Ecuador's flourishing agricultural industries, particularly coffee and cotton. At Jipijapa, a side road climbs into the damp, luxuriant hills of southern Manabí before descending to the coast near **Puerto de Cayo**, a fishing village with pristine beaches.

A large tract of the surrounding area was designated the **Parque Nacional Machalilla** in 1979. It protects a 55,000-hectare (135,910-acre) expanse of tropical dry forest, which is home to a wide variety of bird and animal life, as well as a stretch of coast and two islands. You can enter the park from the coast road, or from the Manta to Guayaquil highway south of Jipijapa. Park admission costs $12 for the mainland parks, $15 for Isla de la Plata, or $20 for both, and tickets can be purchased at the park office in Puerto Lopez (Alvaro and Moreno; daily 7am–6pm) or at the park.

The well-worn coast road passes through **Machalilla ⓭**, the center of the culture of the same name that flourished between 1800 and 1500BC. It is rich in archeological remains, especially in the vicinity of **Salaite** and **Agua Blanca**, where there is a small archeological museum. A pleasant 45-minute walk from Machalilla brings you to the deserted horseshoe beach called **Los Frailes** (the Friars). About 10 km (6 miles) further south, fleets of heavily laden fishing boats dock in the village of **Puerto López** each afternoon at about 4pm, and the skippers sell their catch there and then.

Some 15 km (9 miles) offshore is **Isla de la Plata**, an ancient Manteño ceremonial center currently undergoing excavation. The island is named after an incident in the late 16th century, when Sir Francis Drake captured a silver-laden galleon and made camp on the island to tally his spoils. Recently, there have been a number of archeological finds from pre-Columbian times. It is today inhabited only by sea turtles, blue-footed boobies, and a number of frigate birds such as the albatross, and can be reached by hired motorboat – a trip of two hours. Look out for shells of the spondylus oyster, which in pre-Columbian times served as a unit of currency, and as such was regularly interred in the tombs of tribal chieftains. There is good diving and snorkeling here as well, and a number of agencies in Puerto Lopez can provide gear and transportation.

Digging for the past

About 5 km (3 miles) south of Puerto López is **Salango**, a small fishing village close to a site where dozens of people took part in the largest archeological dig in the country, providing insights into the fragmentary history of pre-Columbian Ecuador. The relics of a host of successive cultures – Valdivia, Machalilla, Chorrera, Engoroy, Bahía, Guangala, and Manteño – that inhabited this fertile stretch of coastline as early as 2000BC were painstakingly recovered. A museum here is filled with artifacts found in the area. ❑

PANAMA HATS

Prohibition gangsters loved them, but do they have a future?

Montecristi is the capital of Panama hat-making: for 150 years the best *superfinos* have been woven in this peaceful, nondescript town. It is here that tourists come to buy the genuine article directly from the weavers' hands, thereby circumventing the demarcated process that the hats undergo before they appear in the shops.

The process extends from the weaver to the *comisionista*, or middle-man, who buys the untrimmed hat and sells it to the factory, which is often owned by the exporter. There it is trimmed, bleached, and hand-ironed and pounded into its finished shape, before being exported. And why is it called a Panama if it comes from Montecristi? A mistake, apparently, attributed to some 19th-century gold-miners who forgot where they bought their innovative headgear.

The Panama hat production trail begins in the low hills west of Guayaquil, a region cooled by the sea breezes of the Humboldt Current, and where rainfall is plentiful but not excessive. Although found from Bolivia to Panama, it is here, in these conditions, that *Carludovica palmata* – named after King Carlos IV and his wife Luisa by two Spanish botanists in the late 18th century – thrives.

The plant is not often found growing wild these days. It is more commonly cultivated in fields divided according to the families' seniority in the trade. The stalks of the plant can grow as high as 6 meters (20 ft) and are topped by slender leaves. But it is the material inside the stalks that is needed, the new shoots con-

BELOW: a dealer displays a *superfino* in his Cuenca store.

Map on pages 174–5

aining dozens of very fine fronds, each about a meter long and a few millimeters wide. These fronds are boiled in water for an hour, and sun-dried for a day. The procedure is repeated to ensure maximum strength when woven.

The finest weaving is done at night or on dull days, as direct sunlight makes the fronds too brittle, and hot sweaty hands don't produce tight weaves. Women and children make the best hats, because their fingers, being smaller, are more agile. A *superfino* – as the best hats are called, those most tightly woven with the thinnest, lightest straw – takes up to three months to complete. The test of a true *superfino* is that it should, when turned upside down, hold water without any leakage. It should also fold up to fit neatly in a top pocket without creasing.

No one knows exactly how long straw hats have been woven in Ecuador, but the craft certainly preceded the Spanish Conquest. The *conquistadores* were impressed by the headgear worn by the indigenous inhabitants of Manabí Province, and adapted it for their own use.

A few of the Panamas were sent to the United States in the late 18th century, and by the middle of the following century exports were growing, although it wasn't until the Spanish-American War of 1898, when the hats were considered ideal headgear for soldiers fighting in the Caribbean and the Philippines, that the export market to the US really took off. The hats first hit Europe in 1855 at the World Exposition in Paris, and, as illustrated by many of Renoir's paintings, they soon became a debonair item of contemporary fashion.

Chicago chic

Why tropical military headgear should have proved so irresistible it is hard to say, but America fell in love with the Panama, and for the next 50 years kept the industry going. The gangsters of the Prohibition period took such a shine to it that the Manabí manufacturers still call the wide-brimmed variety the *El Capone*.

Ever a mirror of popular taste, Hollywood embraced the Panama hat: a hero, or a villain, wearing a Panama was a man to be reckoned with, regardless of the fact that in Ecuador the hat identified its wearer as a manual laborer – but then much the same could be said of the modern fashion for suntans, once only seen on those who had to labor in the sun to earn their living.

The industry peaked in 1946, when 5 million hats were exported, constituting 20 percent of Ecuador's annual export earnings, a figure exceeded only by cacao, coffee, and bananas. In those days every household in Montecristi produced top-quality Panamas, but numbers have now dwindled to a handful. The international demand has fallen steadily since the early 1950s. China and Taiwan now produce cheaper imitations that are sufficiently like the genuine item to satisfy all but the most discerning, and many of the weavers of Manabí now earn their living by making mats and wickerwork furniture.

There are some in the business who believe that the manufacture of *superfinos* will not survive for much longer. For the sake of the weavers' livelihoods, and Ecuadorian pride, let's hope that is an over-pessimistic view, but the heyday of the hat is undeniably gone – probably for ever. ❏

BELOW: Panama hats before they are trimmed.

Bird-watching

Ecuador is a bird-watcher's paradise. The wide variety of habitats, from tropical rainforests to windswept highlands, from mangrove swamps to hilly forests, provide a wider range of species than any other country in the Americas. More than 1,500 bird species have been recorded here, twice as many as in the US and Canada combined.

In the *páramo* (plateau) habitat of Cotopaxi National Park, a place high on the list of many bird-watchers, one of the most surprising sights is a tiny hummingbird, the Andean hillstar, which survives the freezing nights by lowering its body temperature from about 40°C (104°F) in the daytime to about 15°C (59°F) at night – a remarkable feat for a warm-blooded creature. At the other end of the size scale is the Andean condor, which, with its 3-meter (10-ft) wing span, is one of the largest flying birds in the world.

Other *páramo* species include the carunculated caracara, Andean lapwing, Andean gull, páramo pipit, great thrush, and bar-winged cinclodes. If you camp out, you may hear the loud hoot of the great horned owl as it searches for prey, or the eerie drumming of the Andean snipe's outer wing feathers as it careens by in the dark.

The Andes of Ecuador are split into two ranges between which lies the temperate central valley. The less extreme elevation of 2,800 meters (9,200 ft) ensures a pleasant climate and attracts a variety of fascinating birds. Hummingbirds are great favorites. They begin to increase in number as the elevation drops and the climate becomes milder. More than one-fifth of Ecuador's 120 or so species of hummers are found here.

The Fundación Natura, Ecuador's leading conservation agency, runs Pasochoa Nature Reserve, an hour's drive from the capital. In one of the last original stands of temperate forest in the central valley, 11 hummingbird species, plus a variety of doves, furnarids, tapaculos, tyrant flycatchers, honeycreepers, and tanagers can all be seen.

Spend a couple of days driving to Mindo down the Chiriboga and Nono roads, heading toward the western lowlands, looking for the cock-of-the-rock, plate-billed mountain toucans, and mountain tanagers.

On the eastern Andean slopes the road to Coca takes you over the Papallacta Pass through the *páramo*, dropping down through cloud forest, with its barred fruit eaters and gray breasted mountain toucans, into the Amazon Basin. Once there, bird-watching can get a little tricky. Most transportation is by dugout canoe and the lush vegetation hides a huge diversity of birds. You will need considerable patience and experience if you are to see them.

Many people find that the best strategy is to take an organized tour or have a guide to point out some of the 550 bird species found in the area. Parrots, toucans, macaws, vultures, kingfishers, puffbirds, antbirds, herons, and hummingbirds are all there, waiting for the patient bird-watcher. Sacha or La Selva Lodge, or the Tiputini Biodiversity Station, are good options if you are looking for experienced guides. *(See Travel Tips pages 335–340 for more details.)* ❑

RIGHT: the Andean cock-of-the-rock.

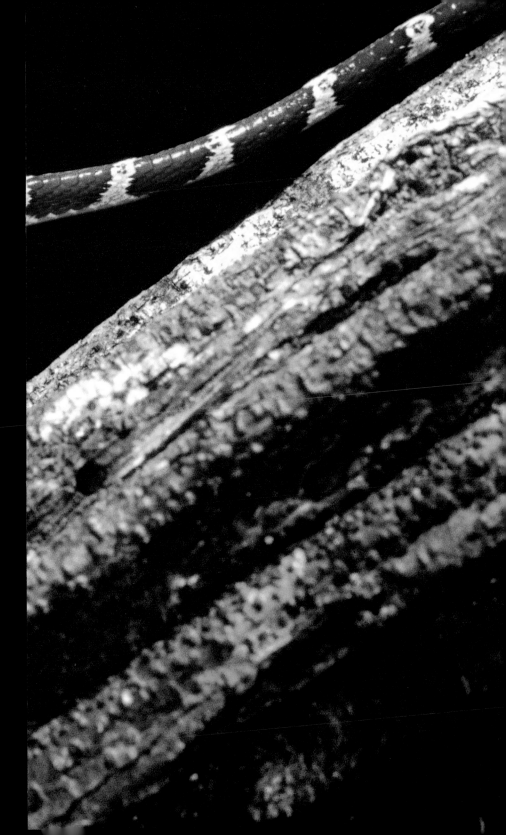

THE ORIENTE

Reptiles, anacondas, piranhas, toucans, howler monkeys, and jumping spiders all await you in the Amazon Basin. Your transport can vary from floating hotel to dugout canoe

Map on pages 174–75

You may go to the Oriente only once in your life, so it is worth asking yourself what you want from your trip. How important is comfort? Do you need a specialist guide and are you more interested in wildlife, plants, or indigenous culture? Also, what impact is your visit going to have on the rainforest? When you've answered these questions, you can start making plans. Options include a wide range of jungle lodges, an Amazon riverboat, or the burgeoning number of "adventure tourism" groups. Trips can be organized from Quito or arranged in Misahuallí, Baños, Tena, or Coca. If you are looking for an expert guide or a comfortable lodge, it is best to organize the trip in Quito, although they can be cheaper elsewhere. *See Travel Tips pages 351–8 for details of tour operators.*

River trips

For the adventurous, the best way to experience primary tropical rainforest is a week-long canoe trip down one of the rivers of the Oriente. Several qualified guides organize float trips on the Río Tiputini or in the Reserva Cuyabeno where you can see wildlife close up. During the day you will see woolly and howler monkeys grazing in the trees, toucans or parrots in flight, or if you are lucky an anaconda lazing in the sun. At night you will be serenaded by a symphony of insects and an occasional unidentified animal.

Floating hotel

At the other end of the scale from canoe trips is the *Manatee Amazon Explorer*. Especially designed for cruises in the Ecuadorian rainforest on the Río Napo, the three-level riverboat allows travelers to dip into the rainforest and return to a certain amount of luxury. Small but comfortable cabins provide the amenities of a modern hotel, while the flotel has a bar, observation deck, and dining room where excellent meals are served. Unlike traditional jungle lodges, the slow but sure flotel allows visits to different parts of the river, and permits deeper penetration of the rainforest, and therefore more opportunities to see wildlife. Passengers are taken ashore to visit a local Amerindian community, to trek into the rainforest, and to marvel at the bird life from a jungle observation tower.

Most people who have arranged river tours or visits to jungle lodges in advance will arrive by air, leaping suddenly from one climate to another. Daily flights dive from Quito to the towns of Lago Agrio and Coca deep in the jungle, covering in only 30 minutes the same distance that can take 12 grueling hours by land, as well as providing spectacular aerial views of the changing landscape. The dazzling white of the snowcapped Andes gives way to an endless mattress of green stretching into the horizon. Dozens of rivers snake beneath huge gray clouds, ready to drop their loads of moisture onto the rainforest.

PRECEDING PAGES: sinuous tributary of the Amazon; vine snake hypnotizes its prey. **LEFT:** giant tree in the rainforest. **BELOW:** a jungle river trip.

Making friends with a boa constrictor.

The highway from Quito

Travelers who want to observe from the ground the subtle shifts in flora between the Sierra and Oriente gladly sacrifice comfort and speed for a bus window seat along the eastern highway. An hour east of Quito, the bus labors over the snow-covered **Papallacta Pass** – at 4,100 meters (13,400 ft), one of the highest points in Ecuador that can be reached by public transport. The narrow gravel road then plunges down in a series of ear-popping curves to the Oriente and the landscape alters dramatically.

The Oriente (the East), as Ecuador's Amazonian region is called, lies less than 100 km (60 miles) from the Papallacta Pass as the vulture glides. But the eastern slopes of the Andes tumble precipitously, and the road passes lush cloudforests full of giant Andean tree ferns, spiky bromeliads, delicate orchids, and brightly colored birds. This is the very rim of the Amazon basin, and the steepness of the terrain combines with the thick vegetation to make it almost impenetrable. The heavily forested subtropical slopes of this transitional area are the haunts of a variety of wildlife, including the spectacled bear. Bird life is more conspicuous and colorful than wildlife in the cloudforest, with iridescent quetzals, glittering hummingbirds, and gaudy tanagers. Each elevation has its own distinct set of bird species, and the same occurs with the plants, resulting in a biological mosaic of unparalleled diversity. The northern Andean cloudforests have a total plant diversity as great as that of the entire Amazon basin, though they cover only a twentieth of the basin area.

Thirty minutes' drive past the Papallacta Pass is the town of **Papallacta** and its nearby hot springs – ideal for anyone in need of a little relaxation. The road drops toward the jungle taking the line of least resistance – a river valley. Ama-

BELOW: the *Manatee Amazon Explorer.*

zonian climate patterns ensure heavy rainfall almost year round, and there are hundreds of minor and major rivers flowing down the eastern Andes toward the Oriente. Although at this point they are only 240 km (150 miles) away from the Pacific, these rivers will merge with the waters of the world's greatest river system and finally join the sea at the Atlantic 3,200 km (2,000 miles) away.

Map
on pages
174–75

An area of strategic importance

The road follows the valley of the Río Papallacta, and finally ends up in the first important Oriente town, **Baeza** ⑰, near the Río Quijos (named for an indigenous tribe that lived in the region at the time of the conquest). Baeza is a small, ramshackle, subtropical outpost whose tin-roofed appearance belies its long and interesting history. Since before the Spanish conquest, lowland forest natives stopped here on their way to the highlands on trading expeditions. Recognizing the area's strategic importance, the Spaniards founded a missionary and trading outpost here in 1548, just 14 years after conquering Ecuador.

Perched on the edge of the Amazon basin at 1,400 meters (4,600ft) above sea level and 80 km (50 miles) east of Quito, Baeza remained Ecuador's last outpost in the northern Oriente for more than four centuries. Today, it is its gateway, and can also be reached by a popular road from Baños further south, via the jungle town of **Puyo**. On clear days you can see the Sangay and Altar volcanoes from town. If you are a wildlife enthusiast, tours deeper into the jungle can be arranged.

Transformed by oil

Until the middle of the 20th century, this Andean rim of the Amazon basin was as far as colonists and travelers went. Wildlife and indigenous groups lived rel-

BELOW: the jumping spider.

atively undisturbed further on in the Oriente. This suddenly changed in the late 1960s with the discovery of oil in the jungle. Almost overnight, a good all-weather road was pushed from Quito beyond Baeza and deep into the heart of parts of the Oriente which until then could be reached only by difficult river travel or by light aircraft. The new 180-km (110-mile) road stretches from Baeza to **Lago Agrio**  (literally "Sour Lake"), an oil town built in a trackless region in the middle of the jungle. For much of its length, the road to Lago Agrio parallels the trans-Ecuadorian pipeline, which pumps oil 495 km (310 miles) from the oil fields of the Oriente, up across the Andes and down to the Pacific coast for processing and export. At irregular intervals along the pipeline, little communities have been created. Some are next to oil pumping stations, whilst others have been founded by colonists near flat pieces of land that they have cleared.

The famous **San Rafael Falls** are on the Río Quijos, about half way between Baeza and Lago Agrio. With a height of about 145 meters (475 ft), they are the highest falls in the country. They can be glimpsed from the bus as it travels along the new road, but for an impressive close-up look you should get off at the NECEL electricity station at **Reventador**. From here, it is a 30-minute walk down an overgrown trail through lush forest to a viewpoint where, if the wind is right (or wrong depending on your point of view) you can be sprayed by the light mist caused by the crashing water. Sometimes the spray can be so thick that it obliterates the view of the cascading river; at other times the mists clear for a magnificent sight of the falls. This is also a great place for birdwatching. Nearby Volcán Reventador, the most active volcano in the Cordillera Real, shows its peak above the cloud forest.

In November 2002, after 26 years of dormancy, Reventador erupted spectacularly, shooting a column of ash and rock 15 km (9 miles) into the sky, which

The new road makes life a lot easier for travelers, but has had detrimental effects on the environment.

BELOW: crucifix and canoe in a mission chapel.

enshrouded Quito and the rest of central Ecuador. Smaller eruptions have occurred since then and heavy rainfall has caused ash deposits in the area to shift, in turn creating major landslides and causing damage to the oil pipeline. It is currently too dangerous to trek to or explore Reventador.

Lago Agrio itself is one of the fastest-growing places in Ecuador, although not much to look at. It's officially called Nueva Loja (New Loja), named by the first Ecuadorian colonists in the area who mainly came from the province of Loja in the south of the country. It was homesick North American oilmen working for Texaco who nicknamed the town Lago Agrio for the small Texan oil town of Sourlake, and despite what it says on the maps, that's what everyone calls it.

Lago Agrio was part of the huge jungle province of Napo, whose capital is Tena, an all-day drive away over ill-maintained roads. Tena is not an oil town and the citizens of Lago felt that their very different interests were not represented. But Lago's importance became apparent after an earthquake in 1987 isolated the town, cutting the oil flow and bringing the economy to a grinding halt. In 1989, Lago Agrio was made the capital of Sucumbios, while in 1998 the new province of Orellana was created to the south. A hot and humid climate pervades the town. Even the newest buildings begin to look decayed within a few months. The unpaved streets are often filled with mud, and rubber boots are the usual footwear. Yet it is a lively and progressive place; late-model Jeeps churn the mud in the streets and the bustling market is thronged with shoppers. Sadly, it is also a frontier town that has suffered from the growth of drug trafficking and armed groups in neighboring Colombia, and travelers are advised to make enquiries about safety before visiting the region.

Map on pages 174–75

LEFT: the San Rafael waterfall.
RIGHT: a woolly monkey.

Tena lies 75 km (47 miles) south of Baeza and is the kayak and rafting capital of Ecuador. Straddling the Río Tena, it has the feel of a jungle town. The charming main plaza overlooks the river, on the other side of which is the *malecón* (pier). There is a small island on the river, reachable by a thatched bridge, where there is a private nature reserve (admission charge) with great walking trails. You can see a number of species of monkeys in the trees, but sadly most of the animals, including a tapir, an ocelot, and a jaguarundi, are in cages. About a 1-hour bus ride and 3-hour hike from the town brings you to the Comunidad Capirona (www.ricancie.nativeweb.org), a network of nine Quichua communities located within the Grand Sumaco National Park Biosphere Reserve, an extremely diverse and threatened area. There are opportunities to volunteer with development projects in the community.

Meet the capybara – the world's largest rodent.

Into the jungle

If there are no current security problems, it is well worth making the effort to get from Lago Agrio to the **Reserva de Producción Faunística Cuyabeno** ⑲, up toward the Colombian border, where some 655,000 hectares (1.6 million acres) of incredibly bio-diverse land, consisting of a great deal of flooded and pretty much intact forest, have been turned into a national park. It's a full day's travel by bus and motorized canoe along the Río Aguarico to reach the reserve itself. Most tour companies use *cabañas* (cabins) – open-sided platforms or tents – as accommodation. Visits to the Siona-Secoya communities on the reserve can sometimes be arranged.

Other, longer, trips take you down the Río Napo. One destination is **Lago Pañacocha**, a beautiful lagoon on the Río Panayacu, located in a small protected

BELOW: a spectacled caiman enjoying the sun.

area of 56,000 hectares (138,400 acres) between the Napo and Aguarico rivers. Colonists, deterred by so much flooded forest, have not taken over here. There is some provision for tourists, with several modest *cabañas* and shelters. Walks along remote trails offer a good chance of seeing birds, butterflies, and fresh jaguar tracks. Some agencies attempt to bring a dozen tourists into the reserve at a time which makes it far more difficult to see animals, so insist on a group of no more than eight people.

Map on pages 174–75

Close encounters with piranhas

There may be the opportunity on one of these trips to try some piranha fishing. Small pieces of raw red flesh are used as bait on hand-lines, bringing the infamous creatures out in their hundreds. These small fish are surprisingly easy to catch, although watch your fingers as you bring them aboard: their small, triangular-shaped teeth are razor sharp. Piranhas make a fine meal and you can keep their jaws as a souvenir of the jungle.

Contrary to popular belief, it is quite possible – if not exactly relaxing – to swim in piranha-infested waters. The variety of piranha found in Ecuador will only ever turn nasty on large mammals, such as humans and horses, if there is a huge quantity of blood in the water. Even so, such is the reputation of the fish that swimming here is rather unnerving, and many prefer to endure the Amazonian heat rather than test the murky waters.

Another unforgettable Oriente experience is night-time caiman-watching. Slip out on a canoe at night and shine a flashlight into the reeds by the lakeside: hundreds of red eyes stare back, the reflections from caimans' retinas (rather like the "red eye" effect in flash photography). The more adventurous guides

BELOW: the notorious piranha.

TIP

Contact Aves y
Conservación (the
Ecuadorian Ornithology
Foundation), for more
information on birds
and their habitats.
*See Travel Tips page
349 for details.*

will take the boat right in among these harmless but vicious-looking reptiles – an experience that can feel a little too adventurous if you happen to be in an unstable dugout canoe. Some guides will even grab a small caiman by the tail, to bring it alongside the canoe and give everyone a closer look.

If you have a few days to spare it is possible to visit **Limoncocha** (Lime Lake) downriver from Coca. Oil production has had some impact on the area, but the swamp and surrounding forest remain intact. This unique ecosystem harbors white caiman and over 400 species of bird. Boat trips can be made at the park headquarters of the **Reserva Biológica Limoncocha** ⓴ near the town of Limoncocha. Although there is no formal lodge, an extended stay can be arranged at the SEK University research station or in the Limoncocha community.

A museum of curiosities

About 8 km (5 miles) from Limoncocha is the Capuchin mission of **Pompeya**. Among the houses on wooden stilts there is an altar with a crucifix above a colored canoe, as well as a curious museum. Here you can handle the various blowpipes used by Amazonian peoples to hunt – many are surprisingly long and heavy, often used to shoot directly upward into the trees with a dart coated with natural venom that paralyzes the prey. Opposite Pompeya is **Isla de los Monos** (Monkey Island), where you can wander freely and spot howler monkeys high in the trees above. You will need a little patience, but you should be well rewarded. There have been regrettable changes, however: not long ago the island was literally packed with monkeys, but the Ecuadorian Army chose this location as the site for survival training, and hundreds of these endangered creatures ended up in the soldiers' stews.

BELOW: artifacts
at a museum
in Pompeya.

Amazon lodges

Not every visitor to the Oriente wants to bathe in a jungle river and sleep on the floor of a native hut at the end of a hard day of hiking in the jungle. For those wishing to visit the virgin rainforest, yet return to a comfortable room with a private shower at night, there are several options. *See Travel Tips pages 335–340 for details of the lodges mentioned in this chapter.*

La Selva Jungle Lodge ㉑ is perhaps the best-known of the lodges. The journey there is half the adventure: first in a twin-propeller aircraft to the jungle town of Coca, then a motorized dugout canoe for 2½ hours followed by a rough boardwalk through the rainforest to Laguna Garzacocha and finally a dugout canoe to the lodge. The buildings at La Selva, up on stilts and with thatched roofs, have been constructed from secondary rainforest materials to withstand the extremes of jungle climate. Rooms are lit with kerosene lamps, and the lack of a thumping generator outside the cabins ensures that guests are able to hear the myriad sounds of the rainforest. La Selva is a magnet for birdwatchers: parrots, tanagers, toucans, and numerous other species can be seen. Expert naturalists, many of them English-speaking, can guide visitors on jungle walks and canoe rides and there is a new observation tower.

Sacha Lodge is another excellent option offering plenty of creature comforts (including electricity and hot water) and a great variety of trails and trips. Just north of the Río Napo, it is reached by a 3-hour motorized canoe trip from Coca. The lodge's observation tower enables you to climb 40 meters (130 ft) into the canopy for an unobstructed view of miles and miles of intact rainforest, close-up views of plants and birds, and maybe the occasional sloth hanging from a tree top. (A lodge with an observation tower is essential.) After a long day exploring

There are English-speaking guides available at Sacha Lodge to make your tour more informative.

BELOW: the award-winning Kapawi Ecolodge.

Panning for gold on the Río Napo.

BELOW: thatched transportation on the Río Napo.

the magic of the rainforest a dip in the Pilchicocha Lagoon in front of the lodge may be a welcome form of relaxation.

If you are short of time, on a budget, and just want a taste of the rainforest, there are plenty of trips on offer starting from the small town of **Misahuallí ㉒** in the headwaters of the Río Napo. Here guides can be hired for about $30–40 a day. The area has been colonized and the forest here is secondary growth. The large mammals and birds have mainly been hunted close to extinction, but a short trip will give you an experience of the jungle and a look at a variety of plants, insects, and smaller birds.

Near Misahuallí, on the Río Napo, is **Reserva Biológica Jatún Sacha**, a center dedicated to conservation, education, and research, where a number of unknown species have been discovered. Next door are the **Cabañas Aliñahui** (also known as the Butterfly Lodge) offering comfortable cabins, canoe trips, visits to indigenous communities, and walks along a great variety of trails in the area. Tourists can visit the reserve and see field work in progress. For butterfly lovers this area is paradise: besides hundreds of birds and plants, an astonishing 765 butterfly species have been identified at Jatún Sacha.

One aspect of forest life that can be observed around Misahuallí is colonization: small coffee *fincas* (estates), oil-palm plantations, cattle ranches, and yucca plots are prevalent. As you journey down the nearby river, you may occasionally notice workers washing and sifting material. They are panning for gold – modern descendants of the long line of settlers obsessed with dreams of El Dorado. A little farther down the Río Napo is **Yachana Lodge**, run by Funedesin, a non-profit organization. Innovative community projects are being developed as role models for sustainable ways of living in the rainforest. Funedesin

(www.funedesin.org), which is a foundation for the education and development of indigenous peoples, can be contacted in Quito at Vicente Solano 12–61 and Avda Oriental, tel: 02-223 7133. If you speak Spanish and are interested in staying with an indigenous community there are several Quichua families in the Tena area that welcome visitors.

One of the most conservation-oriented places is at **Delfin's Cabañas** in Pimpilala, a 45-minute ride from Tena, where you can stay with a Quichua family. Delfin will lead you through the 30 hectares (74 acres) of primary forest he has protected, giving details of the medicinal plants and explaining local legends along the way.

Kapawi Ecolodge on the Pastaza River near the border with Peru, is one of the most highly regarded lodges in the world. Accessible only by air, it is set in an area of 5,000 sq. km (1,930 sq. miles) with a population of 4,500 people in 56 communities. The lodge is run in partnership with the Federation of Achuar Indigenous People in Ecuador (FINAE) and was built in accordance to the Achuar concept of architecture.

The fragile ecosystem

It is imperative that anyone thinking of visiting the Oriente region ask themselves whether they are harming the environment and the lifestyles they are so keen to see and to preserve. This is a particularly pertinent question when it comes to visiting indigenous communities. One group that has so far resisted significant contact with outsiders is the Huaorani, who live in relative isolation in an area around the Río Cononoco. The political organization ONHAE is working to protect the Huaorani from colonization, following the discovery of oil in the region, but it is difficult to predict whether Ecuador will be able to walk the tightrope between economic development and protecting the Huaorani and the rainforest ecosystem. Most of the Huaorani people, who maintain a hunter-gatherer way of life, do not welcome tourist visits to their communities and it is advisable to respect their wishes, but conversely, some Huaorani are turning to eco-tourism to protect their culture, and it is possible to spend time with the Huaorani community of Quehueri'ono by prior arrangement.

Living along the Río Aguarico, a small group of Cofan natives work with the help of US-born Randy Borman to encourage tourists to visit their village of **Zabalo** on carefully organized tours. Once there, visitors experience the Cofan lifestyle, traveling in dugout canoes and hiking into the jungle in search of medicinal plants. The ideal behind the enterprise is to hold on to the jungle and to offer the Cofan group the opportunity to control the rate of change, so that they can retain their language and their sense of themselves as a people. Some people feel that bringing tourism to a region in need of preservation is self-defeating, but Borman and the village leaders disagree. All the money generated goes to the Cofan, who are able to use and display their traditional knowledge of the Oriente, both for personal survival and as their singular contribution to a changing world (*see The Gringo Chief, page 99*). ❑

Map on pages 174–75

BELOW: Oriente settlers.

ORIENTE WILDLIFE

*Everyone wants to see the armadillos and tapirs, the big cats
and the prolific birdlife. But the armies of insects that
most people try to avoid are no less interesting*

Map
on pages
174–75

Quito
ECUADOR

The Oriente has such a diverse variety of wildlife that for many people the chance to see some of it in its natural habitat is reason enough to travel to Ecuador. Whether your interest is in birds, beasts, reptiles, or insects you will find fascinating species in the Amazonian forest.

Fantastic bird life

Some 550 species of birds have been recorded in the Napo region alone, and professional and amateur ornithologists and birdwatchers flock to the area to see species with such exotic names as green and gold tanager, greater yellow-headed vulture, purple-throated fruitcrow, puffbird, and toucan. For many visitors, the parrots and macaws are the favorites. One of the highlights in a trip to La Selva or Sacha Lodge *(see Travel Tips pages 335–40 for details)* is a boat ride further downriver to two large patches of soil laden with mineral salts. These natural salt licks attract hundreds of parrots that require the mineral in their diets. Birdwatchers at dawn can witness a magnificent display of hundreds of squawking, squabbling parrots feeding at the *saladeros*, as the salt licks are known. Species such as the blue-headed, orange-cheeked, and yellow-crowned parrot as well as the dusky-headed parakeet and scarlet-shouldered parrotlet have been observed here.

Mammals of the rainforest

The salt licks also attract a variety of jungle mammals. Most of these feed at night and leave only footprints for the curious visitor to observe in daylight. An adventurous person could spend the night by a salt lick and perhaps be rewarded with moonlit glimpses of a variety of mammals. These may include the nine-banded armadillo, or a rodent called the paca which has spotted fur, weighs up to 9 kg (20 lb) and is considered excellent food by local hunters, or perhaps the capybara, the world's largest rodent weighing around 64 kg (140 lb).

Some salt licks attract a huge, strange mammal, the South American tapir. The largest land mammals in Amazonia, tapirs can weigh in excess of 270 kg (600 lb). Their closest relatives are the other odd-toed ungulates, the rhinoceros and the horse. Members of the tapir family are among the most primitive large mammals in the world and are well adapted to life in the jungle. Their short sturdy legs, thick, strong necks, and barrel-like bodies covered with incredibly tough skin enable them to shove through the dense forest undergrowth like a living tank. One of their strangest features is a short trunk, which gives them an excellent sense of smell and is used to pull leaves off bushes and into their mouths.

Tapirs are much sought-after game animals. Local hunters are able to feed an entire village if they are fortunate enough to shoot one. Apart from the meat, the

LEFT: the great egret.
BELOW: a golden tanager.

tapirs' fatty tissues yield an oil that is much prized for cooking, and the thick skin makes good-quality leather. The South American tapir lives in the Oriente lowlands and the mountain tapir inhabits the upper Amazonian basin and the Andean flanks. Hunting is not as much of a threat to the latter as is habitat destruction, and the mountain tapir is regarded as an endangered species by the Ecuadorian conservation organization, the Fundación Natura.

Apart from man, the tapir's greatest enemy is the big cat of Amazonia – the jaguar. A fully grown male can reach 113 kg (250 lb) in weight and, when hungry, will attack almost any large animal it comes across. Jaguars will leap onto tapirs' backs and attempt to kill them by breaking their necks in their powerful jaws. The tapirs' defense is twofold: the fact that the thick neck is protected by the tough, leathery skin and a bristly mane, and their habit of charging wildly through the dense undergrowth when threatened, thus making it difficult for a predator to hold on long enough to deliver the fatal bite.

Jaguars do not roar, as do most other big cats. Instead, they emit a low, coughing grunt, especially when courting. Generally, jaguars are afraid of humans and only the luckiest of visitors catches a glimpse of them in the wild. Most travelers in the Oriente must be content with footprints in the soft earth or thrilling stories told by local residents.

You are also unlikely to see another resident, the spectacled bear, because it is a very shy creature, which is perhaps why it has survived for so long. The only bear found in South America, its habitat ranges from 200 meters (650 ft) to 4,200 meters (13,800 ft) on the heavily forested subtropical slopes. It is mainly vegetarian, often climbing trees in search of succulent fruits. The bear's habitat is increasingly being encroached upon by colonists, and it is protected by Ecuadorian law.

The toothless armadillo is armed with bands of bony plates.

LEFT: a red howler monkey.
RIGHT: a young puma.

A multitude of monkeys

The mammals that visitors most often get to see, however, are the monkeys. The most vocal of these is the very aptly named howler monkey. The males of this species have a specialized, hollow, and much enlarged hyoid bone in the throat. Air is passed through the hyoid cavity producing an ear-splitting call, which can easily carry for well over a kilometer in the rainforest. This is an astounding feat when one remembers that the forest vegetation has a damping effect on sound. When heard in the distance, the call has been variously described as sounding like the wind moaning through the trees or like a human baby crying. Close up, the call can be quite terrifying to the uninitiated visitor.

The purpose of the call is to advertize a troop's presence in a particular patch of rainforest. This enables troops to space themselves out in the canopy and thus avoid competing as they forage for succulent young leaves. Occasionally, troops do meet in the tree tops and the result is often chaotic with howling, chasing, threatening, and even fighting. The energy used in these meetings is better expended in feeding and thus it pays for a troop to make its presence known by frequent howling.

Several other species of monkey are frequently seen, including woolly, squirrel, spider, and tamarin monkeys. Often, the best way to observe monkeys is from a dugout canoe floating down a jungle river. A local trained guide will spot a troop of monkeys early enough to stop the boat in a position that offers a clear view of the animals foraging in trees along the banks. From within the rainforest, on the other hand, animals may be difficult to see in the tree tops. In addition, monkeys may display their displeasure at human intrusion by hurling sticks, fruit, and even feces down on the unfortunate visitor's head.

Map on pages 174–75

BELOW: a stunning blue butterfly.

Map on pages 174–75

Wildlife beneath your feet

Many people come to the Oriente hoping to see exotic birds and mammals, while trying to avoid the myriad insects. Yet it is the insects that are the most common and, in many ways, most fascinating creatures of the rainforest. Some are simply beautiful, such as the breathtaking blue morpho butterflies whose huge wings flash a dazzling electric blue as they leisurely flap along jungle rivers. Other species have such complex life cycles that they are still not fully understood by tropical ecologists. Among these are hundreds of ant species, particularly the army ants and leaf-cutter ants, both of which species are commonly observed in the forest.

Colonies of leaf-cutter ants numbering hundreds of thousands live in huge nests dug deep into the ground. Foragers search the vegetation for particular types of leaves, cut out small sections and, holding the leaf segments above their heads like small umbrellas, take them back to the nest. The ants can be quite experimental, bringing back a variety of leaves and even pieces of discarded plastic wrappers. Workers within the nest sort out the kinds of leaves which will mulch down into a type of compost; unsuitable material is ejected from the nest after a few days. The composted leaves form a mulch on which a fungus grows. Ants tend these fungal gardens with care, for they provide the main diet for both the adult ants and for the young that are being raised inside the nest.

The story does not end there. When a particularly good source of leaves has been located, ants lay down a trail of chemical markers, or pheromones, linking the nest with the leaf source, often 100 meters (330 ft) or more away in the forest. People frequently come across these trails in the jungle, with hundreds of ants scurrying along carrying leaf sections back to the nest, or returning empty-handed for another load.

BELOW: a tree boa, ready to strike.

Other species, for example army ants, may want to prey on this ready and constant supply of foragers. To combat this the leaf-cutter ants are morphologically separated by size and jaw structure into different castes. Some specialize in tending the fungal gardens; others have jaws designed for cutting the leaf segments; and yet others are soldiers, armed with huge mandibles, who accompany the foragers and protect them from attackers. Close observation of the foragers will sometimes reveal yet another caste, a tiny ant so small that it can ride on the leaf segments without disturbing the foragers. Biologists suggest that they act as protection against parasitical wasps, which may try to lay their eggs on the ants.

A colony of leaf-cutter ants may last for a decade or more. New colonies are founded by the emergence of a number of potential queens, who mate and then fly off to found another nest, carrying some of the fungus used for food. This is essential to "seed" the new nest. The rest of the new queen's life is spent laying tens of thousands of eggs, destined to become gardeners, foragers, soldiers, riders, or even queens.

Such complicated interactions make the rainforest interesting to biologists and tourists alike. A day with a trained naturalist guide will bring to light many such stories about the habits of the forest's vast population of creatures great and small. ❏

The Vanishing Rainforest

The plight of the world's tropical forests is becoming increasingly well known. Huge areas of forest are being logged or burned every day; so much deforestation is occurring that, at the present rate, with more than 25,900 sq. km (10,000 sq. miles) being destroyed for ranching, farming, and logging each year in Brazil alone, some scientists have predicted that 40 percent of the rainforest will disappear by 2050. Of the almost two million known species of plants and animals, about half live only in the rainforest. Estimates of species yet to be discovered are numbered in millions. Most of these unknown species live in the tropical forests, which have by far the greatest biodiversity of any region on the globe. Thus deforestation is causing countless extinctions, with many of the plants and animals as yet unknown.

Numerous medicines have been extracted from forest plants, ranging from malarial prophylactics to anesthetics, from antibiotics to contraceptives. Many more useful drugs will undoubtedly be discovered in the forests, if they are not destroyed first.

The diversity of species growing in the rainforests also comprises a storehouse of new strains of agriculturally important plants that may be destroyed by disease or drought. For example, if banana crops were to be seriously threatened by disease, scientists could search the rainforests for disease-resistant strains to cross with the commercially grown varieties and eradicate the problem.

The forests are also essential for the survival of indigenous peoples. Hundreds of discrete communities living in the jungles of Latin America, and in Africa and Asia, are threatened by rainforest loss.

On a worldwide scale, the moderating effect of the rainforest on global climate patterns is only recently becoming understood. Deforestation could cause severe global warming, leading to melting ice caps, rising ocean levels, and flooding of coastal regions.

Climates would be altered to the extent that some major crops, such as wheat, would no longer grow.

The main reason the rainforest is being cut down is migration of poor *campesinos* from other parts of the country looking for free land to make a living. Generally the soils are not well suited for agriculture and are quickly depleted of scarce nutrients. The short-sighted colonization policies causing this damage are now at last being re-evaluated and solutions being sought, but the forest is still being cleared at an alarming rate.

Debt-for-nature swaps, whereby foreign debts are paid off by the lenders in return for protection of the rainforest, are a move in the right direction, but the developed countries that lend the money must ensure that such incentives reflect the full value of the forests.

Sustainable use, such as rubber-tapping and brazil-nut harvesting, also help to a certain extent. Rainforests such as the Oriente are vital for the planet's survival. Whatever the methods used, it is essential that they are protected. ❏

RIGHT: the rainforest is vital for the survival of the planet.

RAILWAY JOURNEYS

Train journeys in Ecuador can be slow, crowded, and completely idiosyncratic, but they can also be a remarkably exhilarating experience

Ecuador's trains are a colorful part of the landscape, much-loved by tourists, but they are becoming increasingly uneconomical and, as roads and long-distance bus services improve, they are increasingly seen as time-consuming and inconvenient. Soon these idiosyncratic steam trains and "iron cars" may become the preserve of dedicated train enthusiasts rather than travelers, so enjoy them while you can.

THE IRON CAR

The Ibarra–San Lorenzo line was opened in 1957 after two French companies spent five years hacking a route through the wilderness. Until the recent construction of a highway, this was the only means of overland access to the coastal port of San Lorenzo in the north-western tip of the country. The service has recently been restricted to the first 45 km out of Ibarra.

COTOPAXI AND THE CHIVA EXPRESS

The three-hour train ride south from Quito to El Boliche station, near Cotopaxi National Park, offers good views of the Andean peaks. A more reliable option is the Chiva Express, a bus-cum-railcar service to Cotopaxi, which runs on Tuesdays, Thursdays, and Saturdays. A highlight is to ride on the roof of the train.

▷ **BUCAY BELLE**
Ecuador's favorite locomotive steams out of Bucay station.

△ **IRON CAR**
This train is actually an antiquated bus, an *autoferro* ("iron car"), complete with brakes that feed on sand, mounted on a train's chassis and fitted with a diesel engine. It seats 56 and half as many again huddle in the aisles and on the roof for this slow, but scenic journey.

▽ **MUSEUM PIECE**
Steam locomotives such as this romantic red monster draw many train enthusiasts to Ecuador. It still runs through the mountains, but in many countries these engines would be proudly displayed in railway museums.

△ **PIG STOP**
At Huigra station, about halfway between Bucay and Alausí on the Nariz del Diablo route, there's a stop for rather unconventional refreshments – slices from a whole roast pig *(asado)* are popular snacks. The image of the Virgin above the counter bestows a blessing on travelers.

△ **ROOF-TOP VIEW**
Riding on the roofs of trains is an Ecuadorian custom, and a way of escaping the heat of the carriage. Watch out for low-roofed tunnels.

GETTING UP THE DEVIL'S NOSE

Train travel in Ecuador began in 1910, when the Quito–Guayaquil line was opened after more than 30 years and a great deal of money had been spent on its construction. Built with US technical and financial assistance, it was immediately acclaimed as one of the "great railway journeys of the world," and reduced to two days a former nine-day trek along a mule path impassable half the year due to rain.

The most hair-raising train journey in Ecuador, and said to be one of the most spectacular in the world, is the section called El Nariz del Diablo (the Devil's Nose, pictured above) on the Quito–Guayaquil line between Alausí and Bucay. The elderly red steam train switchbacks down the precipitous descent, crossing spindly bridges over heart-stoppingly deep ravines – usually with passengers sitting on the roof, a rather alarming Ecuadorian custom, but one that ensures the best view.

Much of the track was destroyed by landslides during the devastating El Niño floods of 1997–98 but the Riobamba/Sibambe section has since been repaired. Metropolitan Touring (see page 356) operates its own motorized railcar on the Riobamba–Sibambe route, which runs whenever they have a minimum number of passengers.

▷ **WATER BREAK**
Having completed the most exciting part of its route, the steep descent from Alausí, the steam train stops to take on more water before continuing its journey to Sibambe. The adrenaline rush over, many people get off at Bucay and take the bus the rest of the way and on to the larger town of Guayaquil.

▷ **HIGH-STREET TRACK**
In Milagro, near Guayaquil, the train makes stately progress through the main street and no one hurries out of the way.

THE AVENUE
OF THE VOLCANOES

Map on page 242

The "spine" of Ecuador has hot springs and markets as well as a long line of breathtaking snowcapped mountains

The Andes are often thought of as the spine of Ecuador, but a ladder is a better analogy. Think of the Eastern and Western cordilleras as the sides of the ladder, with the lower east–west connecting mountains (called *nudos* or knots) as the rungs. Between each rung is an intermontane valley at about 2,300 to 3,000 meters (7,000 to 9,000ft) in elevation, with fertile volcanic soil.

The valleys are heavily settled and farmed today and were the territory of different ethnic groups in pre-Inca times. Both the Pan-American Highway and the railroad run north–south between the cordilleras, bobbing up and down over the *nudos* past fields, farms, and startled cows beneath a range of dormant and active volcanoes, some of which have permanent snowcaps.

In 1802 the German explorer Alexander von Humboldt named this route the "Avenue of the Volcanoes." Ecuador's position on the equator means that you can travel through the avenue past orchids and palm trees, with tundra vegetation, glaciers, and snow visible in the mountains above. By leaving the valley and hiking or climbing up, you can pass through all the earth's ecological zones from subtropical to alpine.

A splendid way of traveling down the avenue is by train, but you will need to check which lines are running. If open, the railroad does allow you to get an intimate look at life along the tracks, traveling through people's back yards, so to speak, rather than down the main road. The route suggested in this chapter, however, takes the Pan-American Highway, with detours and side roads to places of interest on the way.

PRECEDING PAGES: Cotopaxi crater. **LEFT:** the basilica at Baños against an Andean hillside. **BELOW:** man from the bleak *páramo*.

The road south

Leaving **Quito ❶** by car or bus for the south can seem to take forever, as the streets leading to the Pan-American Highway are usually jammed. However, there is a bypass, the Nuevo Oriental, which connects with the Pan-American Highway on the outskirts of south Quito, and makes driving much less stressful. The road goes through the **Valle de los Chillos** and connects with the main highway about 8 km (5 miles) farther south. The traffic eases a bit as you wind down off the Quito plateau and into the first intermontane valley. Way off to the east the snowy peak of **Volcán Antisana** (5,750 meters/18,720ft) can be seen.

Looming over the region is **Volcán Cotopaxi** (5,897 meters/19,347ft), Ecuador's second-highest peak and one of the world's highest active volcanoes. On a clear day you can see its symmetrical, snowcapped cone from Quito. In the Western Cordillera, almost directly across from Cotopaxi, is **Volcán Illiniza** (5,265 meters/17,280ft)

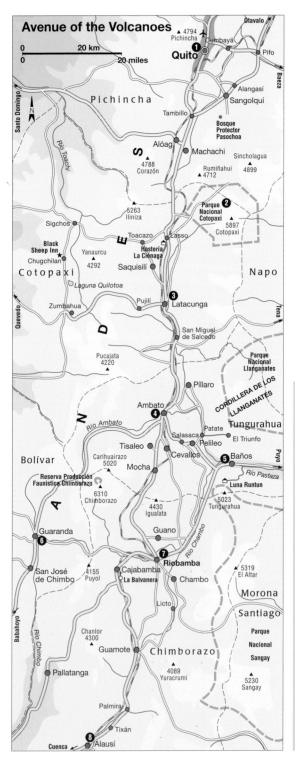

Avenue of the Volcanoes

– or the Illinizas as they are called, for there are actually two peaks. The lower, northern peak is a satisfying climb for non-technical climbers and hikers, while the southern one, Illiniza Sur, is only for those with experience.

Some 32 km (20 miles) beyond Machachi, just over the first pass, is the entrance to the magnificent **Parque Nacional Cotopaxi ②**.

Both sides of the highway are covered by a dense forest of Monterrey pines, many of them dying from a fungal disease. The pines are not native; they were introduced from California for a forestry project and are a textbook example of the dangers of monoculture: the pines have crowded out the indigenous vegetation and the fungus has spread rapidly from tree to tree.

The national park centers on Cotopaxi, of course, but there are several other peaks that attract rock climbers, including **Rumiñahui** (4,710 meters/15,430ft), and there is also a great variety of

FIESTA DE LA MAMÁ NEGRA

Latacunga's festival of the Virgin of the Mercedes, commonly known as the Fiesta de la Mamá Negra (the Festival of the Black Mother) takes place on September 23 and 24. It's a lively event with obvious indigenous influences despite its Christian name and outward trappings, which of course include paying homage to the figure of the black-faced Virgin Mary.

There are huge street parades with allegorical figures, often making satirical social or political points; masquerades; local bands; noisy firework displays; and dancing in the streets until all hours of the night. There is also a solemn Midnight Mass (*misa del gallo*) although some of the celebrants are a little less than solemn. It is one of the best-known such fiestas in the country and well worth seeing, if your visit happens to coincide with these dates.

wildlife, ranging from falcons and highland hummingbirds to tiny deer and the endangered, and rarely seen, Andean puma.

Map on page 242

Haciendas and markets

As elsewhere in Latin America the prime agricultural land in the valley was taken from the indigenous population soon after the Spanish conquest and turned into large Spanish-owned haciendas (estates), many of which still exist and include vast landholdings, despite the Agrarian Reform of 1964. Back on the highway, at Km 68 from Quito, you come to **Tambo Mulaló** (tel: 09-972 7934; www.tierradelvolcan.com), a hacienda converted for tourist use, offering excellent typical food *(comida criolla)*. A *tambo* in Inca times was a way station or inn for travelers. During the colonial era, Tambo Mulaló was a retreat for Jesuits, then an inn for travelers on the road to Quito. It is now a dairy farm with a small bullring and horseback riding facilities. A hop down the road is the tiny town of **Lasso** and the turn-off to the west is for the **Hostería La Ciénega** (tel: 02-271 9052). Now a hotel and restaurant, its main house – a stone mansion with huge windows, stone-cobbled patios and Moorish-style fountains – was built in the mid-1600s for the Marquis de Maenza and was occupied by his family for more than 300 years. The stone chapel has a bell, still rung on Sunday mornings, which was installed in 1768 in thanksgiving when Cotopaxi ended 20 years of devastating eruptions. Von Humboldt stayed here in 1802 when he surveyed Cotopaxi, and the de Maenza-Lasso family plotted Ecuador's independence from Spain on this site in the 1800s. The comfortable rooms are well furnished. Besides opportunities for excellent birdwatching in the gardens you can ride horseback from here and make day trips to Cotopaxi National Park.

BELOW: horseman on the windswept Sierra.

The Hostería La Ciénega.

The little towns in the valley, and the larger city of **Latacunga ❸** (pop. 50,000), are interesting primarily for their fiestas and market days. Some 90 km/ 54 miles from Quito, Latacunga is somnolent and pleasant, with a number of buildings constructed from local gray volcanic rock. It was founded in 1534 on the site of an Inca urban center and fortress. There are busy Saturday and Tuesday markets, where crafts are sold, especially *shigras* (bags), baskets, and ponchos.

Latacunga's town hall *(municipio)* and cathedral are on the main plaza, the Parque Vicente León, which has topiary and a well-maintained garden. Behind the cathedral is a colonial building housing an arcade with shops, offices, and an art gallery. Five blocks west down Calle Maldonado at Calle Vela is the **Casa de la Cultura** (open Tues–Fri 8am–12pm and 2–6pm, Sat 8am–3pm; admission charge), built on the remains of a Jesuit monastery and the old Montserrat water-mill. The museum houses pre-Colombian ceramics and weavings, and a library, theater, and gallery. After that, it's easy to get the small-town blues, but Lata-cunga makes a good base for trips to other parts of Cotopaxi province.

Some 10 km (6 miles) west of Latacunga is **Pujilí**, which has a lively market on Sunday, but otherwise very little going for it except the Corpus Christi fes-tivities in June, the most colorful celebration of this fiesta you will find.

A wild and scenic loop west of Latacunga takes you through the market towns of Zumbagua, Chugchilan, Sigchos, and Saquisilí, then back to Latacunga. Zum-bagua's market on Saturday is stocked with colorful fresh produce. Half an hour's drive further on is Lake Quilotoa, an azure volcanic crater, still considered active. Indigenous people from the Tigua valley nearby sell naïve, brightly colored enamel paintings on sheepskin at the crater rim. On the way north from here to the village of Chugchilan is the Black Sheep Inn (tel: 03-281 4587; www.blacksheepinn.com),

an ecological farm with delicious home cooking and great views over the sierra. The whole loop back takes several hours along mainly dirt roads, so a stop here is a welcome break. **Saquisilí** only comes out of its torpor on Thursday market day. The market is an economic hub for the surrounding region, with *indígenas* buying and selling everything from cattle to cotton. The market is decidedly a local, rather than tourist, affair and a favorite with many travelers for that reason.

Back in Latacunga, the Pan-American Highway continues south, deep into the central Sierra. About 11 km (7 miles) from Latacunga on the outskirts of San Miguel de Salcedo is the Hostería Rumipamba de las Rosas (tel: 03-272 6128), another converted hacienda. Rumipamba serves the best food in the region and an especially good Sunday buffet, with folk musicians playing traditional music. It's a good place to stay, with comfortable rooms, a gym and sauna, swimming pool, and a playground for children.

Some 10 km (6 miles) further south you cross the provincial boundary and enter Tungurahua province, named after the area's dominant volcano. The region is known for its relatively mild climate and production of vegetables, grain, and fruit, including peaches, apricots, apples, pears, and strawberries, and you will encounter roadside vendors along the highway on both sides of Ambato.

Provincial center

Some 128 km (80 miles) from Quito, **Ambato** ❹ is the capital of Tungurahua province. Arriving in the city brings you abruptly face to face with the 21st century. Ambato was almost totally destroyed by an earthquake in 1949 and then rebuilt, so virtually nothing of the colonial town remains. With a population of about 150,000, the city is the fourth largest in Ecuador. Industries include some

Map on page 242

BELOW: the Quilotoa crater lake.

*Guinea pig for sale:
for a pet or the pot?*

textiles (especially rug weaving), leather goods, food processing, and distilling, but the most interesting aspect of Ambato is its enormous Monday market, the largest in Ecuador. Thousands of *indígenas* and country people come into town for the different activities, which take place in various parts of the city. Several plazas contain nothing but produce vendors, while the streets are lined with kiosks selling goods of all kinds. To reach the textiles, dyes, and crafts (ponchos, ikat blankets and shawls, *shigras* bags, belts, beads, hats, and embroidered blouses) follow Calle Bolívar or Cevallos about 10 blocks north from the center of town to the area around Calle Abdón Calderón.

After the market is a good time to visit Ambato's two central plazas. The main one, the **Parque Montalvo**, is named for the writer Juan Montalvo (1833–99), and has an imposing statue of him. Montalvo's nearby house, at calles Bolívar and Montalvo, is open to the public. On the north side of the Parque Montalvo is Ambato's modern **cathedral**, with some fine stained-glass windows. Opposite it is the post office. The **Parque Cevallos**, a few blocks to the northwest, is green and tree-lined, and is the site of the **Museo de Ciencias Naturales** (Natural Science Museum; open Mon–Fri 8am–noon and 2–5.30pm; tel: 03-282 7395; admission fee), packed with stuffed animals and birds of the region. The Río Ambato flows through a gorge to the west of the town center. A walk south along the river leads to the suburb of Miraflores, where there are several fine old *quintas* (country homes) which have gardens open to the public. A paved road leads out of Ambato to the east, past Volcán Tungurahua and down into the Oriente, forming one of the main east–west links between the jungle and Sierra.

BELOW: a colorful
Tigua painting on
sheepskin.

From Ambato, catch a bus or truck 20 km (12 miles) northeast to the small town of **Píllaro**. This is the way to get to the **Parque Nacional Llanganates**,

Map
on page
242

erpetually wrapped in fog and covered with virtually impenetrable cloud forest egetation. These remote mountains appeal to the Indiana Jones in all of us ecause of various accounts of General Rumiñahui hiding Quito's gold here, efore Benalcázar and the *conquistadores* could get to it.

efiant and distinctive

bout 14 km (8 miles) east of Ambato on the road to Baños is **Salasaca**, the me of a small, beleaguered indigenous group, which is struggling to hold on its land and maintain its customs in the face of enormous pressure from *iollos* in the surrounding communities. The Salasaca are said to have been *itmakuna,* part of the Incas' divide and rule policy, under which groups of eople were moved from one part of the empire to another. They are said to have riginated in Bolivia and been sent to Ecuador by the Incas as punishment for a evolt, although there seems to be no documentary evidence for this.

Salasaca men wear black and white ponchos and handmade white felt hats with road, upturned brims at the front and back. Unique to Salasaca are the men's urple or deep-red scarves dyed with cochineal, a natural dye that comes from e female insects that live on the Opuntia (prickly pear) cactus. Salasaca women ear the same hats as the men, brown or black *anakus,* cochineal-dyed shoulder raps, handwoven belts with motifs, and necklaces of red, Venetian glass beads.

A few kilometers past Salasaca is **Pelileo**, a little town in which you wouldn't ant to invest in property: it has been leveled by earthquakes four times in the ast 300 years. As the last quake was in 1949, the present Pelileo is an entirely odern town. There is a small Saturday market, which is attended by many *indí-enas* from Salasaca. It is also Ecuador's major production center for blue jeans.

BELOW: Salasaca *indígenas* returning from market.

Subtropical climate

Beyond Pelileo the highway drops 850 meters (2,780ft) to Baños in only 24 km (15 miles), following various tributaries and then the Río Pastaza itself in its headlong rush to the Amazon basin. The region produces sugar cane for distilled alcohol, and many kinds of fruits and vegetables.

Baños ❺ has always been famous for its thermal hot springs bubbling out of the side of the wild and unruly **Volcán Tungurahua** (5,020 meters/16,465ft). In 1999 the volcano started erupting again and the town was evacuated. Residents fought their way back in at the beginning of 2000 at their own risk, even with the volcano spewing hot rocks and ash only 7 km (4 miles) away. Tungurahua still presents a danger to Baneños and tourists but geologists are keeping a close watch on the peak and will evacuate the town again if activity increases. Eruptions can be viewed safely from Loma Grande (just past Salasaca).

The gentle, subtropical climate and vegetation around Baños (altitude 1,800 meters/5,886ft) is another draw, especially after the chill of the highlands. The region is a hiker's paradise, though obviously you should stay away from Tungurahua. Instead, head along the road between Baños and Puyo skirting the deep canyon of the Río Pastaza, surrounded on all sides by steep mountains covered in cloud forest.

The mountains north of the road are on the edge of one of Ecuador's least known national parks, **Los Llanganates**, where the lost treasure of Atahualpa is supposedly buried. The mountains south of the road are part of another national park, **Sangay**, one of the most biologically diverse areas in the world. Hiking possibilities are infinite, especially near Río Verde (where the spectacular Pailon del Diablo waterfall, about 20 km/12 miles from Baños, deserves a visit) and Machay. With luck and patience, four kinds of monkey, spectacled bears, mountain tapirs, and birds such as the cock-of-the-rock and black and chestnut eagle can be found in the forest away from the road. These forests also contain an exceptionally high diversity of plants, many still unknown to science. A recent study here of just one genus of orchid has turned up 14 new species.

Travelers come here for the hot springs, hiking, and adventure activities. Thousands of Ecuadorians come to pay homage to the Virgin of Baños, known as **Nuestra Señora del Agua Santa** (Our Lady of the Holy Water), whose statue is housed in the basilica in the center of town. The Virgin is credited with many miracles, including delivering people from certain death in a fire in Guayaquil, and saving the lives of travelers when a bridge over the Pastaza River collapsed. The walls of the basilica are hung with paintings depicting these events. The basilica grounds have a small museum with moldering stuffed tropical birds and the Virgin's changes of clothing.

A mountain detour

From Baños, return to Ambato (buses are frequent and the journey takes about an hour) and make a trip to the west. A paved road circles around **Volcán Carihuairazo** (5,020 meters/ft) and **Volcán Chimborazo** (6,310 meters/20,571ft) and heads for Guaranda and the coast.

Baños has its own version of the Hard Rock Café, called the Jack Rock Café. It's a quaint little place in the middle of a strip of bars.

BELOW: thermal baths beneath a waterfall in Baños.

Chimborazo, of course, is the highest peak in Ecuador and it looms over the provinces of Chimborazo, Bolívar, and southern Tungurahua like a giant ice-cream, dominating the landscape *(see pages 119–122 for climbing information)*. The **Reserva Producción Faunística Chimborazo** (Chimborazo Fauna Reserve) is also worth a visit. For more information visit www.ambiente.gov.ec.

The Western Cordillera outside Ambato is the land of emerald mountains. Every inch of the hillsides is farmed by the Chibuleo *indígenas,* turning the land into a patchwork quilt of every shade of green. Every so often, either Carihairazo or Chimborazo pokes its snowy head out above the clouds. The road climbs to the *páramo* above 4,000 meters (13,000 ft), with some superb views of Chimborazo, then drops again to Guaranda, which is 85 km (53 miles) from Ambato. Midway through the journey you enter Bolívar province.

Art and fireworks

About 90 km (55 miles) from Ambato, the capital of Bolívar province, **Guaranda** ❻ (2,670 meters/8,725ft) is a small, sleepy town of 21,000 people that comes alive on Saturday with the weekly market. It is set among seven hills, one of which, Cruz Loma (Cross Ridge), has a giant statue of an indigenous chief, **El Indio de Guarango**, a *mirador* (lookout), and a small, circular museum with pre-Hispanic and colonial artifacts. There are three other small museums in the town with mixed collections including colonial art and ethnographic material: the **Museo Municipal**, the **Museo de la Casa de la Cultura Ecuatoriana**, and the **Museo del Colegio Pedro Carbo**. Opening hours are variable: check on arrival at the tourist information office located on García Moreno (open Mon–Fri 8am–noon and 2–6pm.) The **Parque Central** has a monument to Simón Bolívar, which was a gift from

Map on page 242

TIP

The Manto de la Novia, San Miguel, San Pedro, and Inés María waterfalls near Baños can all be reached by *chiva* bus tours.

BELOW: hotels, bars. and Coca Cola on the main street of Baños.

A pregnant Virgin Mary in the Riobamba museum.

the government of Venezuela. Guaranda is the market center for the **Chimbo Valley**, a rich agricultural region that produces wheat and corn *(maiz)*. A 16-km (10-mile) ride through the valley south from Guaranda takes you to **San José de Chimbo**, an ancient town with colonial architecture and two thriving craft centers. The *barrio* (neighborhood) of Ayurco specializes in fine guitars, hand-made from high-quality wood grown in the province. Tambán *barrio* produces hunting guns and fireworks, but these aren't just any old fireworks. Bamboo frames *(castillos,* or castles) are fabricated in the shape of giant birds, huge tow-ers, or enormous animals, with fireworks attached. They are set off to striking effect at fiestas throughout the country. It's not uncommon for the *castillo* to fall over, shooting sky rockets directly into the crowd. Gringos generally jump for cover behind the plaza fountain, but the Ecuadorians love it.

Ancient center

There is a rough dirt track from Guaranda to **Riobamba ❼**, capital of Chimb-orazo province, but most people return to Ambato and travel the 65 km (40 miles) on the Pan-American Highway. The road climbs up to the *páramo* past the small town of Mocha, skirts the eastern slopes of Carihuairazo and Chimbo-razo, crosses the pass and then drops down into the Riobamba valley. However, a new road is being constructed from Guaranda to Riobamba.

In 1541 the Spanish chronicler, Pedro de Cieza de León, began an epic 17-year horseback journey in Pasto, Colombia, riding south along the Royal Inca High-way through Ecuador, Peru, and Bolivia. By 1545 Cieza was in central Ecuador heading for Riobamba. "Leaving Mocha," he wrote, "one comes to the lodgings of Riobamba, which are no less impressive than those of Mocha. They are situated

BELOW: mules cautiously cross a mountain bridge.

in the province of the Puruhás in beautiful fair fields, whose climate, vegetation, flowers, and other features resemble those of Spain." Chimborazo is still primarily an agricultural province, growing crops such as wheat, barley, potatoes, and carrots, with some grazing land for small herds of sheep, llama, and cattle.

It's only an hour from Ambato to Riobamba, but for each half hour of travel you feel as if you are going back a century. Two more dissimilar provincial capitals located so close to each other would be hard to imagine.

Although Riobamba, at 2,750 meters (8,993ft) is only 180 meters (589ft) higher than Ambato, it feels much colder, perhaps because of the wind sweeping down off the glaciers of Chimborazo. The original Riobamba was founded by the Spanish on the site of a major Inca settlement 21 km (13 miles) away, where the modern town of Cajabamba stands, but the old town was flattened by an earthquake in 1797 and a new location was chosen. The new Riobamba (pop. 150,000) has the architecture and ambiance of an 18th-century town; stately, quiet, and slow – except, of course, on market day, which is Saturday.

Indigenous peoples

Chimborazo province was the pre-Inca territory of the Puruhá tribe. Modern towns such as Guano, Chambo, Pungalá, Licto, Punin, Yaruquies, Alausí, Chunchi, and Chimbo were Puruhá settlements. But, as elsewhere, the Incas moved people around: they settled *indígenas* from Cajamarca and Huamachuco, Peru, in the Chimbo region and moved many Puruhá people to the south.

Today, Chimborazo has an amazing mixture of people who wear different kinds of traditional dress, although there aren't necessarily special names for all these groups. Chimborazo was the site of many *obrajes* (textile sweatshops)

Map on page 242

BELOW: the town of Riobamba, beneath Mount Chimborazo.

in colonial times and after independence. The indigenous population became increasingly impoverished and marginalized through succeeding centuries as they were pushed by new settlers into the mountains or became attached to the country haciendas as *wasipungeros* (serfs).

The Chimborazo *indígenas* did not take mistreatment and injustice lying down. There have been many revolts over the centuries including an uprising of 8,000 *indígenas* around Riobamba in 1764, a revolt in Guano in 1778, and a rebellion in Columbe and Guamote in 1803. Land shortages are still a problem and men from many communities frequently migrate temporarily to the larger cities in search of work. Chimborazo has also seen intensive Protestant Evangelical activity, which has often exacerbated tensions.

The most obvious ethnic marker in Chimborazo is hats. While *indígenas* are increasingly using dark, commercially made fedoras, a large number still wear the handmade white felt hats, especially for fiestas and other special occasions. In the Guamote market you can spot as many as 15 different kinds of white handmade hats being worn. Such variations as the size and shape of the brim and crown and the color and length of the streamers, tassels, or other decorations all indicate the wearer's community or ethnic group.

Dark fedoras are taking over from the traditional white.

BELOW: festival time in Riobamba.

Two areas of the Riobamba market are of particular interest to visitors. Traditional indigenous garments, including such items as hats, belts, ponchos, *ikat* shawls, fabric, *shigras,* hats, and old jewelry (beautiful beads, earrings, and shawl pins) are sold in the **Plaza de la Concepción** on Orozco and 5 de Junio, along with baskets and *ikat* blankets. In one corner of this plaza people set up their treadle sewing machines and mend clothes or sew the collars on ponchos, while other vendors sell aniline (synthetic) dyes. Just south of this

plaza on Calle Orozco is a small cooperative store selling crafts made by the *indígenas* of Cacha.

Another important craft of the Riobamba region is *tagua* nut carving. The egg-sized seeds of the lowland tagua palm are soft when first exposed to air but then harden to an ivory-like consistency. *Tagua* is carved into jewelry, chess sets, buttons, rings, busts, and tiny kitchen utensils. Stores opposite the train station on Avenida Primera Constituyente sell *tagua* crafts. (The Avenue of the First Constitution acquired its name because, after winning independence from Spain, Ecuador's first constitution was written and signed in Riobamba on August 14, 1830.)

About eight blocks northeast of the *artesanías* plaza is the **Plaza Dávalos**, where *cabuya* fiber (made from the Agave americana cactus, the century plant) and products are sold. *Cabuya* crafts have been an important local industry in the region since colonial times. *Indígena* women spin the fiber into cordage, used for the soles of espadrilles, rope, sacks, and saddlebags.

After the market has finished, the town empties rapidly and lapses into somnolence for another week. This is your opportunity to visit the **Museo de Arte Religioso** (open Tues–Sat 9am–12pm and 3–6pm; tel: 03-296 5212; admission charge), housed in the Convento de la Concepción on Calle Orozco at España. Among the items on display are statues, vestments, and a fabulous gold monstrance encrusted with diamonds and pearls.

Four other museums are worth visiting. The museum in the **Colegio Nacional Pedro Vicente Maldonado** (open Tues–Sat 9am–12pm and 3–6pm) at Avenida Primera Constituyente 2412, has natural history exhibits; the **Museo de la Casa de la Cultura** (open Tues–Sat 9am–12pm and 3–6pm) displays archeology; while the **Museo del Banco Central** (open Mon–Sat 8.30am–1.30pm and 2.30–4.30pm; tel: 03-296 5501; admission charge), in the new bank building downtown, has ethnographic and modern art exhibitions. The **Museo de la Ciudad** (open Mon–Fri 8am–12.30pm and 2.30–6pm, Sat 9am–4pm; tel: 03-295 1906) has temporary and permanent exhibits, and concerts on Fridays. Opening times for all these museums can be erratic, so it is worth checking at the tourist information office on Calle 10 de Agosto, near the main plaza. Riobamba also has some majestic old churches, including the **cathedral** on 5 de Junio and Veloz and the circular **basilica** (the only one in Ecuador) on Veloz and Alvarado in the Parque La Libertad.

At sunset, climb to the top of the **Parque 21 de Abril** (located on Calle Argentinos north of the center of town). With luck you can catch the last light on mountains Chimborazo, Carihuairaso, Tungurahua – and **Altar** (5,319 meters/17,457ft), the brooding hulk south of the city in the Eastern Cordillera, known in Quichua as *Capac Urcu* (Great or Powerful Mountain).

Exploring the region

Riobamba is a good base for excursions to the rest of Chimborazo province. For a day trip to buy rugs and visit the artisans at work, catch a bus or cab 12 km (7 miles) north on a subsidiary road, not the Pan-American Highway, to **Guano**. The town is known for its cottage-industry production of fine rugs, handknotted on huge vertical-frame looms. Most shops have a

Map on page 242

BELOW: elegant park and statue, Riobamba.

workshop attached where you can watch the weavers at work. Just a kilometer or two beyond Guano (there is a bus service) is the small town of **Santa Teresita**, which specializes in the production of carrot or potato sacks woven from *cabuya* fiber. Many of the weavers have enormous warping frames in their yards, with hundreds of meters of *cabuya* on them, and you may also see the woven yardage stretched out along the road. At the edge of town is the **Balneario Las Elenas**, with two cold-water swimming pools and one warmer pool, all fed by natural springs, and a cafeteria.

Most of Chimborazo province lies to the south of Riobamba, and it's a part of Ecuador worth exploring. The road to Licto climbs above Riobamba and offers good views of the city and the volcanoes.

A quiet, but extremely traditional Sunday market, drawing *indígenas* from the Laguna Colta area and the usual assortment of vendors, is held in **Cajabamba**, 13 km (8 miles) south of Riobamba on the Pan-American Highway. This was the site of the old Riobamba, which was originally a Puruhá community and then the Inca settlement of Liripamba when it had fine, mortarless stonework, including a temple of the sun, a house of the chosen women, and a royal *tambo* (lodge).

The stones from the Inca buildings were incorporated into the Spanish town, which was destroyed in the 1797 earthquake and subsequent landslide. The only building surviving from the 18th century is the chapel.

About 2 km (just over a mile) beyond Cajabamba is the tiny town of **Balvanera** (also spelled Balbanera), on the shores of **Laguna Colta**. Colta *indígenas* graze their cattle and sheep along the marshy shores of the lake, and use the totora reeds in the lake to make mats *(esteras)* and baskets *(canastas)*.

Cabuya fiber comes from the agave plant and is similar in texture to cotton.

BELOW: *indígenas* farming near Alausí.

Locals claim that the town's little church, with its image of the Virgin of Balvanera, is the oldest in Ecuador, constructed by the *conquistador* Sebastián de Benalcázar and his troops after a victory over the Inca forces, but there is no documentary evidence to support this.

If the journey from Ambato to Riobamba takes you back two centuries, the trip to **Guamote** (51 km/32 miles south of Riobamba) is yet another time warp. The Thursday market is the major weekly fair for the southern part of the province. *Indígenas* on horseback or leading llamas laden with produce arrive from communities where no road reaches. At the animal market much of the bargaining takes place in Quichua, but at the food and clothing markets more vendors speak Spanish. You will see more *indígenas* in different kinds of traditional dress here than at any other market in Ecuador.

Switchback railroad

From here, the highway drops down past Tixan and into **Alausí ❽** (2,356 meters/7,704ft). Alausí was once used as a resort to escape from the heat of Guayaquil, and now it has the feel of a place past its prime. But it has charm, and an interesting Sunday market.

Alausí is still famous, however, for the **Nariz del Diablo** (Devil's Nose) railroad that switchbacks between here and Sibambe, dropping precipitously, on its way between Quito and Sibambe. The railroad used to run all the way to Guayaquil but many switchbacks were washed away in the El Niño storms of 1982–83, and only the part between Riobamba and Sibambe has been repaired. Sibambe is just west of the Devil's Nose, so the most hair-raising part of the trip is still running. *(For more details, see pages 236–37.)* ❑

Map on page 242

BELOW: llamas transport produce to market.

THE SOUTHERN SIERRA

Beautiful colonial Cuenca, the Inca ruins of Ingapirca,
and the valley of Vilcabamba are just three of many reasons
for visiting Cañar, Azuay, and Loja provinces

Map
on page
265

The southern Sierra, consisting of Cañar, Azuay, and Loja provinces, was until recently the least-visited part of the highlands, mainly for reasons of accessibility rather than for lack of attractions. Once a very isolated region, it is now a major stop on the gringo trail from Ecuador to Peru due to improved roadways and an expanding tourist infrastructure. The Andes broaden and flatten out somewhat here, with none of the dramatic snowcaps of the central and northern highlands, but with plenty of stunning green vistas and mountain roads guaranteed to give you an adrenaline rush.

Hub of the south

The jumping-off point for most trips in the south is **Cuenca ❶**, capital of Azuay province, with a population of 600,000, making it Ecuador's third-largest city. Until about 35 years ago, Cuenca was isolated from the rest of Ecuador by the lack of good roads, but now it is connected to both Guayaquil and the northern Sierra by paved highways, as well as by daily flights to Quito and Guayaquil, and (when the railroad is working) *autoferro* connections with the Guayaquil-Riobamba-Quito line at Sibambe.

The Cuenca basin is a major *artesanías* center, producing ceramics, *paja toquilla* (Panama) hats, baskets, and Christmas ornaments, gold and silver jewelry, and *ikat* shawls, ponchos, and blankets. Other industries include textiles, furniture, and automobile tires. The city is the economic and intellectual center of the southern Sierra, with a state university and a long history as the birthplace of artists, writers, poets, and philosophers.

Cuenca is considered to be Ecuador's most beautiful city and in 1999 it was declared a UNESCO World Heritage Site. Cuenca means river basin or bowl in Spanish, and the city is situated at 2,549 meters (8,335 ft) on the banks of the **Río Tomebamba**. It has retained its colonial architecture and feel, with new construction in a neo-colonial style that is compatible with existing structures. The blue domes of the new cathedral dominate the skyline. Because of its cobblestone streets, interior patios, and public plazas overflowing with flowers and greenery, and whitewashed buildings with huge wooden doors and ironwork balconies, Cuenca is a walker's delight.

Originally, Cuenca was a major Cañari settlement. After the Inca conquest, it became an important city called Tumipampa, the Plain of the Knife (Hispanicized as Tomebamba), intended to be the Cuzco of the north. Very little of that Inca city remains. If you follow Calle Larga southeast as it goes downhill along the Tomebamba River (near the junction of Calle Tomás Ordoñez with Calle Larga) you will come to the ruins of **Todos**

PRECEDING PAGES:
patchwork fields of
the southern Sierra.
LEFT: colonial
streets of Cuenca.
RIGHT: after a storm
on the *páramo*.

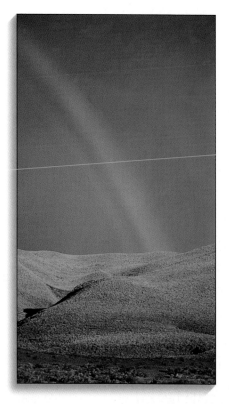

Santos. This small site includes four perfect Inca trapezoidal mortarless stonework niches, and the remains of the colonial mill of Todos Santos, which was constructed with stones taken from Inca buildings. There are remains of Inca walls on the hill side above the mill, where ceramics and other evidence of Inca occupation were excavated.

Colonial culture

In 1532 the Inca armies retreated north before the advancing forces of Sebastián de Benalcázar. Cuenca was founded on this site in 1557, and named Santa Ana de los Cuatro Ríos de Cuenca. As soon as the Spanish arrived in an area they built a church, and Cuenca was no exception. The **Catedral Vieja** Ⓐ (Old Cathedral), on the east side of the main plaza, the Parque Calderón, was begun the year the city was founded. But the city outgrew this simple old church and construction on the **Catedral Nueva** Ⓑ started in 1880. The new church was built to hold 10,000 celebrants during religious events and is opposite the old cathedral on the Parque Calderón. The neo-gothic New Cathedral was intended to be 42.5 meters (141 ft) wide and 105 meters (351 ft) tall, which would have made it the largest church in South America. But the architect miscalculated and designed bell towers too heavy for the structure to support, so work on the towers was halted before completion. It is constructed from alabaster and local marble with floors of pink marble imported from Carrara, Italy.

The **Parque Abdón Calderón** is Cuenca's main square, with the *municipio* (town hall) on the south side. The plaza is busy during the day with locals who come to relax on the many niches amid the tall conifers, orchids, and other plant life. Just off the southwest corner of the square, on Calle Sucre, is the **Casa de**

The bells for Cuenca's cathedral, donated by Germany, have remained at the entrance to the nave ever since construction of the towers had to be abandoned.

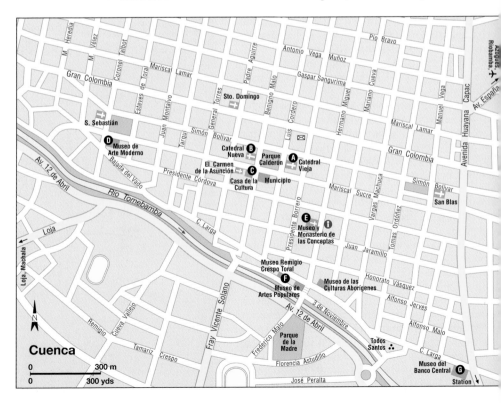

la Cultura Ecuatoriana **C** (open Mon–Fri 9am–7, 8, or 9pm depending on events program). This small colonial-style building frequently has good exhibitions of local art. On the same block is the **Monasterio del Carmen de la Asunción**, founded in 1682. The church has a fine carved stone facade and the pulpit is gilded and embellished with mirrors. However, the building is often closed. A daily flower market is held in the tiny plaza in front of the church and for a few coins you can brighten your hotel room considerably.

The **Museo de Arte Moderno D** (Modern Art Museum; open Mon–Fri 8.30am–1pm and 3–6pm, Sat & Sun 9am–1pm; tel: 07-283 1027) is also on Calle Sucre, at Coronel Tálbot. This museum has rotating exhibitions of contemporary art as well as art workshops for children.

If you're not tired of churches (Cuenca has 27), go back along Calle Sucre and turn right at Calle Hermano Miguel to the **Museo y Monasterio de la Conceptas E** (Church and Museum of the Conception; museum open Mon–Fri 9am–5.30pm, Sat 10am–1pm; tel: 07-283 0625; admission charge). The entrance to the church contains 17th-century tombstones. The cloister, built 1682–1729, has been restored by the Banco Central. The cloister's museum contains an unusual collection of religious art including toys presented to the convent by novices entering the order, a silver nativity scene, and an altarpiece of carved wood and gold by the sculptor Manuel Machina. The museum houses a great collection of lithographs by Oswaldo Guayasamín *(see page 114)*.

The **Museo Municipal Remigio Crespo Toral F**, which is on Calle Larga 7-25 in front of Plazoleta La Merced, is undergoing much-needed restoration but usually houses a wide selection of artifacts, from pre-Hispanic ceramics and goldwork of the Cañari and Chordeleg cultures to colonial paintings,

Map on page 260

BELOW: cupolas in Cuenca.

Detail of a mural in El Turi, Cuenca.

furniture, and religious sculptures. The **Museo del Banco Central Pumapungo** (open Mon–Fri 9am–6pm, Sat 9am–1pm; tel: 07-283 1255; admission charge) is located on Avenida Huayna-Capac across Calle Larga, above the Tomebamba ruins where Inca and Cañari remains and artifacts were unearthed; they now form part of the museum's permanent archeological and ethnographic collection. Colonial and republican art, as well as old photographs of Cuenca, are also on display. The museum inherited the collection of Father Crespi, a Salesian priest who died in the late 1980s. Father Crespi's artifacts consist of an amazing variety of pieces from pure junk to fine pre-Inca ceramics, which the museum is in the process of sorting and dating. Crespi firmly believed that Ecuador was settled by the Phoenicians who sailed up the Amazon.

Also try the **Museo de las Culturas Aborígenes** (open Mon–Fri 8.30am–12.30pm and 2.30–6.30pm, Sat 8.30am–12.30pm; tel: 07-283 9181; admission charge) at Avenida 10 de Agosto 4–70, on the south side of the Río Tomebamba. It holds a fascinating collection of pre-Columbian archeological finds from various cultures throughout Ecuador.

A blending of cultures

Many of the Cuenca valley people occupy an intermediate position between *indígenas* and whites. They are generally artisans and country people and are called *cholos cuencanos*. They represent a mixture of Inca, Cañari, and Spanish blood. The rich *cholo* culture is slowly disappearing as young people adopt modern-style clothing and move to the cities or to work in the United States.

In rural areas and especially at the markets in Sigsig, Gualaceo, Chordeleg, and sometimes in Cuenca you will still see people in traditional *cholo* dress,

Art in Cuenca, past and present: **LEFT:** cathedral door, **RIGHT:** mural in El Turi.

which includes Panama hats for both men and women and colored ponchos, especially burgundy and red, for men. For fiestas, many *cholo* men wear beautiful handwoven *ikat* ponchos *(see chapter on Artesanías, page 107, for details).* If you're in Cuenca for the Thursday weekly fair or for the smaller Saturday market, check out the plaza between Calle Mariscal Lamar and Sangurima off Calle Hermano Miguel, where *artesanías* are sold, including baskets, wool, and *ikat* shawls *(paños).* The permanent food market is on the other side of town, on Calle Cordova off Padre Aguirre.

Southern Ecuador is well-known for its crafts. The Organization of American States has a permanent center in Cuenca for the preservation and promotion of traditional *artesanías:* the Centro Interamerico de Artesanías y Artes Populares (CIDAP); the offices and museum are on the stairs where Calle Hermano Miguel intersects Calle Larga and descends to the Río Tomebamba.

Excursions into the country

Gualaceo is about 36 km (22 miles) from Cuenca on paved roads. Buses run regularly between the two places, heading north of Cuenca on the Pan-American highway, turning east at El Descanso and following the Río Paute. It is a pretty town situated on the banks of the Río Gualaceo and is the site of *quintas*, summer homes for people from Cuenca and Guayaquil. The slightly lower elevation makes it ideal for growing peaches, apricots, apples, cherries, guavas, and custard apples. There are several good restaurants along the river, and an inn, the Parador Turístico Gualaceo *(see Travel Tips pages 341–5 for details).*

Chordeleg, a pre-Inca Cañari town, has artisans of all kinds: *ikat* poncho weavers, Panama hat and basket weavers, potters, embroiderers, and jewelers.

Maps on page 260 & 265

BELOW: laundry drying on the outskirts of Cuenca.

The town is just a few kilometers up the mountain south of Gualaceo, a 10-minute trip in the local bus. The road leading into Chordeleg from Gualaceo is lined with stores selling silver and gold jewelry at very reasonable prices in styles ranging from colonial filigree to modern. Other local *artesanías* and textiles from Otavalo are sold in shops around the main plaza. CIDAP has a small but excellent ethnographic museum on the plaza, with displays of local crafts and a gift shop. The exhibit showing the process used in making *ikat* textiles is especially informative.

There are pre-Inca ruins in the Chordeleg area, including an enormous snake-shaped stone walkway near the entrance to the town, and sites on nearby hill tops that have been excavated. Chordeleg has a small Sunday market, but most people from the town attend the larger market in Gualaceo. From the plaza in Chordeleg you can catch a bus to **Sigsig**, 20 km (12 miles) farther south. Sigsig is a tiny colonial town with an equally tiny Sunday market, but the trip along the river is gorgeous. Two archeological sites, Chobshi and Shabalula, are close by; ask residents for directions.

If you are more interested in wilderness adventures consider visiting the **Area Nacional de Recreación Cajas**, 30 km (19 miles) northwest of Cuenca. The park has hundreds of clear, cold lakes, streams, and rivers at altitudes from 3,500 to 4,200 meters (9,000 to 13,000 ft) on the *páramo* beneath jagged mountain cliffs. You can go swimming (if you're brave), or fishing for rainbow trout, and there are miles of good hiking trails, camping grounds, and even a small refuge.

Herds of llamas and alpacas have been brought in as part of a breeding program to re-introduce these animals to the southern highlands. It is also a wonderful spot for bird-watching, especially around the lakes, where numerous exotic species can be found, including hummingbirds and the occasional condor. Buses to Las Cajas (as the park is known) leave in the early morning from the church of San Sebastián, at calles Bolívar and Talbot in Cuenca, and return late in the afternoon. August to January is the best time to visit and it is a good idea to arrive early in the morning, as the afternoon tends to bring fog, mist, clouds, rain, and sometimes snow. Be sure to bring a good map and compass. Hikers who have come insufficiently prepared have lost their lives here.

Independent traditions

Cañar Province, north of Cuenca, home of the Cañari *indígenas*, has the largest and the most complete accessible Inca ruins in Ecuador. While Cañar is considered a highland province, about one-third of its territory is in the western lowlands, where sugar cane, cocoa, bananas, and other tropical fruits are grown. In both the lowlands and Sierra, extensive territory is given over to cattle grazing on large tracts of land owned by *hacenderos*, despite the Agrarian Reform of 1964.

The Cañaris have never had an easy time of it, at least not since the arrival of the Incas in the 15th century. They were once the principal indigenous group throughout southern Ecuador. At first they resisted the Incas fiercely, at one time defeating them and driving them back to Saraguro.

When civil war broke out in 1527 between two claimants to the throne, Atahulapa in Quito and Huascar in Cuzco, the Cañaris sided with Huascar. Atahualpa

TIP

It is worth noting that entrance to the Cajas National Park costs $10, but a taxi to the information center in the heart of the park will set you back about $15–20.

BELOW: pots for sale.

routed Huascar's army at Ambato and in revenge killed most of the men and boys of the Cañari tribe, despite their surrender. A year after the Spanish captured and killed Atahualpa in Cajamarca, a Spanish force under Sebastián de Benalcázar marched north to plunder Quito. When Benalcázar reached Tumipampa he was joined by 3,000 Cañari warriors, eager for revenge against the Quito Inca forces. The Cañaris fought with the Spanish throughout the conquest of Ecuador, but received scant recognition from the Spanish for their help. By 1544 many thousand Cañari men were working in the gold and silver mines of southern Ecuador and the tribe was so reduced that in 1547 the Spanish chronicler Pedro de Cieza de León noted that the ratio of women to men was 15 to 1.

Currently there are about 40,000 Quichua-speaking Cañari *indígenas* scattered throughout Cañar, the highest province in Ecuador. Most are farmers, but some are sheep- and cattle-herders. They are, on the whole, averse to outsiders and have a reputation for being bellicose.

Cañari men's dress includes the *kushma,* a fine *ikat* poncho for fiesta use, black wool pants, a white cotton shirt with embroidery on the sleeves and collar and an

Map on page 265

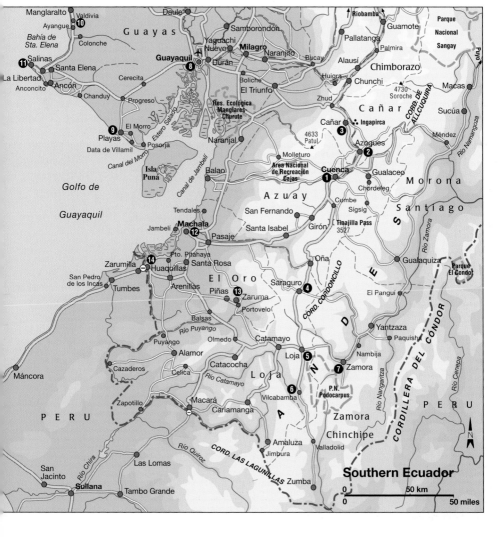

Southern Ecuador

Temporary housing
for dispossessed
Cañari people.

BELOW: hoof-cutting
in the Sierra
near Cuenca.

extremely fine double-faced belt with motifs from local life. Like the men of Saraguro and Otavalo, Cañari men wear their hair in a long braid. The sheepherders wear sheepskin chaps and carry a small whip with a wooden handle, which is worn over their shoulder. The typical Cañari hat, worn by both men and women, is handmade of white felt with a small round crown and narrow brim, turned up at the front. Cañari women wear an embroidered blouse, a shoulder wrap held shut with a *tupu* (shawl pin), and a woolen *pollera* skirt in various colors.

Exploring Cañar

The Pan-American Highway climbs out of Cuenca to **Azogues ❷**, the capital of Cañar province with 28,000 inhabitants. Azogues has a quiet colonial air, with wooden balconies and shutters aslant on ancient whitewashed houses. *Azogue* means mercury, and the town was named after the nearby mercury mines. The **Convento de San Francisco** towers above Azogues on a hill to the southeast. The Spanish practice of building churches on pre-Hispanic Inca holy places *(wakas),* many of which were located on mountain tops, accounts for the large number of churches that are perched at ridiculous heights. If you need the exercise and want the view, it's a half-hour climb to the top.

Azogues has two museums: the **Museo Ignacio Neira** in the Colegio Julio María Matavalle has zoological, archeological, and mineralogical displays, but is open only on request; and the **Museo del Colegio de los Padres Franciscanos**, which houses religious art and archeological artifacts (opening times vary – check when you arrive.)

The Pan-American Highway winds past Azogues and into **Cañar ❸**, which is 65 km (40 miles) from Cuenca and 36 km (22 miles) from Azogues. Cañar is

high and chilly at 3,104 meters (10,150 ft); this is barley, potato, *quinua* (a highly nutritious grain), and cattle country. The town has a fascinating market on Sundays, when *indígenas*, including mounted Cañaris with *ikat* ponchos, whips *(chicotes)*, and sheepskin chaps *(zamarro)* come down off the *páramo* to buy, sell, and trade. The Cañari men's belts are beautifully made in a complex inter-mesh double-faced technique. The best place in town to buy belts is the jail (Centro de Rehabilitación Social), where *indígenas* doing time don't waste time, but spend it weaving. The jailer will unlock the door and let you into the main patio where you will be besieged (in a friendly manner) by prisoners with belts and sometimes ponchos to sell.

Map on page 265

Ecuador's greatest ruins

Many people visit Cañar for the market and then go on to **Ingapirca** (open daily 8am–6pm; admission charge). There are several ways to reach the ruins. You can catch a bus from Cañar, wait by the side of the road for a truck to come along, rent a taxi for the day in Cuenca, rent your own vehicle, or go on an organized tour. Ingapirca can be reached by roads on either side of Cañar. About 2 km (1 mile) south of Cañar a sign on the east side of the Pan-American Highway announces the ruins, which are 15 km (9 miles) down an unpaved road. A kilometer (½ mile) north of Cañar a better, shorter, road (8 km/5 miles) goes east through El Tambo. Alternatively, there is a hiking trail to the ruins, which takes three days from Achupallas, east of Alausí *(see page 117).*

Ingapirca means "Inca stone wall"; the name was given to the site by the Cañaris. We know that the Inca Huayna-Capac built Ingapirca in the 15th century on the royal highway that ran from Quito to Cuzco and stationed soldiers there to keep the Cañaris under control. Throughout the Inca Empire, outlying Inca settlements had multiple functions and were intended to be models of Cuzco on a much smaller scale. From what remains of Ingapirca, the site probably had storehouses, baths, a royal *tambo* or inn for the Inca, dwellings for soldiers and others, and a sun temple, the remains of which can be seen in the beautiful elipse, made of green diorite and modeled after the Koricancha, the main temple in Cuzco. The high-quality stonework indicates that Ingapirca was a very important site.

BELOW: woman from Cañar.

The Incas often chose hill tops for their settlements, both for defensive reasons and to free flat valley land for cultivation. Much of Ingapirca was dismantled over the centuries by local people who used the stones for domestic buildings.

Various other remains surround the main buildings. The Ingachungana, or Inca's playground, is a large rock with carved channels that may have been used for offerings or for divination, with water, *chicha*, or the blood of sacrificed llamas or guinea pigs poured in the channels. Near the Ingachungana is a chair or throne cut in to the rock and called the **Sillón del Inca** (the Inca's Chair). Below in the gorge are several zoomorphic rock carvings that appear to be a monkey and a turtle, and the **Cara del Inca** (the Inca's Face), a large stone outcropping that is probably natural, rather than carved. The site also houses a small museum (open Mon–Sat) with ethnographic and archeological exhibits. The displays include such artifacts from the Cañari and Inca cultures as ceramics, jewelry, and textile fragments. Less than a mile away is the village of **Ingapirca**, which has a crafts cooperative store next to the church and a basic restaurant where the food looks better and better as the day goes on. On Fridays the village plays host to a small but attractive indigenous market.

The far south

Tucked away deep in southern Ecuador between Azuay province and the border with Peru, Loja province is the least visited of the highland provinces, mainly because of its isolation. There are flights to the capital city, Loja, from Quito and Guayaquil, but not from Cuenca, so travelers heading directly south from Cuenca must go overland along the paved Pan-American Highway. Loja is primarily rural and agricultural and there are only a few small towns along the road.

The highway south of Cuenca passes through rich, green land until **Cumbe** (14 km/9 miles), where it begins to climb to **Tinajilla Pass** at 3,500 meters (11,445 ft). It then traverses the *páramo* of **Gañadel**, which is usually misty and fogged in. In the middle of this wilderness, figures bundled in shawls and ponchos will appear out of the fog to flag down the bus.

The clouds sometimes part to surprise you with extensive views of the Western Cordillera and sunlight streaming through in the distance, a sight that looks like a Renaissance artist's idea of the dawn of creation.

From here the road twists a few miles to **Saraguro** ❹, a high, chilly town of about 19,000 inhabitants, mainly *mestizos* and whites. It is the social and commercial center for the Saraguro *indígenas,* relatively prosperous farmers and

Saragueños are said to be descendants of the Incas, who replaced the indigenous Palta people sent to Bolivia by Tupac-Yupanqui.

BELOW: ruins of Ingapirca, Ecuador's major Inca site.

cattle traders who live in small communities *(barrios)* surrounding the town.

The Saragureños are said to be descendants of the Inca conquerors of Ecuador, who were brought to the region after the Inca Tupac-Yupanqui's conquest of the area around 1455. Under Inca rule, each ethnic group was required to retain its traditional costume, especially its headdress and hairstyle. The Spanish outlawed certain kinds of Inca headgear and introduced brimmed hats, but in typically conservative fashion each ethnic group insisted on wearing a distinctive style, which accounts for the plethora of hat styles seen in the Andes today.

The *indígenas* of Saraguro were never serfs on the *haciendas* or laborers in textile sweatshops. They have survived as farmers and cattle traders, supplying much of the beef for southern Ecuador. Because of a shortage of pasture in the Saraguro region the Saragureños drive their cattle over the continental divide and down into the jungle around Yacuambi. The cattle are fattened and driven back up over the Andes to be sold at the Sunday Saraguro market. The people of the Saraguro value education and are among the best-educated *indígenas* in Ecuador, with their own high school, and many young adults attending the universities in Cuenca and Quito. The community has its own doctor and nurse.

Remembering the Inca

Saragureño dress is black or dark indigo-blue wool, which many *indígenas* say they wear in mourning for the death of the Inca Atahualpa. Most of the clothes are handspun and handwoven and everywhere you travel in the Saraguro region you will see women and girls with distaffs and spindles, spinning wool for their family clothing. Most striking, though, is the women's jewelry. Several jewelers in Saraguro specialize in making the large nickel or silver shawl pins *(tupus)*

Map on page 265

BELOW: fine Inca masonry at Ingapirca ruins.

that women use to fasten their shoulder wraps. Fine silver *tupus* are heirlooms passed down through from mother to daughter, as are filigree earrings. Women also wear beaded necklaces. One style has rows of tiny seed beads strung in zig zags, and the colors of the beads and number of rows indicates her community.

Saraguro has two very basic *pensiones* and a couple of bad restaurants, but is worth visiting for the Sunday market. Some crafts, especially the traditional jewelry, are sold in small shops in the main market building and surrounding streets. The town was also an Inca settlement and there are extensive ruins, which are impossible to find without a guide, outside the town in the forests on the slopes of Mount Acacana. The ruins, called **Inca Iglesia** (Inca Church), are large, but overgrown, and contain fine mortarless-stonework walls and channels carved in the rock for the water system.

The Cuenca–Loja bus continues on to Loja after a stop in Saraguro to pick up passengers. If you decide to stay in Saraguro a local Saraguro–Loja bus also makes the round trip between the two places several times a day. Loja is another 61 km (38 miles) from Saraguro, a 2-hour ride along a dizzying corkscrew road.

Woman with a distaff, a common sight in the Saraguro area.

BELOW: skipping Mass in Saraguro.

Colonial center

With improved roads and an influx of tourists heading south, **Loja** ⑤ has caught the eye of passers-by who stop there to enjoy its new amenities and access to Cajas National Park and the surrounding region. It is the capital of the province, and provincial it is: provincial and old. Because the Spanish invasion of Ecuador began in Piura on the north coast of Peru, Ecuador was conquered and settled from south to north. Loja was founded in 1548, which makes it one of the oldest cities in the country. The city has been rebuilt twice due to devastating earthquakes, the last

being in the 1880s. Cieza de León commented on the prosperity of the region and on the vast herds of llamas, vicuñas, and guanacos when he rode through Loja on the Royal Inca Highway, but the Spanish conquerors soon hunted them to extinction. Loja has about 120,000 inhabitants and is nestled among the mountains at a pleasant 2,225 meters (7,275 ft). Because it is so close to the Oriente it is a major entry point to the southern jungle and the province of Zamora-Chinchipe.

A short tourist circuit runs across the town. Begin at the Puerta de la Ciudad (the Door to the City) just north of the center. This castle-like structure was built in 1998 as a replica of a Spanish fortress that was built in Loja in 1571 but later torn down. There is a small modern art gallery and cafe, which has a panoramic view of the city. The path then leads to the pleasant Parque Bolívar and from there to Parque Central, the city's main square.

The city has two universities, one of which has a law school and a music conservatory. It has the inevitable colonial art collection housed in the **Convento de las Conceptas** near the main plaza. A permit from the bishop of Loja is necessary in order to see this collection. A local branch of the **Museo del Banco Central** (open Mon–Fri 9am–1pm and 2–5pm; tel: 07-257 3004; admission charge) occupies a colonial mansion at 10 de Agosto and contains archeological, ethnographic, and colonial art collections.

The **cathedral** and the churches of **San Martín** and **Santo Domingo** have nicely painted interiors, but are otherwise nothing to write home about. The statue of the Virgin of Cisne is kept in the cathedral from August to November. The fiesta of the Virgin takes place on September 8. The religious observances and the accompanying agricultural fair attract pilgrims from throughout northern Peru and the southern part of Ecuador. Further south, just past the Plaza de

Map on page 265

BELOW: Saraguro women at a bus stop.

Map on page 265

TIP

Hostal Madre Tierra (tel: 07-258 0269; www.madretierra1. com) provides an inexpensive and totally relaxing place to stay in Vilcabamba, and horseback riding can be arranged in the valley.

BELOW: old man from Vilcabamba.
RIGHT: young cousins in Saraguro.

Independencia is Lourdes Street, several blocks of which have been restored to highlight their wooden balconies and cobblestone patios. The buildings are home to a wide variety of artisans and galleries.

Valley of the ancients

A popular excursion using Loja as a base is to **Vilcabamba** ❻, 62 km (38 miles) due south. Vilcabamba gained a certain reputation in the 1970s as the valley of the ancients, where an unusual percentage of old people were said to live to be 100 to 120 years old. Disappointingly for those looking for the fountain of youth, these tales turned out to be exaggerated. One book on Vilcabamba, for example, contained a document purporting to be a birth certificate proving that one man was 128 years old. The document, on closer scrutiny, turned out to be a land title in his grandfather's name, which his descendant shared.

Vilcabamba is located at a comfortable, mild 1,500 meters (4,905 ft) and is a visual delight: green, gentle, and pretty. In the past few years the town has become a popular retreat for visitors who want to slow down the pace of their travels and enjoy the tranquil surroundings. There are also plenty of opportunities for horseback riding and hiking up into the nearby **Parque Nacional Poducarpus** (admission charge), one of the most beautiful cloudforest areas in Ecuador. With one of the most diverse ecosystems in the world, it is home to many rare species, including the Andean spectacled bear, and is great for bird-watching. Look out for macaws, Andean cock-of-the-rocks, toucans, hummingbirds, and jocotocos which are endemic to the park. The park is named for the romerillo tree *(Poducarpus montanus)*, a conifer that can grow upwards of 40 meters (130 ft) and lives for more than 1,000 years. Trekking guides can be hired in Loja.

Gold-rush outposts

Although strictly speaking part of the southern Oriente, **Zamora** ❼ is only 60 km (40 miles) from Loja, but they are slow and bumpy miles. A colony was founded here by the Spanish in 1549 at about 970 meters (3,180 ft) above sea level in the headwaters of the Río Zamora. This colony was wiped out by indigenous attacks but undaunted, the Spaniards re-established it and pursued their feverish quest for gold. Around 1560 they refounded the colony, giving it the fanciful title of the Royal Mining Village of the Rich Hill of San Antonio of Zaruma. Gold was successfully extracted for some 70 years before the colony died out once more. Several attempts were subsequently made to re-establish Zamora, the most recent in 1869. It has held on to its existence somewhat precariously since then. In the 1930s there were fewer than a dozen buildings, but by 1953 it had become the capital of the isolated province of Zamora-Chinchipe even though the only access was by mule. The first vehicle made it to Zamora in 1962.

In the 1980s, a new lode of gold was discovered some 15 km (10 miles) northeast of Zamora, in the **Nambija** area, traditional mining grounds of the Incas. Ecuadorian prospectors, hoping to strike it rich, make their way to the Zamora area with their hopes as high as those of their predecessors. The urge to find gold is not something that goes out of fashion. ❑

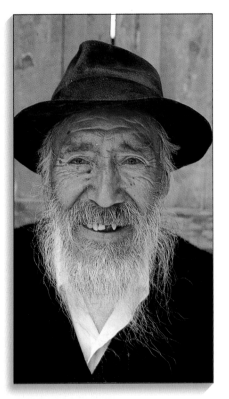

GUAYAQUIL AND THE SOUTH COAST

The vibrant port city of Guayaquil and the beach resorts of the Santa Elena peninsula show a different side of Ecuadorian life

Map on page 265

Many visitors to Ecuador are surprised to learn that the seaport of **Guayaquil ❽** is the country's largest city, with an unofficial population of close to 3 million, nearly half as large again as Quito. This bustling commercial city offers the nation's finest hotels, restaurants, and shopping, along with plenty of mosquitoes. Guayaquil is not for the meek. Situated on the west bank of the busy Río Guayas, navigable for the biggest of ocean vessels heading in from the Pacific via the Golfo de Guayaquil, this city handles 90 percent of Ecuador's imports and 50 percent of its exports. Having previously lacked in tourist attractions, the city has redefined itself amid a flurry of building projects and investments in several districts. The regenerated Malecón 2000, formerly Malecón Simón Bolívar, now has parks, malls, restaurants, museums, and markets. The faded Las Peñas district has been completely restored and become a much friendlier place.

During the rainy season, January to April, the heat and humidity are oppressive, but from May to December the climate is pleasant with little or no rain and cool nights. And Guayaquil, with its new image, is dotted with wide concrete boulevards, spacious parks, and colorful gardens, as well as beautiful monuments, attractive residential neighborhoods, museums with rich archeological and art collections, and excellent restaurants. Its most obvious attraction is the **Guayas** itself. The chocolate-colored river teems with ships, small boats, dugout canoes, and rafts loaded with produce from the inland villages and plantations. Considered one of the cleanest deepwater ports in this part of the world, it is also a controversial spot. Although Ecuador is not considered a major drug-trafficking country, Guayaquil figured prominently in a drug scandal several years ago when 3 tonnes of cocaine in boxes labeled "Ecuadorian cocoa" were shipped from here to the United States. But the so-called Great Chocolate Cocaine Caper was an exception to the mostly legitimate traffic that moves on the Río Guayas. In Guayaquil, a number of travel agencies offer river tours, taking visitors past small settlements, farms, and cattle ranches along this lush, tropical river and through locks into the Salado estuary where the city's seaport area is located.

A name inspired by tragedy

Although Spanish explorer Francisco de Orellana – credited with discovering the Amazon River – claimed to have founded Guayaquil, it was inhabited long before the Spanish arrived. The Valdivia people flourished in the area around 2000BC, followed by the Huancavilcas. Legend has it that the Huancavilca chieftain, Guayas, killed his beautiful wife Quil then drowned himself so

PRECEDING PAGES: gathering shrimp larvae in the province of Guayas. **LEFT:** The Malecón 2000 development. **BELOW:** the city's bustling center.

Cementerio General

Julian Coronel
Julian Coronel
Julian Coronel

Vicente Piedrahita

Galecio

Quito

Lorenzo de Garaicoa

Riobamba

Jimena

Avenida Boyacá

Loja

Baquerizo Moreno

Moreno

Galecio

García

Avenida Machala

Avenida

Pedro Moncayo

Alejo Lascano

Escobedo

Chimborazo

Mendiburo

General Córdova

Avenida Rocafuerte

Banco Central

Antepara

TARQUI

Luis Urdaneta

José de

Rumichaca

Padre Solano

ROCA

Riobamba

Junín

Luis Urdaneta

Roca

Avenida 9 de Octubre

Casa de Cultura

Parque del Centenario

Victor Manuel Rendón

La Merced

Plaza La Merced

Durán Ferry

de Arte Contemporáneo

Piscina Olímpica, Hotel Oro Verde

Vélez

Avenida Machala

Avilés

Avenida 9 de Octubre

Panamá

San Francisco

ROCAFUERTE

Aguirre

Luque

Avenida

Boyaca

Chile

Vélez

La Rotonda

Quito

Parque Victoria

Juan Pio Montúfar

Clemente Ballén

Francis

Aguirre

Pedro Carbo

Museo Nahim Isaías B.

Malecón Simón Bolívar

Pedro Moncayo

Avenida

Colón

10 de Agosto

Catedral

Unicentro

Parque Bolívar

Palacio de Gobierno

Malecón 2000

6 de Marzo

Rumichaca

Sucre

Avenida Boyaca

Museo Municipal

Pedro Carbo

Pichincha

Palacio Municipal

Torre Morisca

Alcedo

Pedro Pablo Gómez

Fco. Campos

Avenida Olmedo

Chimborazo

Colón

BOLÍVAR

Benalcazar

Larayen

Chile

Mercado La Bahia

Ayacucho

Luzarraga

Simón Bolívar

Malecón 2000

Río Guayas

Franco Dávila

Lorenzo de Garaicoa

Noguche

OLMEDO

Avenida Olmedo

Huancapac

Malecón

N

Guayaquil

0   300 m
0   300 yds

Manabi

Chimborazo

Huancavilca

Map
on page
265

hat the Spaniards would not capture them. The tragedy of this doomed couple s allegedly to be what inspired the city's name.

While fairly calm and conventional Quito was worrying only about infrequent earthquakes, Guayaquil spent its first 400 years fending fires. The last major blaze, in 1896, destroyed a large number of Guayaquil's charming wooden houses. The different natures of Quito and Guayaquil – one a sophisticated center for art and culture, the other a center of commerce occupied by tattooed sailors and hard-working, hard-drinking laborers – bred a rivalry between the cities. It is common for competing presidential candidates to be from one or the other, and while Quiteños think the Guayaquil residents rough and unrefined, Guayaquil dwellers think the residents of the capital are dull and backward, not to mention foolish for living in a city with no nightlife and no beaches. Guayaquileños claim that they make the country's money and the Quiteños spend it.

Brassy wealth

Despite its development problems Guayaquil is a growth area, a center of industry with oil and sugar refineries, cement mills, breweries, and all types of manufacturing. It is an attractive destination for visitors seeking luxurious hotels, fine restaurants, clubs for tennis, golf, yachting, and swimming, exciting nightclubs and upscale shopping – including a bevy of duty-free stores. The once high crime rate has been drastically reduced in many areas of the city, particularly in the Las Peñas district.

There is no straightforward way to see the sights of Guayaquil, but a suggested route is to visit the scattered downtown places of interest first, then follow the extensively refurbished Malecón along the water's edge, past the docks

BELOW: Guayaquil's urban sprawl.

A model ship in the Museo del Banco Central.

to Las Peñas. Start with a visit to the neo-Gothic **cathedral** on the west side of Parque Bolívar, on Calle Chile between 10 de Agosto and Clemente Ballén. The cathedral was built in 1948, with lovely stained-glass windows and a Cuenca marble altar. Its side altars are overwhelmed by innumerable votive candles lit by the devout; some people even hold candles in their hands while walking around the church praying. The original wooden cathedral, built in 1547, burned down in one of the city's many fires.

Parque Bolívar (more correctly known as Parque Seminario) is perhaps the most interesting park in the city, The old, well-maintained botanical garden earned its nickname from its equestrian statue of Bolívar; around the statue's base are bas-relief depictions of that mysterious Guayaquil meeting between Bolívar and San Martín (*see page 282*). The pavilion and gates in this century-old park came from France. The park is best known, however, for the hundreds of green tree iguanas – some of them a meter in length – that roam freely in the park. Try to visit at feeding times when they come down from the trees. A small pond is home to several species of turtles and tortoises.

On the other side of the park is the **Unicentro Shopping Center**. The **Uni-hotel** at this sparkling indoor gallery of shops and services has gained a reputation for its cocktails, including its *jipijapa*, a blend of orange *aguardiente*, grenadine, and lemon served with a slice of pineapple.

From here, walk two blocks along Calle Chile to the plaza and church of **San Francisco** . The church was built in 1603 and beautifully restored in 1968. You'll also see that many streets in the central district preserve porticos protecting pedestrians from the the elements. Going west along Avenida 9 de Octubre you will come to the **Parque del Centenario**, the city's largest plaza,

covering four city blocks. It is filled with monuments, the most important being the patriotic liberty monument with the likenesses of Ecuador's heroes, and smaller statues representing history, justice, patriotism, and heroism.

Map on page 278

Pre-Columbian artifacts

Just outside the park on 9 de Octubre and Moncayo is the **Casa de Cultura Ecuatoriana ❻** (Tues–Fri 10am–6pm, Sat 9am–3pm; admission charge) with a display of pre-Columbian artifacts found in archeological digs on the country's coast. This museum once had an impressive collection of gold items – reported to be Ecuador's most valuable pre-colonial gold collection – but many of them mysteriously disappeared; those that remain at the museum are not publicly displayed. Current exhibits range from clay whistles known as *ocarines* to molds for casting gold masks and colonial art. Other artifacts – including ceramics, textiles, gold, and ceremonial masks – are located at the **Museo Nahim Isaias del Banco Central de Ecuador ❼** (Pichincha and Clemente Ballén; open Wed–Sat 10am–6pm; Sun & holidays 10am–5pm; tel: 232 4182; admission charge; free Sun), three blocks to the west on the same street, beside the US Embassy and opposite the **Hotel Oro Verde**, the best spot in town for a gringo breakfast.

Go south from here down Calle García Moreno, and you will find the **Piscina Olímpica ❽** (Olympic Swimming Pool). To reach the most intriguing museum in town walk four blocks south then turn left on Calle Sucre and head back toward the Malecón to the **Museo Municipal ❾** (open Tues–Sat 9am–5pm), which has a macabre collection of the Jivaro *tzantzas* – or shrunken heads – prepared by jungle tribes using secret processes scientists are still unable to unravel. There are theories on how the human heads were reduced to fist size without losing their

BELOW: monument to the meeting between Simón Bolívar and José de San Martín.

original features, but there is no consensus. A 1988 sale at Christie's auction house in London brought in bids of several thousand dollars apiece for such shrunken heads. Tourists in Ecuador are occasionally offered *tzantzas* for sale, although authorities say these are not only illegal but are almost certainly monkey – not human – heads. This museum also displays Inca and pre-Inca ceramics from the Huancavilca and Valdivia peoples, colonial art, modern art, and local handicrafts.

On the waterfront

Running along the Río Guayas from Las Peñas at the north end to the very exclusive Club de la Unión is the tourist-friendly promenade Malecón 2000, or Malecón Simón Bolívar. The tree-lined boardwalk is filled with restaurants, roaming vendors, parks, monuments, and activities for families. At the Las Peñas end is the new **Museo Antropológico y de Arte Contemporaneo** (MAAC; Wed–Sat 10am–6pm; Sun & holidays 10am–4pm; tel: 230 9400; admission charge; free Sun), which combines the ancient and the new with more than 50,000 archeological pieces and 3,000 works of modern art. There is an independent movie and IMAX theater next door. Further north are three postmodern monuments known as the Torres de Aire, Agua, y Tierra (Air, Water, and Earth).

At the **Torre Morisca** ⓖ, a Moorish clock tower dating from 1770, climb the narrow winding stairway to the room containing the clock workings, from where there is an excellent panoramic view of the city. The clock tower's gardens are a favorite meeting spot for young couples in the early evening. Across the street is the stately colonial **Palacio Municipal**, separated from the severe **Palacio de Gobierno** by a plaza with a statue dedicated to General Sucre, hero of Ecuador's war of independence.

Moving south, you will find the replica of Henry Morgan's pirate ship. One-hour rides are offered in the afternoons and evenings. Just past the Club de la Unión at Plaza de la Integración you will find the Eiffel-designed Antiguo Mercado Sur de 1907, now known as the **Palacio de Cristál**, or Crystal Palace. It is an exhibition hall and gallery displaying temporary exhibits.

Meeting place of the liberators

At the foot of Avenida 9 de Octubre at Malecón 2000 you will see the semicircle of **La Rotonda** ⓗ. Its statue commemorates the historical but mysterious meeting between the continent's two great liberators, Venezuelan Simón Bolívar and Argentine General José de San Martín. Bolívar had freed the countries to the north and San Martín was responsible for the independence of Argentina and Chile but their final plans differed – Bolívar wanted the countries united under a democracy with an elected president and San Martín envisioned a monarchy. The meeting resulted in the Acuerdo de Guayaquil (Guayaquil Accord), which established the short-lived Gran Colombia, uniting Venezuela, Colombia, and Ecuador. There was no witness to the exchange between the two men and the only thing that is known for sure is that when the meeting ended, Bolívar remained and San Martín went into exile in France. La Rotonda is built so that people can stand on either side of the statue, whisper, and hear one another. From here

If you like a party, come to Guayaquil on July 24/25, when riotous celebrations mark Bolívar's birthday and the founding of the city. You'll need to book a hotel room well in advance.

BELOW: the Moorish-style clock tower on Malecón 2000.

you can enjoy an impressive view of the hill known as Cerro del Carmen and, far beyond, the Guayaquil-Durán bridge – the country's largest at 4 km (2½ miles) long and the link to the Durán rail terminal.

At the upper end of the Malecón, past restaurant boats, working docks, and the Durán ferry exit, Calle Numa Pompilio Lloma mounts the side of Cerro Santa Ana and enters the picturesque bohemian district of **Las Peñas**. Here, the wooden architecture shows the influence of the Pacific naval yards during the period of Spanish colonization. On the small **Plaza Colón**, where the narrow winding street with its original cobblestone paving begins, two cannons commemorate the defense of the city against pirate invasions. Continued investment in the area has paid off and it is filled with tourists who climb the scenic 444 steps up through the district to the *mirador* above. At the top there is a small fortress with canons, naval artifacts, and the Pirate Bar, a great place to catch your breath after the climb.

The romantic 19th-century neoclassical houses bordered by jasmine bushes are today inhabited mostly by artists and are filled with craft shops, cafes, bars, and galleries. No. 186 is the home of the well-known painter Hugo Luís Lara. From the top of the **Santa Ana** hill there is a spectacular view of the city, salt estuaries, the new port, and the river. Although security has dramatically improved, it is not advisable to climb the hill after dark. This area also has an open-air theater – Teatro Bogotá – and, just behind, the oldest church in Guayaquil, **Santo Domingo**, founded in 1548 and undergoing extensive restoration. A patio at the left-hand side of the church's nave contains a spring credited with miraculous healing powers. Stairs to the right of the church and the steep Buitron Street lead to **Cerro del Carmen**, topped by the Cristo del Consuelo monument. (Because of the isolation of this spot and crime problems, this is best visited on an organized tour.) At the foot

Map on page 278

BELOW: images of urban regeneration in Guayaquil: Las Peñas district and Malécon 2000.

of the hill is the dazzling white cemetery, the **Cementerio General**, with its avenue of royal palms leading to the grave of 19th-century President Vicente Rocafuerte, elaborate marble sculptures, and imposing Greco-Roman mausoleums.

Beaches of the south

Selling salsa by the sea.

Guayaquil is an important meeting city for business executives but rarely the sole destination of tourists. Rather, it is the jumping-off point for the beaches of Ecuador's southern coast. There has been a surge of development on the coast from Guayaquil to Manta and resorts have appeared where once there was only dirt road. Miles of sandy beaches are lapped by warm salt water and toasted by the tropical sun. People with fair skin should take precautions under these burning rays; sometimes less than half an hour of unprotected sun can cause severe sunburn. Although weekends and the December to April vacation season see much beach activity, the area is all but deserted during the week. The road south from Guayaquil passes through dry scrubland, with the scenery undergoing an astonishing change from wet fields of rice and bananas to an arid – but attractive – landscape with strange bottle-shaped kapok trees and scattered bright flowers.

BELOW: a bus will take you to the beach.

Traffic on the coastal road, which passes the busy villages of **Cerecita** and **Progreso** about 70 km (42 miles) outside of Guayaquil, is heavy from January to April during local vacation months, and on weekends. In Progreso (officially called Gomez Rendón), the road forks off to the right to Salinas and Santa Elena. A left-hand fork leads to the popular beach resort of **Playas ❾** (officially known as General Villamil), an important fishing village. Old balsa rafts, similar to craft used in pre-Inca times, line the beaches, and are found only in this area. They are still used by some of the fishermen who bring in a catch every afternoon. However,

the main focus of this little town is tourism, and the sandy beaches are the lure for weekend crowds. An alternative to the main beach with its hotels, including the popular Playas and Rey David, and the villas used as escape destinations for Guayaquil residents, is the beautiful beach to the north, called the Pelado. It is a long and lonely stretch set against the backdrop of a cliff. For overnight stays in Playas, the best lodgings are to be found in the more expensive *hostería* Bellavista (tel: 04-276 0600) on the main road to Data just outside the village.

About 14 km (8 miles) south along the coast from Playas is **Data de Villamil**, interesting for its traditional wooden shipbuilding industry. An inland road from here passes the old village of El Morro with its huge wooden church, and farther along is the fishing village of Posorja with commercial boats and hundreds of seabirds wheeling around the **Canal de Morro**, used by overseas vessels bound for Guayaquil. Shrimp farming produced an economic boom in the village, which has grown rapidly over the past few years. This is a pleasant stop on a day trip even though the beaches are not really good for swimming.

Opposite Posorja is the large island of **Puná**, which was already inhabited in pre-Inca times as evidenced by the traces of two settlements from the Valdivia culture that archeologists have found there. The island is quite difficult to reach as there is no public transport, although boats can be hired for the trip in Guayaquil: contact the Capitanía del Puerto or the Yacht Club for details.

Cactus and tuna

Lined with new hotels and resorts, and countless seafood restaurants, the stretch of road from Salinas to Manta is known as the Ruta del Sol (the Sun Route). To reach the Santa Elena Peninsula you must go back to Progreso, and take the right-

Map on page 265

BELOW: *ceviche carts on the beach at Montañita.*

hand road to Salinas through an increasingly dry, cactus-covered landscape. At Km 35.6 outside Progreso is the road to the fishing village of **Chanduy**, a mecca for archeologists who have made important discoveries while excavating the remains of Valdivia, Machalilla, and Chorrera indigenous settlements. This is considered to be the oldest agricultural settlement on the continent where ceramics were made, and may have been a ceremonial center. Nowadays, as in all the fishing villages along this route, the biggest catches are brought close to the shore with the cold Antarctic-born Humboldt Current. The tuna and marlin feed here on smaller, warm-current fish.

Fragments of multi-colored female figures have been unearthed during archeological digs on Valdivian sites.

Just before reaching Chanduy is the recently inaugurated **Museo Real Alto** (daily 10am–5pm; admission charge), which takes the form of two giant huts covered with straw roofs. Poorly marked, it is to the left of a directional sign reading *Fabrica Portuguesa*. Among the exhibits at this museum is one demonstrating how the local inhabitants live.

Back to the main roadway, at Km 49.5, a right-hand deviation in the road leads to the **Baños de San Vicente**, a large complex in which water is channeled into swimming pools and mud baths that are said to have curative powers. Farther down the main road is **Santa Elena**, interesting only for its church and usually bypassed in favor of La Libertad and Salinas. However, on the outskirts of the town near a Mormon temple with a small tower is the **Museo Los Amantes de Zumba** (The Lovers of Zumba) archeological site. Two human skeletons estimated to be 3,500 years old are caught in an after-life embrace in the grave, which falls under the auspices of the Archeological Department of the Banco Central in Guayaquil. **La Libertad**, the largest town on the peninsula with over 70,000 inhabitants, is a busy port with a market that serves as the hub for bus services far-

ther north. Take the right-hand fork in the road going north toward Manglaralto. There are several fishing villages along this stretch of coast, where Guayaquileños have vacation homes, but there are no restaurants or hotels. **Punta Blanca** has an exquisite, isolated beach that attracts shell collectors. **Ayangue**, 45 km (28 miles) farther north, has white beaches, a gentle slope, and no big waves, making it ideal for children. **Valdivia ⑩**, 5 km (3 miles) up the coast, is the center of Ecuador's oldest culture, established around 3000BC, and has an interesting museum of local finds (although its best pieces are in museums in Quito and Guayaquil).

A few kilometers north, **Montañita**, which for many years was simply a locally known surf spot, has blossomed into the largest surf resort in the country and one of Ecuador's largest backpacker hangouts. Many cheap hotels, jewelry stands, restaurants, and bars and clubs line the cluster of streets. The town is a good base for arranging tours into Machalilla National Park, Isla de Plata, and for whale-watching, paragliding, or kitesurfing. The beach is crowded during the summer months and filled with umbrellas, beer vendors, surfers, and carts selling *ceviche de ostra* (oyster ceviche). More up-market accommodations can be found at the north end of the beach, known as Baja Montañita, and in the town of Olon a few kilometers north. Some 3 km (2 miles) south of Montañita is **Manglaralto**, which is a small, cozy town with several small yet decent hotels offering great value for money, such as Hotel Manglaralto just off the beach beside the central park.

Some 6 km (4 miles) south of Salango is an interesting ecological resort, called the **Centro Turístico Ecológico Alandaluz** (Alandaluz Ecological Tourist Center), with buildings constructed of locally grown, easily replenishable bamboo and palm-leaf thatch. The cabins and towers are set out attractively among organic gardens overlooking the sea. The gardens produce much of the food that is served in the restaurant, water and rubbish are recycled, and innovative organic bathroom facilities convert human waste into fertilizers for the land.

Map on page 265

Summer beach mecca

Retrace your steps down the coast to reach Ecuador's most fashionable resort town, **Salinas ⑪**, lying in a half-moon bay on the tip of the **Santa Elena Peninsula**, a total of 150 km (90 miles) from Guayaquil. It has pleasant beaches, tall buildings, excellent hotels, good restaurants, a casino, and a yacht club that lure throngs of swimmers and sun baskers. It is also the site of a naval base.

About 9 km (5 miles) from Salinas is **Punta Carnero** with a beach several kilometers long. From the Hotel Punta Carnero (tel: 04-294 8477), situated on a cliff, you have a marvelous view of the ocean and the hotel has a good restaurant. Fishing charters can be arranged from here, and it's also a good spot to see whales (July–September) and wading birds. For the best seafood in Salinas, try the Mar y Tierra; for vigorous nightlife there is the Oyster Catcher nightclub.

The deep south

To get to the next destination you must return to Guayaquil and take the road to Azogues, turning off after about 20 km (12 miles) toward Machala in **El Oro**, the

BELOW: the sandy beach at Salinas.

Map on page 265

TIP

Machala has a wide range of inexpensive Chinese restaurants, known in Ecuador as *chifas*.

southernmost of Ecuador's provinces, which owes its name to the rich gold deposits mined here during the 16th century. It is now Ecuador's leading banana and shrimp-producing region. The fields here are blanketed by massive banana plantations, the ripening fruit protected by plastic bags. **Machala** ⑫, the main city, is known as the "World Banana Capital." The International Banana and Agricultural Festival is held here every year in late September and draws large crowds. With 200,000 inhabitants, Machala is Ecuador's fourth-largest city. Although not particularly attractive, it is a thriving town with some comfortable hotels and an international port, **Puerto Bolívar**, near the popular **El Coco** beach. Some 1 million tonnes of banana and shrimp exports pass through Puerto Bolívar annually, and from its boat pier motorized dugouts can be taken to the archipelago of **Jambelí**, an extraordinarily beautiful area that is little explored by visitors to the region.

Other side trips are available from Machala, including a journey to the pleasant farming center of **Santa Rosa**, on the Loja road, and then on to the beautiful old coffee-growing town of **Piñas** (take a left-hand turn about 20 km/12 miles from Santa Rosa) before reaching the mining town of Zaruma. The road is flanked by banana, coffee, and cacao plantations.

Town among the ruins

The road from Piñas continues to **Portovelo** from where you can see the town of **Zaruma** ⑬ stuck to the mountainside like a swallow's nest. This mining town of 8,000 inhabitants was founded during the colonial-era gold boom and recently attracted renewed interest with the discovery of pre-Columbian ruins at Chepel, Trencillas, Payama, and Pocto. Although the ruins have not yet been fully excavated, they have led archeologists to conclude that the area was densely populated in pre-Inca times.

The town conserves much of its colonial past: its wooden houses, elaborately decorated balconies and church are well worth seeing. From the main plaza, there is a fantastic view of the surrounding valley.

Interesting visits to abandoned gold and silver mines can be arranged through the city council, the Consejo Municipal, or with local travel agents. A stop at the **Museo Municipal** (open Wed–Sat 8am–noon & 2–6pm, Sun 8am–noon), with displays of archeological artifacts, colonial art, and Zaruma's history, is also recommended.

To the far south of Machala, the route ends at **Huaquillas** ⑭, next door to Peru. Maps have been reprinted to show the new border along the Cordillera del Condor, which was agreed on in 1998. Since the signing of the peace treaty, relations between the two countries have been cordial. This border not only marks the beginning of Peruvian coastal desert, but is one of the continent's main cross-border commercial centers – although much of what is bought and sold is contraband.

Huaquillas is a busy, dusty, and unattractive town with stagnant water lying on its rutted roads and a reputation for pickpockets – who generally seek out tourists, sometimes returning stolen passports if a reward is proffered and no charges are pressed. The only decent hotel is the government-run Parador Turistico, north of town, with a restaurant and swimming pool, the latter being a welcome relief from the insufferable heat and dust, but most people stay overnight in Machala.

The main street of Huaquillas leads to the **International Bridge** into Peru and is lined with street vendors, moneychangers, police and border officers, and people offering to carry luggage. Travelers must cross the bridge on foot unless they are driving their own car or on a direct bus to Tumbes, Peru. ❏

ABOVE: Machala is the banana capital of Ecuador.
RIGHT: a parade in Guayas province.

THE GALÁPAGOS ISLANDS

"Seeing every height crowned with its crater, and the boundaries of
most of the lava streams still distinct, we are led to believe that
within a period geologically recent, the unbroken ocean was here
spread out. Hence, both in space and time, we seem to be brought
somewhat near to that great fact, that mystery of mysteries – the
first appearance of new beings on this earth."
— CHARLES DARWIN, *The Voyage of the Beagle*

The Galápagos Islands had their fame guaranteed in 1835 when the 26-year-old naturalist Charles Darwin landed on one of their black volcanic coasts. Darwin had begun revealing his extraordinary powers of observation during a voyage around the globe on HMS *Beagle*. No other place would prove to be quite as fertile for his work as the Galápagos. Some 20 years later (in 1859), Darwin published *The Origin of Species*, making the creatures of the Galápagos a cornerstone of his theory of evolution by natural selection, in one stroke overturning the whole train of Western scientific thought. Wildlife is still the main reason why visitors fly the 960km (570 miles) from mainland Ecuador to the Galápagos archipelago, which was designated a World Heritage Site in 1979 and subsequently a World Biosphere Reserve by UNESCO in 1985.

The islands are the ultimate natural zoo, where bizarre fauna exist totally free and fearless of man. Giant lumbering tortoises, blue-footed boobies, and equatorial penguins carry on their daily routine, indifferent to their audience of human visitors only feet away. Baby sea lions play with swimmers in the water and perform somersaults. Come as close as you like, and the marine iguanas sunning themselves on black rocks will just sit and stare blankly back.

Although these animals have been able to thrive on the Galápagos, the islands' landscapes are mostly bleak and sunparched. Until recently, permanent human settlement had been kept to a minimum. In 1959, the Ecuadorian government declared the islands a national park and restricted human settlement to the small outposts already established. Today the Charles Darwin Research Station on Santa Cruz, founded in 1964, and the Marine Research Reserve, created in 1986, have their hands full trying to restore the Galápagos to the days before humans began to upset the delicate ecological balance. In December 2001, UNESCO also declared the Marine Reserve around the islands a World Natural Heritage Site in an attempt to stop illegal fishing and in recognition of the conservation issues it faces.

But the sad fact is that however hard the conservationists, scientists, and authorities work together, it is possible that the only way the islands and their inhabitants will be preserved unharmed is by ending tourist visits altogether.   ❑

PRECEDING PAGES: volcanic eruption on Isla Isabela; marine iguana colony, Punta Espinosa; giant tortoises near Volcán Alcedo.
LEFT: marine iguanas sunbathe on the cliffs at Plaza Sur.

THE GALÁPAGOS: DARWIN'S ZOO

Map on page 318

The volcanic archipelago teems with rare bird and marine life that can be seen nowhere else in the world

The "living laboratory" of the Galápagos archipelago is set in the Pacific Ocean some 960 km (570 miles) west of the Ecuadorian coast. It consists of 13 major islands, six small ones, and 42 islets that are barely more than large rocks. All are of volcanic origin and spread over roughly 80,000 sq. km (30,000 sq. miles) of ocean. Their highest point is Volcán Wolf, at 1,707 meters (5,600 ft) on Isabela, which, at 4,600 sq. km (1,800 sq. miles), is by far the largest island.

Visited at different times by explorers from around the world, most of the islands have two or even three different names. British pirates gave them solid, Anglo-Saxon names like Jervis and Chatham; the Spanish dubbed them from their standard stock of place names, such as Santa Cruz and Santa Fe; while the Ecuadorian Government in 1892 tried to clear up the confusion by giving the islands official titles: the effort was unsuccessful and each usually has at least two names still in use. Even the name Galápagos has been changed several times before being officially restored in 1973: taken from a Spanish word for tortoise, it refers to the giant creatures that most astonished the first explorers.

An eccentric climate

The Galápagos year can be divided into two seasons: the "hot" or "wet" season lasts from January to early May with an average temperature of 28°C (82°F), while the "cool" or "dry" season from May to December has an average of 18°C (64°F). The cooler period is also referred to as the *garua* season, named after the bank of clouds that generally settles over the islands at this time.

Altitude also has an effect on the climate: it can be hot and dry in the low-lying parts of the islands, and almost cold and humid in the highlands (above 22 meters/72 ft). The winds, the marine currents, and the geological formation of the soil can alter the climatic conditions considerably: generally speaking, the beaches with white sands are cooler on the feet, while stretches of black lava can reach temperatures of up to 50°C (120°F).

Two marine currents pass along the archipelago. The cold Humboldt Stream originates in the south of Chile and brings the *garua* with it in May. It has a moderating effect on the whole climate of the Galápagos, which should be more punishing than it actually is, given the islands' position directly on the equator.

The other current is the warm northern stream called El Niño, "the boy child," because it arrives around Christmas time, although its effects are rarely welcome: it brings heavy rains and – on occasion – floods and tidal waves to the Ecuadorian mainland.

LEFT: king of the islands.
BELOW: the naturalist Charles Darwin, who visited the islands in the early 1830s.

Geology of the islands

What we see of the Galápagos Islands is the tips of various gigantic "shield vol-canoes" poking up some 10,000 meters (30,000 ft) from the ocean floor and composed entirely of basalt. Some scientists once believed that the islands were the remains of a sunken continental platform that was linked to the South American continent during the Miocene era. But today it is widely accepted that the archipelago was formed mainly by the accumulation of lava from successive underwater volcanic eruptions.

Preserving the surface.

It appears that the earliest of the islands were formed roughly 4 to 5 million years ago, and that some of the western islands, such as Fernandina and Isabela, are only 1 million years old. The process of island formation is still going on. The Galápagos lie on the northern edge of the Nazca tectonic plate – one of the several huge landmasses that, over millions of years, slowly move around the earth's surface.

Over time, this gradual continental drift takes them toward the southeast – precisely over one of the world's so-called "hotspots." These volatile, unmoving points beneath the tectonic plates build up heat over time to create a volcanic eruption that will rise above the ocean's surface. The southeastern islands of the Galápagos were the first formed in this way, and the more recent, western islands still have active volcanoes. The US scientist Benjamin Morrel witnessed an eruption on Fernandina in 1825 that sent the surrounding sea to a temperature of 65°C (149°F). On Isla Isabela, Volcán Cerro Azul continuted to be active into the late 1990s, while Volcán Sierra Negra erupted as recently as 2005.

BELOW: cactus thrives on lava flows.

Relatively fresh basalt lava flows can still be seen around Isabela, often making fascinating patterns. They include "pahoehoe" or "ropy" lava – where the

skin of the lava flow has been wrinkled by the heat of the still-flowing lava beneath. Another type is "aa" – pronounced "aah aah" – that looks like twisted black toffee.

Map on page 318

Colonization

The volcanic lumps that first burst forth from the Pacific 4 million years ago were utterly devoid of life. Yet now the islands are teeming with plants and animals. Somehow they must have made their way from South America – and, since the islands were never connected to the continent, this fauna and flora must have crossed the 1,000-km (620-mile) stretch of water.

Only certain types of creatures could survive the journey: this explains the present-day predominance of sea birds (that could fly), sea mammals (that could swim) and reptiles (that apparently floated across from the American coast on accidentally formed vegetation rafts and, unlike amphibians and land mammals, could survive for long periods without food or water). Meanwhile, plant seeds and insects could have come across stuck to birds' wings or in animals' stomach contents. Once they had landed on the bleak islands, only certain animals could survive. Those that did found that their traditional predators had been left behind on the South American coast. The animals' lack of timidity probably stems from this general absence of predators – a fact that also explains why recently introduced domestic goats and pigs are able to wreak havoc so easily.

Charles Darwin was the first to observe how each arriving species had adapted over time in order to thrive and survive. The most famous case is "Darwin's finches" – the 13 similar species of finches that probably descended from one original species. Each modern species has differences that suit its particular

Thor Heyerdahl is among those who believed that the Inca Tupac-Yupanqui organized an expedition to the islands in the 15th century, but there is no evidence to support this theory.

BELOW: Sullivan Bay and Pinnacle Rock, Bartolomé Island.

environment: some have short, thick beaks so that they can split seeds; others have long, thin bills to catch insects.

Many years after his visit to the Galápagos, Darwin attributed the process to natural selection. After their arrival on the Galápagos, each finch produced offspring that were imperceptibly different from the parent. In this strange new environment, some chicks were better able to survive. They were the ones that reached maturity and produced young, passing on new genetic traits to their offspring. Over thousands of generations, some traits were thus "selected" as fitting the finches' new home – until the differences between the new creature and the original qualified it to be re-named as a new species.

Darwin propounded this theory in his classic work *The Origin of Species*. It became particularly controversial when applied to man, not only suggesting that the animal kingdom did not spring ready-made from the hand of God, but that man is in many respects no different from other forms of animal life.

The human history

There is a possibility that the Inca Tupac-Yupanqui organized an expedition to the Galápagos during his rule in the 1400s, but most historians accept that the islands were first discovered by accident in 1535 by the Spanish cleric Fray Tomás de Berlanga, bishop of Panama. On the way to Peru, his boat was becalmed and drifted to the Galápagos. The cleric landed in search of water but "found nothing but seals and tortoises, and such big tortoises that each could carry a man on top of itself" and birds "so silly that they do not know to flee." He dubbed the islands "Las Encantadas," the Bewitched Ones, because they tricked his navigator's eyes and seemed to appear and disappear in clouds of mist.

BELOW: National Park wardens measure a giant tortoise.

For the next two centuries, the islands, far from the Spanish trade routes, were hideaway for Dutch and English buccaneers. They began the practice of killing rge numbers of giant tortoises for their meat – having found that the creatures)uld be stacked upside-down in their ships' holds without food and water for ver a year and still be turned into fine soup. This practice was taken up most evastatingly by 19th-century whalers. Between 1811 and 1844 there were said be more than 700 whaling ships in the Pacific, and many of them called into e Galápagos Islands to stock up on tortoise meat.

The first permanent colonist on the Galápagos was an Irishman named Patrick 'atkins, who arrived at Floreana in 1812. His story is included in a series of etches called *The Encantadas* by Herman Melville. Melville's portrait of the lands was not a flattering one: "Take five and twenty heaps of cinders dumped ere and there in an outside lot; imagine some of them magnified into moun-ins, and the vacant lot the sea; and you will have a fit idea of the general aspect the Encantadas."

When the Ecuadorian Government claimed the islands in 1832, Floreana was ven as a reward for bravery to a local Creole officer. He brought 80 people)m the mainland and kept them enslaved using giant dogs. But the so-called)og King of Charles Island" was forced to flee when his slaves rebelled. A utal penal colony was set up on San Cristóbal in the 1880s, with the prisoners orked hard, flogged mercilessly, and marooned on desert islands to die slowly thirst as punishment for misdemeanors.

When the United States entered World War II, it chose the Galápagos as a fense base against attacks on the Panama Canal. An airstrip was built on Bal-a Island that is still in use today. In 1958 the last convict colony was closed,

Map on page 318

BELOW: a graceful diving penguin.

and in the 1960s regular passenger flights began to operate. Since then, touris‹ has been ever-increasing. In September 1995, the islands' tourist trade w‹ brought to a halt when locals, led by the Deputy of the Galápagos, Eduar‹ Veliz, seized San Cristóbal airport, the National Park office and the Charles D‹ win Center, demanding more control of and benefits from tourism. Some kind peace was secured, but only after two weeks of fierce protesting, complete su‹ pension of all visits, and intense negotiations in Quito.

Concern for conservation

Scientists have been observing the Galápagos periodically ever since Darwir‹ work in the mid-19th century. In the 20th century, it became obvious that ma‹ of the animals introduced by man had turned feral and were devastating the natu‹ ecology of the islands. Everything from goats to pigs, rats, dogs, and cats we‹ breeding furiously. They were taking other animals' food, devouring turtle eg‹ and baby land iguanas, eroding the soil, and destroying the plants.

In 1930 an expedition led by Gifford Pinchot from the USA suggested creati‹ a wildlife sanctuary in the archipelago. Five years later, laws were passed to pr‹ tect the fauna of the islands, but it was not until 1959 that the Galápagos we‹ declared a national park, with the aim of protecting the islands and encouragi‹ scientific research.

Also created in 1959 was the Charles Darwin Foundation for the Galápag‹ Islands, an international organization under the auspices of UNESCO and the Inte‹ national Union for the Conservation of Nature. In 1964 the foundation establish‹ the Charles Darwin Research Station, with scientific, educational, and protecti‹ objectives. The scientific program provides assistance for experts and biolo‹ students who visit the islands. The educational progra‹ is aimed at improving environmental awareness, parti‹ ularly among students. And the protective progra‹ attempts to overcome the negative effects of introduc‹ animals, and prevent other man-made disasters.

Various protective programs have been undertak‹ in cooperation with the national park administration. ‹ far, they have been successful in eliminating black ra‹ on Bartolomé and wild goats on Santa Fe, Españo‹ (Hood), and Rábida. A campaign against dogs, whi‹ attack young tortoises and land iguanas, started recent‹

A law has been passed restricting human colonizatio‹ Only residents and their children are allowed to live pe‹ manently in the Galápagos Islands. This has slowed t‹ tide, but illegal migration does continue and the islan‹ have a resident population of over 18,000.

Tourism takes off

Before the 1960s, a visit to the Galápagos involved‹ long and uncomfortable sea voyage on the old sh‹ *Cristóbal Carrier*, which ran once a month fro‹ Guayaquil to the archipelago. Travel between t‹ islands was often nearly impossible: travelers som‹ times had to wait weeks to find a boat heading whe‹ they wanted to go. Not surprisingly, most visitors we‹ wealthy and could afford their own yachts and cru‹ the islands at leisure. All this changed when regular scheduled air transportation was made available to t‹

An iguana posing for the camera.

BELOW: great frigate male with fully inflated pouch.

public, and passenger ships began running by Ecuadorian tourist agencies. In 1970, an estimated 4,500 tourists arrived; in 1978 the figure was 12,000; in 1990, it was 66,000; more than 100,000 visitors a year are now estimated to come to the islands. Wildlife and vegetation are in danger of being severely affected if tourism continues at this rate. Although tourism is tightly controlled, further measures need to be taken to preserve the islands for future generations. There are some 56 visitor sites and 62 marine sites where tourists are allowed outside of towns – and then only in the company of trained guides. Trails are marked with small stakes painted in white to stop you crushing plants and animals underfoot, and also to keep crowds away from crater borders, where serious erosion can occur.

Map on page 318

A range of plant life

Every island in the Galápagos is unique, although only a committed naturalist would plan to visit them all. Many are virtual deserts. Others, more mountainous, are relatively lush. Thanks to the icy Humboldt Current, the islands are not as hot as you would expect, but the sun can still be punishing, and few can stand more than a few hours' hiking steep trails. There are six different vegetation zones on the Galápagos, beginning with the shoreline and ending with the highlands. The low islands are the driest, as clouds pass by here without discharging. Meanwhile, the mountainous islands often block clouds, which turn into fog, drizzle, or rain showers and help flora to thrive.

The area of the shoreline or littoral zone is populated by plants that can tolerate high levels of salt – mangrove, saltbush, myrtle, and other minor aquatic plants. Next comes the arid zone, characterized by thorny plants with small flow-

BELOW: *opuntia* cactus grows in the arid zone.

The scalesia zone.

ers: different types of cactus (particularly *opuntia* and *cereus*), brushwood *(matorrales)*, the ghostly-looking *palos santos*, carob trees *(algarrobos)*, and lichens *(liquenes)*. In the transition zone, perennial herbs and smaller shrubs are dominant, among them the *matazarnos* and the pega pega *(Pisonia floribunda)*.

The high humid area – called scalesia after the zone's dominant tree, typically covered with bromeliads, ferns, and orchids – extends between 200 and 500 meters (650 and 1,650 ft) above sea level. Several typical plants are found in this zone: locust and guava trees, *passiflora* and fungus. Above 500 meters (1,650 ft) is the miconia zone, which is also the main area used for cultivation and pasture on the inhabited islands, where coffee, vegetables, oranges, and pineapples are planted. In the highest zone, called fern-sedge, grow mainly ferns and grasses, including the giant Galápagos fern tree, which can sometimes reach 3 meters (10 ft) in height.

Of the 875 plant species so far recorded on the islands, 228 are endemic. But all the plants did come originally from the South American continent, and have since adapted to the harsh new environment.

Fascinating wildlife

Fifty-eight resident bird species have been recorded here, of which 28 are endemic. The others are either found in other parts of the world or are migratory, spending some part of the year living or breeding away from the islands. They can be classified into sea birds and land birds: among the latter are the famous Darwin finches, mockingbirds (distinguished by their gray and brown streaks), the Galápagos dove, and the endemic Galápagos hawk.

Sea birds tend to be more impressive for non-naturalist visitors. The world's entire population of 12,000 pairs of yellow-billed, waved albatrosses nest on the

BELOW: waved albatrosses perform their courtship dance.

single island of Española (Hood). These magnificent creatures are famous for their extraordinary courtship displays, dancing about and "fencing" with their beaks – literally, standing face to face and clicking their beaks together at a great rate.

One of the most common birds is the blue-footed booby, which is not endemic. They are an unforgettable sight, as their feet really are a bold, striking blue. They were named "boobies" after the Spanish word "bobo" (dunce) by early sailors, who were amazed that the birds would not fly away when men approached. The boobies have a somewhat comical courtship ritual: they "dance" toward one another, plodding about with blue feet working up and down, "skypoint" (pushing their wings up to the heavens) and give one another twigs as presents. They are often seen diving into the water from heights of 20 meters (65 ft) to catch fish.

Another common sea bird is the frigate. They can look quite sinister when hovering overhead, and are not above preying on other birds' young. The males' puffed scarlet chest sack makes an impressive sight when they are mating. With only 400 pairs still alive, the Galápagos lava gull is said to be the rarest bird species on earth. The Galápagos also have the world's only two flightless sea birds: the Galápagos penguin and the flightless cormorant. The penguin is a big favorite, clumsily waddling about on land but speeding like a bullet under the waves. They are the most northerly penguin species, probably first coming up from the south with the icy Humboldt Current. They are mostly found on Isabela and Fernandina, although they can also easily be seen on Bartolomé. Like the penguin, the endemic flightless cormorant makes an entertaining sight – if you are lucky enough to spot one, since there are only 700 pairs in existence, found on the remote, far coasts of Isabela and Fernandina. The flightless cormorant has no enemies to fear, so does not suffer from its inability to fly – it scampers

BELOW: flightless cormorant drying its wings, Isla Fernandina.

along flapping what look like the shreds of lost wings. It is, however, a good diver and can easily catch the fish it needs for its food.

Prehistoric creatures

It was Darwin who called the Galápagos "a paradise for reptiles." Most common are the endemic black marine iguanas, often found sunning themselves on cliffs and shorelines. Darwin himself found their dragon-like appearance rather horrifying: he called them "imps of darkness… of a dirty black color, stupid and sluggish in [their] movements." They are probably relatives of a land-going reptile species that died out 100 million years ago. But these creatures have adapted themselves to the ocean to feed on seaweed, often diving to 12-meter (40-ft) depths. They have developed unusual glands connected to their breathing systems that accumulate the excess of salt in their bodies. Every so often the salt is snorted out through the nose – not an attractive sight. While they are usually black, the males change color during mating to orange, red, and blue.

The rarer-to-spot land iguanas are yellow in color and often larger than their sea-going relatives. They are one of the species that was hardest-hit by the animals introduced by man. Tiny lava lizards can be found on all the Galápagos islands, frequently seen doing somewhat absurd "push-ups" on pathways, which is a sign that they are marking out their territory against intruders.

Slow-moving giants

The most famous of the Galápagos reptiles is the giant tortoise. Countless thousands were killed for their flesh by whalers during the 18th and 19th centuries, and now only an estimated 15,000 remain. There were 14 subspecies of giant tortoise

The flightless cormorant cannot fly because it lost the keel of its breastbone long ago. Its aquatic mating dance routine can last for 40 days.

BELOW: marine iguana with young.

ere – distinguished most easily by the different shell shapes – but three are now xtinct (the last example of one species was found at the turn of the 20th century by n expedition from a San Francisco museum: the scientists promptly dispatched the reature in order to study its shell).

The giant tortoise is one of the most ancient of reptiles, but also among the rarest it exists only here and on the island of Aldabra in the Indian Ocean. Weighing p to 250 kg (550 lbs), it has two types of shell: the dome-shaped type is found in umid environments such as Santa Cruz, where vegetation is low and abundant; his type of tortoise has a short neck and short legs. The second type has a shell nat resembles a horse's harness and lives on islands with uneven soil and no low rass, such as Española (Hood). These tortoises are more agile (relatively speaking) nd have long legs and necks in order to feed themselves. The shell indentation llows them to protrude their necks further.

Legend has it that these tortoises can live for centuries. One, given to the Queen of Tonga by Captain Cook in the 1770s, is said to have survived until 966, but there is no certain evidence for them living for more than 100 years.

Saving these magnificent creatures has been a major task of the Darwin Research Station: a program of breeding seems to be successful. On Española Hood), only 10 males and two females of a subspecies were still alive until, fter years of breeding in captivity, some 100 healthy specimens were eturned to the island. But the tortoise population is still at risk: on Santa Cruz mysterious disease killed several of them in 1996 and for a while visitors vere banned.

There is only one survivor, however, of one subspecies from the island of 'inta, and he goes by the name of Lonesome George. He was discovered on the

Map on page 318

BELOW: a giant tortoise munches leaves.

island of Pinta in 1971, during a period of goat removal, and was transferred t the captive breeding program at the Charles Darwin Research Station soon afte He is estimated to be 70–80 years old. Despite a $10,000 reward for a femal of the species, no mate has been found for him to carry on the line. Attempt have been made to interbreed George with similar species, but without succes Hope has not been surrendered, however, and scientists at the Charles Darwi Research Center are still searching for a female counterpart.

Easier to spot in the wild is the Pacific green sea turtle, which snorkelers ca often observe underwater.

There is a serpent in paradise: the Galápagos snake. There are three endemic species, they grow up to 1 meter (3ft) long, but are not poisonous and very rarely seen.

Playful sea lions and dolphins

There are fewer land mammals than there are birds or reptiles in the Galápago because they were much less likely to survive the journey across from coasta South America. Storms may have blown the hoary bat to the Galápagos, whil the rice rat may have made it across on a vegetation raft. Sea mammals, howeve simply followed the currents to the islands, and these days they make up som of the Galápagos' creatures most popular with visitors.

Topping the list is the sea lion, related to the Californian species. Clumsy o land, they are super agile underwater. The young are incredibly cute and play ful – they will swim about snorkelers and tease them, even staring into you goggles and pretending to charge you before turning away. The *machos*, c older males, do, however, stake out their territory very jealously. They can tur aggressive and have been known to bite swimmers, so a degree of cautio should be used in their presence (guides will know which areas are the pre serve of the bull lions).

BELOW: swimming with sea lions.

Fur seals have more hair than sea lions, they are smaller and very shy: they prefer to live in colonies, on distant cliffs. Bottle-nosed dolphins are often seen surfing the bow spray of boats, while no less than seven whale species have been sighted at or near the Galápagos archipelago, although getting a close look at them is fairly unlikely.

Map on page 318

An underwater world

Under the waves, snorkelers will be constantly surrounded by many of the 307 species of fish recorded in the Galápagos – and more are being discovered every year. Schools of brightly colored tropical fish pass over the sea floor and around rocks, making a spellbinding sight.

There is also a variety of shark that can be seen in the waters around the islands, but they are not dangerous. They are much too well fed to bother about attacking humans, and have never attacked a swimmer in the Galápagos. The grace of these creatures is particularly impressive.

Keep an eye out for the different types of rays that glide majestically along the ocean floor. The giant manta ray can sometimes be spotted leaping out of the sea and landing with a loud slap on the waves. None of the rays are dangerous except for the stingray – on some beaches they lie in shallow water beneath a layer of sand, and can give quite a sting if trodden on. It's worth giving the sand a shuffle with your feet to scare off any basking rays.

Invertebrates (animals that do not have backbones) such as jellyfish, sponges, mollusks, and crabs, proliferate. The most commonly seen of these is the bright yellow and orange Sally Lightfoot crab, which can be found on almost every rock in the Galápagos.   ❑

LEFT: a Sally Lightfoot crab.
RIGHT: a blue-footed booby.

BIRDS OF THE GALÁPAGOS

From the marbled godwit to the black-necked stilt, the birdlife on the Galápagos Islands, which taught us about evolution, is still rich, rare, and rewarding

Where else will birds practically come out to greet you? Life without predators has made the birds of the Galápagos fearless, which means that many of them are easy to spot. There are 58 resident species, of which 28 are endemic, as well as about 30 migratory birds. The seabirds are the most frequently seen: in the dry coastal areas you are likely to spot three species of the booby family, the waved albatross – found nowhere in the world except on the island of Española – and the world's only flightless seabirds, the Galápagos penguin and the flightless cormorant. The best time to come is in winter (October to February) when most migrants are visiting, and birds are reproducing.

Then, a serious ornithologist might see 50 species in a week, and even a dilettante should be able to spot two dozen.

There are dangers in paradise, however: the introduction of domestic animals has been bad news. Some prey on the birds, others destroy or compete for their habitats. Farming on the inhabited islands also destroys habitats, and a natural phenomenon, the *El Niño* current, brings mosquito-carried disease and disrupts the food chain.

△ **PEREGRINE FALCON**
The endangered peregrine falcon *(Falco peregrinus)* originates in Canada and the US, and winters in South America. It is frequently seen on the islands of Española, Isabela, Baltra, and Santa Cruz. The world's swiftest bird, this falcon can reach speeds of 320 km/h (199 mph) when it is swooping to attack prey.

◁ **GALAPAGOS HAWK**
The female Galápagos hawk *(Buteo galapagoensis)* is larger than the male of the species. While the males are monogamous, females will mate with up to seven males per season in order to ensure that breeding will be successful. The female and her males take turns in guarding the nest.

◁ **BLUE-FOOTED BOOBY**
The blue-footed booby *(Sula nebouxii excisa)* has a wonderful courtship ritual, in which the male ostentatiously displays his brightly colored feet in order to attract a mate. Two or three eggs are laid and both of the parents share the task of incubating them. Once they have become independent, the young birds leave the islands and do not return to breed until some three years later.

THE SECRET OF DARWIN'S FINCHES

The finches of the Galápagos were vitally important in the development of Charles Darwin's ideas about evolution and the formation of species. When he set off on his voyage around the world on HMS *Beagle* (1831–36), he believed, like most people of his time, in the fixity of species. But on the Galápagos he observed that 13 different species of the finch had evolved from a single ancestral group, and it was this (together with his observations of the islands' tortoises) which led to his contention that species could evolve over time, with those most suited to their natural environment surviving and passing on their characteristics to the next generation.

The main differences he noted between the finches was the size and shape of their beaks, leading him to conclude that the birds which survived were those whose beaks enabled them to eat the available food.

The 13 species of finch are divided into two groups: ground finches *(pictured above is the large ground finch, geospiza magnirostris)* and tree finches, of which the mangrove finch, found only in the swamps of Isabela Island, is the most rare. You are unlikely to see all of them on a short visit, but it's a challenge to see how many you can spot.

◁ **VERMILLION FLYCATCHER**
The vermillion flycatcher *(Pyrocephalus rubinus)* is an attractive little bird and quite unlike any other bird to be seen on the Galápagos Islands. It has a high-pitched, musical song and builds a distinctive cup-shaped nest, on which the female incubates the eggs.

△ **FRIGATE BIRDS**
The magnificent frigate bird *(Fregata magnificens magnificens)* and its close relation, the great frigate bird, can be seen near the coasts of many islands. Both males and females have long forked tails and the male is remarkable for the red gular pouch which puffs in the mating season.

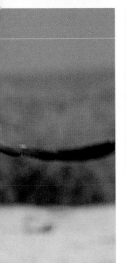

◁ **LAVA GULL**
The lava gull *(Larus fuliginosus)* is believed to be the rarest species in the world It roosts on the shores of saltwater lagoons and builds solitary nests along the coast.

△ **BROWN PELICAN**
The brown pelican *(Pelecanus occidentalis urinator)* is a huge, cumbersome bird which can often be seen following fishing boats in search of food.

VISITING THE ISLANDS

Map
on page
318

*Uncontrolled, tourism could destroy this Pacific paradise.
The thousands of visitors who follow in Darwin's
footsteps need also to follow strict guidelines*

Most travelers to the Galápagos arrive by air, except for a few who have pre-arranged trips on one of the larger cruisers that occasionally depart from Guayaquil. Flights leave from both Quito and Guayaquil. TAME flies daily to the island of Baltra, from where a bus and ferry will take you across to Puerto Ayora on Santa Cruz, and three times a week to San Cristóbal. Aerogal offers thrice-weekly flights to San Cristóbal. On arrival, you must have your passport ready and $100 entrance tax to the Galápagos – without these two essentials, you will not be able to enter the islands.

Many travelers will have pre-arranged their cruise around the islands on one of the larger luxury ships. Two of the best on offer are the *Galápagos Explorer II*, a liner operated by Canodros, which leaves from Baltra island; and the *Santa Cruz*, run by the Ecuadorian agency Metropolitan Touring, which leaves from San Cristóbal *(see Tour Operators pages 356–7)*. Both offer all the comforts of a five-star hotel, with excellent food, swimming pools, evening slide shows, and the like. They have English-speaking guides who are all qualified naturalists. Although the capacity of these ships is 90 people, they operate with groups of no more than 20 – landing them by small dinghies called *pangas* for twice-daily excursions. The large boats have the advantage of covering a lot of territory by night, easily reaching the more remote islands without unduly rough passages. Smaller luxury boats carrying 16–20 passengers, such as the *Beluga* run by Angermeyers, offer a more intimate experience.

Independent and budget travelers often choose to organize their own cruise on one of the dozens of smaller boats on the islands. This can be arranged in Quito or Guayaquil, but is cheapest when done in Puerto Ayora (relatively few small boats operate from San Cristóbal). The idea is to take your time, meet up with other like-minded travelers, find a captain, and agree a price. This usually takes two or three days, but if you have more time than money it's worth doing. The main advantage of organizing your own trip is flexibility: you can choose which islands you want to visit, for how long, and when. However, the guides often don't speak English, and rough weather conditions can make night journeys on these boats difficult for those with delicate stomachs. For younger, independent travelers, this is definitely an experience not to miss.

A guide to the visitor sites

The only places that boats may land on the islands are at the 56 designated visitor sites, and even then visitors must be accompanied by a guide. Some of the more fragile sites are further restricted so that only small groups are allowed to visit, or limits are imposed on the numbers each month. The landing by *panga* is either

PRECEDING PAGES:
the lunar landscape
of Isla Bartolomé.
LEFT: siesta hour at
the Hotel Sol y Mar,
Puerto Ayora.
BELOW: transport to
the islands.

Dried lava patterns.

wet or dry – your guide will tell you which. Wet landings simply mean that you leap into the water up to your ankles (sometimes up to your knees), so keep your shoes aside; dry landings are at natural or man-made jetties, where you should keep your shoes on.

The most densely populated island in the Galápagos (in human terms), as well as its second largest (at 986 sq. km/380 sq. miles), is **Santa Cruz ❶**. Most tours start here at the township of **Puerto Ayora**, and even those that begin at San Cristóbal call here to visit the **Charles Darwin Research Station ❷**.

Puerto Ayora has grown in size and population in recent years, but has still has the air of a relaxed fishing village. The wide turquoise **Academy Bay** is full of small boats and makes a picturesque sight, while the town docks are usually crowded with small children running, swimming, and playing with sea lions. Ayora has plenty of small hotels and restaurants, the most eccentric being the Sol y Mar *(see Travel Tips pages 335–40 for details)*. It sits right on the water-line and its porch is always crowded with marine iguanas (the little beasties will walk over your feet while you're having breakfast, which can be something of a surprise until you get used to it).

The main attraction is the research station. This is the classic place to have your photo taken with one of the giant tortoises: mature specimens of several subspecies are kept in pens here. While you often see pictures of tourists riding tortoises, this can damage their shells and is prohibited. The station has a tortoise breeding house, where the young can be seen, and a small museum and information center. Paths run from the station into littoral vegetation: fine examples of many varieties of cacti can be found, as well as thick expanses of mangrove.

There are several trails from Puerto Ayora that are worth exploring. Some

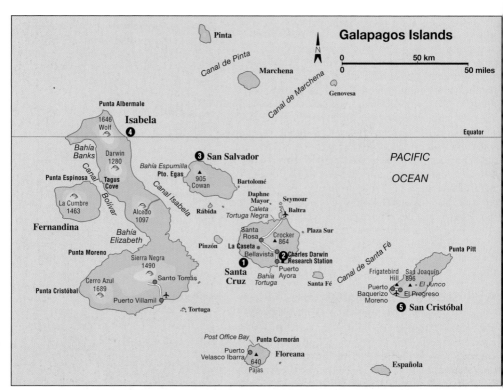

7 km (4 miles) westward is **Tortuga Bay** (Turtle Bay), with fine white sands and waters rich in lobsters. You can go there to swim and relax without a guide, although the fish and animals are still protected. The highland interior of Santa Cruz, in the national park, offers several attractions: the lava tubes are long underground tunnels made when lava solidified on the surface of a flow but kept going underneath. Climbing **Cerro Crocker**, an 860-meter (2,800-ft) high hill, shows the range of vegetation zones on the island. And a day excursion can be made to the **Tortoise Reserve**, which is one of the few places to see giant tortoises in the wild; organize your trip beforehand with a tour guide in the town or visit independently: you need to hire a Jeep and then take a two-hour walk to see these creatures wallowing in the mud.

Map on page 318

The central islands

The islands close to Santa Cruz are the most often visited, although not necessarily the most interesting for naturalists. Day trips are run by various agencies from Puerto Ayora: this means a lot of traveling time on the water if you want to visit more than one. It is more fun and – if properly organized – only slightly more expensive to visit several on your own cruise.

Only 24 km (15 miles) from Puerto Ayora is **Isla Santa Fe** (also known as Barrington). A compulsory wet landing is the start of a short trail into a dry landscape crowded with opuntia cacti. Santa Fe is one of the best places to see the shy land iguana, but the steep path is one of the more difficult on the Galápagos, so a swim from the beach near the landing site comes as a welcome relief.

On the northeastern coast of Santa Cruz is the tiny island of **Plaza Sur**. Only 13 hectares (32 acres) in area, its coast is so crowded with sea lions that every-

BELOW: the harbor at Puerto Ayora.

one on the *panga* needs to clap and shout to clear a landing space. Swimming is not encouraged here, since the *macho* or bull sea lions are particularly aggressive. Plaza Sur is unusually crowded with animal life; there are plenty of land iguanas and the impressive black cliffs are populated with sea birds, as well as the rare Galápagos hawk. Nearby is a convalescent home for bachelor *macho* sea lions: after losing a brawl over territory, they come here to recuperate before returning to the fray.

Isla Seymour is separated from the larger island of **Baltra** by a channel. Baltra has little to interest a visitor, whereas Seymour is one of the Galápagos' best breeding grounds for sea birds: blue-footed boobies are so common that visitors have to be careful not to step on any of the nests that may have been built on the trails.

The strange, block-shaped island of **Daphne** is 10 km (6 miles) away. Access is restricted to only a few boats a month. Landing here is difficult, with a leap onto nearly sheer rocks that becomes somewhat hair-raising in rough weather. But it is worth the effort: at the end of a trail, a large crater is dotted with hundreds of blue-footed booby nests, making a decidedly surreal sight.

Volcanic rock and iguanas

One of the larger islands, relatively close to Santa Cruz, is known as either **Santiago** or **James**, although its official title is **San Salvador ❸**. It has a number of landing sites, by far the most popular being **Puerto Egas** on the west coast. This is one of the best places to see hundreds of marine iguanas sunning themselves on black volcanic rocks, while fur seals can be spotted swimming nearby. The **Sugarloaf Volcano** dominates the horizon here. Swimming is good at Espumilla Beach

BELOW: preparing lunch on a charter boat.

and Buccaneer Cove. If you are in a small group, try snorkeling at the **fur seals' grotto**. You can swim with these characters for hours through the pools that have formed under natural stone archways.

Sitting off the west coast of San Salvador, the small 120-hectare (300-acre) island of **Bartolomé** is one of the most photographed in the Galápagos. The centerpiece of a visit is the steep climb up **Cerro Bartolomé**: the view is spectacular, looking over lunar fields of dried lava, craters, and out over the jutting, honeycombed **Pinnacle Rock**. The heat is also quite intense, so after working up a sweat, transfer to the second landing site, one of the most pleasant beaches on the islands. The snorkeling is excellent, especially around Pinnacle Rock itself: apart from the tropical fish moving in formation, you have a chance of spotting teams of penguins hunting underwater. A path leads over to the other side of the island, where dozens of reef sharks patrol only meters from the edge of the water.

South of Santiago is the island of **Rábida** (Jervis), which has a dark-red sand beach (due to its high iron-oxide content) along which lounge hundreds of bloated sea lions. Indolent and clumsy on land, they are surprisingly energetic in the water: this is a great place to observe the baby sea lions.

A path into the interior of the island passes a marshy lake full of bright pink flamingos (the pinker the flamingo, the healthier it is – the feather color comes from the diet of shrimps they sieve through their beaks). In the trees by the beach are a large number of brown pelicans.

Another unusual point on Rábida that is well worth visiting is **Caleta Tortuga Negra** (Black Turtle Cove). This tidal lagoon leads into a maze of mangroves: it can be visited only by *panga*, cutting the motor and paddling quietly through the natural tunnels made by trees. The brackish waters of the area are full of white-tipped sharks and mustard rays. But it is most famous as a mating spot for the green Pacific turtles. With luck, you can spot the two heads coming up for air during copulation, which lasts for many hours.

When cruising the south coast of Jervis/Santiago, keep an eye out for **Sombrero Chino** – literally "Chinese Hat," named for the island's sweeping conical shape. One of the more recent islands, it has a 400-meter (1,300-ft) path around its circumference, along which sea lions relax in abandonment.

Map on page 318

The western islands

At 4,588 sq. km (1,770 sq. miles), 120 km (75 miles) in length and shaped like a seahorse, **Isabela ❹**, is the largest of the Galápagos Islands. It is still recovering from fires that blazed across the island in 1994. The fires were eventually extinguished, but not without a severe impact on vegetation. One of the island's main attractions, the giant tortoises, were rescued by helicopter and taken to the other side of the island to the safety of a breeding center. Isabela is one of the islands that still has volcanic activity, and there are five cones still visible: **Wolf** at 1,645 meters (5,395 ft); **Alcedo** at 1,097 (3,600); **Sierra Negra** (also called Santo Tomás) at 1,490 (4,885); **Cerro Azul** at 1,690 (5,540), and **Darwin** at 1,280 (4,200).

BELOW: Galápagos penguin surveys the scene.

Some 1,600 people live on Isabela, mostly in and around **Puerto Villamil** on the south coast. Cruise ships rarely visit the outpost since it is difficult to enter the bay, especially when the sea is rough. It does, however, have a fine sandy beach, an old cemetery, and several basic hotels and restaurants. About 18 km (11 miles) away is the village of **Santo Tomás** and the "Wall of Tears" – built of lava stone in the convict colony that was closed in 1959. The crater Santo Tomás has a diameter of 10 km (6 miles), making it the second largest in the world, while Alcedo has a still-steaming fumarole and scores of giant tortoises living at its rim. The volcano is closed until further notice while the authorities attempt to eliminate feral goats.

Most of the visitor sites on Isabela are situated on the west side of the island. Probably the most popular is **Tagus Cove**. Here you can climb up a path to see the lava fields. A *panga* ride along the cliffs reveals colonies of penguins, as well as a range of sea birds. It is probably also the best place to see the unique flightless cormorant. Other landings can be made at **Urbina Bay**, **Elizabeth Bay**, and **Punta Moreno**. The flightless cormorant was common at **Punta García** but it has become more difficult to sight in recent years.

On the other side of Isabela is **Isla Fernandina**. One of the least-visited islands because it is so remote, it is also the most westerly in the Galápagos. It has one visitor site at **Punta Espinosa**, with some impressive lava flows (this was probably the most recently formed major island, and still has some volcanic activity). Along its shores are more penguins and hordes of marine iguanas.

A whalers' post box

Of historical interest on **Isla Floreana**, to the south of the archipelago, is the post box at **Post Office Bay**, where whalers used to leave mail in the late 18th century. Having been replaced several times, the box is still in use. It is the custom to look through the mail and take anything addressed to your home country, putting a local stamp on it when you arrive there and sending it on its way.

Of the visitor sites on Isla Floreana, **Punta Cormorant** is a sandy beach with a greenish tinge from the tiny crystals of olivine, a mineral silicate. From here a trail leads to a lagoon, where occasionally some magnificent pink flamingos nest and circle around. Nearby is a second beach called Stingray which has glistening white sands. The **Devil's Crown** is a sunken crater that forms a semi-circle of rocks: this is perhaps the best site for diving in the whole archipelago. Apart from the schools of brilliant tropical fish, you will probably be joined by some baby sea lions who will race snorkelers through a natural underwater archway.

The outlying islands

The most southerly island in the Galápagos is **Española** (Hood). Española is famous for its sea birds – particularly the waved albatross. Twelve thousand pairs nest here, almost the world's entire population. During the mating season, they begin "fencing" by knocking their beaks together and waddling about "like drunken sailors," as one observer put it.

The whole astonishing range of sea birds can be seen on this island, as well as the beautiful beach of Gardner's Bay. Keep an eye out for the blowhole, which spouts water 50 meters (165 ft) into the air whenever waves hit. At the eastern point of the archipelago lies **San Cristóbal ❺** (Chatham), the second human population center after Santa Cruz: some 3,000 people live in the sleepy town of **Puerto Baquerizo Moreno**. The introduction of flights here caused a development boom, and several hotels and restaurants service the town, which is the capital of the province of Galápagos. There is a small **museum** run by the Franciscan fathers, a monument to Darwin and, at the entrance of the port, a rock called **León Dormido** (Sleeping Lion), which can be climbed for a good view of the island.

A road leads from the capital to the village of **El Progreso** and the 895-meter (2,935-ft) high **Volcán San Joaquín**. The **El Junco Lagoon**, a freshwater lake, is situated within a crater, and surrounded by ferns. **Frigatebird Hill** is, as the name suggests, a good place to see frigate birds and is only a short walk from the town. The Galápagos National Park Visitor Center (tel: 252 1538; daily 7am–6pm), near Frigatebird Hill, has a number of exhibits about the island's natural history and ecosystems. **La Loberia** is a beach crowded with sea lions and **Puerto Grande** a small cove particularly popular for swimming.

Other far-flung islands include **Marchena**, **Pinta**, and **Genovesa** (Tower). Genovesa is home to the main colony of red-footed boobies, three types of Darwin's finch, and everything from red-billed tropic-birds to storm petrels.

Preserving the islands

Tourism to the Galápagos has been described as a two-edged sword: it can be a force to preserve the islands; or, uncontrolled, it can destroy them. The following are guidelines to ensure that the Galápagos are left unaltered by your visit.

Map on page 318

BELOW: messages at Post Office Bay, Isla Floreana.

Map
on page
318

● No natural object – plant, animal, shell, bone, or scrap of wood – should be removed or disturbed. It is illegal and alters the islands' ecological conditions.

● Be careful not to transport any live material to the islands, or from island to island. Before leaving the boat, check your shoe soles for dried mud, as it may contain plant seeds and animal spores. Inadvertent transport of these materials represents a special danger to the Galápagos: each island has its own unique fauna and flora, and introduced plants and animals can quickly destroy them. Obviously no other animals or plants should be brought to the islands. One of the most destructive forces in the Galápagos are domesticated species gone wild.

● For the same reason, do not take any food to the uninhabited islands. Together with the food may come insects or other organisms that might threaten the fragile island ecosystems. Fresh fruits and vegetables are especially dangerous: a dropped orange pip, for example, may become a tree.

● Animals may not be touched or handled. They will cease to be tame if fondled by humans. Young animals that have been handled may be rejected by their mothers because of their smell. They soon die as a result.

● Animals may not be fed. Not only can it be dangerous but in the long run it can destroy the animals' social structure and affect their reproduction.

● Do not startle or chase any animal from its resting or nesting spot. Exercise extreme caution among the breeding colonies of sea birds, such as boobies, cormorants, gulls, or frigate birds. These birds will fly from their nests if they are startled, often knocking the egg or chick to the ground or leaving it exposed to the sun. (A recently hatched booby chick will die in 20 to 30 minutes if it is exposed to the sun; frigate birds will also eat any unguarded chick.)

BELOW: a dip in the waters off Isla Bartolomé.
RIGHT: dolphins ride a boat's spray.

● Do not leave the designated visiting sites. Where trails to points of interest are marked with wooden stakes, you should remain within the stakes.

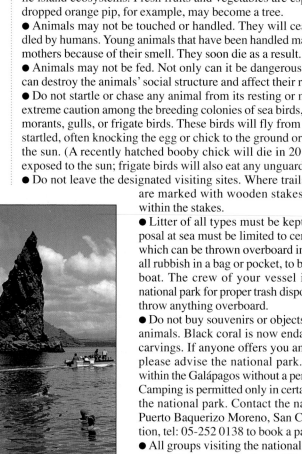

● Litter of all types must be kept off the islands. Disposal at sea must be limited to certain types of garbage which can be thrown overboard in selected areas. Keep all rubbish in a bag or pocket, to be disposed of on your boat. The crew of your vessel is responsible to the national park for proper trash disposal. You should never throw anything overboard.

● Do not buy souvenirs or objects made from plants or animals. Black coral is now endangered by islanders' carvings. If anyone offers you any of these souvenirs, please advise the national park. Camping anywhere within the Galápagos without a permit is against the law. Camping is permitted only in certain sites designated by the national park. Contact the national park office in Puerto Baquerizo Moreno, San Cristóbal, for information, tel: 05-252 0138 to book a package.

● All groups visiting the national park must be accompanied by an approved, qualified guide. The visitor must follow the guide's instructions, while the guide must ensure compliance with the national park regulations relating to the conservation of the flora and fauna.

● Notify the national park service if you see any serious damage being done. You may be a decisive factor in the preservation of the islands. The office is a 10-minute walk east of the main town of Puerto Ayora (tel: 05-252 6511; Mon–Fri 7am–12.15pm and 1.45-4.30pm). ❏

INSIGHT GUIDES

TRAVEL TIPS

ECUADOR

TRAVEL TIPS

TRANSPORTATION

GETTING THERE
AND GETTING AROUND

GETTING THERE

By Air

Ecuador has two international airports, at Quito (Mariscal Sucre) and Guayaquil (José Joaquín de Olmedo). While business travelers may want to visit Guayaquil, most tourists will be heading for Quito. However, the largest airplanes cannot land at Quito airport, and some airlines will take you only as far as Guayaquil. You then take the connection to the capital. The flight time is approximately 30 minutes, and the views can be stunning. If Guayaquil is your gateway to Quito make sure that your international ticket includes the onward connection, otherwise you will need to buy a ticket in Guayaquil airport yourself.

Always reconfirm your return flight before you fly. In Ecuador this is not just a formality.

Flights from the US and Canada

Travelers heading to Ecuador from the US can fly directly to Quito with **American Airlines** from Miami or with **Continental Airlines** from Houston. Continental also flies direct from New York to Guayaquil. **Delta Airlines** has daily flights via Atlanta. **TACA** operates flights from several US cities including Dallas and New York. **Copa** (Panama), **Lacsa** (Costa Rica), and **Avianca** (Colombia) also have flights from Miami and other US cities connecting in their respective countries. Other options include **LAN** from Miami.

Travelers from Canada will need to go via the US with Air Canada, American Airlines, or Continental.

American Airlines
Quito Hotel Hilton Colón, Av. Patria and Amazonas. Tel: (02) 299 5000
Guayaquil Córdoba 1021 and 9 de Octubre. Tel: (04) 259 8800
Cuenca Hermano Miguel 8-67. Tel: (07) 283 1699

Avianca
Quito Av. Coruña 1311 and San Ignacio. Tel: (02) 255 6715
Guayaquil Av. Francisco de Orellana, Manzana 111. Tel: (04) 230 3211
Cuenca Presidente Córdoba 8-40 and Benigno Malo. Tel: (07) 283 4484

Continental Airlines
Quito Av. Naciones Unidas and República del Salvador. Tel: (02) 225 0905/1 800 222 333
Guayaquil Av. 9 de Octubre and Malecón, Edificio Banco La Previsora, 25th Floor. Tel: 1 800 222 333
Cuenca Padre Aguirre 1096 and Mariscal Lamar. Tel: 1 800 222 333

Copa
Quito Av. República del Salvador 361 and Moscú. Tel: (02) 227 3082
Guayaquil Av. 9 de Octubre and Malecón. Tel: (04) 230 3211
Cuenca Mariscal Lamar 989 and Padre Aguirre. Tel: (07) 284 2970

Delta Airlines
Quito Av. 12 de Octubre and Cordero (World Trade Center). Tel: 1 800 101 060
Guayaquil Galerías Colón, Hotel Hilton Colón, Av. Francisco de Orellana. Tel: 1 800 101 060

LAN
Quito Av. Amazonas and Pasaje Guayas E3-131. Tel: 1 800 101 075

Guayaquil Galerías Colón, Hotel Hilton Colón, Av. Francisco de Orellana. Tel: (04) 269 2850

TACA
Quito Av. Naciones Unidas and República del Salvador 1033. Tel: 1 800 008 222
Guayaquil Av. Pichincha 406 and Luque. Tel: 1 800 008 222
Cuenca Mariscal Sucre 7-70 and Luis Cordero. Tel: 1 800 008 222

Flights from Europe

KLM flies direct between Quito, Curazao, and Amsterdam six days a week. **Iberia** flies direct from Madrid four times a week. Otherwise, you must go via the US or South America.

Iberia
Quito Av. Eloy Alfaro 939 and Amazonas. Tel: (02) 256 6009
Guayaquil Av. 9 de Octubre 101 and Malecón. Tel: (04) 232 9558

KLM
Quito Av. 12 de Octubre N26-97 and A. Lincoln. Tel: (02) 396 6728
Guayaquil José Joaquín de Olmedo Airport. Tel: (04) 216 9070

International Airlines

The following airlines operate flights to Quito and Guayaquil.
American Airlines www.aa.com
Avianca www.avianca.com
Continental Airlines www.continental.com
Copa www.copaair.com
Delta Airlines www.delta.com
Iberia www.iberia.com
KLM www.klm.com
LAN www.lan.com
TACA www.taca.com

TRANSPORTATION ◆ 331

TRANSPORTATION

ACCOMMODATIONS

EATING OUT

ACTIVITIES

A – Z

LANGUAGE

Air Travel Taxes

• There is a 12 percent tax imposed on all air tickets bought within Ecuador.
• A $31.60 departure tax is levied on international flights from Ecuador. It is payable at the airport in cash.
• There are no departure taxes for domestic flights.

Flights from Australia, New Zealand, and Asia

Travelers have only three options: take the **Aerolíneas Argentinas** (tel: 800 333 0276) transpolar flight from Sydney via Auckland to Buenos Aires, then a connecting flight to Guayaquil; take the LAN flight from Australia to Santiago, then connect with Ecuador; or fly to Los Angeles and take one of the several connecting flights from there.

Alternatively, **American Airlines** fly from Sydney to Los Angeles, from where you can fly to Miami for a connection to Guayaquil.

Getting to and from Airports

Mariscal Sucre International Airport (UIO) in Quito, tel: (02) 244 0080, is located 8 km (5 miles) north of the New Town. There are no luggage deposit boxes at the airport. Most of the large hotels have a shuttle service; otherwise a taxi to the New Town will cost about $3.5, and $5–6 to the Colonial Center.

The new José Joaquín de Olmedo International Airport (GYE) is located 5 km (3 miles) north of Guayaquil city center, right next to the old one. If you already have a reservation, make arrangements with your hotel to pick you up. Otherwise, taxis marked "airport taxi" can be found to the left of the exit. There is no pre-pay stand, but the journey to the city center should not cost more than $6. There is a casa de cambio (bureau de change) at the airport as well as a small information office.

Cuenca's airport is a 5-minute walk beyond the bus terminal and is easily accessible by city bus or taxi.

Upstream from Esmeraldas, there is a bridge over the river at San Mateo which connects with General Rivadeneira Airport, 25 km (15½ miles) away. Taxis to the airport wait in front of the TAME office and will cost $5–6. Buses go to and from the Terminal Terrestre (Central Bus Terminal) every 30 minutes.

By Land

It is common for backpacking travelers to travel overland into Ecuador, crossing at either Huaquillas or Macará on the Peruvian border or Tulcán/Rumichaca on the Colombian side, although currently there are serious safety issues in this region due to increased drug trafficking and the activities of illegal armed groups. At both borders, minibuses and trucks run between bus centers on both sides for a small fee. The borders are usually open from around 8am to 6pm. Make sure you get an entry stamp and tourist card when you come in.

Several companies run comfortable buses on the more lengthy routes, including **Panamericana Internacional** and **Rey Tours**, which run international services from Quito and Guayaquil to Lima. However, it is more expensive than buying a ticket to the border, walking across and buying another ticket straight away – and they make you change buses anyway, so there is no real advantage in doing this, although it may sound more convenient.

GETTING AROUND

Until the 20th century, transport and communications in Ecuador were poorly developed. When the Guayaquil–Quito railway line was completed in 1908, it provided for the first time an effective inter-regional link and cut the travel time between the two cities from 12 days to 12 hours.

Today the rail system is more of a tourist attraction than a commercial link, as much of the network has fallen into disrepair because of mudslides, flooding, and lack of government funding.

The road network, on the other hand, has expanded considerably since World War II, and the main roads are generally quite good, although many have been badly affected by landslides and flooding and have dangerous potholes. Of the 38,000 km (23,560 miles) of highways, about 18,000 km (11,160 miles) are open all year and about 7,000 km (4,340 miles) are paved.

By Car

Traveling by private car is generally more convenient in Ecuador than in other Andean countries; first, because the main roads are in a comparatively better state; second, because the running costs are economical; and third, because the country is safer than in neighboring republics.

Nevertheless, when touring by car, beware of bus drivers, who often go very fast, and make sure that your car has good ground clearance. As insurance and rental costs become more prohibitive and incidents of ambushes at night increase in certain regions, more travelers tend to opt for buses rather than driving themselves.

Car Rental

Car rental is as expensive as in Europe or in the United States. Charges are about $35 a day, with mileage increments. Extra insurance costs may be charged, and most rental agencies prefer credit cards.

A valid driver's license from your home country is usually accepted, but some rental companies require an international license. It is worth applying for one before you leave if you plan to hire a car.

It is often more economical to hire a taxi for several hours, which will take you to remote areas or to another town: be sure to agree the costs beforehand.

Car Rental Agencies

In addition to the locations listed below, all of the following agencies have branches at Mariscal Sucre Airport in Quito and José Joaquín de Olmedo airport in Guayaquil.

Avis
Av. de las Américas, Centro Comercial Olímpico, Guayaquil. Tel: (04) 228 5498.
www.avis.com
Budget
Av. Amazonas and Colón, Quito. Tel: (02) 223 7026.
Av. de las Américas 900 and Alejandro Andrade, Guayaquil. Tel: (04) 228 4559.
www.budget.com
Expo Rent a Car
Av. América 21-66 and Bolivia, Quito. Tel: (02) 222 8688.
Av. Juan Tanca Marengo, Km 1/2, Guayaquil. Tel: (04) 239 3453.
www.exporentacar.com
Hertz
Panamericana Norte 9900 and Murialdo, Quito. Tel: (02) 241 1677.
Av. de las Américas and E. Arboleda, Guayaquil. Tel: (04) 228 0910.
www.hertz.com

Taxis

Taxis in Ecuador are very cheap for domestic consumption, but meters are only used by taxi drivers in Quito. In Guayaquil, meters are installed by law but drivers do not use them: be sure to ascertain the fare beforehand, or you could be overcharged. In smaller towns, meters do not exist; at weekends and at night fares are 25 to 50 percent higher.

Automobile Club

The Asociación Nacional Ecuatoriana de Turismo y Automobilismo (**ANETA**) is located on Avenida Eloy Alfaro 218 and Berlín, tel: (02) 250 4961. Office hours: 9am–1pm and 3–7pm. It offers an emergency breakdown towing and repair service to members. www.aneta.org.ec (in Spanish)

By Bus
Local Buses

Local buses run frequently and are inexpensive. Destinations are shown on the front of the vehicle. All the main towns and cities are served by urban bus lines. The buses are mostly small and usually extremely overcrowded, especially at peak hours. Beware of pickpockets.

There is a smart trolley system operating between the north and south of Quito, but this, too, gets very crowded at peak hours. The large *selectivo* buses running in Quito's New Town area are a pleasant exception.

Since taxis are very cheap in

Guayaquil, buses and *colectivos* are mostly avoided by foreign visitors, but *busetas* or minibuses are safe to ride. *Servicio especial* buses, marked with blue-and-white diagonal stripes, are slightly more expensive but relatively efficient.

If you want to get off a local bus, shout ¡baja! ("down") or ¡esquina! ("corner") – the driver will stop at the next corner.

Long-Distance Buses

Bus travel is not always comfortable, but often preferable to hiring a car, and numerous companies connect all the main towns at frequent intervals, as well as serving smaller localities, and the fares are incredibly low.

In general, buses leave from central bus terminals. The new luxury buses leave on time; regular buses may or may not. One can usually buy tickets one or two days in advance and choose the seat number; note that the front seats tend to have slightly more leg room than the back seats. During long holiday weekends or special fiestas, buses are generally booked up for several days in advance, so early booking is recommended.

Try to travel by daylight, as there are fewer road accidents and also less likelihood of being held up by bandits or armed gangs.

Four types of buses are used:
• small buses *(busetas)* for 22 passengers, which have cramped leg room and are not very comfortable;
• larger buses *(buses),* which have more space;
• luxury buses *(autobuses de lujo),* which have recently been introduced

on routes between major cities;
• trucks with roofs, open sides, and wooden plank seats, called *rancheros,* which are found mainly around the coast.

Buses from Quito

Long-distance buses leave mainly from the Terminal Terrestre in the southern Villa Flora district, at Maldonado and Cumandá. There are about two dozen bus companies with offices at the terminal. It is worthwhile booking in advance. There are also private companies that operate more comfortable buses from terminals in the New Town.

There are many buses a day to major destinations, including Ambato (3 hours), Bahía de Caráquez (8 hours), Baños (3½ hours), Coca (12 hours), Cuenca (9–14 hours), Guaranda (5 hours), Guayaquil (8 hours), Lago Agrio (10 hours), Latacunga (2 hours), Loja (14–18 hours), Machala (11 hours), Manta (8 hours), Portoviejo (6 hours), Puyo (7 hours), Riobamba (4 hours), Santo Domingo (2½ hours), Tena (9 hours), Esmeraldas (6 hours), Otavalo (2½ hours), Ibarra (2½ hours), and Tulcán (5½ hours).

There are no direct buses to Peru or Colombia. **Reytur** (E. Gangotena 158 and Orellana. Tel: (02) 256 5299/254 6674) runs an "international" bus to Lima, but this involves a change at the border. **Ormeño Internacional** (Los Shyris N34-432 and Portugal, opposite Parque la Carolina. Tel: (02) 246 0027) also offers services to Buenos Aires, Santiago, and Lima. It is cheaper to take a bus to Huaquillas, cross the border, and take a *taxi colectivo* to Tumbes in Peru, where regular buses connect with Lima.

Panamericana (Av. Colón and Reina Victoria. Tel: (02) 250 1585 operates a deluxe service from Quito to Huaquillas and other cities in Ecuador. Both Panamericana and Reytur offer services to Colombia, but this again involves changing buses at the border.

Buses from Esmeraldas

There is no central bus terminal in Esmeraldas. **Aerotaxi**, the fastest line, leaves for Quito from the main plaza (journey time 5 hours, frequent departures); **Panamericana** has a luxury service to Quito once a day, leaving from Hotel Casino; **Transportes Occidentales** and **Trans-Esmeraldas**, Av. Piedrahita 200 operate slower buses (to Quito 7 hours, Santo Domingo 3½ hours, Guayaquil 9 hours, Machala 12 hours); **Cooperativa Sudamericana** runs

BELOW: all aboard the *ranchero* bus to Baños.

buses to Ambato (8 hours); Reina del Camino to Portoviejo (9 hours) and Bahía de Caráquez (8 hours).

Provincial buses leave from *La Costenita,* or the waterfront area (Atacames and Sua 1 hour, Muisné 3½ hours). Frequent departures. Buses run also to La Tola (3 hours). The road is good until Río Verde; there is a combined bus/boat service to San Lorenzo.

Buses from Cuenca

All long-distance buses leave from the Terminal Terrestre on Avenida España, northwest of the city center. here. Destinations include Riobamba (5½ hours), Ambato (7½ hours), Quito (10½ hours), Loja (5–6 hours), Guayaquil (4 hours), Macas (10 hours), and Gualaquiza (6 hours).

Passport Checks

On buses, always carry your passport with you. There are police checks on all the roads leading out of main towns, and you can get into serious trouble if you are unable to present your documents when requested.

Buses from Guayaquil

The Terminal Terrestre is near the airport and the bridge over the Guayas River, and all long-distance buses leave from here. Destinations are: Quito (8½ hours), Cuenca (5 hours), Riobamba (5 hours), Santo Domingo de los Colorados (5 hours), Manta (3 hours), Esmeraldas (8 hours), Portoviejo (3½ hours), Bahía de Caráquez (5½ hours), Machala (3½ hours), Huaquillas (5 hours), Ambato (6½ hours), and Alausí (4 hours). There are also frequent buses to Salinas (2½ hours) and Playas/General Villamil (2 hours). There is a shared-taxi service to Machala (2½ hours) leaving from next door to the Hotel Rizzo, downtown.

By Rail

Many hundred kilometers of Ecuador's train system were totally destroyed during the 1982–3 floods. There are now only three train journeys available in Ecuador: Riobamba to Sibambe, Quito to El Boliche (near Cotopaxi), and an erratic service from Ibarra to Primer Paso. For further information on these journeys, contact the relevant local tourist office.

The Devil's Nose section of the Riobamba–Sibambe route is one of the most spectacular train rides in the world, famous for its spectacular

switchback. The train from Riobamba to Sibambe departs on Wednesday, Friday, and Sunday at 7am.

Metropolitan Touring (*see page 356*) operates its own Chiva Express service, a comfortable, converted bus with toilets, a bar, and space for 34 passangers, which runs on the historic Trans-Andean railway line. The Chiva Express runs one- and two-day tours departing from Quito and can be combined with cross-country tours to Cuenca.

Quito's train station is 2 km (1 mile) south of the center, on Avenida P. Vicente Maldonado near Llanganates (tel: (02) 265 6144). Trains run from here to Cotopaxi on Saturday and Sunday at 8am, returning at 2.30pm. Tickets cost around $5 and can be bought in advance at Bolívar 443 and García Moreno (tel: 02-258 2927) or on the day at the station.

By Air

Air transport is fairly well developed. The Oriente is the one area where airlines have virtually no competition from other forms of transport. There are many villages whose only contact with the rest of the country is by air; besides numerous small strips, 34 airports can handle bigger planes, some of them modern jet aircraft.

There are domestic flights between all the main cities. **AeroGal, Icaro,** and **TAME** connect the principal urban centers of the country – Quito, Guayaquil, and Cuenca – by jet service, with several flights daily each way. Flying time between Guayaquil and Quito is about 30 minutes. TAME flies from Quito to Esmeraldas, Manta, Portoviejo, Tulcan, and Loja (via Guayaquil), and from Guayaquil to Machala. In the Amazon jungle Lago Agrio, Coca, and Macas are served.

There are military flights in the

Domestic Airlines

AeroGal Av. Amazonas 7797, Quito. Tel: (02) 292 0495; José Joaquín de Olmedo Airport, Guayaquil. Tel: (04) 216 9023; www.aerogal.com.ec
icaro Palora 124 and Amazonas, Quito. Tel: (02) 299 7400; José Joaquin de Olmedo Airport, Guayaquil. Tel: (04) 263 0602; www.icaro.com.ec
TAME Av. Amazonas 1354 and Colón, Quito. Tel: (02) 396 6378; Av. Fco de Orellana, Hotel Colón, Guayaquil. Tel: (04) 269 2967; www.tame.com.ec

more remote Amazon areas but they are not generally available to foreign travelers. Air taxis (Cessnas or Bonanzas) can be rented. Small airlines' offices are found at the Guayaquil and Quito airports.

Flights to the Galápagos Islands are heavily booked, so you should confirm and reconfirm your seat and check in early at the airport, unless you have booked your cruise through an agency – in which case, they will reconfirm for you.

TAME has two daily flights in the morning to Baltra, with connecting buses making the short trip to Puerto Ayora. Many cruises pick up their passengers directly at the airport and return them there. **TAME** and **AeroGal** both fly to San Cristóbal three times a week. Check carefully with the cruise operator which flight to book as it can be quite difficult to travel between the islands.

All non-Ecuadorian travelers to the islands must pay a $100 entrance fee on arrival at the airport. Payment must be made in dollars and not by credit card. Keep the receipt: you may have to show it again.

There are also regular flights between some of the islands with **Emebete,** a local airline, subject to demand. Tel: (05) 252 6177. You will be restricted to luggage of 13 kg (30 lbs) or less (non-negotiable). There are flights three times a week between Baltra and Isabela, as well as between Baltra and San Cristóbal.

With the exception of flying to the Galápagos Islands, domestic flights are fairly inexpensive (a return flight Quito–Guayaquil is about $80). Passengers are required to show up one hour before the departure of domestic flights, for baggage handling and check-in procedures. Many flights give marvelous views of the snow-capped Andes, so it is worth getting a window seat. Seats are given on a first-come, first-served basis.

There are no departure taxes for domestic flights.

By Boat

It is possible to travel by boat from Cuenca. Enquire at the *capitanía del puerto* (harbormaster's office) about boat departures (occasionally to Guayaquil and Manta, more often to Limones).

Traveling by boat is the principal means of transport in the Amazon and many lodges are only accessible by motorboat or canoe. The *Manatee Amazon Explorer* floating hotel (*see page 219*) offers a more luxurious way of visiting the area.

Cruises in the Galápagos

The Galápagos archipelago is almost entirely a national park, and no visitor is allowed to enter it without a qualified guide on an organized tour. There are various ways that this can be done. Some travelers choose to take a series of different day trips from Puerto Ayora to the islands nearest Santa Cruz, but, while this is cheap, it is not very satisfying (tour operators on the island will offer these for about $50 a day). The great majority of visitors go on cruises around the islands, taking at least three nights – the more, the better. If you are going to spend the cash to come all this way, it is a pity to miss out on one of the world's great travel experiences.

Large Cruises

For many, a trip on one of the largest cruisers is the most comfortable and convenient way to visit the islands. The *Galápagos Explorer II*, operated by **Canodros**, is the most luxurious boat touring the islands. Contact any travel agency that specializes in Latin America, or see www.canodros.com. The *Santa Cruz*, run by **Metropolitan Touring** (*see page 356*) has all the comforts of a luxury liner, including excellent food. By traveling overnight, these cruisers can easily reach outer islands that smaller yachts sometimes struggle to get to. The going is smoother on a large ship as well.

Both boats are based in the Galápagos, taking around 100 passengers on three- or four-day cruises – one covering the northern islands, the other the southern. You can combine both trips to make a seven-day cruise. Passengers visit the islands in groups of 10 on motorboats *(pangas)* accompanied by English-speaking naturalist guides who all have university degrees in their fields.

The cost is between $200–300 per person per night on a twin-share basis (all inclusive, except for bar and air fare), depending on cabin and length of cruise.

Bookings for the *Santa Cruz* can be made at **Metropolitan Touring** in Quito or Guayaquil, or their US agents **Adventure Associates** (*see page 357*).

Smaller Yachts

Dozens of yachts carrying 8–20 people operate cruises around the islands. Most work out of Puerto Ayora, although a growing number are now based in Puerto Baquerizo Morena. The boats are categorized into five classes – luxury, first class, superior tourist, standard tourist, and economy class. Tours on these boats can be booked on the mainland from a number of agencies, or beforehand through a travel agency specializing in Latin America. **Quasar Naútica** (*see page 357*), for example, offers a selection of luxury yachts. These trips are more costly than on the larger cruises, but are also more intimate and allow more time on the islands. One of the most reliable companies offering both luxury small yachts and tourist-class yachts is **Enchanted Expeditions** (*see page 356*). They offer the *Beluga*, a luxury 16-person yacht, *Angelito*, a comfortable mid-range yacht, and two cheaper options, the *Sagitta* (a sail-boat) and *Cachalote*.

Cheaper tours on small boats can also be arranged at places such as **Galasam Galápagos Tours** on 9 de Octubre 424 and Córdova, Guayaquil. Tel: (04) 234 5446; www.galasam.com.ec. When booking in Quito or Guayaquil, expect to pay around $90–$150 a day including food for a reasonable boat. Check with the South American Explorers Clubhouse in Quito (*see page 355*) for the latest reports on smaller operators to make sure you aren't being ripped off.

Ecoventura operates a variety of cruises from three to seven nights, and can be booked in the US through **Galápagos Network**, 6503 Blue Lagoon Drive, Suite 140, Miami, FL 33126, tel: 305 262 6264, fax: 305 262 9609 or www.ecoventura.com. One of the UK's leading dive specialists, **Scuba Safaris**, tel: 01342 851196, www.scuba-safaris.com, have exclusive use of *Galápagos Agressor I* and *II*.

Organizing Your Own Tour

There are many economy-class boats that can be booked in Quito quite cheaply or at the last minute. Dozens of backpackers turn up at Puerto Ayora and begin getting people together to charter a boat – if you look like a candidate, they are likely to stop you in the street and ask about your plans. The only drawback is that you need a few days to get the required number of people together and arrange a boat, so it's not a good idea to try to set it up in a hurry.

Boats take 8 or 12 people, and the cheapest cost from $60–80 a day with all meals but excluding tips for the crew. However, if your budget allows, it is worth paying for a more expensive boat as the cabins are likely to be bigger, the food better, and the guides more informed. The South American Explorers Club (*see page 355*) keeps lists of reports from travelers

Foreign Exchange

If you are taking a tour on one of the large cruise ships in the Galápagos Islands, there is no problem about paying your bill in dollars, and exchange facilities are available. Independent travelers can change foreign currency in Puerto Ayora, but at a poor rate, so bring whatever you need in dollars from the mainland.

indicating which of the many boats are the best, and offers the following hints for travelers doing this:

• Boat owners like to fill their boats to capacity. The group is usually expected to share the cost of any unsold passenger space.
• When dealing directly with the boat owner, bargaining is expected.
• Bottled drinks are not included in the cost of the cruise. Bring as much mineral water as you think you will need; it is sold at the Puerto Ayora supermarket (at the docks).
• Boat travel to outer islands such as Española and Genovesa can be quite rough, especially from September to November.
• Make sure the boats have enough sets of snorkeling gear. The water is cold from July to December and wetsuits are recommended.

Traveling between the Islands

INGALA (Instituto Nacional de Galápagos) has official inter-island passenger services between Santa Cruz, San Cristóbal, Isabela, and Floreana, as well as services between Puerto Ayora and San Cristóbal. The INGALA office in Puerto Ayora is next to the hospital, tel: (05) 252 6199. In Puerto Baquerizo Moreno on San Cristóbal, it is on the road leading inland at the edge of the town, tel: (05) 252 0133.

Alternatively, if you have the time to be flexible, check with the *capitanía del puerto* (harbormaster's office) for details of other boats, such as the converted cargo ship the *Estrella de Mar*. This travels from Isabela to Santa Cruz. The trip takes between six and seven hours. To move from Santa Cruz to Isabela or San Cristóbal you can also pay a private speedboat to take you to the other islands. Try to negotiate a price, especially if there are several of you.

A CCOMMODATIONS

HOTELS, YOUTH HOSTELS, BED & BREAKFAST

Hotels

There is no shortage of hotels in Ecuador. Every little town, no matter how remote, has somewhere to lay one's head. However, if you want hotels of an international standard, the options are more limited. Five-star luxury accommodations can be found in Quito, Guayaquil, Cuenca, and the resort areas of Esmeraldas and Santa Elena, and there are first-class jungle lodges in the Oriente. Most other areas rely on basic but clean country inns (hosterías), pensiones, or residenciales.

In high season (June to September in the Sierra, December and January on the coast), during fiestas, and the night before market days (in Otavalo particularly), finding accommodations can be tight, so it is worth making a reservation; at other times just turn up.

A room in a luxury hotel might cost $150–200 a night; in a first-class hotel, $80–$100, while a double room with private bath in a perfectly comfortable residencial can be had for $20. Decent backpacker hotels with shared bathrooms can generally be found for $3–6 per person in even the remotest areas. In most places, apart from budget hotels and hostels, service (10 percent) and tax charges (12–14 percent) will be added to the bill.

It is often cheaper and easier to arrange accommodation as a package through a tour operator or local travel agency.

Camping

Camping is a cheap and popular option in many coastal areas, and most campsites provide access to bathrooms and running water. There are three official sites on the island of Santa Cruz: near the Darwin Research Station, at the Tortuga Bay, and near the caseta in the tortoise reserve. For more information about camping sites and special permits contact ex-INEFAN (see box on page 350 for address).

ACCOMMODATIONS LISTINGS

QUITO

Hilton Colón
Av. Amazonas and Patria
Tel: (02) 256 0666
Fax: (02) 256 3903
www.hilton.com
The Colón has a shopping mall, several restaurants and bars, a coffee shop, a casino, a hairdresser, and a range of sports facilities (swimming pool, sauna, masseur, gymnasium). All rooms have cable TV (US programs). There are facilities for disabled visitors. $$$$
Hotel Plaza Grande
García Moreno and Chile
Tel: (02) 251 0777

www.plazagrandequito.com
This 16th-century house, formerly the Hotel Majestic, was reopened in December 2006 and overlooks the Plaza de la Independencia. Most consider it to be the country's best hotel. $$$$
Hotel Spas Termas de Papallacta
Km 67, Vía Quito–Baeza
Tel: (02) 256 8989
Fax: (02) 254 9794
www.papallacta.com.ec
A range of cabins and rooms set in the most luxurious spa in the country, near a popular

hot spring 67 km (41½ miles) east of Quito. $$$$
Radisson Royal Quito
Av. 12 de Octubre and Luís Cordero 444
Tel: (02) 223 333
Fax: (02) 223 5777
www.radisson.com/quitoec
Hotel located in the World Trade Center with 24-hour room service and cable TV. Has good sports facilities, a barber, a beauty salon, and a gift store. $$$$
Swissotel
Av. 12 de Octubre 1820 and Luís Cordero
Tel: (02) 256 7600

Fax: (02) 256 8079
www.swissotel.com
A luxury hotel with numerous rooms, including executive suites. Has five restaurants, a bar, sports facilities (heated pool, fitness center, and spa), and a business center. $$$$
Café Cultura
Robles 513 and Reina Victoria
Tel: (02) 250 4078
Fax: (02) 222 4271
www.cafecultura.com
Converted mansion, surrounded by gardens, which mixes traditional English-style decor with modern touches. Serves

ABOVE: an international welcome at the Swissotel in Quito.

great Danish breakfasts. **$$$**

Chalet Suisse
Reina Victoria 312 and Calama
Tel: (02) 256 2700
Fax: (02) 256 3966
Modern hotel with a restaurant serving excellent food, a nightclub, and a casino. **$$$**

Hotel Quito
Av. González Suárez 2500
Tel: (02) 254 4600
Fax: (02) 256 7284
www.hotelquito.com.ec
Large, but quiet hotel with splendid views and pleasant gardens. Includes several restaurants and bars, a coffee shop, a nightclub, and a heated pool. All rooms have cable TV (US programs). **$$$**

Hotel Sebastián
Diego de Almagro 822 and Luís Cordero
Tel: (02) 222 2400
Fax: (02) 222 2500
www.hotelsebastian.com
Comfortable rooms, friendly staff, restaurant. **$$$**

Mansión del Angel
Wilson ES-29 and Juan León Mera

Tel: (02) 255 7721
The most elegant option in the New Town, set in a restored colonial mansion with wood floors, a fine restaurant, and lavish bedding. **$$$**

Marriott
Av. Orellana 1172 and Av. Amazonas
Tel: (02) 297 2000
www.marriott.com
City and volcano views add to the resort feel of this very large hotel. **$$$**

Nü House Hotel
Plaza del Quinde
Tel: (02) 223 0567
This recently opened boutique hotel has transformed the area around Plaza del Quinde and offers style and modern amenities for a reasonable price. **$$$**

Sheraton Four Points
Av. Naciones Unidas and Av. República del Salvador
Tel: (02) 297 0002
www.sheraton.com
Very modern and comfortable hotel with all the necessary amenities. Popular

with business travelers. **$$$**

La Casa Sol
José Calama 127 and Av. 6 de Diciembre
Tel: (02) 223 0798
www.lacasasol.com
Owned by the same people as the Casa Andina in Otavalo. Includes internet, breakfast, and cozy rooms with cheery Andean decor. **$$**

Hotel Finlandia
Finlandia 227 and Suecia
Tel: (02) 224 4287
www.hotelfinlandia.com.ec
25 cozy rooms in Quito's New Town with Wifi, cable TV, and an excellent restaurant. **$$**

La Rabida
La Rabida 227 and Santa María
Tel: (02) 222 1720
www.hostalrabida.com
Eleven rooms in an attractive building. Good service. **$$**

El Cafecito
Luís Cordero 1124 and Reina Victoria
Tel: (02) 223 4862

www.cafecito.net
Friendly hotel with shared rooms in a great central location in the New Town. Excellent cafe downstairs, with live music at weekends. **$**

Crossroads Cafe & Hostal
Mariscal Foch 678 (E5-23) and Juan León Mera
Tel/fax: (02) 223 4735
www.crossroadshostal.com
Remodeled house with restaurant, use of kitchen and terraces. **$**

Magic Bean
Mariscal Foch 681 and Juan León Mera
Tel: (02) 256 6161
Fax: (02) 290 6105
www.ecuadorexplorer.com/magic
Attractive house with choice of shared or private rooms. Good restaurant downstairs. Centrally located. **$**

Posada del Maple
Juan Rodriguez E8-49 and Av.6 de Diciembre
Tel: (02) 254 4507/223 7375
www.posadadelmaple.com
Friendly atmosphere with kitchen and cable TV room. **$**

APARTHOTELS

For longer stays, self-catering apartment hotels are sometime a good option. Prices start at around $60 per night, but vary depending on the length of stay.

Amaranta
Leonidas Plaza N20-32 and Jorge Washington
Tel: (02) 254 3619
Luxurious apartments with their own kitchens. There is also a bar and restaurant on site.

Antinea Apart Hotel
Juan Rodríguez 175 and Diego de Almagro
Tel: (02) 250 6839
Tel: (02) 250 4404
www.hotelantinea.com
Offers a selection of duplexes and apartments, some of which have access to a terrace or private garden. Located in the Mariscal Sucre district.

E ATING OUT

RECOMMENDED RESTAURANTS, CAFES & BARS

What to Eat

Ecuador has a rich, plentiful, and varied gastronomic culture, different from that of other Latin American countries. Ingredients and seasonings from other parts of South America and from Europe have blended to create some exciting tastes. The following local dishes are well worth trying:

Cuy: whole roasted guinea pig is a traditional food dating back to Inca times. Certainly not served in fancy restaurants, but rather at markets and street stands.

Tamales: a pastry dough made from toasted corn flour or wheat flour and filled with chicken, pork, or beef, wrapped in a leaf and steamed.

Humitas: a pastry (sweet or savory) made from corn (*choclo*), crumbled cheese, egg, and butter and wrapped in a corn husk.

Tortillas de maíz: tasty fried corn pancakes filled with mashed potatoes and cheese.

Empanadas de morocho: a delicious small pie stuffed with pork meat and fried, served with hot sauce.

Empanadas de verde: a pie of green plantain, filled with cheese or meat.

Ceviche: raw seafood marinated in lemon, orange, and tomato juice and served with popcorn and sliced onions. Types of seafood include fish, shrimp, mussels, oysters, lobster, or octopus. Very popular on the coast.

Locro: a yellow soup prepared from milk, stewed potatoes, and cheese, topped with an avocado. It may also contain watercress, meat, lentils, and pork skin.

Lechón hornado: roast suckling pig, a specialty of Sangolqui, near Quito.

Asado (literally, "roasted"): generally means whole roasted pig. It is found in many parts of the country.

Llapingachos: potato and cheese pancakes usually served with *fritada* – scraps of roast pork and salad.

Seco (stew): it can be based on chicken (*gallina*), goat (*chivo*), or lamb (*cordero*) and is usually served with plenty of rice.

Fanesca: a kind of fish soup with beans, lentils, and corn. Eaten mainly during the Easter week, *fanesca* is filling and rich.

On the coast, there is also an amazing richness of gastronomic combinations. Seafood is very good. The most common fish are white sea bass, called *corvina*, shrimp (*camarones*), and lobster (*langostas*). Look out for *encocada* (coconut) dishes, and the *sal prieta* of Manabí, a sauce of peanut butter and corn flour.

A surprisingly tasty dessert (*postre*) is *helados de paila*, ice cream made with fruit juice and beaten in a large brass pot (*paila*), which is rotated in another pot filled with ice.

Where to Eat

Quito has a very good selection of restaurants serving everything from local dishes to international cuisine. Surprisingly, there are few good restaurants in Guayaquil, apart from in the bigger hotels, where excellent food is served. In the provinces it is possible to eat well at reasonable prices. A restaurant need not be fancy to serve delicious and healthy food, but avoid shabby places.

Most of the best restaurants in Quito are in the New Town, around Amazonas, Colón, and 6 de Diciembre. There are several outdoor cafes along Amazonas where you can take in the sun and street life during the day.

In Quito and Guayaquil there are some very expensive restaurants, but in a good restaurant you can have a full meal for approximately $5–10

plus 20 percent service charge and tax. If you order a bottle of wine, however, the bill will be much higher, because wine is imported. It is customary to leave an additional tip of 5–10 percent for the waiter if you have had especially good service.

Restaurants are open for lunch from noon until about 3pm. They often offer inexpensive "executive lunches." Dinner is from 7pm until midnight. In the evening, ordering is à la carte. Most restaurants are closed on Sunday or Monday, but hotel restaurants are open every day.

Drinking Notes

There is an amazing choice of juices (*jugos*) such as *mora* (blackberry), *naranja* (orange), *maracuya* (passion fruit), *naranjilla* (a local fruit tasting like bitter orange) and papaya. Beers such as Pilsener, Club, and Loewenbrau are quite drinkable. All other beers are imported and rather expensive. The usual soft drinks are known as *colas*, and the local brands are very sweet. The excellent mineral water is called Guitig (pronounced gwee-tig) after the best-known brand.

Coffee is often served after meals. A favorite Ecuadorian way of preparing it is to boil it for hours until only a thick syrup remains. This is then diluted with milk and water. Instant coffee is common. Espresso machines are found only in the better hotels and in a very few restaurants and cafeterias.

Finally a word about alcoholic beverages: rum is cheap and good (commonly drunk with Coca-Cola in a *cuba libre*); tequila is also cheap; whisky is fairly expensive, and imported wines (from Chile and Argentina) cost much more than they do in their country of origin. Local wines cannot be recommended.

RESTAURANT LISTINGS

QUITO

International

Mea Culpa
Plaza de la Independencia
Tel: (02) 295 1190
Perhaps the best and most expensive restaurant in the city, overlooking Plaza de la Independencia from the Palacio Arzobispal, which was constructed in 1545. Serves an array of international and Mediterranean dishes. **$$$**

Magic Bean
Mariscal Foch 681 and Juan León Mera
Tel: (02) 256 6181
Cafe/restaurant serving coffee, brownies, pancakes, felafel salads, kebabs, and pizzas. Great meeting place with a relaxed atmosphere. **$$**

Theatrum
Manabí, between Guayaquil and Juan José Flores
Tel: (02) 257 1011
www.theatrum.com.ec
Set inside the Teatro Nacional Sucre, this is one of the hottest new restaurants in the city, with numerous creatively prepared, contemporary international dishes. **$$**

Magic Wrap and Garden Grill
Corner Mariscal Foch 476 and Diego de Almagro
Tel: (02) 252 7190
Same owners as the ever-popular Magic Bean. Serves wrap and *empanadas*. Outdoor Garden Grill open in the evenings. Espresso bar. **$**

Zocalo
José Calama 469 and Juan León Mera
Tel: (02) 223 3929
Inexpensive terrace restaurant and bar with international food. **$**

Cuban

La Bodeguita de Cuba
Reina Victoria 1721 and La Pinta
Tel: (02) 254 2476
Good Cuban food, pleasant atmosphere. **$$**

Ecuadorian and Fusion

Astrid y Gastón
Av. Coruña N32-302 and Av. González Suárez
Tel: (02) 250 6621
www.astridygaston.com
A clone of the enormously popular restaurant in Lima, Peru, which pairs South American dishes with a contemporary touch and a hip, elegant setting. **$$$**

Ceuce Wine Bar
Mall El Jardín, Av. Amazonas and República
Tel: (02) 298 0259
Excellent fusion dishes in a funky, elegant setting blanketed in white. The focus is on the vast wine list. **$$$**

Zazu
Mariano Aguilera 331 and La Pradera
Tel: (02) 254 3559
www.zazuquito.com
One of the leading New Andean restaurants in Ecuador, with a worldly wine list. **$$$**

La Boca del Lobo
José Calama 284 and Reina Victoria
Tel: (02) 223 4083
Chic, fashionable vibes with Ecuadorian and international fusion dishes and a crowd of beautiful people. **$$**

Mamá Clorinda
Reina Victoria 1144 and José Calama
Tel: (02) 254 4362
One of the best choices in Quito for Ecuadorian fare and often has live music. **$$**

Su Cebiche
Juan León Mera 24-204 and José Calama
Tel: (02) 252 6380
A great lunch spot serving Manabí-style ceviches and seafood in an unassuming location in the Mariscal. **$**

French

Rincón de Francia
General Roca 779 and 9 de Octubre
Tel: (02) 255 4668/222 5053
www.rincondefrancia.com
French restaurant with a very good reputation. Reservation necessary. **$$$**

Italian

Il Risotto
Pinto 209 and Diego de Almagro
Tel: (02) 222 0400
Authentic Italian cooking. Home-made pasta and good tiramisu. **$$**

Il Pizzaiolo
Juan León Mera 1012 and Mariscal Foch
Tel: (02) 254 3900
Italian restaurant serving delicious, inexpensive pasta dishes and pizzas. **$**

Oriental

Sake
Paul Rivet N30-166 and Whymper
Tel: (02) 252 4818
Very hip, upscale sushi

BELOW: fine dining at Cueva del Oso in Quito.

restaurant with a creative selection of rolls, sashimi, and other Japanese dishes. $$$

Siam
José Calama E5-10 and Juan León Mera
Tel: (02) 379 2035
Thai place with cool East Asian decor and a terrace overlooking the center of the Mariscal. A wide selection of dishes. $$

Steak Houses

Adam's Rib
José Calama 329 and Reina Victoria
Tel: (02) 256 3196
Excellent steak house in the Mariscal Sucre district with even better desserts. $$$

Shorton Grill
José Calama 216 and Diego de Almagro
Tel: (02) 252 3645
Formal steak house with a large wine list. For those who don't fancy steak, the menu also includes a number of seafood and international dishes. $$$

Vegetarian

El Marqués
José Calama 443 and Av. Amazonas
Inexpensive vegetarian

restaurant which is particularly popular at lunchtimes. $

Local Dishes

La Cueva del Oso
Chile and Venezuela
Tel: (02) 258 3826
Fancy restaurant serving a variety of Ecuadorian dishes. $$$

El Cebiche
Juan León Mera 1232 and José Calama
Tel: (02) 252 6380
As the name suggests, a good place to try the local ceviche. $$

Las Redes
Av. Amazonas 845 and Veintimilla
Tel: (02) 252 5691
Delicious ceviche and seafood specialties served in informal surroundings. $$

Taberna Quiteña
Av. Amazonas 1259 and Luís Cordero
Tel: (02) 223 0009
Restaurant serving good Ecuadorian food and also hosts live entertainment. $$

La Choza
12 de Octubre 1821 and Luís Cordero
Tel: (02) 223 0839
Well-made food served in pleasant surroundings. $$

ABOVE: a leisurely lunch at the Pallapacta springs near Quito

CAFES

Café de la Cultura
Robles 513 and Reina Victoria
Tel: (02) 222 4271
www.cafecultura.com
Delicious breakfasts. Also open for lunch and afternoon English tea.

Cafecito
Luís Cordero and Reina Victoria
Tel: (02) 223 4862
www.cafecito.net
Popular cafe with good service and atmosphere.

Café Sutra
José Calama 380 and Juan Léon Mera
Tel: (02) 250 9106

Trendy internet cafe/bar.
Coffee Tree
Plaza del Quinde
Enormously popular cafe with good coffee, juices, sandwiches, and snacks.

Crepes & Waffles
Quicentro Shopping Center, La Rábida 461 and Francisco de Orellana
Tel: (02) 243 6058
Clean and modern Colombian chain that specializes in sweet and savory crepes, waffles, and ice creams.

THE NORTH AND THE PACIFIC COAST

Otavalo

Alli Alpa
Plaza de Ponchos
Local dishes such as *trucha* (trout) prepared in a number of ways, plus reasonable set meals. $$

Shenandoah Pie Shop
Plaza de Ponchos
This shop on the plaza has some of the best pies, milkshakes, and desserts in the country, plus a decent breakfast. $

Cotacachi

El Colibri
End of Calle 10 de Agosto
Tel: (06) 291 5237

Gourmet restaurant set in the gardens of the lavish La Mirage hotel and spa. Worth making the hour and a half drive from Quito just for lunch. $$$

Ibarra

Café Floral
Bolivar and Gómez de la Torre
Friendly cafe serving a number of dishes including crêpes and fondue. Swiss owners make their own cheese. $$

Esmeraldas

Budapest
Manuela Cañizares 214 and Bolívar

Hungarian-owned restaurant. $

Chifa Asiático
Mañizares and Bolívar
The best of the *chifas* (Chinese restaurants) in Esmeraldas. $

Las Redes
On the main plaza
Restaurant serving inexpensive fish dishes. $

Manta

El Marinero
Malecón and Calle 110 in Tarquí, this is one of the better typical Manabí seafood restaurants. Good ceviches and other seafood dishes. $$

Bahía de Caráquez

Muelle Uno
On the pier for the San Vicente boats
The best grill and seafood restaurant in town, with a number of wonderfully prepared dishes. $$

Arena Bar
Bolívar and Arenas
Great and wildly popular place for pizza. $$

PRICE CATEGORIES

Categories are based on the cost of a meal for two people, excluding wine:
$$$ = $20 or more
$$ = $10–20
$ = $10 or less

ORIENTE AND THE CENTRAL HIGHLANDS

Puyo

El Alcázar
10 de Agosto 936
Tel: (03) 288 5330
Great Spanish restaurant with good value set meals. **$$**

Coca

Parrilladas Argentinas
Cuenca and Amazonas
This Argentine-style grill is the only good restaurant in town. **$$**

Tena

Café Tortuga
Orellana s/n
Tel: (06) 529 5419
Great cafe located right on the *malecón* (pier), serving a variety of international dishes. **$**

Ambato

El Alamo Chalet
Cevallos 1179
Swiss-owned restaurant serving a variety of Ecuadorian and international dishes. Open late. **$$**

Baños

Le Petit Restaurant
16 de Diciembre and Montalvo
Tel: (03) 740 936
www.lepetit.banios.com
With a great garden setting and Parisian owners, this is the best restaurant in the city. Serves a variety of international dishes. **$$$**
Casa de la Abuela
Ambato and 16 de Diciembre
Tel: (03) 274 0923
A variety of traditional dishes, such as *llapingacho*, plus

international fare. **$$**
Pancho Villa
Montalvo and 16 de Diciembre
Nice variety of Mexican food in a pleasant atmosphere. Makes a nice change from the other places in town. **$$**
Ali Cumba
Calle Maldonaldo
This small yet charming Danish-owned cafe is situated on a terrace overlooking Parque Central. Serves muffins, pastries, light meals, and good espresso coffee. **$**
Café Blah Blah
Ambato and Haflants
Small sidewalk cafe serving light meals and coffees. **$**
Casa Hood
Martínez and Alfaro
Tel: (03) 740 537
A range of food from vegetarian to Southeast Asian, with a good book

exchange and maps for sale. **$**

Riobamba

D'Baggio Pizzeria
Av. Borja and Miguel Angel
Tel: (03) 296 1832
Wood-fired, Neopolitan-style pizza in a clean, modern setting. **$$**
La Gran Havana
Borja 42–52 and Duchicela
Good value Cuban restaurant serving sandwiches, rice, and beans, plus a number of international dishes. **$**

SOUTHERN SIERRA

Cuenca

Café Eucalyptus
Gran Colombia 9-41 and Benigno Malo
Tel: (07) 284 9157
Sparkling, colonial-style bar and restaurant that has been visited by presidents and celebrities. They serve excellent international cuisine, and there is a lengthy sushi menu and cocktail list. Hosts a lively salsa night on a Saturday. **$$$**
El Jardín
Presidente Córdova 7-23
Tel: (07) 283 1120
This is one of Ecuador's best restaurants – pricey but worth it. Serves a variety of international dishes. **$$$**
El Jordán
Larga 6-111 and Presidente Borrero
Tel: (07) 285 0517
www.eljordanrestaurante.com
Arabian dishes paired with a few Ecuadorian ones served in an elegant setting with nice views of the river. The hand-painted walls are an interesting

feature. **$$$**
Goda Restaurant and Delicatessen
Gran Colombia 7-87 and Luís Cordero
Tel: (07) 283 1390
Situated in the El Dorado Hotel, this place has two sections – a good deli with soups and sandwiches, and a trendy, modern restaurant with some of the most cutting-edge dishes in town. **$$**
Raymipampa Café
Benigno Malo 859
Tel: (07) 282 7435
Best budget restaurant in Cuenca, popular with locals. Inexpensive steaks and chicken, and excellent chocolate milkshakes. **$$**
Sankt Florian
Larga 7-119 and Luís Cordero
Tel: (07) 883 3359
www.sanktflorian.com
Extremely elegant restaurant and bar on the Barranco serving classy international dishes. Has a fine wine list. **$$**
Café Austria
Benigno Malo 5-99

Tel: (07) 284 0899
Pleasant corner cafe serving hot drinks, cocktails, pastries, and light meals. It's a popular choice with locals and tourists. **$**
El Cafecito
Honorato Vásquez 736 and Luís Cordero
Tel: (07) 283 2337
Popular place for a light meal, coffee, or beer, particularly with the younger crowd. **$**
New York Pizza Restaurant
Gran Columbia 10-43
Tel: (07) 284 2792
Good pizzeria serving large pizzas and filling *calzones*. **$**
Poncho
Larga 579
Tel: (07) 580 4075
Excellent American-owned, Californian-style cafe serving tacos, burritos, and other fast, but somewhat healthy, goodies. **$**
Rancho Chileno
Av. España 1317
Tel: (07) 286 4112
Chilean restaurant with a pleasant ambience. **$**

Loja

Jose Antonio
Eguiguren 12-24
The best restaurant in the city. Serves classic French cuisine and a number of international dishes. **$$**
Mi Tierra
10 de Agosto 1144
Tel: (07) 420-431
Typical regional dishes such as *cecina* (salty fried pork) in a pleasant rustic setting. **$$**

Vilcabamba

La Terraza
Vega y Bolívar
Sidewalk setting on the main plaza with good Mexican and international dishes. Popular with the backpacker crowd. **$**

SOUTH COAST

ABOVE: a typical coastal dish of deep-fried seafood.

Guayaquil

Blu Restaurant
Victor Emilio Estrada 707 and
Ficus, Urdesa
Tel: (04) 288 4954
Mediterranean and
international dishes and
one of the most complete
wine lists in Guayaquil. $$$
**Guayaquil Club Naval
de Yacht**
Malecón Simon Bolívar and Aguirre
Tel: (04) 244 6366
A nice place for the happy
hour or sunset. Serves
international dishes and
seafood. There is also a
smaller, but less
atmospheric, restaurant on
the first floor with very
economical menus. $$$
Lo Nuestro
Victor Emilio Estrada 903 and

Higueras, Urdesa
Tel: (04) 238 6398
Excellent Ecuadorian food.
The most famous steak
house in Guayaquil. $$$
Aroma Café
Jardines del Malecón 2000
Tel: (04) 239 1328
Pleasant cafe on the
Malecón overlooking a
small pool and gardens.
$$
Barandua Inn
Circunvalación Norte 528 B, at the
shore of the Salado estuary
Tel: (04) 238 9407
Excellent seafood. $$
Ciao Restaurant
Samborondón Centro Comercial
Piazza, Local 4C
Tel: (04) 283 7349
The best Italian restaurant
in town, with eclectic
contemporary dishes. $$

El Caracol Azul
9 de Octubre and Los Ríos
Tel: (04) 228 0461
White-tablecloth place with
a Peruvian chef who cooks
excellent meat and seafood
dishes. $$
El Parque
Top floor of Unicentro, Aguirre,
between Chile and Chimborazo
Very good buffet lunch;
overlooks Parque Bolívar. $$
**La Canoa at Hotel
Continental**
Chile and 10 de Agosto
Tel: (04) 232 9270
Good local food. $$
La Casa del Cangrejo
Av. Plaza Dañin
All types of crab dishes. $$
La Parrillada del Ñato
Victor Emilio Estrada 1219, Urdesa
Tel: (04) 238 7098/288 8599
Good grilled meat,
Argentine-style. $$
Restaurant Nuvó
Av. Alzibar and Edificio Torres del
Norte Torre B, Local 7
Tel: (04) 268 7758
Very modern, elegant
restaurant with
international fusion cuisine
and a lengthy wine list. $$
Trattoria da Enrico
Bálsamos 504
Tel: (04) 238 7079
Very pleasant Italian
ambiance, rustic, yet
elegant; excellent food. $$
Tsuji
Victor Emilio Estrada 813 and
Guayacanes, Urdesa
Tel: (04) 288 1183
Exquisite Japanese food. $$
El Cantonés
Av. Guillermo Pareja and Calle 43,

La Garzota
Tel: (04) 223 6333
Reasonably priced *chifa*
(Chinese restaurant) with a
pleasant atmosphere. $
Sion Lung
Victor Emilio Estrada 619 and
Ficus, Urdesa
Tel: (04) 228 7949
Great *chifa* (Chinese
restaurant) that will even
deliver to your hotel room. $

Salinas

Mar y Tierra
Malecón and Valverde
Tel: (04) 288 4954
Perhaps the best seafood
restaurant in Salinas. Has
a number of good meat
dishes as well. $$$
La Bella Italia
Malecón and Calle 17
Tel: (04) 288 4954
A nice pizza menu is paired
with a good selection of
international dishes. Very
popular. $$

Montañita

Tiburón
In the town
Well-run restaurant serving
ceviche, fish dishes, and
seafood *empanadas*. $$
Zoociedad
In the town
It has a thatched roof, but is
still the most sophisticated
restaurant in town. Pastas,
meats, and a nice wine list
chosen by the Italian chef.
The *lomo de pimienta verde*
is highly recommended. $$

THE GALÁPAGOS

Isla Santa Cruz

The main area for
restaurants and cafes in
the Galápagos is along
Avenida Charles Darwin
in Puerto Ayora, Isla
Santa Cruz.
La Garrapata
Av. Charles Darwin,
Puerto Ayora
Tel: (05) 252 6264
Popular meeting place for
travelers serving
sandwiches and main
dishes. $$$

**Red Sushi Bar &
Restaurant**
At the Red Mangrove Inn,
Av. Charles Darwin,
Puerto Ayora
Tel: (05) 252 7011
Japanese restaurant with a
long sushi and sashimi list.
They will even deliver to
your hotel or yacht. $$$
Café Habana
Av. Charles Darwin and Naveda,
Puerto Ayora
Lively bar at night, although
during the day it has a good
set lunch. $$

Hotel Sol y Mar
Av. Charles Darwin,
Puerto Ayora
Tel: (05) 252 6281
Good place for breakfast on
terrace with iguanas. $$
Las Cuatro Linternas
Av. Charles Darwin,
Puerto Ayora
Good Italian food. $$
Limón y Café
Av. Charles Darwin,
Puerto Ayora
Popular thatched bar
serving drinks and snacks.
Open evenings only. $$

El Chocolate Galápagos
Av. Charles Darwin,
Opposite Banco del Pacífico,
Puerto Ayora
Recommended for snacks
and delicious chocolate
cake. $

PRICE CATEGORIES

Categories are based on
the cost of a meal for two
people, excluding wine:
$$$ = $20 or more
$$ = $10–20
$ = $10 or less

A CTIVITIES

FESTIVALS AND HOLIDAYS, THE ARTS, NIGHTLIFE, SHOPPING, SPORTS, AND TOURS

THE ARTS

Art Galleries

Quito

Artists display their works in the Parque El Ejido, near the big arch on Av. Patria, at weekends.
El Centro Cultural Mexicano
Suiza 343 and República del El Salvador.
Tel: (02) 225 5149.
Often shows Ecuadorian and Latin American artists.
Centro de Promoción de Artistas, Casa Blanca, Parque del Ejido.
Tel: (02) 252 2410.
Fundación Posada de las Artes Kingman
Diego de Almagro 1550 and Pradera.
Tel: (02) 222 0610.
Exhibitions and cultural events.
Exhibits of Eduardo Kingman's work.
Gold Mask Gallery
Jorge Washington 656 and Av.Amazonas.
Tel: (02) 254 2120/247 3817.
Centro de Arte Viteri
Orellana 473 and Whymper.
Tel: (02) 256 1548.
Exhibition of Oswaldo Viteri's work.

Cuenca

Galería de Arte Contemporáneo Illescas
Calle Alvear 1-91 and Solano.
Tel (07) 283 5764.
Ariel Dawi
Borrero 7-40.
Tel (07) 282 2935.

Theaters

Quito

Teatro Prometeo (Teatro de la Casa de la Cultura)

6 de Diciembre and Tarqui.
Tel: (02) 290 2272.
Adjoining the Casa de la Cultura Ecuatoriana.
Teatro Sucre
Calle Flores and Guayaquil.
Tel: (02) 257 2823.
www.teatrosucre.com (in Spanish)
The most fancy and most traditional of the theaters (plays, concerts, shows).
Humanizarte
Leonidas Plaza N24–226 and Lizardo García.
Tel: (02) 222 6116/250 6302.
www.humanizarte.org
Contemporary dance shows.
Teatro Bolívar
Flores 421 and Junín.
Tel: (02) 258 2486.
www.teatrobolivar.org
A variety of festivals and events are held in this recently restored colonial gem of a building.

NIGHTLIFE

Quito

The Mariscal Sucre district is filled with numerous bars and clubs around Plaza del Quinde, Foch, and Mera.
Huaina, Foch E5-12. An often crowded bar and dance hall with cheap drinks and loud music.
The Lounge, Foch E5-25.Glitzy lounge with Victorian furniture and a laid-back atmosphere.
Naranjilla Mecánica, Tamayo and Veintimilla. Trendy with a labyrinthine layout and good cocktails.
No Bar, Calama 380. Young crowd with popular music and a lively dance floor.
Nucanchi, Av. Universitaria and Armero. Tel: (02) 254 0967. One of

the best *peñas* in town where you can hear live local folk music.
El Pobre Diablo, La Católica and Galavis. Frequent live jazz nights ($5–8 entrance) with a pleasant atmosphere.
Reina Victoria Pub, Reina Victoria and Roca. Tel: (02) 222 6369. British pub with a good selection of imported beers and microbrews. Serves classic British dishes such as fish and chips, and curry.
Sport Planet, Av. Naciones Unidas and América. Tel: (02) 226 7790. Sports bar with a full menu. The best place to catch a game away from home.
Vulcano Bar, At the base of the Teleférico. Tel (02) 223 5195. One of the "it" clubs of the moment, with high covers and pricey drinks.

Baños

Amenitay, 16 de Diciembre and Espejo. Tel: (03) 274 1713. Decades-old *peña* with live music every night of the year.
Jack Rock Café, Eloy Alfaro 541. Longtime travelers' favorite, with great mixed drinks and a pool table.
Mocambo, Eloy Alfaro and Ambato. Sprawling bar with lounge areas and small dance floors over three levels.

Guayaquil

There are a number of frequently changing clubs near the Malecón 2000, the Malecón del Salado, the Urdesa suburb, and the Kennedy Mall.
Rincón Folklórico, Malecón 208 and Montalvo. Popular *peña* that stays open late on the weekends.
    Party-goers should also try **La Chiva** city tour – a lively open bus with music (and rum) on Friday nights. Contact **Royal Tours**, tel: (02) 232 6688, or **Viajes Horizontes**, tel:

(02) 228 1260. Some of the most pleasant places to drink and dine are along the recently refurbished Malecón waterfront.

Cuenca

Café Eucalyptus, Colombia 9-41 and Benigno Malo. Tel: (07) 284 9157. Salsa night on Saturdays is the liveliest place in Cuenca. Ladies' night on a Thursday is also popular. **Wunderbar**, Hermano Miguel 3-43 and Larga. Tel: (07) 283 1724. Pasta, sandwiches, and a few German dishes round out this friendly restaurant-cum-bar with a few pool tales.

Puerto Ayora

Bar Bongo, Av. Charles Darwin and Berlanga, 2nd Floor. Popular place for a drink. There are also a number of other bars near by.

Entertainment

There are many cinemas in Guayaquil which show English-language movies with Spanish subtitles. Look in the local newspapers or at the reception desks of the more expensive hotels

about what is going on. *El Universo* has information on movies and events. *Peñas* (folk music evenings) normally take place at weekends: recommended is **Rincón Folklórico**, Malecón 208 and Montalvo.

SHOPPING

Quito

There are dozens of *artesanías* stores and kiosks in Quito, especially in the Avenida Amazonas area. Several have outstanding selections of high-quality folk art and clothing. They include:
Folklore Olga Fisch
Av. Colón 260.
Tel: (02) 254 1315.
www.olgafisch.com
There is also a branch in the Hotel Colón.
Centro Artesanal
Calle Juan León Mera 804.
Tel: (02) 254 8234.
Exedra
Carrión 243 and Plaza.
Artesanía center.
Tel: (02) 222 4001.

Cinemas

Cinemark, Plaza de las Américas, República and Naciones Unidas, Quito. Tel: (02) 226 2026, www.cinemark.com.ec
Popular multiplex.
Fundación Octaedro, El Zuriago E8–28 and los Shyris, Quito. Tel: (02) 246 9170, www.octaedro.org.ec
Shows arthouse films.
Multicines, CCI Shopping Mall, Amazonas and Naciones Unidas, Quito. Tel: (02) 225 9677, www.multicines.com.ec
Eight screens, good sound quality, and the latest movies.
IMAX, Malecón and Loja, Guayaquil. Tel: (04) 230 9400, www.imaxmalecon2000.com
IMAX and movie theater right on Malecón 2000. Also on the same site is MAAC Cine, which shows indie films.
Cinemark, Mall del Sol, Guayaquil. Tel: (04) 208 5106, www.cinemark.com.ec
Popular multiplex.

Galería Latina
Calle Juan León Mera 833 and Veintimilla.
Tel: (02) 254 0380.
www.galerialatina-quito.com
La Bodega Exportadora
Calle Juan León Mera 614.

Cuenca

There are several handicraft shops along Gran Colombia, near the El Dorado Hotel.
Artes Artesanias y Antiguedades
Borrero and Córdova.
Textiles, jewelry, and antiques.
Artesa
Luís Cordero 10–31 and Gran Colombia.
Ecuadorian ceramics (including Vega designs).

High-quality Panama hats are made by **Homero Ortega**, Av. Gil Ramirez Davalos 3–86. Tel: (07) 280 1288. www.homeroortega.com
The factory near the bus station is open for tours. You can see these famed and misnamed straw hats being made. They were originally crafted by hand in Montecristi and then exported to Panama.

Guayaquil

Guayaquil has several smart shopping centers, including:
Mall del Sur
Av. 25 de Julio, between Cuadra and Albán.
Tel: (04) 208 5000.
Large mall with many European and

BELOW: Quito has some great clubs and bars and Quiteños know how to party.

Calendar of Festivals and Events

Each month sees numerous festivals take place in Ecuador. Typical festivities involve fireworks, processions, masquerades, and folkloric dancing. Bullfights and horse racing are common in rural areas. Here is a calendar of Ecuador's principal festivals, including national holidays.

January

1st – National holiday: New Year's festivities.
6th – National holiday: Epiphany. **Ambato** (Tungurahua) and **Cuenca** (Azuay): Children's Mass (*masa de niños*), processions, carols.
Gatazo Grande (Chimborazo) and **Lican** (Chimborazo): Fireworks, hymns, election of the *prioste* (Steward of the Festival) and kings.
Montecristi (Manabí): Bands, dances.
Tisalleo (Tungurahua): High Mass, paying homage to the Christ Child in the crib.
Calpi (Chimborazo): Marimbas, processions with "La Mamá Negra."
15th – Quito-Chillogallo (Pichincha): Dances of the Innocent, masquerades, bands.

February

1st – Mira (Carchi): Festival of the Virgin of Charity (Virgen de la Caridad); fireworks, dances, glove ball games *(pelota nacional)*, vaca loca (crazy cow) rodeos.
12th – (All Ecuador): Anniversary of the "discovery" of the Amazon River *(Día del Oriente)* – Fairs in Puyo, Tena, Macas, and Zamora; day of the province of Galápagos – civic events.
27th – (All Ecuador): Patriotism and National Unity day to commemorate the battle of Tarqui in 1829.
Changeable date – (All Ecuador): Carnival preceding Lent.

March

2nd to 5th – Atuntaqui (Imbabura): Sugar cane and Craftsmanship Festival, *verbenas* (open-air dances).
4th to 10th – Gualaceo (Azuay): Peach Festival.

April

19th to 21st – Riobamba (Chimborazo): Farming, cattle, handicraft, and industrial fair.
Changeable date – (All Ecuador): Holy Week. Celebrations on Good Friday and Easter Sunday.

May

1st – (All Ecuador): Labor day – workers' parades.
2nd – Quito: Festival of Las Cruzes at La Cruz Verde quarter (corner of Bolívar and Imbabura streets).
3rd – Quito: Festival of La Cruz at Champicruz (Avenidas Prensa and Sumaco).
Checa (Pinchincha): Patron saint's day (of El Señor de la Buena Esperanza).
11th to 14th – Puyo (Pastaza): Farming and industrial exhibition and fair in the Amazon region.
24th – (All Ecuador): National civic festivity to commemorate the battle of Pichincha in 1822.

June

23rd/24th – Otavalo (Imbabura), **Tabacundo** (Pichincha), **Guamote** (Chimborazo): Festival of Saint John (San Juan).
24th – Sangolqui (Pichincha): Corn and tourism festivities.
24th – Calpi (Chimborazo): *Gallo Compadre* and *vaca loca* rodeos.
28th to 29th – Santo Domingo de los Colorados (Pichincha): Canonization anniversary.
29th – Cotacahi and Cayambe (Imbabura), and other communities: Festival of saints Peter and Paul (San Pedro y San Pablo).
Changeable date – (All Ecuador): Corpus Christi.

July

16th – Ibarra (Imbabura): Celebration of Virgen del Carmen.
22nd – Pelileo (Tungurahua): Canonization anniversary.
23rd to 25th – Guayaquil: Guayaquil's foundation anniversary.
24th – National Holiday: Simón Bolívar's birthday.
29th – Pillaro (Tungurahua): Celebration day of the Apostle Santiago the Elder.

August

3rd to 5th – Esmeraldas: Independence Day.
5th to 7th – Sicalpa (Chimborazo): Festival of the Virgin of the Snow (Virgen de las Nieves).
10th – National Holiday: Commemoration of independence in 1809.
Pillaro (Tungurahua): San Lorenzo festivities.
Yaguachi (Guayas): San Jacinto Festival, with popular pilgrimages.
25th – Santa Rosa (El Oro): Agricultural Fair.

September

2nd to 15th – Otavalo (Imbabura): Yamor festivities.
5th to 12th – Loja: Festival of Virgen del Cisne, the patron saint.
6th to 14th – Cotacachi (Imbabura): Jora festival.
8th to 9th – Macara (Loja): Agricultural fair.
8th to 9th – Sangolqui (Pichincha): Bullfights, dances, processions.
11th to 16th – Milagro (Guayas): Agricultural fair.
20th to 26th – Machala (El Oro): International Banana Festival.
23rd to 24th – Quito and **Latacunga** (Cotopaxi): Festival of Virgen de las Mercedes, the patron saint.
24th – Piñas (El Oro): Product fair.
24th to 28th – Ibarra (Imbabura): Festivals of the Lakes.
27th – Espejo (Imbabura): Indigenous handicrafts fair.
29th – Gonzanama (Loja): Agricultural and industrial exhibition.

October

9th to 12th – Guayaquil: National civic festival to commemorate the independence of Guayaquil.
12th – National Holiday: Columbus Day (Día de la Raza).
14th to 18th – Portoviejo (Manabí): Agricultural and industrial exhibition. Many attractions.

November

1st – National Holiday: All Saints' Day.
2nd – (All Ecuador): All Souls' Day (Día de los Difuntos).
3rd – Cuenca (Azuay): Commemoratation of Cuenca's independence.
4th – Manta (Manabí): Manta Day.
11th – Latacunga (Cotopaxi): Independence of Latacunga.
21st – El Quinche (Pichincha): Day of the Virgen of El Quinche, the patron saint.

December

1st to 6th – Quito (Pichincha): Anniversary of the Foundation of San Francisco de Quito.
25th – National Holiday: Christmas Day.
**28th – All Fools' Day.
31st – (All Ecuador): New Year's Eve celebrations. Parades and dances culminate in burning of life-size dolls representing politicians, artists, and *el año viejo* (the old year), particularly in Quito, Guayaquil, and Esmeraldas.

North American shops.
Mall del Sol
Av. Marengo and Orrantia.
Tel: (04) 269 0100.
Mall and entertainment complex with many international shops, restaurants, and bars.
Centro Comercial Malécon
Malecón 2000, between Olmedo and Colón.
Tel: (04) 232 0245.
Large mall on the waterfront with over 200 stores and a range of international restaurants.

For good-quality handicrafts, **Lo Nuestro** and **Galería Guayasamín** (both at Policentro) and **Artesanías de Ecuador**, 9 de Octubre 104 and Malecón, are recommended. The **Mercado Artesanal** between Av. Loja and Montalia is also good, but be wary of pickpockets.

Shopping at the Bahía (black market), along Calles Pinchincha and Olmedo, is very popular.

Galápagos
Food and drink are available in several stores on the main islands of Santa Cruz, San Cristóbal, and Isabela, although dearer than on the mainland, but medicines, sun lotions, and film are either not available or extremely expensive.

Never buy souvenirs made from black coral, turtle, and tortoiseshell, as these animals are protected.

Bookstores

Quito
Confederate Books
Calama 410
Tel: (02) 252 7890
www.confederatebooks.com
Good for books in Spanish on Ecuadorian culture.
Ediciones Abya Yala
12 de Octubre 1430
and Wilson
Tel: (02) 250 6251, 250 6247
www.abyayala.org
Good for books in Spanish on Ecuadorian culture.
Librería Científica
Luque 225 and Chile
Tel: (04) 232 8069
Sells books in English.
Libri Mundi
Juan León Mera N23-83 and Wilson
Tel: (02) 223 4791/252 9587
Also at the QuiCentro Shopping Mall
Tel: (02) 246 4473
www.librimundi.com (in Spanish)
Books in English, German, French, and Spanish; large selection of maps, international magazines, and records.
Nuevos Horizontes
6 de Marzo 924

ABOVE: sea kayaking in Elizabeth Bay in the Galápagos Islands.

Book exchange.
Selecciones
Albán Borja Mall
Has books and magazines in English.
Tower Records
QuiCentro Shopping Mall
Tel: (02) 292 0413
Has a variety of magazines.

SPORTS

Quito
There is a **public swimming pool** at Av. Universitaria and Nicaragua and also one at Cochapata, near Villarroel and 6 de Diciembre.

The El Condado Country Club has an **18-hole golf course, heated swimming pool**, and **horseback riding facilities** (temporary membership available).

You can join some of the top hotel **gym clubs** if staying a while. Membership is about $100 a month. Hotel Hilton Colón often has special discount rates for its gym.

A variety of **paragliding** courses is offered by TerranovaTrek. Tel: (02) 225 3327; www.terranovatrek.com

Guayaquil
There are many sports clubs in Guayaquil. Guests of the Hotel Oro Verde can use the facilities of the **Tennis Club Guayaquil** on request. Near by, there is an **Olympic swimming pool**, open to the public. There is also a swimming pool at **Malecón Simón Bolívar 116**. Guests of the Gran Hotel Guayaquil can use the facilities of the **Terraza Racquet Club** (with two squash courts, gymnasium and sauna).

Horseback Riding

Horseback riding trips can be arranged from most major tourist destinations (see also page 123).
The Green Horse Ranch
Casilla 17-12-602, Quito
Tel: (02) 237 4847
www.horseranch.de
Monta Runa
Hermano Miguel 4-46 and Calle Larga, Cuenca
Tel: (07) 282 8593
Fax: (07) 282 0085
www.montaruna.ch
Horseback riding.

Mountain Biking

Biking tours can be booked through specialist tour agencies, such as the ones listed here. It is also possible to hire bikes in major destinations including Quito, Cuenca, Riobamba, and Baños.

Diving

Galápagos Sub-Aqua
Guayaquil office:
Tel/fax: (04) 230 5514
Galápagos office:
Av. Charles Darwin, Puerto Ayora, Isla Santa Cruz
Tel/fax: (05) 252 6350/252 6633
www.galapagos-sub-aqua.com
Offers scuba and diving tours and diving instruction.
Scuba Iguana
Av. Charles Darwin, Puerto Ayora, Isla Santa Cruz
Tel/fax: (05) 252 6497
www.scubaiguana.com
Offers a wide choice of courses and dives.

National Parks

For information on National Parks contact:
Ministerio del Ambiente y Turismo (Parks Section: ex-INEFAN), 8th Floor, Av. Amazonas and Eloy Alfaro, Quito. Tel: (02) 256 3429. www.ambiente.gov.ec
The main conservation organization is:
Fundación Natura
Calle Elia Liut N45-10 and El Telégarfo 1, Quito. Tel: (02) 227 2863. www.fnatura.org

Biking Dutchman
Foch 714 and Juan León Mera, Quito
Tel: (02) 256 8323/254 2806
Fax: (02) 256 7008
www.bikingdutchman.com
Moggely Tours
Calama E4-54 and Av. Amazonas, Quito
Tel: (02) 255 4984
www.moggely.com
ProBici
Constituyente 23-51, Riobamba
Tel: (03) 295 1759
www.probici.com

White-water Rafting

With the Andes and one of the highest concentrations of rivers in any country, it's no wonder rafting in Ecuador is world class. Baños, Tena, and Puyo are great bases for rafting class III and IV rapids, including the Upper Río Napo (Class III) and Río Misahuallí (Class IV and IV+). The Río Toachi (Class III–III+) is also popular due to its proximity to Quito. The following agencies specialize in rafting trips.
Explorandes Ecuador
Presidente Wilson 537 and Diego de Almagro, Quito
Tel: (02) 222 2699
Fax: (02) 255 6938,
www.explorandes.com
Geo Tours
Ambato and Haflants, Baños
Tel: (03) 274 1344
www.geotoursecuador.com
Ríos Ecuador
Foch 746 and Juan León Mera, Quito
Tel: (02) 290 4054
Tarqui 230 and Días de Pineda, Tena
Tel: (06) 288 6727
www.riosecuador.com
Row Expediciones
Pablo Suárez 151, Quito
Tel: (02) 223 9224,
www.rowexpediciones.com
Yacu Amu Rafting
Foch 746 and Juan León Mera, Quito
Tel: (02) 290 4054

Fax: (02) 290 4055
www.yacuamu.com

Birdwatching

Andean cloudforest and the Amazonian lowlands are extremely diverse and are home to many rare and endemic avian species. Some of the country's ornithological highlights include the area around Mindo north of Quito and Parque Nacional Podocarpus, near Vilcabamba. In the Galápagos you can see Darwin's finches, various boobies, and numerous frigate birds. The following organizations can provide information on birdwatching in Ecuador.
Andean Birding
Salazar Gómez E-1482 and Eloy Alfaro, Quito
Tel/fax: (02) 224 4426
www.andeanbirding.com
Aves & Conservación
(Ecuadorian Ornithology Foundation), Pasaje Joaquín Tinajero E3-05 and Jorge Drom

BELOW: Ecuador is an ornithologist's paradise.

Tel/fax: (02) 227 1800/224 9968, www.avesyconservacion.org
Fundácion Natura
See National Parks box, left.
Tinalandia Ornithological Reserve
Urbanización el Bosque, Calle Tercera 43-78, Quito
Tel/fax: (02) 244 9028
www.tinalandia.com

Fishing

The Guayas and Manabí provinces hold some of the world's best sport fishing; dolphinfish, barracuda, blue and black marlin, and yellow-finned tuna are all found there. Andean rivers and lakes are filled with trout and popular with fly-fishermen, while fishing for piranha in the rivers of the Oriente is a popular activity at jungle lodges. To arrange fishing trips on the Pacific Coast, contact:
Pescatours
Comín 135 and El Oro, Guayaquil
Tel/fax: (04) 244 3365
www.pescatours.com.ec (in Spanish)

A – Z

A HANDY SUMMARY OF PRACTICAL INFORMATION, ARRANGED ALPHABETICALLY

A dmission Charges

Charges for museums and national parks are no more than a few dollars each, and rarely that.

B udgeting for Your Trip

Ecuador falls into the middle when comparing prices to other Latin American countries. Since dollarization in 2000, prices have remained steady. Cities such as Quito and Guayaquil remain slightly more expensive than other places, but the difference is hardly noticeable outside the price of a hotel.

Accommodation varies from place to place. In the large cities and major tourist destinations budget accommodation will run from as little as $8 per night to several hundred dollars for a top hotel. In small, rural villages it is easy to find accommodation in hostels and

hospedajes for just a few dollars per person. In the Oriente, lodges tend to be rather expensive, starting at around $50 per day, although this usually includes food and activities.

Getting around by bus is fairly cheap, and journeys are never more than a few hours due to the size of the country. Transportation by bus averages about $1 per hour, depending on the level of comfort. Trains are also economical, although less reliable. Within cities, taxis are cheap and everywhere, and rarely will a ride within a city, even Quito or Guayaquil, cost more than a few dollars. Some locations in the Oriente, as well as the Galápagos, can only be reached by airplane, which can be expensive. A round-trip plane ticket to the Galápagos will cost about $350.

The cost of food varies heavily. In large cities, and especially the Galápagos, rarely will you be able to eat at a restaurant for less than $5, and meals can cost as much as $30

per person for a top restaurant. In rural areas, small local restaurants will serve menus, usually including several hearty courses, for just over a dollar. It may be your only option.

Drinking tends to be relatively cheap, as a beer will generally cost just over a dollar in most bars and pubs, although if you are in a large club in a place such as Quito, you will likely have to triple that price. Cover charges at clubs tend to be anywhere between $3–15.

Business Hours

Government offices in Quito are open to the public Mon–Fri 8am–4.30pm. In Guayaquil, hours are Mon–Fri 9am–noon and 3.30–6pm.

Banks in Ecuador are open Mon–Fri 9am–6pm with some also open 9am–1pm on Sat. They are closed on public holidays. Private companies generally work weekdays 8am–5pm with an hour for lunch.

Stores are generally open Mon–Fri

TRANSPORTATION
ACCOMMODATIONS
EATING OUT
ACTIVITIES
A–Z
LANGUAGE

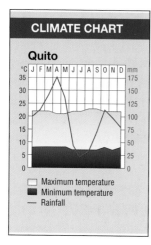

CLIMATE CHART

Quito

☐ Maximum temperature
■ Minimum temperature
— Rainfall

9am–1pm and 3–7pm, then Sat 9am–1.30pm, with many now staying open during lunchtime. Shopping centers and small grocery stores stay open until 8pm. Drug stores *(farmacias)* are open Mon–Fri 9am–8pm and some are listed "on duty" 24 hours a day (see local newspapers for the daily roster).

C limate

Because it is on the equator, Ecuador has only two seasons: wet and dry. Weather patterns vary greatly between the different geographical regions, however.

In the inhabited inter-mountain basin of the Sierra, the temperature changes little between seasons. However, mornings are generally sunny and fresh, becoming warmer toward midday; in the afternoon it often rains, and toward the evenings it gets chilly, and the nights are cold. Thus, in Quito the daily range of temperature is generally 8° to 21°C (46° to 70°F). There is one rainy season in the Sierra, from November to May, when there is frequent rainfall during the afternoon and evening. However, it rains quite often during the dry season too, and the sun shines in the rainy season for at least a couple of hours every day.

Above 3,800 meters (11,400 ft) no plants grow, and temperatures reach freezing during the night.

Electricity

110V/60Hz is the standard current throughout the country. Ecuador uses the North American flat-pronged plug. Travelers from other countries will need to bring an adapter with them.

Occasional snowstorms also occur.

The coastal lowlands and Amazon basin are very hot year-round, with temperatures ranging from 22°C (73°F) at night to 33°C (100°F) during the day. Humidity is extremely high. The rainy season in both areas is from May to December, although tropical downpours are regular in the dry season also. In the Galápagos Islands, there are also two seasons, produced by the ocean currents: the rainy (warm) and dry (cool) seasons. During the rainy season, from January through June, the weather is warm and sunny, while the water temperature is a comfortable 23°C (75°F); heavy, tropical showers occur occasionally. This is the best time to visit. For the rest of the year, a mist called the *garua* settles over the islands and makes the day cloudy, and the water begins to cool. It rarely rains, but it can be windy.

Crime and Safety

Most of Ecuador is relatively safe, although petty theft does occur in large cities. Armed robberies do occur on occasion on isolated mountain trails, although this is somewhat rare. In major cities it is best to only go in marked taxis. Don't walk alone at night and avoid poorly lit streets. In hostels, particularly dorms, secure your belongings in a locker, as thefts among budget travelers are more common than you may think. Take extra precautions along the border with Colombia, although the situation there has improved dramatically in recent years. Although drugs such as marijuana may seem common in areas where many travelers visit, use or purchase is punishable by up to 16 years in prison, where a number of foreigners now reside.

Customs Regulations

Each traveler may bring a liter of spirits, several bottles (a "reasonable amount") of perfume, and 300 cigarettes into Ecuador duty free.

D isabled Travelers

In large cities and major tourist areas, most large hotels and attractions are equipped with ramps and/or elevators. Elsewhere there are few services for the disabled traveler. Most areas of the Galápagos Islands tend to be quite untouched by development for conservation reasons and therefore lack proper facilities for wheelchair

Emergency Numbers

Fire 102
Police 101 (911 in Quito)
Radio Patrol 101
Ambulance/Red Cross 131
General Emergency 111

users. Consult a tour operator to see what types of activities may be accessible.

E mbassies & Consulates
Quito

Australian Embassy
The Canadian Embassy provides assistance to Australian nationals.
British Embassy
Av. Naciones Unidas and República del Salvador, Edificio Citiplaza, 14th Floor. Tel: (02) 297 0800, fax: (02) 297 0809, www.britembquito.org.ec
Canadian Embassy
Av. 6 de Diciembre, 2816 and Paul Rivet, Edificio Josueth González, 4th Floor. Tel: (02) 223 2114, fax: (02) 250 3108, www.quito.gc.ca
Irish Embassy
Yanacocha N72-64 and Juan Procel. Tel: (02) 600 1166, fax: (02) 249 4251. Email: dominiquekennedy@gmail.com
US Embassy
Av. 12 de Octubre and Patria. Tel: (02) 256 2890, fax: (02) 250 2052, www.usembassy.org.ec

Guayaquil
British Embassy
Córdova 623 and Padre Solano Castilla 8598. Tel: (04) 256 0400, fax: (04) 256 2641.
Canadian Honorary Consulate
Córdova and Rendón. Tel: (04) 256 3580, fax (04) 231 4562.
US Consulate
Av. 9 de Octubre and García Moreno. Tel: (04) 232 3570, http://guayaquil.usconsulate.gov

Entry Requirements
Visas and Passports

To visit Ecuador as a tourist, all you need is a valid passport (valid for at least six months before arrival), a return ticket, and proof of sufficient funds during your stay (although visas are required by citizens of some Central American and Middle Eastern countries as well as China, Cuba, India, North Korea, Pakistan, and Vietnam – check with the local Consulate of Ecuador before traveling). Ecuadorian Immigration Police will give you a free T-3 Tourist Card, which you should keep since it is needed when you leave the country (stapling it into your passport is not a bad idea). It is usually given for 30 days (unless you ask for more), although you can easily extend it for up to 90 days by visiting the local immigration authority. Note that tourists can only stay in the country for a maximum of 90 days in any calendar year – but sometimes a one-month extension can be obtained for a few dollars at the end of the 90-day period. You must go to the Dirección Nacional de Migración in Quito (Av. Amazonas 171 and República).

In theory, Immigration Police can ask for an onward ticket or proof of sufficient funds ($20 a day) before allowing entry to Ecuador, although they rarely do.

You should carry your passport, or a photocopy of it, at all times, since the police are empowered to arrest those without ID should a check be made. Foreigners are unlikely to be bothered in this way in Quito, but it is very important to have your passport handy on bus trips in the countryside, where checks are common.

G ay and Lesbian Travelers

As with most Catholic Latin American countries, homosexuality is often shunned. However, in large cities, particularly Quito, gay communities have developed, and homosexuality is slowly becoming more tolerated. The Mariscal Sucre district of Quito tends to be the center of Ecuador's gay scene. For more information for gay and lesbians in Ecuador visit: www.quitogay.net, www.gayecuador.com, www.gayscapre.com.

H ealth and Medical Care

It is a good idea to consult a tropical medicine clinic before traveling. Vaccinations against diphtheria, polio, tetanus, typhoid, and hepatitis A are strongly recommended. A yellow fever certificate is compulsory if arriving from a tropical South American or African region. If traveling into the Amazon or the tropical lowlands, anti-malaria pills should be taken. Remember that the course usually starts one or two weeks before your visit and should be continued for at least four weeks after you leave. Remember, too, to cover exposed areas of skin after dusk and use an insect repellent.

If you are hiking or cycling in rural areas a rabies vaccination will mean fewer post-bite shots if you get bitten by a rabid dog.

The most common illness for tourists is, of course, mild diarrhea – something that hits most visitors at some stage. Sufferers should have plenty of liquids (hot tea without milk is ideal, but definitely no coffee), avoid eggs and dairy products, and rest as much as they can. Rehydration products, such as Dioralyte and Rehidrat, taken regularly, help prevent dehydration. Boiled water with a little sugar and salt added has a similar effect.

The symptoms of diarrhea can be stopped with medication like Imodium. This does not cure the ailment, and is really only useful if you have a long bus journey or flight and don't want a sudden attack. If the complaint continues for several days, consult a doctor. Also, if you suffer severe abdominal cramps, fever, or nausea, or if blood or pus is evident in your stool, you need a test to see if you've caught amoebic dysentery. But in almost all cases, diarrhea is simply a matter of becoming accustomed to strange foods, and the gut returns to normal after a couple of days.

To avoid diarrhea, don't drink the tap water in Ecuador. Ask instead for mineral water (Güitig is the best brand – pronounced gwee-tig). Stay clear of ice, uncooked vegetables, salads that haven't been properly treated, and unpeeled fruits.

Most food in the larger cities, or in the restaurants where most travelers eat, is perfectly safe. Hepatitis is a danger if you eat food prepared in dirty conditions, and it is advisable to have a gamma globulin shot to protect against this. There is also the drug Havirix, which gives 10-year protection, although you need a booster after the first year.

A more everyday health risk is the fierce equatorial sun, a danger even in the cold Sierra. Newcomers to Ecuador should not expose their skin to the sun for long periods, especially during the middle of the day. Bring strong sunscreen lotion. Wearing a hat is a good idea.

Altitude sickness (soroche) can sometimes affect travelers arriving in Quito by air. Most people will need a couple of days to get used to the thin Andean air, so take it easy at first: eat light meals, steer clear of excessive alcohol, and don't go on strenuous walks; a chocolate bar can sometimes help. Drink tea, relax, and let your body become accustomed to the height.

Mountain sickness is a more serious problem for climbers, who may be exerting themselves at altitudes over 5,000 meters (15,000 ft). Symptoms can include vomiting, rapid pulse, and failing blood pressure. The only real cure is to descend to a lower level. Before

South American Explorers

A valuable source of information for backpacking travelers is the **South American Explorers Club**, a non-profit-making information resource center with offices in Ecuador, Peru, Argentina, and the US. Located in the New Town in Quito, this travelers' meeting place keeps up-to-date information on every aspect of Ecuador and is the perfect place to go for advice. Non-members may visit once, but if you want to use the facilities you need to join the club.
South American Explorers Club
Quito Clubhouse
Jorge Washington 311 and Leonidas Plaza
Tel/fax: (02) 222 5228
www.saexplorers.org

starting out, most climbers drink mate de coca (coca leaf tea), which is the local preventative remedy.

There are several good private hospitals in Quito and Guayaquil, but they are expensive. Visitors are advised to take out travel insurance.

Drugstores

Regular medicine can be bought without a prescription in most pharmacies (farmacias). In major cities pharmacies carry a wide range of drugs, antibiotics, and treatments. It is recommended that you use well-known brands. The newspapers list farmacias de turno, which are open on Sunday or at night. In Quito a number are open 24 hours a day – look out for an illuminated "Turno" sign. Most drugstores will give injections as well as disposable serum needles (beware of non-disposable needles).

Medical Services, Quito

Ambulance
Tel: (02) 911/131 for emergencies
Hospital Metropolitano
Av. Mariana de Jesús and Occidental
Tel: (02) 243 1520/226 9030
Best and most expensive hospital in Quito. English-speaking doctors available.
Hospital Voz Andes
Juan Villalengua 0E2-37 and Av. 10 de Agosto
Tel: (02) 225 2142/224 1540
Run by HCJB – an American Christian organization. Has an emergency room. Most of the doctors speak some English.
Clínica Los Andes
Mariano Cueva 14-68 and Pio Bravo
Tel: (02) 284 2942

Clínica de la Mujer
Av. Amazonas N39-216 and Gaspar de Villaroel
Tel: (02) 245 8000
Women's clinic. Laboratory analysis for parasites.
Clínica Pichincha
Veintimilla E3-30 and Paez
Tel: (02) 256 2410/256 2296.
Clínica Santa Ana
Av. Manuel J. Calle 1-104
Tel: (02) 281 4068
Good medical center, 24-hour emergency service.

Medical Services, Guayaquil

Clínica Kennedy
Av. San Jorge and la 9na.
Tel: (04) 228 9666/228 6963.
Best hospital in the city. English-speaking doctors, consulting rooms for external patients.
Clínica Guayaquil
Padre Aguirre 401 and Córdoba.
Tel: (04) 256 3555.
Private clinic. Dr Roberto Gilbert speaks English.

Medical Services, Galápagos

There is a basic hospital in Puerto Ayora. Consultations cost $10.

Internet

An extraordinary number of internet cafes have opened in Quito (Quito is said to be the city with the most cybercafes in the world). You can't miss them in the Mariscal area – particularly the Calama/Juan León Mera/Reina Victoria area. Elsewhere around the country, you shouldn't have a problem finding service, although speed may sometimes be an issue in rural areas. Wireless internet is becoming more and more common in large hotels, resorts, and luxury haciendas and lodges.

Lost Property

Considering that many people in Ecuador live below the poverty line, the chances are that if you lose a bag or an item, you are unlikely to see it again. That said, if you leave an item on a bus, it is worth checking at the bus company's office in case your belongings stayed on until the final destination and are waiting in the office.

Maps

The best selection of maps of Ecuador is produced by the Instituto Geográfico Militar on top of the hill on Avenida T. Paz and Mino, off Avenida Colombia in Quito. Large-

ABOVE: queuing for the bank in Baños.

scale maps of the whole country, ranging from 1:1,000,000 one-sheet maps to 1:50,000 topographical maps, are available here. The Sierra has been covered in detail, but the Oriente and parts of the Western Lowlands are not well served. For a road map, pick up the *Guía Vial del Ecuador*, with 26 partial maps, by Nelson Gómez, Editorial Camino.

Media

In Quito, there are several good newspapers: *El Comercio*, *Hoy*, *Tiempo*, and *Ultimas Noticias* are the most established. In Guayaquil, you can choose from *Expreso*, *El Telégrafo*, *El Universo*, and *La Prensa*. There are also a few English-language publications including the *Ecuador Times* and *Inside Ecuador*.

Public Holidays

Ecuador has numerous public holidays and festivals *(see page 348 for a comprehensive list)*, and it is worth bearing in mind that shops, banks, and services may be closed around these dates.
• When an official public holiday falls at a weekend, offices may be closed on the Friday or Monday.
• When a public holiday falls midweek it may be moved to the nearest Friday or Monday to create a long weekend.
• Major holidays are often celebrated for several days around the actual date.
• Banks and businesses are closed on official public holidays.
• If you plan to travel on a major holiday, book ahead if possible as transport can get very crowded.

TV and Radio

Cable TV in Ecuador carries many of the same channels and shows as the United States. News channels, such as the BBC and CNN, and sports channels, such as ESPN and Fox Sports, are common in most cities, although rural areas may be limited to a few basic channels.
There are a plethora of local radio stations in nearly every part of the country, that you will no doubt hear blasting away on any rural bus. Most play a combination of popular and regional music and they are a great way to find out what each part of the country is listening to.

Money

In September 2000 Ecuador completed its dollarization process when the country's currency was legally changed from the sucre to the US dollar. Travelers' checks and credit cards are more widely accepted than debit cards, and in rural areas it is best to travel with small-denomination notes.
US dollars are by far the best currency to take to Ecuador, but other foreign currencies can be exchanged in banks and *casas de cambio* (currency exchange offices) in the business districts of Quito (Avenida Amazonas), Guayaquil, and Cuenca. Outside major city centers, however, it becomes difficult to exchange other currencies, so it is best to change your money before leaving Quito.
On Sundays and holidays, when banks and *casas de cambio* are shut, you can always exchange money in the major hotels such as the Colón in Quito. It is worth bringing most of your money in travelers' checks for safety, as these can be changed almost as easily as cash. Most people also bring

Street Names in Quito

In 1998 a new street numbering system was introduced in Quito based on N (*norte*), S (*sud*), E (*este*), and O (*oeste*), followed by a street and building number. Many businesses still use the old street names, however, and maps of the city usually show both old and new street names.

a certain amount of cash dollars in manageable denominations (say, $20 bills).

It is easy to have money transferred to Ecuador, through organizations such as Western Union. You can pick up the sum in US dollars and travelers' checks.

Major credit cards (particularly Visa and MasterCard) are accepted in the larger hotels, restaurants, and tourist-oriented shops.

In Quito and Guayaquil ATMs from which you can withdraw dollars using Visa or MasterCard are becoming more common.

Banks in Quito
American Express
Av. Amazonas 329 and Jorge Washington.
Tel: (02) 256 0488
Banco de Guayaquil
Colón and Reina Victoria.
Tel: (02) 256 6800
For cash advance on Visa.
Banco del Pacifico
Av. Amazonas N22-94 and Veintimilla.
Tel: (02) 250 0988
For cash advance on MasterCard.
Banco de Pichincha
Av. Amazonas and Colón.
Tel: (02) 254 7006
For cash advance on Visa/Diners Card.
Western Union
Av. La Prensa 1463 and Zamora.
Tel: (02) 226 4353

Banks in Cuenca
Banco del Pacifico, Benigno Malo 9-75, MasterCard ATM.
Banco del Austro
Sucre and Borrero, Visa ATM.

Banks in Esmeraldas
The **Banco del Austro** and **Banco del Pichincha** can change cash.

Banks in Guayaquil
American Express, 9 de Octubre 1900 and Esmeraldas
For replacement travelers' checks.
Banco de Guayaquil, Pichincha and P. Icaza. Visa & AmEx ATM.
Banco del Pacifico, Fco P. Icaza 200

and Pichincha, 4th Floor. Tel: (04) 232 8333. MasterCard.

There are fewer *casas de cambio* since dollarization. Cambiosa is at Av. 9 de Octubre and Pichincha. On weekends, change money in the larger hotels or at Wander Cambios in the airport.

P hotography

If you plan to shoot with film rather than with a digital camera, bring sufficient film with you: buying camera gear within Ecuador is expensive, and the choice of film is limited. If you are stuck, try one of the photo stores on Quito's Avenida Amazonas and make sure the film date hasn't expired.

Equatorial shadows are very strong and come out almost black on photographs, so the best results are often achieved on overcast days.

Not surprisingly, Ecuadorian *indigenas* may resent having a camera thrust in their faces and often turn their backs on pushy photographers. Unless you are taking a shot from long distance, ask permission beforehand. Many will ask for a small fee or "tip" and it is often more pleasant to comply rather than trying to shoot people without being noticed.

Postal Services

Letters are often slow to be delivered and are sometimes lost. It is worth having your letters certified *(con certificado)* – you get a receipt which won't do much practical good, but means that your letter's existence is recorded somewhere and, in theory, given safer treatment.

DHL, FedEx, and other international courier services can be found across the country.

Quito
The head post office in Quito is at Eloy Alfaro 354 and 9 de Octubre in the New Town, but many travelers use the main office in the Old Town at Espejo 935 and Guayaquil. This is where Poste Restante *(Lista de Correos)* is located. Also, the South American Explorers *(see right)* will hold mail for members. Users of American Express travelers' checks may have their mail sent to the Amex office in the New Town operated by Ecuadorian Tours at Amazonas 399. Mail can be sent care of American Express, Apartado 17-010-2605, Quito, Ecuador.

Packages can be sent from the post office at Ulloa 273 and Davalos, in the New Town. Letters may be dropped at the reception desk of the hotels Colón and Quito.

Stamps can be bought in the hotel bookshops during store hours. Faxes can be sent from most hotels or – inexpensive, but less convenient – the Andinatel office at Avenida 10 de Agosto and Colón (open daily 8am–10pm). Long-distance calls can be made from the same office and English-speaking operators are on duty at all times. Calls are less expensive between 7pm–5am and all day Sunday (with a three-minute minimum charge). New telephone centers are opening across the city all the time.

Guayaquil
Pacifictel and Correo Central (the main post office) are side by side on Aguirre and Pedro Carbo.
Tel: (04) 253 1713.

R eligious Services

Roman Catholic services are held regularly in Quito's churches. Services other than Catholic are held at:
Carolina Adventist Church
Av. 10 de Agosto 3929.
Tel: (02) 223 9995.
Meetings on Saturdays at 9am.
Central Baptist Church
Ríos 1803.
Sunday services 9am and 6pm.
Church of Jesus Christ of the Latter Day Saints
Almagro and Colón.
Tel: (02) 252 9602.
Sunday service 9.30am.
Lutheran Church
Isabel la Católica 1431.
Tel: (02) 223 4391.
Sunday services: 9am in English; 10.15am in German; 11.30am in Spanish.
Synagogue
Versalles and 18 de Septiembre.
Services Friday 7pm.

S tudent Travelers

ISIC (International Student Identity Card) discounts are few and far between. At times you may be able to get airline and bus tickets for a reduced fair, but little else.

T elecommunications

Since 1998, Ecuador's telephone network has been run by Andinatel, Pacifitel, Etapa, and a couple of private companies, and one of the best places to make calls is at the telephone company's office in each town. It is also possible to purchase convenient, if more expensive, debit cards for public telephones, but these are not interchangeable between networks.

Time Zone

Mainland 5 hours behind GMT, the Galápagos 6 hours behind.

Many people will find it more convenient to make collect (reverse-charge) calls from their hotel or buy a charge card before leaving home. If using a hotel line, check tariffs as hefty surcharges are often added. In general, international calls are expensive (about $7 a minute to Europe and the US). Rates may be discounted after 7pm.

Many internet cafes in Quito, Guayaquil, and Cuenca offer a net phone service, which is usually cheap if not always of the best sound quality.

Telephoning Ecuador

The country code for Ecuador is 593. To call a number in Ecuador from abroad, dial the international access code (011 from the US, 00 from Britain), the country code (593) the area code without the 0 (2, 3, 4, 5, 6, or 7 depending on the area) and the seven-digit local phone number. Area codes are divided by province. Examples of codes for popular destinations are:

Quito **02**
Cuenca **07**
Ambato **03**
Baños **03**
Riobamba **03**
Guayaquil **04**
Manta **05**
Galápagos Islands **05**
Esmeraldas **06**
Otavalo **06**

Tipping

In many restaurants 22 percent service and tax is added to the bill, but some cheaper establishments will leave it to your discretion. It is customary to leave a 10 percent tip for the waiter if you have received good service. Airport porters can be tipped about 50 US cents. Taxi drivers do not expect a tip.

Toilets

Most of the toilets in Ecuador are Western, although in some rural areas you may encounter a few that are little more than holes that use pails of water to flush. Regardless, you should almost never flush paper down the toilet. It should be disposed in a small wastebasket beside the toilet. Some large hotels with their own septic systems will allow paper to be flushed.

Tour Operators and Travel Agents

Tours can be arranged through tour operators and travel agents in Europe or the US, but it is simple to organize an itinerary on arrival in Ecuador.

Quito

There are travel agencies all along Avenida Amazonas and in the major hotels. Some of the best include:
Enchanted Expeditions
De las Alondras N45-102 and de los Lirios (Monteserrín), Floralp Building, Office 104.
Tel: (02) 334 0525
Fax: (02) 334 0123
www.enchantedexpeditions.com
A well-established company offering quality excursions throughout Ecuador at reasonable prices. It offers trips to the Galápagos Islands on the boats *Angelito, Beluga, Cachalote, Galápagos Explorer II,* and *Santa Cruz.*
Metropolitan Touring
Head office, 464-702 Av. Republica del Salvador N36–84.
Tel: (02) 298 8200
Fax: (02) 246 4702
www.metropolitan-touring.com
The oldest and largest travel agency network in Ecuador is also probably its most efficient. Tours and ticketing of all kinds can be done here.
Nuevo Mundo Expediciones
18 de Septiembre E4-161 and Juan León Mera.
Tel: (02) 250 9431
www.nuevomundotravel.com

Tourist Information

The Ministry of Tourism has an excellent website (www.vivecuador.com), and its **iTur** tourist offices can be found throughout the country.

Quito
Eloy Alfaro N32-300, Carlos Tobar.
Tel: (02) 250 7559.

Otavalo
Bolívar and Calderón.
Tel: (06) 284 4162.

Esmeraldas
Cañizares and Bolívar.
Tel: (06) 292 1313.

Manta
Paseo José María Egas, between Calles 10 and 11 near Av. 3.
Tel: (05) 262 2944.

Tena
García Moreno and Calderón.
Tel: (06) 288 6536.

Offers tours all over Ecuador, including *Manatee Amazon Explorer* Cruises.
Quasar Naútica
Brasíl 293 and Grande Centeno Edificio IACA, Floor 2
Tel: (02) 244 6996/7
Fax: (02) 225 4305
www.quasarnautica.com
Operates excellent upmarket bespoke tours in Ecuador and a superb selection of boats in the Galápagos.
Gala Cruises
N22-118 9 de Octubre and Veintimilla, Quito.
Tel: (02) 222 4893
www.galacruises.com
Cruise agency for Galápagos boats and a number of other tours.
Sangay Tours
Amazonas and Cordero.
Tel: (02) 255 0176
www.sangay.com
Range of tours from the Galápagos to Amazon lodges and trekking.
Compañía de Guías de Montaña
Jorge Washington 425 and 6 de Diciembre.
Tel: (02) 290 1551
www.companiadeguias.com.ec
Specializes in climbing and trekking tours.
Safari
Foch E5-39 and Juan León Mera.
Tel: (02) 255 2505
Fax: (02) 222 0426
www.safari.com.ec
Sierra Nevada
Pinto 637 and Amazonas.
Tel: (02) 255 3658

Baños
Haflants and Rocafuerte.
Tel: (03) 284 4162.

Guaranda
Calle 10 de Agosto 2072 and García Moreno.
Tel: (03) 294 1213.

Cuenca
Benigno Malo and Presidente Córdoba, Edificio San Agustín.
Tel: (07) 283 9337/283 9338.

Loja
Bolívar 12-39, entrance on Mercadillo and Lourdes.
Tel: (07) 257 2964.

Guayaquil
Plaza Icaza 203, between Pedro Carbo and Pichincha (opposite Banco Pacífico), 5th and 6th Floors.
Tel: (04) 256 8764/256 0514.

E-mail: snevada@accessinter.net
Surtrek
Amazonas 897 and Wilson.
Tel: (02) 223 1534
Fax: (02) 250 0540
www.surtrek.com

Baños

Geo Tours
Ambato and Haflants
Tel: (03) 274 1344
www.geotoursecuador.com
Rainforestur
Ambato 800
Tel: (03) 274 0743
www.rainforestur.com

Bahía de Caraquez

Guacamayo Tours
Bolívar and Arenas
Tel: (05) 269 1412
www.guacamayotours.com

Cuenca

Eco Trek
Calle Larga 7-108 and Cordero.
Tel: (07) 283 4677
Email: ecotrek@az.pro.ec
Expediciones Río Arriba
Corner Hermano Miguel and Córdova
Tel: (07) 283 0116
Email: negro@az.pro.ec
Metropolitan Touring
Mariscal Sucre 662
Tel: (07) 283 7340
www.metropolitan-touring.com
(See right.)
TerraDiversa Travel & Adventure
Hermano Miguel 4-46 and
Calle Larga
Tel: (07) 282 3782
Fax: (07) 282 0085
www.terradiversa.com
Southland Touring
Larga and Miguel
Tel: (07) 393 3087
Email: infosouthland@etapanet.net

Guayaquil

The travel agencies vie with each
other to offer attractive tours to the
Galápagos. To avoid disappointment
it's best to plan ahead, as flights and
cruises around the islands get very
heavily booked.
Canodros Tours
Santa Leonor Mz 5, Local 10
Tel: (04) 228 5711
www.canodros.com
Excellent responsible tour operator
that operates luxury cruises in the
Galápagos and the superb Kapawi
Ecological Reserve in the Oriente.
Ecuadorian Tours
Av. 9 de Octubre 1900 and
Esmeraldas
Tel: (04) 228 7111
Fax: (04) 228 0851
www.ecuadoriantoursgye.com.ec
American Express Agent.
Guayatur
Aguirre 108 and Malecón
Tel: (04) 232 2441
www.guayatur.com
Recommended local operator.
Macchiavello Tours
Antepara 802 and 9 de Octubre
Tel: (04) 228 6079
Metropolitan Touring
Antepara 915 and 9 de Octubre
Tel: (04) 232 0300
www.metropolitan-touring.com
(See left.)

Galápagos Islands

Moorise Travel Agency
Av. Charles Darwin, Puerto Ayora,
Santa Cruz.
Tel: (05) 252 6348.
This excellent travel company is
renowned for its reliable advice.

UK

For a useful list of some of the many
excellent companies offering trips in

Ecuador, check out www.lata.org, the
website of the **Latin American Travel
Association** in the United Kingdom.
They can also give impartial advice
on how to plan a trip to Ecuador.
Austral Tours, 20 Upper Tachbrook
Street, London SW1V 1SH. Tel: (020)
7233 5384. www.latinamerica.co.uk
Crusader Travel, 57 Church Street,
Twickenham, TW1 3NR. Tel: (020)
8744 0474.
www.crusadertravel.com
Journey Latin America, 12–13
Heathfield Terrace, Chiswick, London
W4 4JE. Tel: (020) 8747 8315.
Fax: (020) 8742 01312.
www.journeylatinamerica.co.uk
Select Latin America Ltd,
79 Maltings Place, 169 Tower Bridge
Road, London SE1 3LJ. Tel: (020)
7407 1478. www.selectlatinamerica.co.uk
The director is a former naturalist
guide in the Galápagos.
South American Experience,
47 Causton Street, London SW1P
4AT. Tel: (020) 7976 5511.
Fax: (020) 7976 6908.
www.southamericanexperience.co.uk
The Ultimate Travel Company, 25–7
Vanston Place, London SW6 1AZ.
Tel: (020) 7386 4646.
Fax: (020) 7381 0836.

BELOW: horse-drawn carriage tours are a great way to visit Quito's Old Town.

www.theultimatetravelcompany.co.uk
Quasar Naútica, which operates bespoke tours in Ecuador and the Galápagos *(see left)* is represented in the UK by **Penelope Kellie World Wide Yacht Charters & Tours**, Tel: (01962) 779317, www.pkworldwide.com

US and Canada

Bookings for tours operated by **Metropolitan Touring** *(see left)* can be made in the US through **Adventure Associates**, 13150 Coit Road, Suite 110, Dallas, Texas 75240. Tel: (972) 907 0414. Freephone: 1 800 527 2500. Fax: (972) 783 1286. www.adventure-associates.com
Wilderness Travel, 1102 Ninth Street, Berkeley, CA 94710, USA. Tel: 1 800 368 2794.
eXito Travel, 108 Rutgers Street, Fort Collins, CO 80525. Tel: 1 800 655 4053/(970) 482 3019. www.exitotravel.com
Inti Travel, Box 1586, Banff Alberta, TIL 1BF. Tel: 1 403 760 3565. www.intitravel.com
Off-the-beaten-track hiking trips, climbing expeditions, and tours of the Galápagos .

U seful Addresses

ETAPA
Benigno Malo between Cordóva and Sucre, Quito
Tel: (02) 283 1900
www.etapa.com.ec
Good-value internet access and telephone calls.
Quito Policía de Turismo
Reina Victoria and Roca, Quito

BELOW: Which way now? A signpost in Puerto Lopez.

Tel: (02) 254 3983
Empresa de Desarrollo del Centro Histórico
Pasaje Arzobispal, Plaza de la Independencia, Quito
Tel: (02) 258 6591
Has a range of information on Quito's colonial center. Also arranges tours and horse-drawn carriage rides.
Galápagos Conservation Trust
5 Derby Street, London W1J 7AB, UK
Tel: (020) 7629 5049

W eights and Measures

The metric system is used to calculate distances and weights.

What to Bring

What you bring depends on where you are going to go and what you are going to do. Basic necessities can be found throughout the country, and in the larger cities nearly all the same products can be found that you would find in your own country.

If you intend to partake in any adventure activities, check with your tour operator ahead of time to see what exactly you will need. Often for more technical activities such as climbing it is best to bring your own equipment. You can buy equipment for a number of sports in many towns such as Baños. However, prices tend to be much higher than they would be in the US or Europe.

A few recommended items: antibacterial handsoap, hand wipes, personal stereo, basic first aid kit, sunscreen, sunglasses, Swiss Army knife, and Spanish dictionary.

What to Wear

Ecuador has three very different climatic zones, so what you wear depends completely on where you are headed.

The Sierra is where most travelers begin. Quito is called the "City of Eternal Spring," although eternal fall (autumn) might be more accurate. When the sun is shining, Sierran days are warm and pleasant, but when the clouds roll in and winds begin to blow, you need a warm sweater. Nights can be quite cold, so a warm overcoat or parka is recommended.

Note that Quito tends to be more conservative in its dress standards than the rest of the country. Ecuadorians, like most Latin Americans, like to dress up when they go out to restaurants and night spots – men will often wear a jacket and tie even in relatively casual surroundings, while women can seem to spend hours grooming themselves.

Of course, this doesn't apply to many backpacker hang-outs, and even in the ritzier establishments traveling gringos are forgiven for a more casual appearance than Ecuadorians. But remember that a night out in a restaurant is more of a big deal for an Ecuadorian, and dressing too unkemptly can seem like an insult to the other clients. If in doubt, err on the side of formality.

The coast and Galápagos Islands are tropical regions, so dress for the heat. Take a swimsuit, because swimming and snorkeling on the islands are a joy (most boats have snorkeling gear, so you don't need to bring your own). Guayaquil and the coast are very casual, so shorts for men are widely accepted for many social situations (not so widely for women – a light dress is more appropriate). Remember to use protection against the sun.

Dress in the Oriente is even more functional. All clothes should be light, because of the stifling heat, but long trousers and shirts are recommended to guard against insects. Bring some sneakers for walking.

Rain can strike in any part of Ecuador, whether it's the rainy season or not, so bring a decent raincoat.

Women Travelers

If you can ignore the occasional cat calls, much of Ecuador is safe for women as it lacks the machismo of many other Latin American countries. However, there are a few precautions that it would be wise to take, such as never getting into taxis or walking alone late at night.

LANGUAGE

UNDERSTANDING THE LANGUAGE

Pronunciation and Grammar Tips

Anyone with a working knowledge of Spanish will have no trouble making themselves understood in Ecuador, but there are a few interesting local variations. In order to emphasize an adjective, the ending -aso is added: for example, something that is very good would be *buenaso*. An expression you will hear everywhere, and which is difficult to translate, is *no más*. *Siga no más*, for example, means "Hurry up (and get on the bus/move down the line, etc)." *Come no más* means "Just eat it/It'll get cold/it's nicer than it looks, etc.)." You will soon get the hang of it.

Indígenas almost all speak Spanish, but you will hear Quichua words which have crept into the language: *wambras* translates as "guys," and *cheveré* means "cool."

VOWELS
a slightly longer than in cat
e as in bed
i as in police
o as in hot
u as in rude

CONSONANTS are approximately like those in English, the main exceptions being:
c is hard before **a**, **o**, or **u** (as in English), and is soft before **e** or **i**, when it sounds like **s** (as opposed to the Castilian pronunciation of **th** as in think). Thus, *censo* (census) sounds like *senso*.
g is hard before **a**, **o**, or **u** (as in English), but where English **g** sounds like **j** – before **e** or **i** – Spanish **g** sounds like a guttural **h**. **G** before **ua** is often soft or silent, so that *agua* sounds more like *awa*, and Guadalajara like Wadalajara.

h is silent.
j sounds like a guttural English h.
ll sounds like y.
ñ sounds like ny, as in the familiar Spanish word *señor*.
q is followed by **u** as in English, but the combination sounds like **k** instead of like **kw**. *¿Qué quiere usted?* is pronounced: Keh kee-ehr-eh oostehd?
r is rolled, and more so for double r.
x between vowels sounds like a guttural **h**, e.g. in México or Oaxaca.
y alone, as the word meaning 'and', is pronounced ee.
Note that **ch** and **ll** are separate letters of the Spanish alphabet; if looking in a phone book or dictionary for a word beginning with **ch**, you will find it after the final **c** entry. A name or word beginning with **ll** will be listed after the **l** entries.

Language Classes

Quito is considered one of the best places in Latin America to learn Spanish. There are dozens of cheap places offering classes: they advertise in the hotels, bars, and restaurants frequented by young gringos. Classes can be taken by the hour, by the day, or by the week. Also, many organizations offer intensive courses where you board with an Ecuadorian family and are usually taught on a one-to-one basis.

Other places, including Otavalo, Tena, Baños, and Montañita, also offer language classes, and some schools offer college credit.

The following schools are recommended.

Quito
La Lengua
Av. Colón 1001 and Juan León Mera, Edificio Av. María
Tel/fax: (02) 250 1271

www.la-lengua.com
Simón Bolívar
Leonidas Plaza 353 and Roca
Tel/fax: (02) 223 6688/250 4977
www.simon-bolivar.com

Otavalo
Mundo Andino
Salinas 509
Tel: (06) 292 5478
Email: andinoinn@hotmail.com

Baños
Baños Spanish Center
Cañar and Oriente
Tel: (06) 274 0632
Email: elizabasc@uio.satnet.net
International Spanish School
16 de Diciembre and Espejo
Tel: (06) 274 0612

Cuenca
Sí Centro de Español y Inglés
Jaramillo 7-27
Tel: (07) 284 6932
www.sicentrospanishschool.com

Basics

Please *Por favor*
Thank you *Gracias*
You're welcome *De nada*
Excuse me *Perdón*
Sorry *Lo siento*
Yes *Sí*
No *No*
Hello *¡Hola!*
Good morning *Buenos días*
Good afternoon *Buenas tardes*
Goodnight *Buenas noches*
See you later *Hasta luego*
Bye *Adiós*
My name is... *Me llamo...*
What is your name? (formal)
¿Cómo se llama usted?
Mr/Miss/Mrs
Señor/Señorita/Señora
Pleased to meet you

¡Encantado(a)!/Mucho gusto
I am English/American/Canadian/
Irish/Scottish/Australian
Soy inglés(a)/norteamericano(a)/
canadiense/irlandés(a)/
escocés(a)/australiano(a)
Do you speak English? (formal)
¿Habla inglés?
I (don't) understand *(No) entiendo*
How are you? (formal/informal)
¿Cómo está?/¿Qué tal?
Fine, thanks *Muy bien, gracias*

Finding Your Way

Where is the lavatory (men's/
women's)? *¿Dónde está el baño*
(de caballeros/de damas)?
Where is the (tourist office)?
¿Dónde está la (oficina de turismo)?
town hall *ayuntamiento*
bank *banco*
currency exhange bureau *casa*
de cambio
library *biblioteca*
art gallery *sala de exposiciones*
pharmacy *farmacia*
bus stop *parada de autobús*
train station *estación de tren*
post office *correos*
hospital *hospital*
church *iglesia*
hotel *hotel*
youth hostel *albergue*
camping *camping*
parking *aparcamiento*
discotheque *discoteca*
beach *playa*

straight *derecho*
to the left *a la izquierda*
to the right *a la derecha*
square *plaza*
corner *esquina*
street *calle*

In the Hotel

Do you have a vacant room?
¿Tiene una habitación disponible?
I have a reservation
Tengo una reserva
I'd like... *Quisiera...*

Emergencies

Help! *¡Socorro! ¡Auxilio!*
Stop! *¡Pare!*
Call a doctor *Llame a un médico*
Call an ambulance *Llame una*
ambulancia
Call the police *Llame a la policía*
Call the fire brigade *Llame a los*
bomberos
Where is the nearest hospital?
¿Dónde queda el hospital más
cercano?
I want to report an assault/a
robbery *Quisiera reportar un*
asalto/un robo

a single/double (with double bed)/
a room with twin beds
una habitación individual
(sencilla)/una habitación
matrimonial/una habitación doble
for one night/two nights
por una noche/dos noches
with a sea view *con vista al mar*
Does the room have a private
bathroom or shared bathroom?
¿Tiene la habitación baño privado
o baño compartido?
Does it have hot water?
¿Tiene agua caliente?
Could you show me another room,
please? *¿Puede mostrarme otra*
habitación, por favor?
What time do you close (lock)
the doors?
¿A qué hora se cierran las puertas?
I would like to change rooms
Quisiera cambiar la habitación
How much is it?
¿Cuánto cuesta?/¿Cuánto sale?
Do you accept credit cards/
travelers' checks/dollars?
¿Se aceptan tarjetas de crédito/
cheques de viajeros/dólares?
What time is breakfast/
lunch/dinner? *¿A qué hora es el*
desayuno/el almuerzo/la cena?
Please wake me at...
Por favor despertarme a...
Come in! *¡Pase!/¡Adelante!*
I'd like to pay the bill now, please
Quisiera cancelar la cuenta ahora,
por favor

In the Restaurant

I'd like to book a table *Quisiera*
reservar una mesa, por favor
Do you have a table for...?
¿Tiene una mesa para...?
breakfast/lunch/dinner
desayuno/almuerzo/cena
I'm a vegetarian *Soy vegetariano(a)*
May we have the menu? *¿Puede*
traernos la carta/el menú?
wine list *la carta de vinos*
What would you recommend?
¿Qué recomienda?
fixed-price menu *el menú fijo*
special of the day
plato del día/sugerencia del chef
waiter *mozo*
What would you like to drink?
¿Qué quiere tomar?
Is service included?
¿Incluye el servicio?

Shopping

How much is this? *¿Cuanto*
cuesta/sale?
Do you have it in another color?
¿Tiene en otro color?
Do you have it in another size?
¿Tiene en otro talle/número?

Numbers

1	*uno*
2	*dos*
3	*tres*
4	*cuatro*
5	*cinco*
6	*seis*
7	*siete*
8	*ocho*
9	*nueve*
10	*diez*
11	*once*
12	*doce*
13	*trece*
14	*catorce*
15	*quince*
16	*dieciséis*
17	*diecisiete*
18	*dieciocho*
19	*diecinueve*
20	*veinte*
21	*veintiuno*
25	*veinticinco*
30	*treinta*
40	*cuarenta*
50	*cincuenta*
60	*sesenta*
70	*setenta*
80	*ochenta*
90	*noventa*
100	*cien*
101	*ciento uno*
200	*doscientos*
300	*trescientos*
400	*cuatrocientos*
500	*quinientos*
600	*seiscientos*
700	*setecientos*
800	*ochocientos*
900	*novecientos*
1,000	*mil*
10,000	*diez mil*
100,000	*cien mil*
1,000,000	*un millón*

Days of the Week

Monday	*lunes*
Tuesday	*martes*
Wednesday	*miercoles*
Thursday	*jueves*
Friday	*viernes*
Saturday	*sábado*
Sunday	*domingo*

Months of the Year

January	*enero*
February	*febrero*
March	*marzo*
April	*abril*
May	*mayo*
June	*junio*
July	*julio*
August	*agosto*
September	*septiembre*
October	*octubre*
November	*noviembre*
December	*diciembre*

FURTHER READING

History and Society

Indians, Oil, and Politics: A Recent History of Ecuador by Gerlach, Allen. Scholarly Resources, Wilmington, 2003. A study of Ecuadorian politics since the 1970s.
The Conquest of the Incas by Hemming, John. Pan, 2004. The classic account of the Spanish conquest.
Savages by Kane, Joe. Vintage, 1996. First-hand account of the Huaorani people's struggle to preserve their way of life.

Birdwatching

A Guide to the Birds of the Galápagos Islands by Castro, Isabel, and Phillips, Antonia. Christopher Helm Publishers, 1996.
A Guide to the Birds of Colombia by Hilty, Steven, and Brown, William. Princeton University Press, 1986.
The Birds of Ecuador by Ridgeley, R., and Greenfield, P. Christopher Helm Publishers, 2001.

Crafts

Otavalo: Weaving, Costume, and the Market by Meisch, Lynn. Ediciones Libri Mundi, 1987. A good overview of the textile crafts of Otavalo.

Travel Literature

Personal Narrative of a Journey by Humbolt, Alexander von, abridged and translated by Jason Wilson. Penguin, 1996. The 19th-century scientist's account of his expedition to Ecuador.
The Lost Lady of the Amazon by Smith, Anthony. Constable and Robinson, 2003. The story of Isabel Godin's harrowing journey through the Amazon in search of her husband.
The Panama Hat Trail by Miller, Tom. National Geographic Books, 2002. The story behind the famous hats.
Travels amongst the Great Andes of the Equator by Whymper, Edward. Rocky Limited, 2005. Memoirs of the famous 19th-century British mountaineer.
Maíz y Coca-Cola by Terezakis,

Diane. Xlibris, 2001. One woman's journey through Ecuador, from the Andes to the Amazon.
Living Poor by Moritz, Thomsen. University of Washington Press, 1997. Life as a Peace Corps worker in 1960s Ecuador.

The Galápagos

The Voyage of the Beagle by Darwin, Charles. Penguin, 1989. Shortened journal of Darwin's five-year voyage around the world. A classic.
Galápagos Wildlife by Horwell, David, and Oxford, Pete. Bradt Travel Guides, 2005.
Galápagos: A Natural History by Jackson, M.H. University of Calgary Press, 1988. Without doubt the best guide to the islands.
A Field Guide to the Fishes of the Galápagos by Merlen, G. Wilmot, 1988.
The Galápagos Affair by Treherne, John. Pimlico, 2002. An entertaining account of the scandals and murder occurring on Floreana in the 1930s.
Galápagos by Vonnegut, Kurt. Dial Press, 1999. An apocalyptic satire of human evolution set in the Galápagos.

Other Guides

Among nearly 200 companion books to this one are several guides highlighting destinations in this region. Titles include *Insight Guides* to *South America, Buenos Aires, Brazil, Rio de Janeiro, Venezuela, Peru, Chile, Argentina*, and the *Berlitz Guide to Buenos Aires*. *Insight Guide: Amazon Wildlife* vividly captures the flora and fauna of the world's greatest rainforest.

Feedback

We do our best to ensure the information in our books is as accurate and up-to-date as possible. The books are updated on a regular basis, using local contacts, who painstakingly add, amend, and correct as required. However, some mistakes and omissions are inevitable, and we are ultimately reliant on our readers to put us in the picture. We would welcome your feedback on any details related to your experiences using the book "on the road". Maybe we recommended a hotel that you liked (or another that you didn't), as well as interesting new attractions, or facts and figures you have found out about the country itself. The more details you can give us (particularly with regard to addresses, emails and telephone numbers), the better. We will acknowledge all contributions, and we'll offer an Insight Guide to the best letters received.

Please write to us at:
Insight Guides
PO Box 7910
London SE1 1WE
United Kingdom
Or send email to:
insight@apaguide.co.uk

ART & PHOTO CREDITS

Bill Abbot/Wilderness Travel 98
AKG London 32
Archivo Fotográfico Madrid 38, 40, 46
Andre and Cornelia Bärtschi 20/21, 209, 213, 214/215, 216/217, 221, 224, 225, 230, 232L, 232R, 233, 234
Bruce Coleman Ltd 53, 224T, 231, 232T
Corbis 169R
County of New York Library/ Vautier de Nanxe 45
Courtesy of El Comercio, Quito 93
Katie Dixon 169L
Donna Elmendorf front flap top, 50, 56/57, 60, 61, 63R, 65, 82, 90, 100/101, 187, 188, 194, 195, 223R, 249, 261
Bolo Franco 191R, 196, 198, 274/275, 281, 282, 284, 289
Cesar Franco 197
Robert Frerck/Robert Harding 68
Peter Frost/APA 6BR, 7TL&BR, 8TL, TR&B, 9BR, 54/55, 69, 74, 109, 129, 147, 151, 152, 156, 167, 190, 191L, 200, 201, 219, 245, 332, 336, 337, 340, 342, 343, 345, 347, 349, 350, 354, 357, 358
Eduardo Gil back cover bottom, front flap bottom, 26, 27, 22/23, 29, 37, 42, 58/59, 62, 91, 92, 95, 106, 107, 110, 112, 114, 115L, 115R, 122, 128, 134/135, 136/137, 138/139, 146, 149, 154L, 154R, 155, 157L, 157R, 159, 173, 177, 180R, 206/207, 208, 210, 211R, 212, 220T, 228, 246T, 248, 250, 251, 253, 258, 262T, 262L, 262R, 263, 267, 309, 311R, 325
Nicholas Gill 78, 126, 150L, 161, 252, 283L, 285
Sylvain Grandadam/Hoa-qui 63
Andreas M. Gross 41, 108, 150R, 153, 158, 162, 305, 317, 319

Joseph Hooper 99
Peter Hurley/Wilderness Travel 97
Hutchison Library 79, 83
Jtb Photo/Photolibrary 276
Kaos/SIME-4Corners Images 283R
Shari Kessler 30, 52, 94, 184/185, 202
Oliver Krist 152T, 160T, 168T, 288
Eric Lawrie back flap bottom, back cover left, 10/11, 70/71, 75, 76, 77, 81, 118, 120, 121, 132/133, 140, 144/145, 181, 223L, 241, 243, 244, 246, 247, 250T, 256/257, 259, 266, 270, 270T, 271
Yadid Levy/Alamy 193
John Maier 14, 84/85, 102/103, 172, 179, 182, 235
Courtesy of the Manatee River Explorer 220
Lynn Meisch back cover right, 16, 42/43, 67, 80, 86, 104/105, 176T
Martin Mejia/AP/PA Photos 49
Andriana Meyer/Latinphoto.org 186
Edward Parker 163
Tony Perrottet spine, 18/19, 48, 66, 111, 170/171, 176, 180L, 182T, 183, 218, 222, 296, 301, 316, 318T, 320, 322, 323, 324
Carl & Ann Purcell/Corbis 226
Rob Rachowiecki 96, 116/117, 203, 306T, 321
Tui de Roy 12/13, 290/291, 292/293, 294/295, 302, 303, 304, 305, 306, 307, 308, 310, 311R, 314/315, 326
Juliet Shrimpton/Alamy 192
South American Pictures/Robert Frances 124
Stephen Trimble 4/5, 87, 88, 130, 131, 156T, 166, 189, 199, 211L, 212T, 244T, 252T, 254, 255, 266T, 286, 300, 306T
Selio Villon 125
Harry Walker 148T, 149T, 298

Günther Wessel 64, 196T, 228T, 277, 280, 280T, 287
Corrie Wingate 6T&BL, 9TR&CL
Alison Wright/Corbis 7TR, 227

PICTURE SPREADS

Pages 70/71:
Top row: all Andreas M. Gross; Bottom row from left to right: Andreas M. Gross, Andreas M. Gross, Stephen Trimble, Andreas M. Gross, Stephen Trimble.

Pages 164/165:
Top row from left to right: Stephen Trimble, Andreas M. Gross; Archivo Iconográfico, Barcelona; Bottom row from left to right: Stephen Trimble, Stephen Trimble, Tony Perrottet, Stephen Trimble.

Pages 238/239:
Top row from left to right: P. B. Whitehouse/Millbrook House, Donna Elmendorf, Menaux Photo/ Image Bank; Center row: both P. B. Whitehouse/Millbrook House; Bottom row from left to right: C. M. Whitehouse/Millbrook House, P. B. Whitehouse/Millbrook House, P. B. Whitehouse/Millbrook House.

Pages 312/313:
Top row from left to right: Andreas M. Gross, Andreas M. Gross, Natural History Museum, London; Center row: Stephen Trimble, Andreas M. Gross; Bottom row: all Andreas M. Gross.

Map Production:
Polyglott Kartographie, Berndtson & Berndtson Publications

© 2007 Apa Publications GmbH & Co. Verlag KG (Singapore branch)

INSIGHT GUIDE
ECUADOR

Cartographic Editor **Zoë Goodwin**
Production **Linton Donaldson**
Design Consultants
Klaus Geisler, Graham Mitchener
Picture Research **Hilary Genin**

INDEX

Numbers in italics refer to photographs

INSIGHT GUIDES
The classic series that puts you in the picture

Alaska
Amazon Wildlife
American Southwest
Amsterdam
Athens
Argentina
Arizona & the
  Grand Canyon
Asia's Best Hotels
  & Resorts
Asia, East
Asia, Southeast
Australia
Australia & New Zealand's
  Best Hotels & Resorts
Austria
Bahamas
Bali
Baltic States
Bangkok
Barbados
Barcelona
Beijing
Belgium
Belize
Berlin
Bermuda
Boston
Brazil
Bruges, Ghent, Antwerp
Brussels
Budapest
Buenos Aires
Bulgaria
Burgundy
Burma (Myanmar)
Cairo
California
California, Southern
Canada
Cape Town
Caribbean
Caribbean Cruises
Channel Islands
Chicago
Chile
China
China, Southern
Colorado
Continental Europe
Corsica
Costa Rica
Crete
Croatia
Cuba
Cyprus
Czech & Slovak
  Republics
Delhi, Agra & Jaipur

Denmark
Dominican Republic
  & Haiti
Dublin
East African Wildlife
Ecuador
Edinburgh
Egypt
England
Finland
Florence
Florida
France
France, Southwest
French Riviera
Gambia & Senegal
Germany
Glasgow
Gran Canaria
Great Britain
Great Gardens of
  Britain & Ireland
Great Railway Journeys
  of Europe
Great River Cruises
  of Europe
Greece
Greek Islands
Guatemala, Belize
  & Yucatán
Hawaii
Holland
Hong Kong
Hungary
Iceland
India
India, South
Indian Wildlife
Indonesia
Ireland
Israel
Istanbul
Italy
Italy, Northern
Italy, Southern
Jamaica
Japan
Jerusalem
Jordan
Kenya
Korea

Kuala Lumpur
Laos & Cambodia
Las Vegas
Lisbon
London
Los Angeles
Madeira
Madrid
Malaysia
Mallorca & Ibiza
Malta
Marine Life in the
  South China Sea
Mauritius, Réunion
  & Seychelles
Mediterranean Cruises
Melbourne
Mexico
Mexico City
Miami
Montreal
Morocco
Moscow
Munich
Namibia
Nepal
Netherlands
New England
New Mexico
New Orleans
New South Wales
New York City
New York State
New Zealand
Nile
Normandy
North American &
  Alaskan Cruises
Norway
Oman & the UAE
Orlando
Oxford
Pacific Northwest
Pakistan
Paris
Perth & Surroundings
Peru
Philadelphia
Philippines
Poland
Portugal

Prague
Provence
Puerto Rico
Queensland & The
  Great Barrier Reef
Rajasthan
Rio de Janeiro
Rockies, The
Romania
Rome
Russia
St Petersburg
San Francisco
Sardinia
Scandinavia
Scotland
Seattle
Shanghai
Sicily
Singapore
South Africa
South America
Spain
Spain, Northern
Spain, Southern
Sri Lanka
Sweden
Switzerland
Sydney
Syria & Lebanon
Taipei
Taiwan
Tanzania & Zanzibar
Tasmania
Tenerife
Texas
Thailand
Thailand's Beaches
  & Islands
Tokyo
Toronto
Trinidad & Tobago
Tunisia
Turkey
Turkish Coast
Tuscany
US National Parks West
USA On The Road
USA New South
Utah
Vancouver
Venezuela
Venice
Vienna
Vietnam
Wales
Washington D.C.
The Western
  United States